# Advanced  Programming with Visual FoxPro 6.0

*Markus Egger*

*Donated in Memory of*
*Ceil Silver*

*Hentzenwerke Publishing*

Published by:
Hentzenwerke Publishing
980 East Circle Drive
Whitefish Bay, WI 53217

Hentzenwerke Publishing books are available through booksellers and directly from the publisher. Contact Hentzenwerke Publishing at:
414.332.9876
414.332.9463 (fax) or
www.hentzenwerke.com

Advanced Object Oriented Programming with Visual FoxPro 6.0
By Markus Egger
      Technical Editor: Mac Rubel
      Copy Editor: Jeana Randell

Copyright © 1999 by Markus Egger

All other products and services identified throughout this book are trademarks or registered trademarks of their respective companies. They are used throughout this book in editorial fashion only and for the benefit of such companies. No such uses, or the use of any trade name, is intended to convey endorsement or other affiliation with the book.

All rights reserved. No part of this book, or the .chm Help files available by download from Hentzenwerke Publishing, may be reproduced or transmitted in any form or by any means, electronic, mechanical photocopying, recording, or otherwise, without the prior written permission of the publisher, except that program listings and sample code files may be entered, stored and executed in a computer system.

The information and material contained in this book are provided "as is," without warranty of any kind, express or implied, including without limitation any warranty concerning the accuracy, adequacy, or completeness of such information or material or the results to be obtained from using such information or material. Neither Hentzenwerke Publishing nor the authors shall be responsible for any claims attributable to errors, omissions, or other inaccuracies in the information or material contained in the book. In no event shall Hentzenwerke Publishing or the authors be liable for direct, indirect, special, incidental, or consequential damages arising out of the use of such information or material.

ISBN: 0-96550-938-9

Manufactured in the United States of America

# Dedication

*Ich widme dieses Buch meinen Eltern (Erna und Franz Egger)
sowie meinen Großeltern (Anna und Franz Wimmer, Hildegard und Josef Egger).*

# List of Chapters

# Table of Contents

# Chapter 4: Using Shrink-Wrapped Classes

## SECTION 2—Advanced Object-Oriented Programming   259

## Chapter 8: The Bigger Picture   261

## Chapter 9: Three-Tiered Development   271

## Chapter 10: Patterns   281

## Chapter 11: Object Metrics       295

## SECTION 3—Object Modeling       313

## Chapter 12: The Unified Modeling Language   315

# Acknowledgements

Over a year ago, I started to discuss with Whil Hentzen the possibility of writing a book exclusively about object-oriented programming in Visual FoxPro. I knew Whil was planning a series of books about Visual FoxPro 6.0, and to me, the series just wouldn't have been complete without something on object-oriented development. After all, Visual FoxPro has an excellent object model, and it will be a shame if people don't start using it more than they do now. Luckily, Whil saw it the same way and we decided to do this book. So the first "thank you" goes to Whil Hentzen for letting me do this in the first place.

When I started work on this book, I knew it was going to be a large task. Boy, was I wrong! This task wasn't large—it was enormously huge! When you write about advanced object-oriented programming, there is a large amount of research involved. Also, there is a lot of text and few pictures (unless one draws pictures, but I'm a lousy artist…), so the pages filled up very slowly. Also, the task of writing a book in a foreign language turned out to be not so simple. But again, I was lucky: I had Mac Rubel as a technical editor, who gave lots of helpful input and was of great assistance every time I stumbled over hurdles in the English language. Thanks, Mac, I couldn't have done it without you! The same is also true for Jeana Randell, our copy editor, so also "thanks" to you, Jeana!

I'm not a professional author. My job is to design and write object-oriented applications, mainly as a consultant. I do a good amount of writing, and I also like to speak at conferences and other events, but all of this is more personal pleasure than business. For this reason, writing this book cut deep into my spare time, which wasn't only at my expense, but also at the expense of my best friend and fiancée Martina. I want to use this opportunity to thank her for sticking with me during this time, and even helping me out as much as possible. Thanks, Martina, and I promise to have more spare time from now on!

The initial outline of this book was slightly different from what you hold in your hands now. We decided to make some changes as we went along, mainly due to the fact that I discovered things that weren't obvious before. The chapter that deals with the Fox Foundation Classes is a good example. When I came up with an outline, I knew that there would be new foundation classes, but nobody (not even Microsoft, I think) really knew what they would include. Once I saw them, I realized how powerful and important this set of classes was, so I decided to write much more about them than initially intended. However, this also required a lot of input from Microsoft. Thanks to the entire Microsoft Visual FoxPro team for their help!

Obviously, it took me a while to even get to a point where I could write a book, and I didn't get there all by myself. I want to thank my parents for supporting a crazy teenager who had some wild ideas about writing software for customers all around the world who would be serviced over the Internet. To many of us, this is part of our daily lives now, but then it was science fiction, especially to the bankers. Without having my parents (and the rest of the family) supporting me, I would have given up a long time ago. Thanks for this support!

Once I started my own business, I realized how hard it was to get a foot on the floor without stumbling too much. At this time, people such as Jürgen "wOOdy" Wondzinski, Steven Black, Andrew Ross MacNeill, the German FoxPro Users Group and basically the entire FoxGang were extremely helpful. Thanks to all of you!

—Markus Egger

# Foreword

I met Markus Egger on the VFP 3.0 Beta forum. I'd never heard of him before I saw his name on a whole lot of messages that were asking questions that I only began to comprehend. I remember saying to myself, "Who is this guy?" When I finally met him in person, he was introduced as "the guy that's doing cool things in FoxPro with Rational Rose." I thought, "What's Rational Rose?" It was painfully clear to me that I had some catching up to do. What made it worse was that it all came so *easy* to Max. It still does. That's why I jumped at the chance to do the edit on this book. I may have been the editor, but I was also the first person to benefit from Max's *tour de force* in writing about object-oriented programming for VFP.

If you are like me, you've struggled with OOP for at least six or eight years. I remember sitting in a conference session hearing words like "polymorphism" and "inherited behavior" and not having a clue about what the speaker was trying to tell me. It seems like it was just yesterday, but it was really quite a while ago. Since then I've read book after book on the subject and have even written some code that I considered to be "object-oriented." Bit by bit, I've pulled myself up to the point where I feel comfortable talking about the subject and sitting down at a computer to write some of it.

You can understand my surprise when, in the process of helping Max with the organization of this book and, from time to time, with his English, I started really *learning* from what I was reading. The more that I read, the more I liked what I was reading. This stuff was *good*! Things were falling into place! I was *learning*! (Even editors can learn; it may take longer, but we *can* learn.)

Anyone reading this foreword has to have an interest in object-oriented programming in Visual FoxPro. This is called "natural selection" in computer terms. Until now you could buy good FoxPro programming books and good (sometimes not-so-good) object-oriented programming books, but you couldn't buy a good Visual FoxPro OOP book. It just didn't exist. If you share my experiences, you know the pain of trying to understand C++ book examples of object-oriented programming. The language is different, the projects are different, and the basic outlook on application development is different. The experience is always frustrating, and you walk away from it with less than a complete feeling of satisfaction. *Advanced Object Oriented Programming with Visual FoxPro 6.0* is going to be a breath of fresh air for you.

Max has done all FoxPro programmers a real favor with this book. I recommend it as a good first book for FoxPro 2.x programmers who are just making the move to VFP. I recommend it for people who are in the middle of the learning curve and need a good reference. I also recommend it for people who consider themselves in the top 1% of VFP programmers. *Advanced Object Oriented Programming with Visual FoxPro 6.0* truly has something for everyone. Yes, there's a discussion of inheritance, encapsulation, and polymorphism, but there's also a good discussion of doing two-way work between object models and Visual FoxPro object code.

This book has some of the most comprehensive discussions of the process of object-oriented development that I've seen—*and it's all oriented to FoxPro!* If your "thing" is Java, don't buy this book. If it's Visual FoxPro, you'll want to keep this book in your "Let's See What They Say About This Subject" pile. I kid you not.

—Mac Rubel, New York, February 1999

## Icons used in this book

Paragraphs marked with this icon indicate that the referenced tool or application is available for download with the Developer's Download Files at www.hentzenwerke.com. Future updates to these tools or applications will be available at www.eps-software.com. See the back of the book for instructions about how to download these files.

Information of special interest, related topics, or important notes are indicated by this "Note" icon.

# Section 1
# Basic Concepts

# Chapter 1
# Basic Concepts

**This book does not explain the ideas behind object-oriented programming in excruciating detail. Its intention is to explain how to take advantage of these concepts. However, this chapter briefly introduces the concepts you need to know to make sense of the rest of the book. If you already know them, you can skip to Chapter 2.**

## Encapsulation

Encapsulation is the fundamental idea behind object-oriented programming. This concept can be found throughout all object-oriented languages. It was invented as a result of the need to model real-world problems. Even though procedural languages are extremely abstract implementations of a real-world model, they are mostly influenced by implementation issues rather than concerned about the business problem. As an example, with procedural code, variables (data) and functions (behavior) are separated. Because they are not "contained," the possibilities of reuse are limited.

Encapsulation models a problem according to a real-life situation. Variables and functions are logically bound together in what we call an *object*. Each object has a range of behavior and responsibilities. It also has to maintain its own set of data. Due to the self-contained nature of objects, they are easy to reuse.

Let's assume you want to create an application that takes care of seat reservations for a multiplex movie theater. In this case you'd want to handle reservations for each movie screen separately. In an object-oriented environment, you would most likely create an object for each screen. Each object would be able to count the number of available seats and might also be able to generate some statistics. The functionality and data are *encapsulated* in these objects.

### Classes

Of course, it would be pretty annoying to code 15 different objects because you have 15 different screens. (It's a *big* movie theater.) After all, all these objects are basically the same. For this reason (well, not because of my theater example, actually...), the inventors of object-oriented technology came up with a concept called *classes*.

A class is basically a blueprint for an object. Once you have this blueprint, you can create as many objects out of each class as you want. Defining classes in Visual FoxPro is very easy and intuitive. There are several different ways to create classes, by the way. For now, we'll only look at the plain source code version. Later on we'll learn about visual class design.

To define our theater class in Visual FoxPro, we would write something like this:

```
DEFINE CLASS Screen AS Custom
ENDDEFINE
```

This is quite simple and doesn't require a lot of explanation. Only the "as custom" part might be a little confusing. But I'll get to that a little later.

## Properties

Properties are variables that are encapsulated in an object (they belong to an object). Some other languages like C++ use the term *attribute* instead of *property*.

Other than the fact that properties live inside an object rather than in a program, they are a lot like variables. They can be of different data types (*character*, *numeric*, *date*, and so forth) and their values may change over time. Actually, properties are (just like variables) what I like to call *semi-variants*. That means that you can assign values of a certain type to a property, but you can always switch to a different type on the fly by simply assigning another value. And you can ask FoxPro about the current type using functions like Type() or VarType(). This is unlike other languages that store variables and properties as variants (such as VBScript) that don't have an exact defined type.

Defining properties is just as easy as defining a class. Here's the next incarnation of our theater sample with some assigned properties:

```
DEFINE CLASS Screen AS Custom
   CurrentMovie = "The Sound Of Music"
   AvailableSeats = 150
   Date = {06/20/98}
ENDDEFINE
```

In this example we added three properties and assigned an initial value to each of them. In Visual FoxPro, there is no way to define standard properties without assigning a default value. In other words, standard properties are declared by assigning a value to them in the definition (this doesn't work at runtime). Of course there are some exceptions, but we won't worry about these right now.

Properties can even be arrays. Unlike regular properties, arrays cannot have initial values. Arrays are usually defined using the *dimension* keyword. Property arrays have initial dimensions, but they can always be redimensioned later on.

```
DEFINE CLASS Theater AS Custom
   DIMENSION Screens(15,1)
ENDDEFINE
```

### How to access properties

Because properties belong to objects, a couple of extra rules must be followed to access them. This is fairly easy. In the normal case, all we have to do is add the object's name before our property, and separate the two with a dot.

Let's assume we have an object called *Screen1* (I know—we do not yet know how to turn our classes into objects, but just go with me on this…). In this case we could access its properties like so:

```
Screen1.CurrentMovie = "Terminator"
Screen1.AvailableSeats = Screen1.AvailableSeats - 1
Screen1.Date = Date()
```

Note that this object is of the class *Screen* defined above. Object names and class names can be different and they probably should be. Remember that classes were invented so we wouldn't have to code each object individually. Of course, each object must have its unique name so that we can uniquely identify it.

## Methods

Well, you already guessed it: Methods are functions that are encapsulated in an object. Defining them is just as easy as assigning properties. In order to make our *Screen* class complete, we add functions to make seat reservations:

```
DEFINE CLASS Screen AS Custom
  CurrentMovie = "The Sound Of Music"
  AvailableSeats = 150
  Date = {01/20/98}

  FUNCTION ReserveSeats( NumberOfSeats )
    IF THIS.AvailableSeats - NumberOfSeats >= 0
      THIS.AvailableSeats = THIS.AvailableSeats - NumberOfSeats
    ELSE
      MessageBox("Not enough seats available.")
    ENDIF
    RETURN
  ENDFUNC
ENDDEFINE
```

In this example, we can pass the number of requested seats to the method ReserveSeats(), the method checks for the availability, and finally, the number of seats we requested is subtracted from the number of available seats. Of course, this is just a simple demo function, and there is a lot of room for enhancements. After all, it wouldn't make a lot of sense to make reservations without leaving your name, would it?

Accessing methods works the same way as accessing properties. Here's how we would make a reservation:

```
Screen1.ReserveSeats( 2 )      && Looks like my girlfriend joined in...
```

### THIS—a first look

One keyword used in the example above has yet to be explained: *THIS*. Well, as mentioned above, object names are likely to be different from class names. As we have also seen, we need to know the object's name in order to access its properties and methods. Unfortunately, we do not know what the object name will be until the object is created. And even if we did know its name, we would limit ourselves to create one and only one object out of this class by using the real object name.

For this reason, each class/object knows about itself and grants itself access using the *THIS* keyword. So THIS.xxx always refers to the current object no matter what its real name is. The *THIS* keyword seems to be pretty common in object languages, although some, such as *SmallTalk,* use *SELF* instead.

## How to draw classes

**Figure 1** illustrates the notation I'll be using to draw classes in this book. It shows the above *Screen* class in Unified Modeling Language (UML) notation.

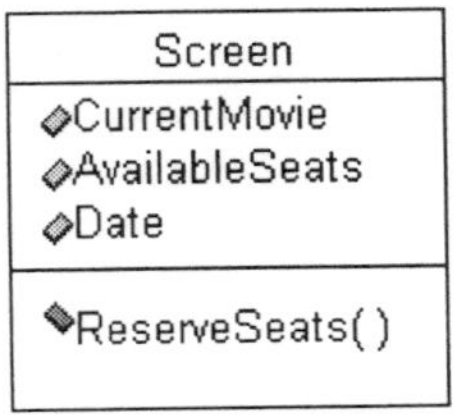

*Figure 1. A simple class in UML notation.*

Each class is drawn as a rectangle with the class name at the top. Underneath are all the properties and methods. These are optional. Sometimes I will draw a class as a simple rectangle with the name in it.

I'll discuss the UML notation in more detail in Chapter 12.

## Inheritance

Inheritance is one of the most mystifying concepts of object-oriented programming. But it's really quite simple. Inheritance is one of the key concepts to software reuse.

Let's stick with our movie theater example. Let's say Markus Multiplex made a lot of money thanks to our great reservation system, so management made a decision to build one more screen that features balcony seating. Now, that sounds great for the audience but it doesn't sound that great to us. After all, our existing classes can't handle balcony seating. What can we do?

We could create another class especially for the new screen. But that would be a shame. After all, we spent months creating the other class and we don't want to rewrite all of that. So this is not an option. We want a way to say, "The new screen is just like all the others, with the exception that we have additional seats in a balcony."

And that's what inheritance is all about. It provides a way to tell Visual FoxPro that one class is basically the same as another with a few exceptions. The way to do that—you guessed it—is by using the keyword *AS* in the class definition. Let's have a look at the very basic definition of our screen class:

```
DEFINE CLASS Screen AS Custom
  ..
  ..
ENDDEFINE
```

*AS Custom* basically means we don't want to inherit anything and start out from scratch. (Well, this is not entirely true, but we'll worry about that later.) In order to create a class that inherits from the class *Screen*, we would define a new class as follows:

```
DEFINE CLASS BalconyScreen AS Screen
  BalconySeats = 80
ENDDEFINE
```

This is called *subclassing.* The new class *BalconyScreen* inherits everything the class *Screen* had. In addition to that, we defined a new property called *BalconySeats* in order to take care of the new possibilities. So internally, the new class now has the properties *CurrentMovie, AvailableSeats, Date,* and *BalconySeats,* and of course it also has the ReserveSeats() method. In addition to that, our new class inherits all of the initial values for each property.

The class *Screen* is also called the *parent class* of *BalconyScreen,* while *BalconyScreen* is the child class from the *Screen's* point of view.

We can assume that the number of seats in the regular seating area has increased, and can take care of this in our new class:

```
DEFINE CLASS BalconyScreen AS Screen
  AvailableSeats = 220
  BalconySeats = 80
ENDDEFINE
```

We have now overwritten the initial value for the number of available seats. Note that we have only one newly defined property in this definition (*BalconySeating*).

One great feature of inheritance is that you can always go back and add features to the parent class. All the subclasses will then automatically inherit all the features. So if some dummy one day has the idea of adding optional headphones to every seat, we are ready. We would simply add headsets as a property of our *Screen* class, and all instances of that class and instances of any subclasses we might have added will automatically inherit the headsets property as well.

## Overwriting code

We have not yet taken care of our reservation method to accommodate the addition of the balcony class. Of course it needs some adjustment, so let's see what the possibilities are. Option number one is to simply overwrite the original method in the subclass:

```
DEFINE CLASS BalconyScreen AS Screen
  AvailableSeats = 220
  BalconySeats = 80

  FUNCTION ReserveSeats( NumberOfSeats, Area )
    IF Area = 1       && Regular seats
      IF THIS.AvailableSeats - NumberOfSeats > -1
        THIS.AvailableSeats = THIS.AvailableSeats - NumberOfSeats
      ELSE
        MessageBox("Not enough seats available.")
      ENDIF
    ELSE
      IF THIS.BalconySeats - NumberOfSeats > -1
        THIS.BalconySeats = THIS.BalconySeats - NumberOfSeats
      ELSE
        MessageBox("Not enough balcony seats available.")
```

```
        ENDIF
      ENDIF
      RETURN
    ENDFUNC .
ENDDEFINE
```

In this example, the ReserveSeats() method has been totally overwritten and redefined. The method now supports another parameter that determines whether we want regular or balcony seating:

```
Screen1.ReserveSeats( 2, 1 )      && Regular seating, 2 seats
Screen1.ReserveSeats( 5, 2 )      && Balcony seating, 5 seats
```

This takes care of our problem. But was it really a good solution? I doubt it! Almost half of the ReserveSeats() method code has been copied from the original method. Suppose that this method had several hundred lines of complicated code. What if that code had bugs? We would have copied them over to the new method. Maybe later on we would fix that bug in the original method, but then we might forget about the copied code in the new method. And even if we didn't forget about it, the code might have been modified so it's hard to locate the bug. Or even worse, the new code might depend on the original bug and we'd break a good amount of code by changing something...

There has to be a better way! And there is. It's called *programming by exception*.

## Programming by exception

The basic idea of *programming by exception* is to define only new behavior, changed behavior or any other cases that might be an exception from the original code. Doing it this way, we would still get all the bugs from the original code, but all the code would be in one place. If we had to go back later to fix something or to add new functionality, we would have to take care of only one class.

So let's take a look at the method in the subclass to see what parts are copied and what is the exception:

```
FUNCTION ReserveSeats( NumberOfSeats, Area )
  IF Area = 1        && Regular seats
    * We already have that in the parent class...
    DoDefault( NumberOfSeats )
  ELSE
    IF THIS.BalconySeats - NumberOfSeats > -1
      THIS.BalconySeats = THIS.BalconySeats - NumberOfSeats
    ELSE
      MessageBox("Not enough balcony seats available.")
    ENDIF
  ENDIF
  RETURN
ENDFUNC
```

We removed all the code that belongs to *Area = 1* and added a DoDefault() function call instead.

## DoDefault()

DoDefault() calls code that has been defined in a parent class. So in the example above, the original code is executed within the first IF statement. As you can see, you can also pass parameters using DoDefault(). This is important because the original code in the *Screen* class expects the number of seats as a parameter. Note that the new version of this method receives two parameters, while we're passing only one parameter to the parent class.

DoDefault() also returns the value of the original method. So the example above is incomplete because we aren't taking care of the return value at all. This would be important, even though the parent class doesn't return anything interesting. We might decide to always return something in a future version of our *Screen* class. One of the problems with that is we don't yet have a clue what this return value might mean. So in this case we should simply pass whatever value we get back:

```
FUNCTION ReserveSeats( NumberOfSeats, Area )
  LOCAL ReturnValue
  ReturnValue = .T.
  IF Area = 1       && Regular seats
    * We already have that in the parent class...
    ReturnValue = DoDefault( NumberOfSeats )
  ELSE
    IF THIS.BalconySeats - NumberOfSeats > -1
      THIS.BalconySeats = THIS.BalconySeats - NumberOfSeats
    ELSE
      MessageBox("Not enough balcony seats available.")
    ENDIF
  ENDIF
  RETURN ReturnValue
ENDFUNC
```

DoDefault() can be called multiple times in one method. This might sound stupid, but it sometimes makes sense, such as when using *CASE* structures. But be very careful doing that. You might end up calling the original code twice, and reserve four seats instead of two.

## The scope resolution operator

When Visual FoxPro was first released (version 3.0), there was no DoDefault() function. People had to use the more complex scope resolution operator (::). To use the scope resolution operator, you have to know the method name (which is easy) and the name of the parent class (which might be tricky).

In the example above, we would use the following command instead of the DoDefault():

```
Screen::ReserveSeats( NumberOfSeats )
```

Just like DoDefault(), the scope resolution operator can pass parameters and receive return values. However, the scope resolution operator has a couple of disadvantages. Obviously it is a lot harder to use than DoDefault(), since DoDefault() knows about all the class and method names by itself.

This might not seem like a big deal, but it really is. Let's just assume you discover that a class structure is incorrect and you decide to change the parent class. In this case you'd have to go through all the code, making sure that the scope resolution operator calls the correct class.

There also are a couple of issues when dealing with more complex scenarios. I'll go into more detail later on; you'll have to trust me for now.

On the other hand, the scope resolution operator allows more fine tuning than DoDefault(). Imagine the following class structure:

```
DEFINE CLASS Class1 AS Custom
  FUNCTION Test
    WAIT WINDOW "Class 1"
ENDFUNC
ENDDEFINE

DEFINE CLASS Class2 AS Class1
  FUNCTION Test
    WAIT WINDOW "Class 2"
    Class1::Test()
  ENDFUNC
ENDDEFINE

DEFINE CLASS Class3 AS Class2
  FUNCTION Test
    WAIT WINDOW "Class 3"
    Class1::Test()
  ENDFUNC
ENDDEFINE
```

In this example, Class2 is a subclass of Class1, and Class3 inherits from Class2. But still, the test method in Class3 bypasses Class2 and calls directly to Class1. This is usually a sign of bad design. In this example, we really should have subclassed Class3 from Class1 rather than from Class2. Unfortunately, scenarios like this can happen in big projects, especially when the implementation phase starts too early. So I encourage you to go back to the design phase when you discover problems that require this kind of design.

If you still can't help doing something "bad," be very careful and make sure to document what you do and why. Otherwise another programmer might just browse through your code and replace the scope resolution operator by a DoDefault(), which would lead to a bug that is very hard to spot.

## What about multiple inheritance?

Maybe you've heard about a feature called *multiple inheritance*. To make a long story short: Visual FoxPro does not support multiple inheritance. I'll explain the concepts briefly so you won't feel uninformed the next time a C++ programmer talks about it.

In all the examples so far, every class had one parent class. (Yes, even the ones that were defined *AS Custom* had a parent class, as you'll see later on.) With multiple inheritance, classes can have more than one parent class. This leads to some tricky scenarios. What if you used a DoDefault()? Which class would be called? Which class would be used for the scope resolution operator? All these issues can be resolved easily as long as none of the parent classes use the same method or property names. But as soon as two classes use the same names, things can get out of control.

C++ programmers might argue that all of these issues can be handled, but I'm still pretty happy that Visual FoxPro does not have multiple inheritance.

## Base classes—a first look

I still haven't explained what *AS Custom* stood for in the examples above.

As I mentioned before, every class in Visual FoxPro must be derived (subclassed) from another class. Unlike other languages, there is no way to start from scratch. No matter what you do in Visual FoxPro, you'll always inherit some basic functionality. FoxPro has a set of default classes called the *FoxPro Base Classes*.

Most of these are visible classes such as buttons, textboxes, forms, and so forth. *Custom* is invisible. Custom is also as close as you will get to starting from scratch, but you might still be surprised at how much functionality this class already has.

I'll use this base class often in my examples. You'll find that this is a pretty accurate reflection of the real world, since most of the classes you will use in Visual FoxPro are subclassed from *Custom*. This, of course, applies only to non-interface classes. When you take a first look at the objects you create using FoxPro, you might be fooled by the number of interface classes you use. But keep in mind that the biggest part of an application is typically the invisible business logic that pulls the strings behind the scenes.

This book was not meant to explain FoxPro base classes; your Visual FoxPro manual already does a good job explaining them. But I'll revisit base classes later on to take a closer look at some of the methods and properties they share, and I'll also pick a couple of special base classes that are worth an in-depth look.

## How to draw subclassing

Since I already explained how classes are drawn in UML, I'll also show how to draw subclassing (see **Figure 2**).

Inheritance is simply drawn as an arrow pointing from the subclass to the parent class. The subclass usually shows only new properties and methods. But you might see some specialized diagrams that also show inherited members, especially in complex diagrams where only part of the inheritance tree is shown.

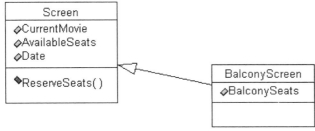

*Figure 2. A simple arrow indicates inheritance.*

# Polymorphism

Polymorphism is, along with encapsulation and inheritance, one of the fundamental forces behind object-oriented programming. The word *polymorphism* comes from the Greek words *poly*, which means *multi*, and *morphos*, which means *form*.

In the world of object-oriented programming, this means that one behavior can be implemented in multiple forms. Because we're talking about behavior, this applies for methods. In plain English, *polymorphism* means that different objects have methods with the same name but they do different things or do equivalent things in a different manner. An example would be a rectangle's draw method that would do something very similar to the draw method of a circle—the act of drawing is similar, but the implementation is very different.

When might this be helpful? Well, consider the movie theater example again. Every screen must have a method to turn lights on and off. This might be implemented like so:

```
DEFINE CLASS Screen AS Custom
   FUNCTION TurnOnLights
     ** Some smart code goes here…
   ENDFUNC
ENDDEFINE
```

Of course we have more than just screens in our theater. We also have rooms such as the food counter, the hallways and the restrooms. They also have lights that must be turned on and off. Let's assume we have an object that turns on the lights in the whole building at 5:00 p.m. Of course, we don't want to implement a different set of messages for each room, so we create the same method in every class. Here is the code for these classes:

```
DEFINE CLASS Hallway AS Custom
   FUNCTION TurnOnLights
     ** Some smart code goes here…
   ENDFUNC
ENDDEFINE

DEFINE CLASS Restroom AS Custom
   FUNCTION TurnOnLights
     ** Some smart code goes here…
   ENDFUNC
ENDDEFINE

DEFINE CLASS FoodCourt AS Custom
   FUNCTION TurnOnLights
     ** Some smart code goes here…
   ENDFUNC
ENDDEFINE
```

Assigning the same function name in every class becomes possible because methods belong to an object and can only be referenced by adding the object name. Otherwise the compiler might get confused.

Now, our light-handler object can simply turn on all the lights like so:

```
Hallway1.TurnOnLights()
Hallway2.TurnOnLights()
FoodCourt.TurnOnLights()
Screen1.TurnOnLights()
Screen2.TurnOnLights()
Screen3.TurnOnLights()
```

All we need to do is make sure that the light-handler object knows about all the rooms we have. I'll explain a generic way to do that later on when I talk about collections.

Another example is the File menu in standard Windows applications. Did you ever wonder how an application can possibly know which item to save when many different documents are open at the same time you click Save? Well, it actually doesn't know. It simply sends a "save" message to the currently active document. Each document might require a different action when it is saved. But the menu item doesn't care about that. It leaves all of this logic to the currently active object, which is completely responsible for saving its contents. The object must have a save method; otherwise, the message sent by the menu won't be received. (We'd get an error message because FoxPro wouldn't be able to find a receiver for the message.)

It might be a while before you can evaluate the power that polymorphism adds to Visual FoxPro, but it's well worth the effort to understand its power.

## Messages

Objects communicate with each other. They do so by sending messages. Objects are always responsible for their own actions. If one object (such as a user interface object) wants another object to do something, the interface object won't take any action other than telling the second object to execute some behavior. This is called *sending messages*. Basically every kind of method call is a *message*.

You've already seen a couple of typical messages:

```
Screen.ReserveSeats( 2 )
Screen.TurnOnLights()
```

Messages consist of three fundamental parts. The first part is the name of the message receiver. The second part is the message that's passed along. This actually is the name of the method that will be executed. The third part contains the parameters that are passed to the referenced method.

In addition to that, there is usually a response to a message. This is the return value that the called method sends back.

## Events

Messages can originate from different sources. Objects may send messages internally. These messages are usually fired in the same sequence and at the same relative point in time. But another kind of message can be sent at any point in time, no matter in what state the system currently is. These messages, called *events*, are usually caused by user interaction or they come from the operating system.

Visual FoxPro relies heavily on events. A modern Visual FoxPro application usually creates an application object and then switches into a waiting mode (*READ EVENTS*). Everything that happens from this point on is originated by an event.

As already mentioned, events are usually created by some kind of user interaction with the computer, through the mouse or keyboard input. But a couple of events are originated by the operating system. These are usually unpleasant events such as errors. And of course, some events are originated by the way the program flows. For example, there are events that fire whenever an object is destroyed or created, or whenever an object changes size or position.

## Events vs. event methods

When an event occurs, Visual FoxPro automatically fires a method that's associated with that event. For example, when the user clicks an object, the Click event happens and the object's Click method fires.

As mentioned above, Visual FoxPro provides a set of classes you can subclass. I'll discuss base classes in more detail later on. All you need to know about them now is that they all come with a set of predefined event methods. You can subclass these classes and add your behavior to them.

Don't confuse these methods with events. An event method is just a method that happens to have the same name as the event, and it gets fired automatically when an event happens. You can also fire those methods yourself, just like any other method. However, this does not mean that the actual event fires, which might be a significant difference. As an example, *MouseDown* events often have assigned methods that require the mouse position to be on top of the object to which the method belongs. If you simply fire this method programmatically, this may or may not be the case.

While this is a logical problem that can be resolved by smart and preventive programming techniques, there are some great differences in internal behavior between handling a real event and firing an event method manually. An example that makes this obvious is the *KeyPressEvent*. This event always fires when the user presses a key while the focus is in a data entry field. However, if you fire this method programmatically, you won't be able to simulate a keystroke because the operating system doesn't know that the method associated with that event exists.

## Access and assign methods

Access and assign methods are new features in Visual FoxPro 6.0, and they are also two of my personal favorites. Basically, they are events that fire when somebody tries to change or access a property. You can trap these events and actually manipulate return and assigned values. Other than that, access and assign methods are regular methods that allow you to do everything you can do with other methods.

Let's say our *Screen* class has a property called *DoorLocked*. This property specifies whether the entrance door is locked. By simply changing the value of this property, we lock and unlock the door.

Of course, not everyone should be able to change this property. Also, not everyone should be able to ask for the status of this property. So let's see how we can accomplish that using access and assign methods:

```
DEFINE CLASS SecureScreen AS Screen
  DoorLocked = .F.

  FUNCTION DoorLocked_Assign( Locked )
    IF oUser.Administrator
      THIS.DoorLocked = Locked
    ELSE
      MessageBox( "Only administrators can lock and unlock doors!" )
    ENDIF
    RETURN
  ENDFUNC

  FUNCTION DoorLocked_Access
    IF oUser.Administrator
      RETURN THIS.DoorLocked
    ELSE
      MessageBox( "Only administrators can check the door status!" )
      RETURN .NULL.
    ENDIF
  ENDFUNC
ENDDEFINE
```

As you can see, access and assign methods are regular methods that have the same name as the property, in addition to the phrase _Access_ or _Assign_. In assign methods, the new value is passed as a parameter. Access methods return the value the user tries to access.

In the example above, I created a subclass of the *Screen* class to keep the sample simple. Of course, I could have added these methods in the original class. Most likely I would do it this way in a real-life scenario. In line 2 of each method, I check for a property called *Administrator* in an *oUser* object. You might wonder where this object comes from. Well, I just assume it exists somewhere in memory. Let's just leave it at that in favor of the simplicity of the example.

Once the program focus is in an access or assign method, the property can be accessed directly. We could now use our class as we would have before. In our example, we could access the *DoorLocked* property in the following manner:

```
Screen1.DoorLocked = .F.      && We open the door
```

Whenever we execute this line, the assign method fires in order to check if we are an administrator, and it may or may not allow us to assign that value.

The same applies for property access. We could ask for a value like this:

```
? Screen1.DoorLocked
```

If we are not an administrator, this would return .NULL., since that would be the return value from the assign method for non-administrators.

So whenever you try to access a property or assign a value to it, Visual FoxPro checks if there is an access or assign method, and if so it is executed instead of talking to the property directly. There is only one exception: Once the program focus is in an access or assign method, Visual FoxPro flips an internal flag that tells it that the methods should now be bypassed. Otherwise we could never assign a new value to a property from within the assign method, because we would only end up firing the method again when we tried to finally assign the value. This seems obvious, but it can get tricky in more complex scenarios. Keep in mind that these methods can do everything regular methods can do, including sending messages and calling other methods. Of course, these methods might then access the same property, but since we are in this special state now, access and assign methods will be bypassed. This can lead to some unexpected behavior and very hard-to-find bugs, so watch out!

Of course, restricting access is only one possibility offered by this feature. Let me give you another example: Let's say our movie theater is doing so well, we finally made enough money to buy another theater at the other end of town. Of course, because we're good businessmen, the theater we purchased is modern and already has some software to manage the screens. Unfortunately, the software is not compatible with ours. But of course we want to manage both theaters with the same application. Let's just assume that using the new theater's software is out of the question. But our new theater has features our software doesn't support. We somehow need to link these features to our application.

Let's say the screen class in the other application does not have a *DoorLocked* property. Instead, there are three methods that allow locking doors, unlocking doors and asking for the current door status. Unfortunately, our application does not support that because it expects the property. So what can we do?

Well, first of all we can add the *DoorLocked* property, just as a dummy. Then we'll add access and assign methods for this property. We can then use these methods to reroute the call to the messages the class supports:

```
DEFINE CLASS TheirScreen AS Custom
   DoorLocked = .NULL.    && This is just a dummy

   FUNCTION DoorLocked_Assign( Lock )
     IF Lock
       * their method
       THIS.LockDoor()
     ELSE
       * their method
       THIS.UnlockDoor()
     ENDIF
   ENDFUNC

   FUNCTION DoorLocked_Access
     RETURN THIS.GetDoorStatus()
   ENDFUNC

   FUNCTION LockDoor
     ** Original code would be here...
   ENDFUNC
```

```
FUNCTION UnlockDoor
   ** Original code would be here...
ENDFUNC

FUNCTION GetDoorStatus
   ** Original code would be here...
ENDFUNC
ENDDEFINE
```

Now we can simply link the foreign object in our application without going through any major rewrite. So what are we waiting for? Let's buy another movie theater from the money we saved on the software!

As you can imagine, access and assign methods are important for object reuse, but they also make maintenance tasks and changes a lot easier. I remember when we first started to use the *Outline* control that shipped with Visual FoxPro 3.0. It allowed creating tree structures just as in the Windows 3.1 File Manager. To fill it with data, you had to send messages and assign values to properties. After all, this was a tricky process.

But shortly after Visual FoxPro 3.0 was released, Windows 95 was introduced, and it replaced the ugly *Outline* object with the new *TreeView* class. Of course, all the customers wanted the Windows 95 look and feel, and I ended up rewriting all my code because the *TreeView* object handled almost everything through methods, and all the property and method names had changed. This was the first time I wished for access and assign methods. Using them, I could have simply redirected all the calls to the new methods. Writing an *Outline*-compatible *TreeView* class would have been a piece of cake.

You can also use access and assign methods to create your own events. A good example would be the *TextBox* base class. It has a property called *Value,* which reflects the current content of the textbox, and it has a couple of events that fire whenever the value changes, like InteractiveChange (which fires when the user enters something) or ProgrammaticChange (which fires when the value is assigned programmatically). However, the value of the textbox can change for other reasons. For example, if the textbox is tied to a field in a database, the value would change whenever the record pointer moves. Unfortunately, no event would fire then. We can create our own event, as demonstrated in the following example:

```
DEFINE CLASS MyTextbox AS Textbox
  FUNCTION Value_Assign( Value )
    THIS.Value = Value
    THIS.OnChange
  ENDFUNC

  FUNCTION OnChange
    * This is only a placeholder
  ENDFUNC
ENDDEFINE
```

In this example, we fire a method called OnChange every time the value property changes. This includes scenarios where the user enters something (which would also fire an InteractiveChange event), when a value is assigned programmatically (which would also fire the *ProgrammaticChange* event) or when the textbox's control source is a field in a table and the record pointer is moved. In subclasses of this class, the OnChange method can be treated like every other kind of event method.

### This_Access

This method has a special status. Unlike other access methods, it is very generic. It uses the THIS pointer to trap every property access, no matter which one it is. The parameter that is passed to this method is the name of the property that is accessed. You cannot reroute the call to a different property. This still has to be done in the access method for this particular property. However, you can actually return a completely different object reference.

Imagine a form that has a command button. In the THIS_ACCESS method of the form, we put the following code:

```
FUNCTION THIS_ACCESS
    LPARAMETERS lcMember
    RETURN THIS.Command1
ENDFUNC
```

This code reroutes every property call from the form to the button. When accessing the form's caption property, you'd actually talk to the button instead. This also works when assigning a value to a property, because you access the object pointer to assign a value to a property. For this reason, there is no need to create an assign method for the THIS pointer.

You can also use this assign method to add properties on the fly. VBScript demonstrates the usefulness of this ability. The idea is to add a property on the fly in case somebody tries to assign a value to a property that doesn't exist. Here's the code that accomplishes that:

```
FUNCTION THIS_ACCESS
    LPARAMETERS lcMember
    IF NOT PEMStatus(this,lcMember,5)
        this.AddProperty(lcMember,.NULL.)
    ENDIF
    RETURN THIS
ENDFUNC
```

# Composition

In a real-world solution, objects don't exist by themselves. They are composed of other objects. A car, for example, might be composed of an engine, tires, seats, and so forth. Of course, we could have one object that had all of those components, but this would raise problems. What if the car should get another engine? We'd have to redefine the whole inheritance tree. Maybe we would break other car classes by doing that. To avoid that, we'd have to create totally separate classes. This would ruin the whole inheritance idea.

For this reason, smart people invented *composition*, which allows us to combine classes and to assemble bigger objects out of simple components. This allows flexibility because we can exchange components independently. Let's go back to our movie theater, which is assembled of screens. Each screen might be assembled of other objects that we haven't discovered so far, such as chairs and projectors.

Another use for composition would be in the user interface. Each form is composed of various objects like buttons, page frames, textboxes and other components.

There are two different kinds of composition: containers and logical composition.

## Containers

Containers are the most common way to achieve composition in Visual FoxPro. When container composition is applied, objects basically live inside other objects. This is mostly true for interfaces, but there are also some reasons to use contained behavioral objects, as you'll see later. For now we'll stick with interface objects such as buttons and textboxes, since the containership is easy to understand this way.

Imagine a simple Visual FoxPro form. The form has visual elements such as buttons, page frames, option buttons, checkboxes and, of course, the form itself. Each of these elements is a single object with a distinct set of properties and methods. It's obvious that most of these objects live within the form. So in this case, the form is the container for the other objects. What's not so obvious is that some of these objects might be containers themselves. Pageframes, for example, are containers that can contain only pages. Each page, on the other hand, can contain almost any kind of object, including other pageframes. Another container would be an option group that includes option buttons. Of course, the user might not even see it, since the container might be borderless and transparent and therefore invisible. Other containers might be totally invisible, such as a form set which is used only to tie a couple of forms together.

Containers have one very important advantage. Once the container is created, all the objects contained in that container (also called *member objects*) are created as well, since the container knows about all the objects that live in it. As a result, containers are easy to use because they hide a lot of the complexity they may deal with.

Most of the FoxPro containers have a very specific use. They can contain only certain objects, such as the pages in a pageframe, interface objects in a form, or columns in a grid. In addition, there is one generic container that can contain almost any kind of object. It is used only to compose objects and has no visual appearance other than an optional border. This might be useful for grouping objects and simplifying the use of that logical group. In our theater example, we could create a user interface that combines fields for the movie name, the schedule, and the number of available seats. We could then use this group of objects on every form that deals with this kind of data simply by dropping the whole container on a form.

Containers can also be subclassed. The child class would inherit information about the objects that live within each container. Take note that only the container itself is subclassed. All the member objects still remain of the same class that they were in the parent container. But we'll get to that in more detail later on.

In the subclass, you can change and overwrite properties and methods of the container, as well as for the members. This means you can move members around if they are visible objects, or you can change their behavior. This is a great feature, especially for rapid application development (RAD), and it's unique to FoxPro. But there are also some issues that come with it. We'll discuss them in Chapter 3 when we talk about pseudo-subclassing and instance programming.

### How to add objects to a container

Defining contained objects with the visual designers is easy. The programmer simply drops an object in a container. Accomplishing the same in source code requires a little more knowledge, but it's still rather obvious. Here's some code to demonstrate:

```
DEFINE CLASS MyContainer AS Container
  ADD OBJECT Button AS CommandButton WITH;
    Caption = "Button 1";
    Left = 100;
    Top = 50
ENDDEFINE
```

In this sample, we create a container and add an object using the ADD OBJECT command. We can also specify the object's class by using the AS keyword, and we can specify default values after the WITH keyword.

This example shows how you can specify member objects in the class-definition level. But there are ways to add objects to containers dynamically once the objects are in memory. All containers have AddObject() and NewObject() methods. They both create an object in a container. Here's how you could create the above button sample dynamically:

```
SomeContainer.AddObject( "Button", "CommandButton" )
```

We'll get into more detail about AddObject() and NewObject() in Chapter 2.

### Referencing objects in containers

Now that we know how to define contained objects, it's time to think about referencing them. So far we've only talked to stand-alone objects, but referencing contained objects isn't much different. All you have to do is add the name of the container.

The following code shows how to reference a button in a form:

```
Form.Button.Caption = "Click me!"
```

As you can imagine, this is simple. Unfortunately, it gets more complex sometimes. Let's assume we have a form that contains a pageframe, which has a couple of pages, and on page 3 we have a button. We would talk to this button like so:

```
Form.PageFrame.Page3.Button.Caption = "Click me on page 3!"
```

These examples show how to reference objects from the outside world. But objects can also be referenced from within the container using the *THIS* keyword. The following sample shows how this would work from a method that belongs to the form:

```
FUNCTION CustomFormMethod
  THIS.PageFrame.Page3.Button.Caption = "Click me on page 3!"
ENDFUNC
```

From within the pageframe, the path would vary because we are one level deeper in the nesting structure:

```
FUNCTION CustomPageFrameMethod
  THIS.Page3.Button.Caption = "Click me on page 3!"
ENDFUNC
```

### Parent vs. ParentClass

Not only does each container know about its members, but each member also knows about its container. It can reference the container using its *Parent* property. The pageframe in the sample above could talk to the form it lives in like so:

```
FUNCTION CustomPageFrameMethod
  THIS.Parent.Show()
ENDFUNC
```

The container an object lives in is also called the *parent object*—not to be confused with the *parent class*. Parent classes are the classes the current class inherits from. A parent object is the object that hosts the current object. There is a big difference in these relationships.

The inheritance relationship is also called an *IS-A* relationship. For example, the *secure screen* we created above *IS A screen*. The container relationship is also called a *HAS-A* relationship. Using the same example we could say: "Each *screen HAS-A projector...*"

To fully understand the difference between these two relationships, it's important to differentiate the terms *class* and *object*.

## Composition by reference

Besides containership, the other form of composition is called *logical composition*. This kind of aggregation (which is another word for composition) is language specific. It might be a simple logical aggregation where one object is simply aware of other objects and knows how to talk to them. Or this might be accomplished by having object references (pointers) to other objects.

Some might call logical aggregation the classical composition, used by many of the object-oriented environments. In FoxPro it's used less often than containers, because containers are easier to maintain and use. They are basically a more evolved form of aggregation.

Let's look at how an object can reference another object without containing it. First of all, we have to create a couple of classes:

```
DEFINE CLASS Screen AS Custom
  MainProjector = .NULL.
ENDDEFINE

DEFINE CLASS Projector AS Custom
  FUNCTION StartMovie()
    ** Some code to start a movie
  ENDFUNC
ENDDEFINE
```

Once the classes are objects in memory (see Chapter 2 for more information about object instantiation), we can establish the logical connection:

```
Screen.MainProjector = Projector
```

As you can see, we use a custom property to reference the projector object. From the screen's point of view, this construction looks a lot like container composition. The projector could be referenced like so:

```
Screen.MainProjector.StartMovie()
```

The other way is more difficult. The projector doesn't know what object it belongs to because parent objects exist only in container relations. The ownership issue can get tricky using logical composition. References can even become cyclic, as in the following example:

```
DEFINE CLASS Screen AS Custom
   MainProjector = .NULL.
ENDDEFINE

DEFINE CLASS Projector AS Custom
   Screen = .NULL.
ENDDEFINE

Screen.MainProjector = Projector
Projector.Screen = Screen
```

In this sample, the projector has a link to the screen it belongs to. Unfortunately, we've lost track of which object is the owner (user) of the other object and which object is being used. But ownership might not be a major issue when using this kind of composition. As a matter of fact, one object could belong to more than one other object at a time:

```
Screen1.MainProjector = Projector
Screen2.MainProjector = Projector
```

In this scenario, both screens reference the same projector. This might not make a whole lot of sense in the movie theater example, but it might in other cases. Imagine two forms that reference the same behavioral objects. This is a very powerful way to share functionality in a resource-friendly way. Or imagine that two or more objects simply refer to something they share, like the cafeteria in the hallway of the movie theater. This kind of aggregation cannot be built using containers because each object can only live within a single host. Also, objects that live within a container cannot move to other objects. With referential aggregation, objects are free to travel and can make themselves at home wherever they find a hosting object.

There are a couple of issues associated with this construction. Obviously, we'll have some overhead in determining when the projector object can be released once it's no longer needed by any other object. But in the basic scenarios, Visual FoxPro keeps track of that and releases the referenced object as soon as all references are gone.

# Abstraction

When designing an object-oriented application, you'll discover that the objects are made up of many objects and classes. Because object-oriented development is programming by exception, the idea is to find as many common methods and properties for these classes as possible. This allows us to create common parent classes that define interfaces and have code that is inherited by all the subclasses.

The process of discovering the common parent classes is called *abstraction*. This process adds a lot of power to object-oriented applications.

It is important to remember that abstraction is not trivial, and it requires good design. If we just start coding, we won't discover those common parts and we'll lose most of the advantages of object-oriented programming. For this reason, I devoted Section 3 of this book to the analysis and design process to help with abstraction.

## Building class hierarchies

Building class hierarchies is one of the most important tasks when creating an object-oriented application. How to build class hierarchies has been and still is an ongoing discussion. I don't think there is one right answer. "It depends" seems to fit here. Some prefer deep class hierarchies, where they build many levels of subclassing. Others prefer broad inheritance structures, where there are lots of subclasses from a single parent class, but the subclassing goes down only one or two levels. You might look at these two different ways of doing things as frameworks (deep structure) and as components (broad structure).

I don't think one-dimensional structures (either broad or deep) are a good way to go. Object-oriented design is not that simplistic after all. I think the idea of components is a good starting point, but I don't buy into the idea of being able to plug all kinds of objects together. Objects have to know about each other. They have to interact in order to do something useful. This seems to work best in a two-dimensional inheritance model. Going this route, you can still plug all the components together. But because they support standard interfaces (see below) and follow basic rules, they will be able to accomplish huge tasks.

I usually like to compare this to the electronics business. If someone wants to build something complex (like a computer), he has lots of standard parts he can use. All these parts seem to be stand-alone objects. But if you look at it in more detail, they all follow general rules and standards.

### Abstract vs. concrete classes

Abstract classes serve only the purpose of building class hierarchies. They are never instantiated. (Repeat after me: "Abstract classes are never instantiated.") They define interfaces, provide common behavior, or are simply added for possible adaptations later. Abstract classes always have concrete child classes.

Concrete classes are the ones that will be instantiated. In a good design, concrete classes have abstract parent classes to make later changes easy and straightforward. Of course, concrete classes can also be subclassed further. In simple scenarios, concrete classes could be the first level of classes in the inheritance structure.

A typical example of abstract and concrete classes is the *Screen* class in the sample above. We might have an abstract *Screen* class that defines everything a typical screen would have, but we would never use this class directly. We'd rather create specialized subclasses for individual screens. We could have a class for the screen with balcony seating, or one class for the big screen, and so on. We'd use these classes in our application.

As you can see in this example, we might have some reasons to directly use the abstract *Screen* class in very simple scenarios. In this case, the *Screen* class might be a concrete class as well as an abstract class, depending on the point of view. However, we would no longer refer to it as an abstract class as soon as we directly used it once.

**Figure 3** shows a simple diagram of abstract and concrete classes.

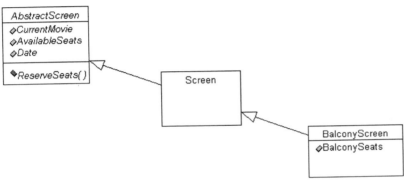

*Figure 3*. *Abstract and concrete classes.*

In this example, we defined an abstract *Screen* class (abstract classes are usually drawn using italic fonts). The *Screen* class that has been subclassed from *AbstractScreen* has no new properties or methods. It might have overwritten ones, but we couldn't tell from this kind of diagram. The *Screen* class has another subclass called *BalconyScreen*, which is also a concrete class. It also has one new property.

## Hiding information

In order to provide clean classes and interfaces, we need a mechanism that allows the programmer to hide complexity inside an object.

There are several good reasons for hiding information. First, you don't want somebody to be able to change internals of your class, because this is a potential source for bugs. Perhaps the object encapsulates sensitive data, in which case you'd want to provide access only to certain properties and methods. After all, it wouldn't make sense to require a password when someone could simply look at the password property.

But even if you are the only user of your classes, there are good reasons to hide information. The first reason is to keep everything simple and easy to use. After all, you still want to be able to use your classes a year after creating them, don't you? If you look at 100 different methods and properties, reuse might be hard. But all you might need to do is to send a handful of messages. If all the implementation-specific methods are hidden, it's very hard to use the object incorrectly. Avoiding mistakes must be one of the highest priorities when developing an object-oriented program. Modern-day business applications have grown so complex, that it's simply impossible to remember every little detail about every single object. Setting a property that is crucial for a certain method can break huge amounts of code. So the simpler an object is to reuse, the higher the code quality and the lower the maintenance costs will be.

Visual FoxPro supports two different ways of hiding properties and methods: *protecting* and *hiding*. Let's see how these mechanisms work and how they differ.

## Protecting properties and methods

Protecting a property or method means hiding it from the outside world. It can be accessed only from a method belonging to the same class. To the outside world, the property or method is totally invisible. If someone tried to access it, she would receive a message that the property or method didn't exist.

In Visual FoxPro, we use the *PROTECTED* keyword to create protected properties and methods, as in the following example:

```
DEFINE CLASS ProtectedDemo AS Custom
   PROTECTED Property1

   PROTECTED FUNCTION Method1
     THIS.Property1 = "Test"
   ENDFUNC

   FUNCTION Method2
     THIS.Method1()
   ENDFUNC
ENDDEFINE
```

In this example, the property *Property1* has been defined as protected. This means that the following call would result in an error:

```
oProtectedDemo.Property1 = "Test"
```

However, *Method1* can still access that property because it belongs to the same class. The method itself is also protected, which means it can't be accessed from the outside, either. But again: *Method2* can access it because it belongs to the same class and it isn't protected—therefore it's visible to everybody.

We could even create a subclass of that class like so:

```
DEFINE CLASS ProtectedDemoSubclass AS ProtectedDemo
   FUNCTION Method2
     DoDefault()
     WAIT WIND THIS.Property1
   ENDFUNC
ENDDEFINE
```

This would still work, because this class would also inherit the protected property. The property would therefore belong to this class, and all the methods in the class could access its protected properties and methods.

Here is a sample that uses protected properties to encapsulate sensitive data:

```
DEFINE CLASS SecureData AS Custom
   PROTECTED Password, CustomerCreditLimit
   Password = "foxpro"
   CustomerCreditLimit = 1000000

   FUNCTION GetCreditLimit( Password )
      IF THIS.Password == Password
        RETURN THIS.CustomerCreditLimit
      ELSE
        RETURN -1
      ENDIF
   ENDFUNC
ENDDFINE
```

This class tells us about a customer's credit limit. Of course, not everybody should have access to this kind of information, so we have a function that allows only authorized users to access it. In order to read the credit limit, we have to supply a password.

Of course, it would be really stupid if just anyone could access these properties. But because they are protected, it looks like they don't even exist. Also keep in mind that these properties might be assigned on the fly, and on top of that, one doesn't necessarily have the source code for this class.

Note that a property must first be declared protected before you can assign initial values. This works similarly to declaring variables where you would use *LOCAL*, *PRIVATE*, and so on, instead of *PROTECTED*.

## Hiding properties and methods

As you saw above, protected properties and methods are still visible in subclasses. Depending on the circumstances, this might not be what you need. In the sample above, we might simply create a subclass of *SecureData*, add methods to retrieve the data, and our security would be useless.

But there is another way to limit access to that data. Using the Visual FoxPro keyword *HIDDEN*, we can actually hide properties and methods not only from the outside world, but also from subclasses. Here is a sample that shows how *HIDDEN* works:

```
DEFINE CLASS HiddenDemo AS Custom
   HIDDEN Property1

   HIDDEN FUNCTION Method1
      THIS.Property1 = "Test"
   ENDFUNC

   FUNCTION Method2
      THIS.Method1()
   ENDFUNC
ENDDEFINE
```

```
DEFINE CLASS HiddenSubclassDemo AS HiddenDemo
  FUNCTION Method2
    DoDefault()
    WAIT WIND THIS.Property1    && This line will fail...
  ENDFUNC
ENDDEFINE
```

In this example, *Method2* in the class *HiddenSubclassDemo* would fail, because it wouldn't have access to the hidden *Property1*. The DoDefault() would still work, because the program focus would move to the parent class (*HiddenDemo*), and the hidden property is visible at this level.

This allows us to hide implementation details from subclasses. Imagine using a framework created by somebody else. It would be a hassle to deal with all the properties and methods needed by the creator of the framework. Some methods might be specific to the problems he had to solve and not useful for you at all, such as the properties *CharBuffer*, *InstanceCounter*, or something else along those lines. It might even break the whole class to access these methods or change the value of these properties.

## Interfaces

The sum of the properties and methods that are visible to the outside world is called the object's *interface*, or *programming interface*.

This term should not be confused with *user interface*. Sometimes it's hard to differentiate between the two, especially when you talk to object gurus. When one object sends messages to another, the sender is also called the *using object*, or simply the *user*. But of course, the same term could also refer to a human user, especially when third-party class libraries or COM/OLE interfaces are involved.

Designing good object interfaces is at least as hard as creating good user interfaces, and you should give it a lot of thought. Interfaces should be very clear and easy to use. They should be self-explanatory or well documented. Therefore, they should hide as much complexity as possible. Once an object's interface has been defined, be careful when making changes. Remember that other objects are depending on a certain protocol when "talking" to each other. Whenever an object's interface changes, all the users have to change the way they communicate with the modified object. This can be a big problem, especially when you create classes for other programmers, or for resale.

Interfaces can be used as wrappers. Imagine you have to use a class that is incompatible with your other classes or framework. In this case, you can subclass the class, hide the original functionality and create the same interface that reroutes all the calls to the different internals. This will enable you to plug this class into your application as if it were designed for it.

The interface should provide straightforward ways to accomplish goals. You should avoid having multiple ways to do a task. This makes maintenance a lot easier and guarantees better reuse. Imagine a screen class in the theater example that has five different ways to turn on the lights. Whenever a new light switch is added, you would have to create another method to turn on that light. Then all the objects that used this interface would have to learn about this new method. This requires lots of changes.

A better way to do this is to provide one method to toggle the switches, even if you need five completely different internal methods. Objects can send a parameter to specify what lights they want to turn on. This has a couple of advantages. First of all, an object might try to turn on a light that doesn't even exist in that room. But instead of calling a method that doesn't exist (and therefore causes an error), the interface catches the mistake and can take proper action to avoid problems. Other objects might not know what lights they can turn on. In this case we could create a smart interface that allows the user to query the existing lights in order to get a list of valid actions. (This is how OLE works, by the way.) Or, the interface method could make an educated guess and turn on the most common lights.

No matter what route you take, the simple, well-defined and unified interface provides more power, more flexibility and better code quality than exposing five different methods. It makes classes easier to use (which is a big step toward code reuse) and it reduces the opportunity to make mistakes (which is a big step toward product release). And it's easy and straightforward to create, so you pay very little and gain a lot. (This should be an easy sale…)

## Interface vs. implementation

A common mistake that programmers make is to confuse the interface with the implementation and vice versa. This usually happens because most people don't differentiate between the two and simply expose implementation methods and properties. This has a couple of disadvantages.

It's pretty hard to keep a clean interface by simply exposing the implementation methods, because objects usually do things that are quite different. When you create business objects, they might have a number of similarities. Actually, they might and should be subclasses of each other. In this case the common interface would be maintained almost automatically, thanks to inheritance. But in larger object systems, an application might deal with totally different objects where the implementation varies greatly. An example of that would be the Start method of a car and the Start method of a movie projector. The actual implementation in those objects will vary greatly. But that shouldn't matter in interface terms. After all, the user should not be concerned with the object's internals.

Common interfaces are often defined in common parent classes, which are abstract classes. Most likely, they don't contain any code because their whole purpose is to provide a standard interface that's inherited by all the subclasses. All the additional methods that contain the implementation code are located in the child classes, and they should be either protected or hidden so as not to pollute the interface.

Another thing to keep in mind is that an interface shouldn't be influenced by coding standards or other personal preferences. Hungarian notation might be a great thing to have, but it shouldn't show in the interface unless you are the only user. This is especially true for class libraries that are sold or given away, or for automation interfaces. How would you like to be stuck with some kind of Delphi or C++ naming convention, just because the programmer of the class liked it that way?

## Polymorphism revisited

As you can imagine by now, polymorphism makes sense only if you have well-abstracted classes and well-defined interfaces. In the sample above, a manager object would be able to handle all the screens in the theater only if every screen object had the same set of methods and properties. If one object violates this interface, the whole idea of polymorphism doesn't work anymore—projects grow too complex and disasters are guaranteed. This shows how important it is to properly design object-oriented applications. Changing interfaces late in development can introduce major problems and is a potential source for bugs.

Earlier, I described how to implement a special screen class that allows customers to buy tickets for balcony seats. I described this by passing another parameter to the ReserveSeats() method. This is an easy and straightforward way to go, but it introduces a couple of problems. We are using polymorphism, but we changed the interface by requiring a second parameter. In order to do that, the object that sends the ReserveSeats() method has to know about two different interfaces. That's not good. In this case we might as well create a second method to buy tickets for the balcony area. This would reduce the risk of confusing two methods that have the same name but different interfaces. Calling the wrong method with the wrong number of parameters would make it hard to find bugs, because everything would look okay in the debugger and the programmer has to remember that he created two different interfaces. Imagine a scenario where a person calls the ReserveSeats() method of a regular screen and passes two parameters in order to reserve a balcony seat. This might easily occur because he might not be aware that the screen he is talking to doesn't feature balcony seating. He would start the debugger and wonder why the method was called with an invalid number of parameters, not knowing that the calling object expected balcony seating. But when the object actually sent a separate ReserveBalconySeats() method, he could figure out immediately what was wrong and why this message was sent. So from a functional point of view, it wouldn't really make a difference because both scenarios would fail at runtime. Even though they would both fail, it's important to remember that it is harder to debug the single-method scenario.

This leads to the question of how to resolve this problem properly once a person found the bug and isolated the problem. There are different ways to do so. The common way seems to be to use a property in the message receiver that determines what the next message is supposed to do, but this method has several problems. Not only do we still have a different interface for this object, but we also have to take two steps. Another way would be to pass an object as a parameter, rather than a single parameter. The properties of the object would specify what kind of ticket we wanted to buy. This would leave the interface clean but would complicate the implementation. Between the two, messing with implementation is always preferred to polluting the design.

There is another way to look at this. It might not be a coding problem after all. Let's think through the scenario one more time: Suppose some manager object makes calls to screen objects in order to make seat reservations. To reserve seats in special areas that are only featured by some screens, the manager object has to know about these features. So we might as well create a second method to make those special reservations. This might again be done in a polymorphic way by providing a ReserveSpecialSeat() method in the example. But in this case I'd recommend using separate method names in order to avoid further confusion.

Don't make the mistake of creating Swiss-army-knife methods. Having clean and generic interfaces is powerful in many scenarios. But no manager object will be able to reserve a balcony seat if it doesn't know these seats exist. As you've seen, it might be better to enhance the interface to avoid confusion and make it hard to find bugs. But this doesn't mean you shouldn't try to reuse code. The special method to reserve balcony seats might just set a couple of parameters and then call the original method.

As you can see, the decision whether to enhance the interface or to enhance existing functionality depends on the particular scenario. Usually, you'll find these gray areas in the analysis and design phase. Yet another good reason to use proper design...

### Naming conventions

Of course, using polymorphism requires the programmer to have naming conventions. It doesn't make sense to call the method to store data "save" in one class and "SaveDocument" in the other. This might be an obvious example, but it gets trickier in more specific scenarios. For this reason, naming conventions are required in order to avoid name mix-ups that would ruin the idea of polymorphism for no good reason.

I describe some naming conventions in Chapter 6. These conventions are just suggestions. Feel free to use them, modify them or come up with your own conventions. It doesn't matter what conventions you use, as long as you use them consistently.

# Chapter 2
# How Things are Done
# in Visual FoxPro

**In Chapter 1, I discussed general object topics and looked at the important object concepts from a Visual FoxPro point of view. However, while the concepts exist in almost all object-oriented development systems, some things are done differently in every language. Let's have a look at some FoxPro-specific issues.**

## Instantiating classes

In Chapter 1, I discussed how to define classes and I assumed objects could be created out of these classes. Now I'll take a closer look at how to create those objects and discuss what strings are attached.

## Constructors and destructors

Often it's helpful to do something whenever a class is created or destroyed. A typical task would be to bring the environment to a proper state or clean up after the object. Often the constructor sets properties of the current object based on certain conditions, while the destructor removes things the object created in order to leave the system as it was when the object was created.

Most object-oriented languages support this in one way or another. Visual C++, for example, has a concept called constructors and destructors. C++ simply uses a naming convention that allows you to attach code to a class that runs whenever the object is created or destroyed. The constructor uses the same name as the class itself.

Visual FoxPro also supports constructors and destructors, but they are implemented a bit differently. FoxPro simply fires events that occur whenever the object is instantiated or dies. The constructor event is called Init() and the destructor event is called Destroy(). However, there are some differences between the events FoxPro fires, and real constructors and destructors as they are used in C++. This is especially true for the event-firing sequence, which I'll discuss later.

All FoxPro base classes support the constructor and destructor events. However, some classes feature other events in addition to the regular constructor. Form classes, for instance, have a Load event that fires even before the Init. This particular event allows changing settings or opening tables that are needed by member objects. Doing so in the Init would be too late, because member objects that are linked to data would have already failed to instantiate at that point.

FoxPro's handling of the constructors has a couple advantages over the C++ way, one of which is subclassing. Whenever you create a subclass in C++, the class gets new name, and therefore the constructor has a new name. This means that the original constructor doesn't fire anymore unless it's called explicitly. This makes programming by exception difficult. In Visual

FoxPro, the name of the constructor is always Init. This allows you to apply regular rules of inheritance and simplifies the class handling.

## Event-firing sequence for Init() and Destroy()

Let's have a look at the firing sequence of constructors and destructors. When there is only one object, the sequence is easy. An object gets instantiated and the Init event fires right away. Then the object is alive and other events may fire. Whenever the object dies, the destructor fires and that's it.

However, this gets more complex when you create composite objects, especially in container scenarios. Imagine you have a form object that contains a command button. If you create this object, the button's constructor fires first, followed by the one belonging to the form. This is pretty weird if you think about it. It would be like installing a bathtub on the second floor when building a house, and adding the framework later. However, in an object world it makes sense. Keep in mind that objects should be black boxes that can live in virtually every container. For this reason it wouldn't make sense to have the container object in place and ready to go whenever the child constructs, because the child object wouldn't have any specific knowledge about the container and therefore couldn't do anything with it. However, an object can have knowledge about member objects that it hosts. For this reason, it makes a lot of sense to have all the member objects already in place when the constructor of the container object fires.

The opposite is true for the destructor. The Destroy method fires for the container first, while the objects contained in it still exist.

## Handling parameters in objects

The Init method can also be used to pass parameters to an object. You could do this with an (L)PARAMETERS statement in the first line of the Init method. Parameters are passed right away, when creating the object (as you'll see a bit later). From this point on, parameters are handled as usual. This includes the fact that the visibility of parameters is either private or local. For this reason, parameters go out of scope after the Init has fired. For this reason, parameters are often saved to custom properties of the object to make them available throughout the object.

When using composite objects, parameters can only be passed to the container objects. If you need to pass parameters to a member object (which usually indicates bad design), you can receive the parameters in the container object's Init and pass them on to the child object. The following example demonstrates this:

```
DEFINE CLASS MyContainer AS Container
   * oCustom is the child object
   ADD OBJECT oCustom AS MyCustom

   FUNCTION Init
      LPARAMETERS Parameter1
      * We fire the init of oCustom again...
      THIS.oCustom.Init(Parameter1)
   ENDFUNC
ENDDEFINE
```

```
DEFINE CLASS MyCustom AS Custom
   FUNCTION Init
      LPARAMETERS Parameter1
      IF Parameters() < 1
         ** No parameters yet...
         RETURN .T.
      ENDIF
      ** This time we received parameters
      WAIT WINDOW Parameter1
   ENDFUNC
ENDDEFINE
```

When you instantiate the *MyContainer* class (which hosts one instance of the *MyCustom* class) and pass a parameter, the Init of the custom class fires first, followed by the Init of the container. (I'll show you the syntax shortly.) Of course, when the Init of the custom class fires, it doesn't receive any parameters, but since it checks for the parameters in the first line, it deals with that and simply does nothing. Then the Init of the container fires and it receives one parameter. It then passes this parameter on to the Init of *MyCustom* by firing the method one more time. This works, because the custom object now exists, which demonstrates how handy the firing sequence of the constructors is.

## The constructor's return value

Not only can the Init method handle parameters, but it also can handle return values. However, the programmer does not have access to the return value because Visual FoxPro itself reacts to this value.

Whenever the Init method returns .T. (which is the default), Visual FoxPro assumes that everything worked out well and finishes creating the object. If the return value is .F., FoxPro assumes something went wrong and destroys the object right away, so it basically looks like the object was never created.

Very often I see programs where people try to decide in the constructor whether or not the object should be created. If it shouldn't, they simply return .F. from that method. However, this is not a smart way to go for reasons of performance and resources. Keep in mind that the object and all its members have already been constructed whenever the form's Init fires. For this reason, the Init should only return .F. when something went wrong while constructing the object. Here's an example that shows when to use the constructor to decide whether an object should be created:

```
FUNCTION Init
   IF NOT VarType(Customer.Name) = "C"
      * The data we need isn't there
      RETURN .F.
   ENDIF
ENDFUNC
```

In this example, the object checks for some data it depends on. If it isn't there, the object won't work, and for this reason we don't even instantiate it. Here is another example that shows a scenario where I wouldn't use the constructor to decide whether the object can be instantiated:

```
FUNCTION Init
   IF oApp.oUser.nLevel < 1
      * The user doesn't have access to this object
      RETURN .F.
   ENDIF
ENDFUNC
```

In this case the object checks whether the user has rights to use it. There might be some good reasons to do this, but if at all possible, I would do this before instantiating the object. Most likely, I would use a special security-manager object or something similar. Checking for access rights at the end of the instantiation process is only a waste of resources.

## CreateObject()

Using the CreateObject() function is one of the simpler ways to create an object. You simply pass a class name and it returns a reference to the created object, as in the following example:

```
oForm = CreateObject("Form")
```

In this case, I'm creating an object based on the FoxPro base class *Form*. Of course I can use CreateObject() to create objects based on classes I created myself. Whenever I do that, I have to make sure that the class definition is in scope. To do so, I can use the SET CLASSLIB (if I use visual class libraries) or the SET PROCEDURE command (if I use PRG files). The class definition would also be in scope if the class was defined in the PRG that actually does the CreateObject(), or if the PRG that has the class definition is in the call stack. For the scope issue, the same rules apply as for finding function definitions. Here's an example that instantiates a user-defined class:

```
SET CLASSLIB TO MyLib.vcx ADDITIVE
oForm = CreateObject("MyForm")
```

## NewObject()

Visual FoxPro 6.0 introduces a new function to instantiate objects called NewObject(). It basically does the same job as CreateObject(), but it allows you to specify the class library as well. Here is the same example as before using NewObject():

```
oForm = NewObject("MyForm","MyLib.vcx")
```

Using NewObject(), Visual FoxPro makes sure the class definition is in scope. You can specify visual class libraries (VCX) as well as PRG files. Also, NewObject() allows you to specify a compiled application that hosts the class definition. This allows you to create class libraries that are distributed in compiled versions rather than in source code.

This all may not look like a big deal, but it really is. Making sure the class library is in scope for CreateObject() becomes complex in real-life applications. The easiest way usually is to make sure all the class libraries are in focus in the startup program. However, this does not work once you start using third-party tools or self-contained components. In this case, the component needs to check if the definition is in scope. If not, it has to set it and eventually release it to leave the environment as it was (remember that objects should never change the surrounding environment).

NewObject() takes care of all these issues for you, but of course it has to do that every single time a new object is created, and this takes time. So you should still use CreateObject() for performance reasons whenever possible. If you know that a library is already set, or if the current object is the only one using it—and therefore you can set it without having to check whether it was set before—there is no reason to use NewObject(). CreateObject() can be used just as easily, and it's a lot faster.

## .AddObject() and .NewObject()

The CreateObject() and NewObject() functions you've seen so far create new, independent objects. However, you'll also face situations where you have to add objects to an existing container (such as adding a new button or textbox to a form). To do this, you can use the .AddObject() and .NewObject() methods. Every container class (container, form, page, and so on) features these methods.

.AddObject() and .NewObject() work similarly to the functions introduced above, but they require another parameter, the object name, since they don't return a new object reference but add it to the container object. If we had a form object called *oForm*, we could simply add a button (on the fly) like so:

```
oForm.AddObject("cmdButton","CommandButton")
oForm.cmdButton.Visible = .T.
oForm.NewObject("cmdButton2","MyCommandButton","MyButtons.vcx")
oForm.cmdButton2.Visible = .T.
```

As you might have already guessed, .NewObject() allows you to specify the library just as the NewObject() function, while .AddObject() requires that the class definition is already in scope. Because the behavior of these methods is similar to the equivalent functions, the same performance issues apply. Also, note that objects added to objects are by default invisible, so you have to explicitly make them visible.

## Passing parameters to objects

As I mentioned earlier, objects can receive parameters. All four functions and methods used to create objects support passing parameters. All the parameters are passed to the methods and functions as additional parameters. You simply need to know how many parameters each of the methods and functions support, and you can pass your parameters in addition to that. Let's have a look at how this works in each case:

```
oForm = CreateObject("MyForm","Parameter1")
```

The CreateObject() function is pretty simple and supports only one internal parameter, so parameter 2 would already be passed on to the instantiated object, where it would end up as parameter 1.

```
oForm = NewObject("MyForm","forms.vcx",,"Parameter1")
```

NewObject() supports two more parameters (the class library and the hosting application). In the example above, I didn't use a library from a compiled application, so I simply left this parameter out.

```
oForm.AddObject("cmdButton","MyCommandButton","Parameter1")
oForm.NewObject("cmdButton","MyCommandButton","MyButtons.vcx",,"Parameter1")
```

These methods work according to their function counterparts, but they require one more parameter in front (the name of the object being added), so the rest of the parameters are shifted back one position.

## SCATTER... NAME...

There are more commands that create objects, one of which is *SCATTER... NAME...*. This command takes the current record of a table or cursor and creates an object that has one property per table field. It also puts the current field values into the properties. Here is an example:

```
USE Customer
LOCAL loData
SCATTER NAME loData MEMO
```

The resulting object doesn't have any methods—not even constructors or destructors. Also, you can't specify a class that is used to create this object because everything is constructed on the fly. For this reason, it would not make sense to provide methods, events, or constructors and destructors.

If property values have been changed, that object's new property values can be saved back to the table using the GATHER...NAME... command.

Using data objects has many advantages over using regular data. You can access multiple records at a time using multiple data objects. Also, data can be handed over to other objects, even across data sessions and through OLE connections. However, this would fill a whole chapter and this book is not about handling data. For this reason, I'll leave this discussion for somebody else.

Besides the SCATTER... NAME... command, there are some others that create objects in a similar fashion. BROWSE...NAME... is one of them. Another one is DEFINE WINDOW... NAME.... As you can see, they all share the added *NAME* clause, which is an indicator that objects are created. Most of these commands are included for backward compatibility, and you should use the newer counterparts instead.

## Object references

Object references are variables that point to objects. In Visual FoxPro you never have direct access to objects, but you can talk to them through references or pointers. This doesn't make a big difference, especially because it's easy to use object references.

To create an object reference to a new object, you use either CreateObject() or NewObject(). Both functions return references to the new object and this reference is copied into whatever variable you provide.

Here's a simple example:

```
oForm = CreateObject("Form")
```

The variable *oForm* is now a reference to the new object. You can create a second reference to the same object by simply copying the existing reference like so:

```
oForm2 = oForm
```

Unlike what many people believe, this does not copy the whole object, but only the contents of the variable, which is the object reference. You could not copy the object itself because you don't have access to the actual object, as mentioned before. To create a second object that is unique to oForm2 you would have to do a second CreateObject().

You can now start communicating with that object, and it doesn't matter what reference you use. There is no real difference between these two lines of code:

```
oForm.Caption = "Changing the caption through oForm"
oForm2.Caption = "Changing the caption through oForm2"
```

## Object lifetime

The lifetime of an object reference determines an object's lifetime. An object stays alive as long as there are references to it. You create an object, provide a FoxPro variable as a reference to it, and the object is alive. As soon as you assign a different value to the variable or simply release it, the object goes away.

Let's continue with the example above. Make sure the form *oForm* is visible, otherwise you'll have a hard time following the example. When we first created the object, we provided the *oForm* reference, which kept the object alive. Later on, we added the second reference, which linked to the same object. The question is: "What happens when the first reference goes away?" Well, let's try it by removing this reference. You can do this with any of the following commands:

```
RELEASE oForm
oForm = .NULL.
oForm = "Something else"
```

As you can see, the form still remains in memory, because *oForm2* is a separate, independent reference to this object.

Now if you think about this, it is powerful as well as dangerous. If you simply copy object references, you also have to clean up after yourself; otherwise you might end up trying to release objects and they simply don't go away. This makes it hard to find bugs, because there is no way to tell what references point to that object.

Many objects also have a Release() method. This is a very good way to remove objects from memory, because these methods try to release all the references that point to the actual object. Let me give you a little example to demonstrate why this is the case. Let's assume you had an object called *oForm*. Later on during runtime, you created additional references to this object. This kind of scenario happens often in large applications. Here's some sample code that constructs such a scenario:

```
oForm = CreateObject("Form")
oForm2 = oForm
```

To release the *oForm* object, the *oForm2* reference must be cleared as well. This could be done by assigning a new value to the references or by releasing them using the RELEASE command:

```
RELEASE oForm
oForm2 = .NULL.
```

Unfortunately, this gets really tricky, especially in generic algorithms. Most likely you won't be able to keep track of all the references using an automated mechanism. Using the Release() method takes care of this issue beautifully:

```
oForm.Release()
```

All known references are automatically released by the object, and we don't have to take care of our own garbage. This saves us many lines of source code and a lot of sleepless nights. This works fine for all variable references. However, it might not work well if you also have property references, which I'll discuss in the next section.

## THIS, THISFORM, THISFORMSET and Parent

The Visual FoxPro keywords *THIS*, *THISFORM* and *THISFORMSET* are special kinds of object references. Visual FoxPro maintains these references on its own. They always point to the current object (THIS) or to an object that's a parent (container) of the current object. *THISFORM* points to the current form and (you guessed it) *THISFORMSET* to the current form set. Here are some examples that use these references:

```
THIS.Execute()
THISFORM.Caption = "Invoice Form"
THISFORMSET.frmToolbar.cmdSave.Enabled = .T.
```

*Parent* is a little different from these references. *Parent* is a property of every object in Visual FoxPro. *THIS*, *THISFORM* and *THISFORMSET* are stand-alone variable references. Also, unlike the *Parent* reference, they change all the time depending on the currently active object.

The *Parent* property of each object that is contained in another object has a reference to the parent that remains the same as long as the object stays in memory. *Parent* is usually used together with *THIS,* as in the following examples:

```
THIS.Parent.Refresh()
THIS.Parent.Parent.cmdOK.Enabled = .F.
```

As you can see, *Parent* references another object that can have a *Parent* reference as well. The second line might be in a *Page* that's in a *PageFrame* that's in a *Container* that has an OK button. If this *PageFrame* were in a form, it could be referenced like this:

```
THISFORM.cmdOK.Enabled = .F.
```

Only use *Parent* in members of composite classes. Don't assume a class will be used in a certain container object, because this would limit the reusability of the class. Keep in mind that every object should be a black box that can exist in any environment whatsoever.

The same logic applies for *THISFORM*, but some objects can only exist in forms, such as CommandButtons. It is impossible to instantiate and use a command button outside a form. For this reason, it's safe to use *THISFORM* as a reference in a command button as long as you don't assume that the form has nonstandard properties or methods.

## Variable references

The most common type of object reference is a variable reference. It is a regular FoxPro variable that points to an object.

Variable references follow all the same rules as regular FoxPro variables. They can be public, private or local, and they can be passed or received as parameters. This simple program demonstrates the use of variable references:

```
LOCAL loForm
loForm = CreateObject("Form")
DisplayForm( loForm )
* Some more code would follow here…

FUNCTION DisplayForm( loFormReference )
* This function is used to set forms visible
IF VarType( loFormReference ) = "O" AND loFormReference.BaseClass = "Form"
   loFormReference.Visible = .T.
ENDIF
RETURN
```

This code defines a local variable that is used as an object reference for a form object. We then call the DisplayForm() function and pass the object reference as a parameter. The function verifies that the reference is valid and displays the form. Then the program focus returns to the previous procedure, some additional code executes, and finally the program ends and the local object reference goes out of scope; the object goes away as well.

As you learned earlier in this chapter, you never have access to the actual object. The only form of access to objects is through the references or pointers. These pointers know the memory address of the objects. If you pass this memory address to another function, it will still point to the same address and therefore to the same object. For this reason, there is no need to pass object pointers by reference, because the result will be almost the same (all right, you might save a byte or two of memory). Many people actually believe that FoxPro checks to see whether the passed parameter is an object, and if so, automatically passes it by reference. For the reasons described above, this is not the case and it isn't necessary.

## Property references

Object references don't have to be variables. They can also be properties of other objects. Here's an example that makes use of this:

```
oForm = CreateObject("MyForm")
oForm.oBehavior = CreateObject("SomeBehavior")

DEFINE CLASS MyForm AS Form
   oBehavior = .NULL.
ENDDEFINE

DEFINE CLASS SomeBehavior AS Custom
   * Lots and lots of code goes here
ENDDEFINE
```

Note that the behavior object created does not become a member object of the form, meaning it's not contained or owned by that form. The form just contains a reference to that object. We could simply create another reference to the behavior object and release the form, and the behavior object would remain in memory.

Using property references is also called "composition by reference." The cool part is that many objects may share one other object (I'll call it a *behavior object* for this example). The first object created also instantiates the behavior object. All other objects would simply create additional references to the existing behavior object. As soon as all objects are released, the last reference to the behavior object also goes away, and the behavior object is released as well. This may or may not make sense depending on the scenario you are dealing with. If you create a *car* object, for instance, every *car* should get its own *engine*, but if you are creating a *house* class, not every *house* should get its own *power plant*.

For some mysterious reason, FoxPro doesn't handle property references as well as variable references. As I mentioned earlier, the Release() method takes care of variable references, but it sometimes forgets about property references. This results in objects that accidentally stay alive. I refer to these objects as *Goof-Monsters*.

## Cleaning up after yourself

Whenever you create new object references or copy existing ones, you take the risk of creating object references that might keep objects alive after they are supposed to be released. For this reason, you need to be very careful and clean up after yourself, meaning you have to release all the references you created. As I mentioned earlier, this is especially true for property references, so the form class I used in the last example should also make sure the property is reset in the form's destructor:

```
DEFINE CLASS MyForm AS Form
   oBehavior = .NULL.

   FUNCTION Destroy
      THIS.oBehavior = .NULL.
   ENDFUNC
ENDDEFINE
```

"But Markus," one might say, "when this object is released the property goes away, so how could this result in an outstanding reference?"

Well, good point. It seems like this would never be a problem, but it is in real-world scenarios. Sometimes object references can become cyclic over many steps. Let's assume you create a form that has a pageframe. The pageframe has several pages and one of them has a button. For some reason, the button has a reference to the pageframe, which has a reference to the form. This is a typical use of a chain of responsibility that could be used to handle errors or to somehow delegate messages. (I'll discuss the chain-of-responsibility pattern in Chapter 10, "Patterns.") Now imagine that the form always sets a reference to the current control. This could be done in the GotFocus event of the button, for instance. In this case you would have a circular reference: from the button to the pageframe to the form and back to the button. This seems like a stupid thing to do, but it could happen very easily, because object systems grow very complex and there is no way to see all the references.

If cyclic relations exist, it might happen that a whole group of objects doesn't go away, because the internal references keep them alive. This can cause some weird effects. Forms remain on the screen, but they aren't functional because they are only kept alive by objects that live within that form. Those objects, on the other hand, can't go away either, because the references to each other keep them alive. However, all public references to these objects are gone and they are linked only internally, making it impossible to communicate with them. They just sit there, eat up your memory, and cause random GPFs every now and then. I've worked on projects where we spent several man-months trying to find mysterious crashes and memory leaks, only to discover that one object reference wasn't released properly. Unfortunately, this kind of bug is extremely hard to find. First, you don't have any tools that show object references, and second, you don't really know where to look because the problem might be in any line of your whole project. Unfortunately, there is no obvious misbehavior, either, when the problem occurs. All you can do is step through the whole code, make educated guesses, make little changes every now and then, and see how the system behaves over the next couple of hours. If nothing has changed, you can start over, step through every single line, make your next educated guess and hope for better luck. If it still doesn't work, you can try again the next day.

I make it a basic rule to reset every property that might have been used as an object reference in the destructor of the class. I usually have a special method that does that. I call this method from the destroy event of the class, or I can decide to clean up during runtime, like after a process has ended. This technique is called a *Garbage Collection*.

## Differences between classes and forms

Classes (I'll talk about subclasses of the *Form* base class later in this chapter) and forms have many similarities. If you look at the Form and Class Designers, you'll discover that they look almost the same. As a matter of fact, they are pretty much the same internally. But there are several differences between real forms and classes that are subclasses of forms. Both have advantages, too, which makes it hard to decide which one to use.

## Instantiating forms

The first big difference between classes and forms is how they are instantiated. I already described how classes are instantiated. Form classes cannot be members of other container classes (FormSets are the rule-proving exception, but I'll talk about these later). For this reason, forms are usually stand-alone objects. (Sometimes they are attached to objects that use properties, as an object reference, but that doesn't really make a difference.) So the only way to instantiate a form class is to use the CreateObject() and NewObject() functions (not the .NewObject() method!).

In order to use one of these functions, you have to provide a reference name for the new object, as in the following example:

```
oForm = CreateObject("Form")
```

Form classes always instantiate with the *Visible* property set to .F., so in order to make the form visible you have to issue one of the following commands:

```
oForm.Visible = .T.
oForm.Show()
```

Both would have the same result. Until Visual FoxPro 5.0, I preferred to use the Show() method. This would allow me to add additional functionality if I needed some behavior every time a form was displayed. Now, I tend to use the first option (setting the property) because I can always add behavior using an assign method. Setting the property is a little faster, too (about 25 percent, according to my performance tests).

So far, this has been easy. You created an object and displayed it. However, it gets even easier once you start using forms instead of classes. Here's how you would create a form:

```
DO FORM Form.scx
```

This command makes FoxPro look for a form called *Form.scx* (the .scx is optional). It creates the form and displays it right away. I guess FoxPro figures that forms don't do any good unless they are visible. With classes, this is a totally different story. In fact, most classes never become visible or don't even have a visible property or any visible appearance.

However, you might want to run a form and leave it invisible. The DO FORM command lets you do that as well:

```
DO FORM Form.scx NOSHOW
```

This would create the form object, just as the CreateObject() or NewObject() functions do, and keep it invisible. You can make the form visible later on using the method or property introduced above. In order to do that, you need to know the object's name, which might be tricky every now and then. To make this easier, I recommend using the NAME clause wherever possible:

```
DO FORM Form.scx NOSHOW NAME oForm
** Lots of code goes here...
oForm.Visible = .T.
```

If you can't use the NAME clause (for reasons described later), I recommend using the Forms() collection, which FoxPro automatically maintains as a property of _Screen (see the Collections discussion in this chapter). You could try to use the form's name (name of the .scx file), but I don't recommend that because you might end up talking to the wrong form, especially when instantiating the same form twice.

This brings us quickly to the next point: How do you run multiple instances of the same form? With real forms it's easy. All you have to do is issue the DO FORM command several times:

```
DO FORM Form.scx
DO FORM Form.scx
```

This would start two instances of the same form. They would be two different and fully functional objects. Because these forms are regular FoxPro objects, both need to have object references, of course. But you don't have to worry about them because FoxPro creates these references itself. Every one of these references has to be unique, which is the tricky part, because once you instantiate a form multiple times, these reference names will change. That's the reason why I recommended using the Forms() collection instead. Using the NAME clause wouldn't work either, because you'd have to use a new name each time so you couldn't approach this generically.

Creating multiple instances of form classes introduces a similar problem as with the NAME clause. The reference you use has to be unique, so in order to instantiate two form classes you would do something like this:

```
oForm1 = CreateObject("Form")
oForm2 = CreateObject("Form")
```

This would create two forms of the same class, just as in the example with the DO FORM above. Unfortunately, this code is not generic, because every time I create a new instance I have to think of another reference name. Another way of doing this is to use an array as the object reference, like so:

```
DIMENSION ApplicationForms(2)
ApplicationForms(1) = CreateObject("Form")
ApplicationForms(2) = CreateObject("Form")
```

I could take this code and put it in a method to make it more generic. The method and the array could be members of a form-handler object, which leads me to my first example of how objects work together:

```
DEFINCE CLASS FormManager AS Custom
   DIMENSION ApplicationForms(1)

   FUNCTION NewForm( FormClass, FormClassLib )
      * We check if we have to redimension the array
      IF Alen(THIS.ApplicationForms,1)=1 AND NOT ;
         VarType(THIS.ApplicationForms(1))="O"
         DIMENSION THIS.ApplicationForms( Alen(THIS.ApplicationForms,1) + 1 )
      ENDIF

      * Now we create the new form and show it
      IF Empty(FormClassLib)
         * The classlib has to be set already
         THIS.ApplicationForms(Alen(THIS.ApplicationForms,1)) =;
            CreateObject(FormClass)
      ELSE
         * We also deal with the classlib
         THIS.ApplicationForms(Alen(THIS.ApplicationForms,1)) =;
            NewObject(FormClass,FormClassLib)
      ENDIF

      * We check if the form has been created
      IF VarType(THIS.ApplicationForms(Alen(THIS.ApplicationForms,1)))="O"
         * Form has been created
         THIS.ApplicationForms(Alen(THIS.ApplicationForms,1)).Visible = .T.
         * We return a reference to the new form
         RETURN THIS.ApplicationForms(Alen(THIS.ApplicationForms,1))

      ELSE
         * Form hasn't been created,
         * so we have to delete the reference from the array
         IF Alen(THIS.ApplicationForms,1) = 1
            * The array only has one item, so we can't make it any smaller
            THIS.ApplicationForms(1)=.NULL.
         ELSE
            * We shrink the array
            DIMENSION THIS.ApplicationForms(Alen(THIS.ApplicationForm,1) - 1 )
         ENDIF
         RETURN .NULL.
      ENDIF
   ENDFUNC
ENDDEFINE
```

In a real-life scenario, this class would be instantiated when the application started, and it would always be available. To create a new form, I would pass the form's class name. The class library is optional, which makes the code somewhat more complex but easier to use (I like to make my code more complex so it's easier to use for others). When the form has been created, the manager returns an object reference to the new form. The following example shows how this works:

```
LOCAL NewForm, NewForm2
NewForm = oFormManager.NewForm( "MyForm", "Forms.vcx" )
NewForm2 = oFormManager.NewForm( "Form")
```

However, I really need to check if the reference that has been returned is an object. If an error occurred and the form couldn't be created, the form manager would return *.NULL.* instead of a real object reference. This also makes the code above a bit more complex than it would be in its purest form. But still, the form manager is not quite ready yet. Keep in mind that you might want to pass parameters to the new form, which wouldn't be possible this way. In fact, passing parameters with a form manager usually turns out to be a real nightmare, so I won't go into details about this problem.

In the example above, I created two local variables that I used as references for the new forms. However, I wouldn't really need them. They are just convenient in case I want to talk to the new forms. They won't cause any troubles, either, because they go out of scope (since they are local) and won't result in outstanding object references. The form itself is kept alive by the array that's a member of the form manager. This requires that the form manager stay alive until the application finishes; otherwise, all the forms would disappear, too.

As you can see, this is a lot of work compared to the simple DO FORM command above. So there are definite advantages to real forms when it comes to instantiation, especially multiple instantiation.

Current score: forms 1, form classes 0.

## DataEnvironment

When I started to write this book, I was under the impression that I wouldn't have to write about data at all. However, there are DataEnvironments that are somewhat object oriented (after all, they have their own FoxPro base class), even though you can't subclass them or do other cool things.

DataEnvironments can be attached only to forms—not to form classes. It's just as easy as that. No long explanations, no tricks for getting around this restriction. Form classes simply can't have attached data environments. Of course, you can still open tables (or other data sources) yourself and, contrary to popular opinion, form classes can also have their own data sessions. You, as the developer, just have to create them.  For obvious reasons, this makes it a lot harder to work with form classes than with regular forms.

Current score: forms 2, form classes 0.

## Inheritance

After discovering all the disadvantages of form classes, there must be something that's good about them, and there is: subclassing! Forms cannot be subclassed, but classes obviously can. This is a pretty good reason to use form classes instead of forms, and to deal with all the disadvantages. As a matter of fact, most gurus actually use form classes.

This is a big advantage for the form classes. It's hard to give a score, but I'd say that the form classes tied the ball game (at least). So the decision becomes even more difficult. But do you really have to decide?

## Combining form classes and forms

As I discussed earlier, forms cannot be subclassed. However, they can be at the end of the inheritance tree, which means that you can create a form class, subclass it several times, and create a form based on this class.

This combines the advantages of both form classes and regular forms. I usually create all my forms in classes, create a form based on those classes (and don't change a single property, method or member object there), and add a data environment. Whenever I need a subclass, I simply create it in my inheritance tree, create a new form based on that class and add a new data environment there (which is somewhat redundant, but not everything can be perfect).

This way, I combine all the advantages. I have subclassing, I have data environments, and I also have the ease of instantiation using the regular DO FORM command.

That should be an easy sale!

# Templates

Now that you know how to use form classes and forms together, you're missing only one little piece of information: "How do we create forms with a certain base class?"

There are two different ways. One is to use the *AS* keyword in the CREATE FORM command, as in the following example:

```
CREATE FORM NewForm AS MyForm FROM Forms.vcx
```

The other way is to define a default template in the Visual FoxPro Options dialog. The class you define there will be used for each CREATE FORM command, unless you specify a different class using the *AS* clause. **Figure 1** shows where you can find that setting in the Tools/Options dialog.

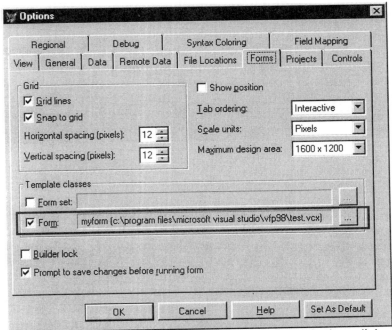

*Figure 1. You can set the default form class in the Options dialog.*

Defining a template class is a good idea if you create many forms based on the same class. This could happen when you create lots of data entry forms, for instance. However, when you create many forms based on different classes, I recommend using the *AS* clause instead.

If you have specified a template class and you want to create a form that is not subclassed from one of your own classes, you can use the *DEFAULT* keyword:

```
DEFINE FORM NewForm DEFAULT
```

# Visual FoxPro base classes

I didn't write this book to explain all the FoxPro base classes and their details. However, I would like to take the time to point out some details that are worth a second look.

## NODEFAULT

Every FoxPro base class method is inherited from some internal class. Most of these methods have default behavior attached. For example, the default behavior of the KeyPress method makes sure the operating system recognizes that a key was pressed.

As I mentioned earlier, you can overwrite methods by adding code to the method in a subclass. If this were also true for original FoxPro behavior, it would be very hard to use FoxPro base classes, especially for beginners. Every time you added code without doing a DoDefault() it would possibly overwrite important default behavior and cause severe misbehavior. For this reason, you can't just overwrite default behavior.

However, there might be some reasons why you would like to overwrite the default FoxPro behavior. In this case, you can use the FoxPro keyword *NODEFAULT*.

When you add code to a method, the original behavior is always executed after all the added code. This is very handy because you can use *NODEFAULT* at any position in a method. You can even use it within IF statements. Suppose you want the user to be able to type only the characters "Y" and "N" in a special textbox. The following code attached to the textbox would accomplish that:

```
FUNCTION KeyPress
   LPARAMETERS nKeyCode, nShiftAltCtrl
   IF NOT (Chr(nKeyCode)="Y" OR Chr(nKeyCode)="N")
      NODEFAULT
   ENDIF
ENDFUNC
```

## Custom classes

The base class *Custom* plays a special role in the set of base classes. It might be the most frequently used class, too. *Custom* is used for most things that are not part of the interface. Custom classes are used to create manager and service objects, behavioral objects, business logic and more.

At first sight, custom classes might look like they don't have a lot of functionality, but they do. Custom classes feature a rich set of properties and methods. They are fully functional containers that feature methods such as AddObject(). They can also be edited using the Visual Class Designer, even though they don't have a visual appearance.

This is one disadvantage of the *Custom* class, because it's not exactly lightweight. For this reason, many people use other base classes, such as *Line* or *Relation*, when they don't need the whole *Custom* functionality. Of course, these classes were never meant to take the place of *Custom*. The *Line* class has a visual appearance, but if it serves as a replacement for *Custom*, its *Visible* property never gets set to .T., so this is not an issue. After all, these classes seem to work just fine and they are not as resource-intensive as *Custom*. This is really important when you instantiate lots of classes, or when performance is a big issue.

When *Custom* is used as a container, it isn't done to create interface classes, because custom classes have no visual appearance. A custom class is used as a container when you want to compose behavioral objects. This is not as obvious as creating composite objects for the interface, but in big applications you'll find more behavioral composition containers than interface containers.

## Control classes

Control classes are one of my personal favorites. They are very similar to the Visual FoxPro *Container* class, but they automatically set all the member objects protected. This means that you automatically create very clean composite classes without having to worry about protecting member objects. In fact, member objects can't even be made visible to the outside world. They can only be accessed through a special interface that talks to these objects.

**Figure 2** shows how a *Control* class looks in the Class Designer.

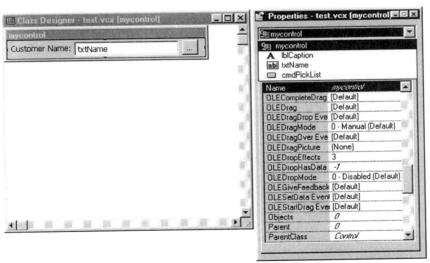

*Figure 2. A sample control class being assembled.*

In this example I created a composite class I can use for all my data-entry forms that require entering a customer name. The user can either enter the name directly, or click the command button to bring up a picklist form.

The class is composed of a control class and three different member objects. You can see the object's structure in the Properties window. Note that all the member objects are visible in the Properties window and can be modified. **Figure 3** shows how this class can be used in a form.

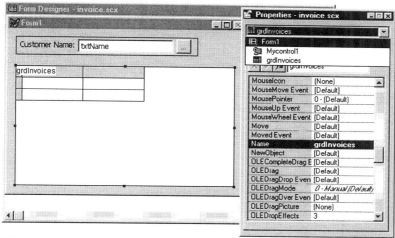

***Figure 3***. *A sample control class used in a form.*

Note that the property sheet for the form does not show the member objects of the control class—just the objects on the form.

## Adding properties on the fly

Visual FoxPro 6.0 supports adding properties on the fly, which is quite straightforward. Every object has a method called .AddProperty() that supports two parameters: the name of the new property and the initial value, which is optional. The default value for the new property is .F. just as it is in the Class Designer. Here is an example of one way to add a new property to the Visual FoxPro _Screen object:

```
_Screen.AddObject("SomeText","Hello World!")
```

Before Visual FoxPro 6.0, there was no internal feature that allowed adding properties on the fly. However, a public domain library called AddProp.fll did just what .AddProperty() does now. Sometimes *ADDPROP* is still useful—for example, whenever you want to add a property to an object created using the *SCATTER...* command— since these objects don't have the AddProperty() method. You can download AddProp.fll from the Developer's Download Files at www.hentzenwerke.com.

### Should you, or shouldn't you?

There has been quite a discussion about whether or not you should add properties on the fly. Object purists argue that it is bad design to do so, and I have to grant them a point. On the other hand, there are some good reasons to add properties on the fly. Most of these are concerned with performance and ease of use.

Imagine you want to create a little component that resizes a form and changes the dimensions of each contained object. The component should be very generic and usable in every application without making any changes to the existing interface classes.

To resize interface objects, you would most likely need to remember the original object dimensions. You could store these values internally in your component, but it might be a difficult and confusing process. On top of that, you could waste valuable resources by keeping those values in memory once the object is already destroyed. Keeping track of objects that get destroyed is not trivial unless you redesign these objects, and that's exactly what you don't want to do. One way to do that would be to use an observer object that keeps track of objects, but this might turn out to be a major performance bottleneck. For this reason, you would most likely keep wasting memory by tracking values that are no longer valid.

The next big issue to deal with is to map the values to objects. You'd have to store the object path, which takes up a lot of resources. Also, object paths might not be unique if somebody reuses object references. Another way of doing this is to store object references, which isn't recommended, because you might end up with outstanding object references.

The easy way to resolve these problems is to add a property to each interface object that stores the original dimensions. These properties automatically go away when the object dies, and it's easy to find them because they are encapsulated in each object. So now, all that's left to do is to code the resize algorithm. But that should be trivial, right?

However, there are a couple of issues attached to adding these properties on the fly. Imagine another component that adds properties with the same name, or maybe the object already has those properties…

I recommend using AddProperty() as sparsely as possible. Only use it in special cases like the example above. Don't consider using AddProperty() as long as you are in the design phase. The need for AddProperty() will arise soon enough. AddProperty() should be used only for implementation-specific reasons, and its use should never be an intentional design decision.

# Collections

Creating a unique object reference for each object you create might not be a good way to go, especially when you create a set of similar objects, like a lot of forms. Even if every object has its own reference, you might want to have an easy way to iterate through objects, for example. Collections provide this functionality.

Collections are arrays of object references. You've already seen a simple collection in the form manager example above. It used an ApplicationForms array to provide object references to all the forms I wanted to launch.

The advantages of collections are obvious. They make it easy to provide object references in a scenario where you need multiple references to similar objects. They also make it very easy to handle these objects. Let's assume you wanted to iterate through all forms. This could simply be done using FOR…NEXT or FOR EACH… loops.

Collections usually follow a simple naming convention. All collections are named in plural to show that they reference multiple objects. That's why I called my form manager collection "ApplicationForms". This is pretty simple and doesn't seem like much, but I always have a hard time remembering what each property, object or collection is called. Bringing the plural rule to mind actually saved me quite a lot of recompilation time.

In the form manager example, I used a collection to actually provide object references that keep the objects alive. However, collections can also host copies of references to simplify object handling. Each FoxPro form, for instance, has an Objects collection that grants us access to every object in that form, even though each object has its very own object reference.

Accessing objects through a collection is very easy; it's a lot like accessing items in an array. You simply use the name of the collection plus the item index instead of the object name. Suppose you have a grid with several columns. You can access each column directly with its name, or you can use the Columns collection. Both ways are demonstrated in the following example:

```
SomeObject.oGrid.colPriceColumn.Header1.Caption = "Price"
SomeObject.oGrid.Column(5).Header1.Caption = "Price"
```

The fifth column is called "colPriceColumn" and it has several member objects, including the header and maybe a textbox.

## FoxPro's collections

Visual FoxPro provides a variety of built-in collections. Most container objects have a *Controls* collection. In addition to that, some objects have special collections that are unique. FormSets have a *Forms* collection, PageFrames feature a *Pages* collection, Grids have a *Columns* collection, and so forth.

Working with these collections is straightforward. FoxPro takes care of everything. It makes sure each item in the collection points to the right object, it makes sure the collection always has the correct number of items, and it also makes sure that there are no outstanding references that keep objects alive that are supposed to die.

The most commonly used collection in Visual FoxPro is *Controls*. It makes accessing member objects of containers very easy and generic. You can iterate through this collection using either a FOR...EACH or a FOR...NEXT loop. When using the FOR...NEXT version, you can use the *ControlCount* property of the container to determine the number of items.

There isn't a lot you can do with these collections other than access objects. You can't just redimension these collections because FoxPro knows the difference between its own collections and arrays. However, some collections provide an interface (such as an AddItem() method) to add or remove items from a collection.

The item order in a collection does not necessarily reflect visible sequences you see on the screen. In a grid, for instance, columns might be dragged all over the place, but the collection would always keep the original sequence. Usually other properties help to query object sequences.

## The collections you create yourself

You can also create collections personally, using arrays as object references, as demonstrated in the form manager example. However, Visual FoxPro does not recognize these collections as real collections. You have to deal with all the details yourself. This means you have to make sure the array gets redimensioned, keep all the items in the array in sync, and make sure your collection doesn't accidentally keep objects alive that are supposed to be destroyed.

Let's have another look at the form manager example. Here is the code that maintained the collection:

```
FUNCTION NewForm( FormClass, FormClassLib )
    * We check if we have to redimension the array
    IF Alen(THIS.ApplicationForms,1)=1 AND NOT
VarType(THIS.ApplicationForms(1))="O"
        DIMENSION THIS.ApplicationForms( Alen(THIS.ApplicationForms,1) + 1 )
    ENDIF

    * Now we create the new form and show it
    *-- more code goes here...

    * We check if the form has been created
    IF VarType(THIS.ApplicationForms(Alen(THIS.ApplicationForms,1)))="O"
        * Form has been created
        THIS.ApplicationForms(Alen(THIS.ApplicationForms,1)).Visible = .T.
        * We return a reference to the new form
        RETURN THIS.ApplicationForms(Alen(THIS.ApplicationForms,1))
    ELSE
        * Form hasn't been created,
        * so we have to delete the reference from the array
        IF Alen(THIS.ApplicationForms,1) = 1
            * The array only has one item, so we can't make it any smaller
            THIS.ApplicationForms(1)=.NULL.
        ELSE
            * We shrink the array
            DIMENSION THIS.ApplicationForms(Alen(THIS.ApplicationForm,1) - 1 )
        ENDIF
        RETURN .NULL.
    ENDIF
ENDFUNC
```

At the very beginning, I check if the collection has to be redimensioned. FoxPro arrays can't have a length of 0, which brings up a bad situation at the beginning. So I simply define an array with one item, and whenever I run through the code, I check if the array has a length of 1. If it does, I check if the first item is an object reference. If it is an object reference, I have to add an item; otherwise, I can simply use the existing one.

Then comes the code that actually instantiates the form. I removed that code from this example to keep it simple.

The next program line checks if the object creation was successful. If not, I have to remove the item from the array. Of course, I can only remove an item if the length of the array is at least two items. Otherwise, I'd end up with a length of 0, which wouldn't be valid in FoxPro.

However, this code doesn't deal with all possible scenarios. What if the user closes a form using the window's Close box? In this case the form would just disappear, leaving a .NULL. value in one item of the collection. In order to handle this scenario perfectly, I'd need to change the form classes so they tell the manager object that they are about to die. This is not a good way to go. Whenever other objects require redesign in order to make other objects work, there is something wrong and you should think of a better way.

In this example, I could simply iterate through the collection before I add a new item, and clean up the collection. This wouldn't be a perfect solution, because it could still throw the collection out of sync from time to time, but for most uses it should do the trick. If this weren't good enough, I'd have to use an observer component which, on the other hand, might introduce a performance problem.

This code iterates through the collection before continuing with the standard behavior:

```
FUNCTION NewForm( FormClass, FormClassLib )
   * First of all, we make sure the collection is OK
   THIS.CleanCollection()

   * We check if we have to redimension the array
   IF Alen(THIS.ApplicationForms,1)=1 AND NOT ;
      VarType(THIS.ApplicationForms(1))="O"
      DIMENSION THIS.ApplicationForms( Alen(THIS.ApplicationForms,1) + 1 )
   ENDIF

   * Now we create the new form and show it
   *-- more code goes here…

   * We check if the form has been created
   IF VarType(THIS.ApplicationForms(Alen(THIS.ApplicationForms,1)))="O"
      * Form has been created
      THIS.ApplicationForms(Alen(THIS.ApplicationForms,1)).Visible = .T.
      * We return a reference to the new form
      RETURN THIS.ApplicationForms(Alen(THIS.ApplicationForms,1))
   ELSE
      * Form hasn't been created,
      * so we have to delete the reference from the array
      IF Alen(THIS.ApplicationForms,1) = 1
         * The array only has one item, so we can't make it any smaller
         THIS.ApplicationForms(1)=.NULL.
      ELSE
         * We shrink the array
         DIMENSION THIS.ApplicationForms(Alen(THIS.ApplicationForm,1) - 1 )
      ENDIF
      RETURN .NULL.
   ENDIF
ENDFUNC

PROTECTED FUNCTION CleanCollection
   LOCAL loObject
   LOCAL lnCounter
   lnCounter = 1
   FOR EACH loObject IN THIS.ApplicationForms
      IF NOT VarType(loObject) = "O"
         * The current item is not an object reference
         IF Alen(THIS.ApplicationForms) > 1
            * We delete the item from the array
            Adel( THIS.ApplicationForms, lnCounter )
            DIMENSION THIS.ApplicationForms( Alen( THIS.AppliactionForms ) -1 )
            lnCounter = lnCounter - 1
         ELSE
            * The array has only one item which has to remain
```

```
         ENDIF
      ENDIF
      lnCounter = lnCounter + 1
   ENDFOR
ENDFUNC
```

As you can see, I created a separate method that makes sure all the items in the collection are object references. Doing it this way, I can check the collection from every method that uses it, just to make sure everything is fine. I could have made this method even more generic by passing the array's name as a parameter. This might be a good idea in a real-world scenario (unless performance is extremely important) but to keep the demo simple, I didn't do that here.

## Creating VB-style collections

Visual Basic handles collections very nicely. They all have a name instead of a numeric index that nobody can remember anyway. In addition, they usually act much like an object. In other words, the collection has properties and methods. The good news is that in Visual FoxPro 6.0 you can create collections that are much like the ones in VB.

I'll deal with the naming part first. Suppose I have a form that has a button and a textbox. I add a collection (array) called "members" that will provide a generic way to access all the members of the form. I can either pass a numeric index to that collection, or the name of the object I want to talk to. I'll use the new access methods to accomplish this goal:

```
FUNCTION Members_Access
   LPARAMETERS lvIndex

   DO CASE
      CASE VarType(lvIndex) = "C"
         DO CASE
            CASE Lower(lvIndex) = "button"
               RETURN THISFORM.Command1
            CASE Lower(lvIndex) = "editbox"
               RETURN THISFORM.Edit1
            OTHERWISE
               IF Type("THIS."+lvIndex) = "O"
                  RETURN THIS.&lvIndex.
               ELSE
                  RETURN .NULL.
               ENDIF
         ENDCASE

      CASE VarType(lvIndex) = "N"
         RETURN THIS.Controls(lvIndex)

      OTHERWISE
         RETURN .NULL.
   ENDCASE
ENDFUNC
```

The first thing the access method does is to check for the type of the parameter. If it is a character, the method checks to see whether it's a "button" or an "editbox". In this case it returns the reference to one of the existing objects. Otherwise, the method checks if there is a member object that happens to have the name that was passed as a parameter. If so, it returns a reference to this object.

In case the parameter is numeric, I simply use the internal *Controls* collection and return the item with the index that was passed.

Suppose I wanted to access the first button object on the form. I can do that in three different ways:

```
? Form.Members(1).Caption
? Form.Members("button").Caption
? Form.Members("Command1").Caption
```

Now I can access all the members in a nice and easy way. This is very useful. I have a class that I use to filter data. It expects a grid to be in the same form. The algorithm goes out and tries to find that grid itself, which works great unless there is more than one grid in that form. Using a generic collection that allows referencing the grid by some generic name instead of the real name that can be different in every form, it allows me to reuse that class in many more instances.

Note that I didn't have to redimension any array or anything else, because I only used the access method to reroute the calls. This makes handling these collections a lot easier. I don't have to worry about outstanding object references or anything like that.

Now I only need to add methods and properties to my collection. To do so, I have to create another object that actually hosts these members. Whenever the collection is accessed without passing an index, I simply reroute the call to that object. To do so, I have to change the code from above just a little bit. All I do is alter the OTHERWISE... case that used to return .NULL.:

```
OTHERWISE
   RETURN THIS.oMembers
```

Of course, this requires that there is an object called *oMembers*. This object can have all kinds of properties and methods. Here are a couple of examples:

```
Form.Members.AddObject("Button2","CommandButton")
Form.Members.Refresh
? Form.Members.Count
```

For these examples, you might not want to reroute the call to a separate object, but to *THIS*. The form object already has a Refresh and an AddObject method. It doesn't have a *Count* property, but that is easy to add. I suggest you create a *Count* property that has an access method that reroutes the call to the *ControlCount* property that's maintained internally:

```
FUNCTION Count_Access
   RETURN THIS.ControlCount
ENDFUNC
```

This way, I created a self-organizing collection that actually grows with the product. It allows me to access every object in the form and all the form's methods in a generic way. At the same time, I don't introduce any major risks. Very cool and very elegant!

## Collections provided by others

Collections can be found in almost all object-oriented applications and components. You might encounter some that are quite different from those I've described so far. This is especially true for COM servers and ActiveX controls. Some might grant you access to each item by simply referencing them. Others require querying collections first, which will then return an array of objects. Sometimes it gets even more complex.

However, it seems that most modern implementations feature the simple way that allows you to access each item directly. Also, a lot of collections have an *Items* subcollection and a *Count* property, which makes the handling even easier. Here's a simple example that uses *Count*:

```
LOCAL lnCounter
FOR lnCounter = 1 TO oObject.Collection.Items.Count
   oObject.Collection( lnCounter ).Execute()
ENDFOR
```

At first sight it might seem weird that a collection is an array of object references, but it can also have properties. But hey, I never said collections and arrays were exactly the same.

# Features you might miss in Visual FoxPro

Visual FoxPro has a powerful object model. However, other object-oriented languages support a couple of things that Visual FoxPro doesn't. With every new version of Visual FoxPro, we get a little bit closer to having full support for all object-oriented concepts. Visual FoxPro 6.0 has only a couple of little things missing, and most of them keep even the experts arguing whether or not they belong in a truly object-oriented system.

## Multiple inheritance revisited

I talked in brief about multiple inheritance, which means that one class inherits from two or more parent classes. Visual C++ allows you to use this feature.

Multiple inheritance introduces a whole set of new possibilities. Let's re-examine the Movie Theater Complex example I used in Chapter 1. I talked about buying other theaters and creating classes for these new theaters that link in the existing set of classes. To do so, I simply created a new subclass of the existing screen classes and added all the methods and properties the screen classes had. However, this might not be the perfect solution, because changes in the theater class would not automatically be inherited in this class.

Using multiple inheritance, I could simply create a new class that inherits from the foreign screen class as well as from my screen class. This way, it would automatically inherit the interface and the original behavior. Unfortunately, this perfect-looking scenario introduces a couple of serious problems. What if both parent classes have methods or properties with the same name? How is FoxPro supposed to know what the parent class is when a DoDefault() is executed?

C++ programmers will assure you that there are perfect solutions for all these problems, and I don't doubt it, but it's obvious that these constructions can end up as a maintenance nightmare. I personally would like to see multiple inheritance in Visual FoxPro, mostly to resolve implementation issues. However, I realize that not having multiple inheritance is not a show-stopper, and that it would introduce problems that would make Visual FoxPro almost impossible to use, especially for beginning and intermediate programmers.

## Friendship relations

There are four different method and property visibilities in an OOP language: *public, protected, hidden*, and *friend*. I've discussed the first three. *Friend* is very similar to *protected*, but it allows you to define that certain classes are friends of others and therefore can see all the protected properties.

This is very useful in complex object systems and in composition scenarios. Without *friend* relations, you'd often end up making properties or methods available to all objects, just because one other class (possibly a container class that hosts the current object) needs access. This often turns a clean design into a badly polluted implementation.

If I could choose one missing feature to be implemented in Visual FoxPro, it would definitely be *friend* relations.

## Static properties

Static properties are shared among objects. This, again, is a technique that's popular in C++. You could define a property as static, instantiate an infinite number of objects of this class, and refer to this property. No matter from which object you talk to this property, you would always talk to the same property. This could be used to count instances, or to save memory by allocating memory for properties that don't change. This is a great feature for a low-level language like C++ that does a lot of things in a hybrid fashion, rather than in a truly object-oriented way. However, it breaks all the rules of encapsulation. Sometimes it seems that Visual FoxPro's object model is cleaner than the C++ model.

## Operator overloading

Overloading operators means that a standard operator like "+" behaves differently than it was initially intended. Certain operators like "+" behave in a well-defined way in Visual FoxPro. If the operator is used with two numeric values, they are added to each other. When this operator is used with strings, they are concatenated. However, there is no associated behavior for this operator when it's used with two objects. This makes sense because there couldn't be a standard way to add an object to another one. The same applies for other variable types.

However, it might make sense to sum up objects of a certain type. If there are two invoicing objects, we could calculate a grand total by simply adding one object to the other. At the same time we calculate the total tax amount, we could come up with a new number of items in stock (by subtracting the ones we sold in that invoice) and so forth. Obviously, FoxPro couldn't know how to do all of this. With operator overloading, we could customize the behavior of the "+" operator (this works with all kinds of operators) for specific items.

This is not an object-oriented feature at all because it works with other items and variable types as well, but it seems to go along great with objects. You could specify how objects are added or subtracted from each other.

This would be a truly great feature to have, but again, it's not object-oriented and there must be better ways to accomplish the same goal in truly object-oriented ways. You could provide methods that do just the same as the operators would. In addition, I don't see a way to implement something like that in Visual FoxPro because C++ compiles its programs in a very different manner from Visual FoxPro.

## Copying objects

In Visual FoxPro, there is no way to create an exact copy or clone of an object at runtime. There is no question that this might be handy in a number of scenarios. Well, maybe in Visual FoxPro 2000.

Note that the Visual FoxPro documentation lists a function to clone objects. However, this does not work at runtime. It is useful only when creating builders to automate processes while creating forms or classes.

# Chapter 3
# What's Not So Obvious

**So far we have discussed all major object-oriented concepts and how they are implemented in Visual FoxPro. However, Visual FoxPro supports a couple of features you won't find in other object-oriented languages. This chapter gives us the chance to discuss these and other issues that aren't as obvious as they might seem.**

## Instance programming and pseudo-subclassing

Visual FoxPro has features called *instance programming* and *pseudo-subclassing*. You may not have heard about them since they aren't widely discussed or generally known; however, almost everybody uses them without even knowing it.

This feature must be easy to use, but every now and then, the lack of specific knowledge brings up some serious problems. For this reason, I'd like to discuss this issue in detail, which should help you to use all the power of pseudo-subclassing and instance programming without running into their potential problems.

### Instance programming

What exactly is instance programming? Well, let me give you a little example. Let's assume we create a form class that contains one command button. We add some code to the command button to release the form when the button is clicked. **Figure 1** illustrates this scenario.

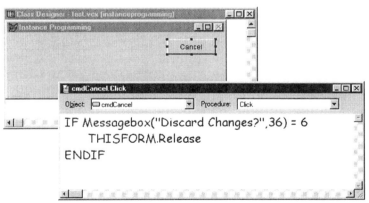

*Figure 1*. Our form class and command button.

To review: We created a new form class (let's call it *IP* for instance programming), which is a subclass of the FoxPro base class *Form*. The *IP* class has a member object called *cmdCancel*, which is a command button. This button is a subclass of ... well ... let's have a look at the Properties window in **Figure 2**.

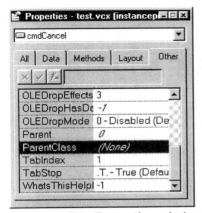

*Figure 2. The Properties window.*

Hmmm ... the Properties window says it doesn't have a parent class. That's strange. After all, I told you we couldn't create a class that didn't have a parent class. So what is the actual class? See **Figure 3**.

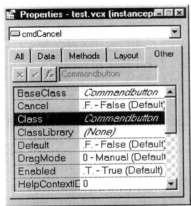

*Figure 3. The current class of the Properties window.*

FoxPro says the current class is *CommandButton*. That's strange, too! We just created a class that doesn't have a parent class, and the current class name is a FoxPro base class. Did we create such a class?

In fact, we didn't! All we created was a subclass of the FoxPro form *class* that had a predefined instance of a command button. There was no subclassing going on with the button. It is just an *instance* of the *CommandButton* FoxPro base class. So theoretically, we shouldn't be able to add code to one of the button's methods. Rather, we should create a button class, add the code there, and drop the button on the form. Everything else would break all kinds of object rules, because we would add code to an object rather than to a class.

However, adding code directly to object instances allows us to develop prototypes and actual applications at tremendous speed; it's one of FoxPro's most important Rapid Application Development (RAD) features.

By the way, creating FoxPro forms is 100 percent instance programming because not even the form itself is subclassed.

## Pseudo-subclassing

Now let's take this a step further and create a subclass of the whole *IP* form class. This class (let's call it *PS* for pseudo-subclassing) inherits everything from the *IP* class, including properties, methods, and all predefined member objects plus their assigned properties and methods.

Take note that only the form has been subclassed, just as in the *IP* class. The button is still of class *CommandButton* and doesn't have a parent class (well, it has, but only an internal one). However, FoxPro is very generous and will still allow you to add code to the button. In fact, you can even overwrite and inherit code just as if it were a real subclass. This is called *pseudo-subclassing*.

Most people use the terms *pseudo-subclassing* and *instance programming* interchangeably. However, they are not the same thing. Internally, pseudo-subclassing and instance programming are handled very differently. As you'll see later (when I explain how visual classes are stored internally), visual classes are stored in FoxPro tables. Each class gets one record in this table, as do all the newly defined member objects. FoxPro stores the code that is added to an instance (instance programming) in each member's record. When applying pseudo subclasses, the new class inherits all the information about the members but does not create a record for each of them, so FoxPro doesn't have a good place to store the new code and the overwritten properties. So it uses a little trick and stores this data directly with the class record. To assign the code and properties to the member objects, FoxPro adds the name of each object. So the button's Click method is now called "Function cmdCancel.Click" rather than "Function Click" as it would be in normal scenarios.

Of course, the user never sees these things, but he might experience some resulting problems. Let's try to fool FoxPro a little. To do so, we go back to the *IP* class and rename the Cancel button *cmdCancelButton*. Now let's look at the button in the *PS* class. The button is still there and it inherited the new name from its parent class. However, for some strange reason, all the code we assigned to this button has been removed. On first sight, this might appear to be a bug, but if you think about it, it's rather simple. As we've just discussed, FoxPro stores the name of the member object in order to assign the code to it. The code that has been removed belonged to an object called *cmdClick*. Of course, this object can't be found anymore because we renamed it. The subclass cannot know that the button in the form is still the same object. It thinks we removed the original object and added a new one. If we want to recover the original code, we need to cancel the current operation, go back to the parent class, and rename the button to its original name. Make sure you don't save the subclass. Otherwise FoxPro simply removes all your code and you'll have to start over from scratch.

This behavior might seem bad, but it used to be worse. In earlier versions, FoxPro thought the class library was corrupt whenever it couldn't find referenced objects, and wouldn't allow us to modify it at all. Imagine if you renamed an object in a class at the beginning of a class hierarchy. You might have to start your whole project from scratch again. Considering these facts, the current situation appears quite acceptable. After all, the advantages outweigh the disadvantages by far, especially when you're aware of the possible problems.

But wait, there's more! If you use DoDefault() in the member object's method, you can move on to the next paragraph, but if you use the scope resolution operator (::), you are in deep trouble. The scope resolution operator requires the name of the parent class, the method name, and possibly some parameters. But as we already know, the command button doesn't have a parent class, so we can't provide the necessary information for the scope resolution operator. This is one of the reasons why DoDefault() was introduced in Visual FoxPro 5.0. However, there are some tricks to make this work, even if you use Visual FoxPro 3.0, which didn't have DoDefault(). Here's an example that uses the previous example to demonstrate how this would work:

```
IP.cmdCancel::Click()
```

This code would go in the Click() event of the button. Remember I told you FoxPro simply stores the methods with the class and adds the name to assign the code to each object? We can now use this fact to our advantage and add the object name in front of the message name. This way, FoxPro can identify the code we try to run and execute it, even if the syntax doesn't seem to match the normal scope resolution requirements.

However, I recommend using DoDefault() instead, even though you might take a bit of a performance hit. I think the ease of maintenance outweighs that by far. Keep in mind that neither instance programming nor pseudo-subclassing is truly object-oriented. They are shortcuts to make the developer's life easier and more productive. If you want to avoid all the troubles this might introduce, you could go the truly object-oriented route. You could create a form class, create a button class, and finally create a subclass of the form class and change nothing but drop the button on it. Whenever you wanted to change the behavior of the button, you would create a subclass of the button and another subclass of the original form, and drop the button on this form as well. This becomes a nightmare if you have many member objects. Imagine a form that has only five members. Depending on how you want to change the behavior, you could end up with as many as 25 different subclasses of the form. Now imagine you have 25 different objects rather than five. In this case, you might end up with 625 different subclasses. This, of course, would be the case only when you wanted to change the behavior of each object independently from all the other objects, which is improbable.

I think you can see the issue, and I believe it's well worth it to accept the disadvantages of instance programming and pseudo-subclassing instead.

## Visual vs. non-visual classes

One of the great features of Visual FoxPro is its Visual Class Designer. It allows you to create classes in a visual way rather than deal with a huge amount of source code. However, you don't have to use the designer. You can always go the source code route; by doing so, you gain a couple of advantages.

## Advantages of non-visual classes

Let's examine a couple of reasons for using source-code-only classes. First, they might be a bit faster. According to my own measurements, classes that are stored in PRGs instantiate about twice as fast as classes that are stored in VCX libraries. This changes from scenario to scenario, but it seems that source code classes are a lot faster, especially for first-time instantiation. Once an instance of a class has been created, FoxPro caches the class definition, and the speed seems to be about equal.

The reason for the speed disadvantages of visual classes is due to the way they are stored. VCX files are simply DBFs with a different extension. When a class gets instantiated, FoxPro scans the table, looks for compiled code that is stored in the table, and checks for information about possible parent classes. If parent classes are found, they have to be searched as well. Classes that are stored in PRG files are one huge chunk of compiled code, and VFP doesn't have to add all the overhead of SEEKing classes and their inheritance information.

Another factor that needs to be considered is class size. The larger the class, the less the difference in instantiation speed. The reason is simple. The bigger the class, the longer it takes to instantiate it. If it takes 50 milliseconds to instantiate a class, it doesn't really matter that it took three milliseconds to search the VCX and only one to find the definition in the PRG file. However, if it only takes a millisecond or two to instantiate the class, an additional overhead of three milliseconds matters a lot.

A couple of handling issues seem to be resolved a lot better in source code classes. Include files (.H extension files), for instance, are hard to handle in visual classes, and you're also limited to a single include file at a time. Further, you cannot use precompiler commands wrapped around methods or property definitions.

Another issue is size. Visual class libraries have a tendency to grow huge, because every time they are modified, FoxPro deletes the old version of your class and adds it again at the bottom of the file. Also, a table with memo fields is always a little bigger than a plain text file. Source code classes, on the other hand, are very compact. Furthermore, because source code classes are stored in regular text files, file corruption isn't a big issue. VCX files, on the other hand, are more fragile and might get corrupted every now and then.

The final advantage I want to point out is the ease of renaming classes, properties and methods, and the ease of redefining class structures. However, this advantage might also turn into a disadvantage because renaming and redefining can lead to other problems further down the road.

## Why not go the visual route?

Going the visual route has many advantages. Almost all of them are a result of the proper internal organization of classes in each library. It's easy to browse source code on a per-class basis. Viewing class hierarchies and inheritance trees is supported by many tools like the Class Browser. Visual design tools consolidate properties and methods from classes and superclasses and display all the available ones in a properly ordered list called *Property-Sheet*.

Using non-visual classes, you're on your own with all these issues. Non-visual class libraries can be a big mess of code that has no particular order or organization whatsoever. Properties and methods are spread over the whole file, possibly even over multiple files, and there is no way to see them all at once. This makes it easy to forget about them, or even to redefine them accidentally, since there is no integrated mechanism to warn you about a possible problem. This gets even trickier if you want to use predefined events. In the property sheet, you can simply pick one of the available events and add code to it. In source code, this isn't so easy. You have to remember the event names for each class and where each class was derived from. Otherwise, you have to look it up, which is a very time-consuming process.

The Visual Class Designer takes care of all the stupid little standard tasks like adding objects to containers, setting properties, and adding code to methods. Following the concept of "information at your fingertips," the whole class definition is broken into pieces to show only the part of the class you're currently working on. This enhances productivity a great deal so you can concentrate on the essentials of programming, which is resolving a business problem—*not* taking care of technical issues.

The majority of the visual design tools have been enhanced in Visual FoxPro 6.0. The Visual Class Designer got a whole new dialog to manage methods, properties and member objects, as shown in **Figure 4**.

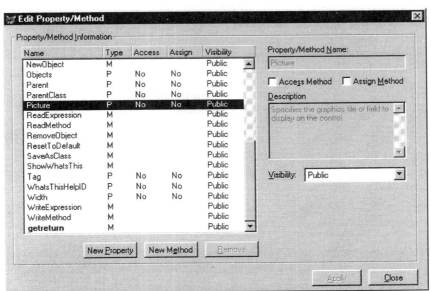

*Figure 4. The Visual Class Designer's new Edit Property/Method dialog for managing methods, properties and member objects.*

Using this dialog, you can create and delete new properties and methods, specify member visibility, and create access and assign methods. After using this dialog for a couple months, it was hard for me to imagine going back to Visual FoxPro 5.0 and living without it.

Another great tool that has been around since the first version of Visual FoxPro is the Class Browser. It has changed a lot since then; it's become easier to use and more powerful at the same time. The new browser also has a slightly different look and feel, as illustrated in **Figure 5**.

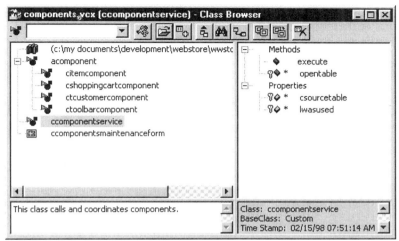

***Figure 5****. The new Class Browser.*

The browser allows you to view classes in hierarchical or alphabetical order, even across class libraries. It also displays class details such as properties, methods and class documentation. We'll examine the Class Browser in more detail in Chapter 5.

Of course, all these tools are only in addition to the centerpiece, which is the Visual Class Designer itself. It consists of four main components: the Class window, the Code Snippet Editor, the Properties window and the Classes/Controls toolbar. See **Figure 6**.

I do not intend to explain the details of the Class Designer because many other people have spent a lot of time doing that already. I think the advantages of this visual design tool are rather obvious.

A further advantage of visual classes is the ability to create builders. Builders can automate tasks while designing a class. The concept of builders is unique to Visual FoxPro. It is based on the fact that FoxPro always uses live objects in the Visual Class Designer. This means that you can talk to classes programmatically, as if they were objects. This way you can assign properties, add code to methods, and instantiate new member objects. Despite the fact that this is an extremely interesting topic, I will leave this one to another book in this set.

Also, keep in mind that most third-party tools are optimized for visual class libraries. Even some tools Microsoft provides rely on VCX storage. A typical example would be the Modeling Wizards that I'll discuss in Section 3 of this book.

## Visual classes: Nintendo for adults?

Here are some of the arguments I keep hearing: "Real programmers don't use visual design tools" and "The Visual Class Designer is like a video game for adults." To make a long story short: *I couldn't agree less!* (This is sort of like the old adage "Real programmers don't use code generators.")

Does a person become a better programmer because he's able to specify a default value for a property in source code rather than in a Properties window? I don't think so! Does one become a better programmer because he is able to identify a method in a huge PRG file rather than getting to it with a double-click in the Visual Class Designer? I don't think so! Does one become a better programmer because she can add member objects programmatically rather than dropping them in a container by a simple mouse operation? I doubt it! Does one create more efficient code when creating PRGs than when using VCXes? Well, maybe! But even if non-visual classes have a slight performance advantage, other issues outweigh that by far. Creating user interfaces in a non-visual way is quite a nightmare and the results are usually rather ugly. And even for non-interface classes, productivity and handling benefits are overwhelming.

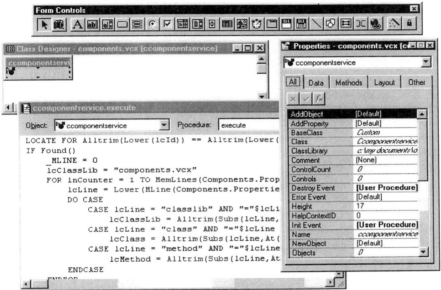

*Figure 6*. The four main components of the Visual Class Designer.

In the end, the only difference between good and bad programmers is the resulting application they produce, and in order to create a good application, highly productive programmers are needed. At the same time, code quality has to remain high.

Visual design tools, property sheets, code snippet editors and the Class Browser are outstanding tools that raise a programmer's productivity and help to maintain code quality at the same time. Let's be more productive!

## Some classes are non-visual only

Unfortunately, not all classes are available in the Visual Class Designer. Among the ones that can only be edited in source code are *Pages* (not *PageFrames*), *Grid Columns* and *Headers*. However, you can subclass all these classes in source code.

Many of the classes that can't be modified in a visual way are specialized containers that can only live in certain other containers. Pages, for instance, can only live in PageFrames, and Columns can only live in Grids. Nevertheless, almost any kind of object can be contained in these classes. Usually you'd modify the container classes in the Visual Class Designer and set some kind of property to instantiate these specialized member objects. In Grids, for instance, you can simply set the *ColumnCount* property and FoxPro will add new columns on the fly. However, all the added columns are of the FoxPro base class *Column* and can't be of a special user-defined class. If you want to add your own column class, you can define that in source code, set the *ColumnCount* property to 0 and add the columns on the fly (at runtime) using the AddObject() method. Because columns have to have some member objects, these must also be instantiated on the fly or defined in the source code. No matter how this is done, you always lose the advantages and power of the visual design tools.

## Creating your own set of base classes

Using Visual FoxPro base classes directly without subclassing is a big no-no. You should subclass each base class before instantiating it or using it in the Form Designer. This adds a lot of flexibility to the design. You can always go back later, change a couple of properties, modify some behavior or add new methods. This is especially important when starting with Visual FoxPro, because it makes a project more forgiving—you can always go back and correct mistakes you made earlier in the cycle.

Creating your own set of classes makes it possible to make system-wide changes within a matter of minutes. Let's assume you discovered a bug that influences your whole system. I just had such a bug. I used the InteractiveChange and the ProgrammaticChange events to discover record pointer movement and other changes in text fields. However, sometimes this event wouldn't fire, so I added an assign method for the *Value* property in my textbox base class that fired an OnChange() method. I basically created my own system-wide event that would fire whenever the *Value* property changed. This helped to resolve a problem that had us hooked for months. After making this change (which took me only a couple of minutes), I was able to remove about 50 items from our bug-tracking system. I could do this only because I had created my own "top-level" entry point.

Using your own base classes does more than help to resolve your own mistakes and problems. You can also use them to change standard behavior or appearance. Maybe you don't like FoxPro's default font. No problem! Go to your base class and change it. It only takes a couple of minutes...

This first level of subclasses is usually referred to as your own set of *base* or *foundation* classes. Once you have this class library in place, you can basically forget about FoxPro's original base classes. Unfortunately, there is no way to tell FoxPro to display these classes instead of the internal base classes. This leaves us with the risk of using the wrong set of classes, which might result in hard-to-find bugs.

Fortunately, there are a couple of tools that check class libraries and force the use of certain base classes. The PowerBrowser is one of these tools. It comes with some wizards that deal with all kinds of base class issues. This tool is freeware and can be downloaded from the Developer's Download Files at www.hentzenwerke.com. Future updates to this tool will be available at www.eps-software.com.

## Some suggestions

When creating your set of base classes, you can take care of some issues you might run into in a later stage of your development cycle.

I'm always concerned with creating applications that provide an interface the user is familiar with. Usually I stick to the Microsoft Office standards. One of the first steps to meet these standards is to change the standard font for all controls from Arial to MS Sans Serif or to the newer Tahoma. Font size should be 8 points. However, this could lead to problems if the user runs large fonts. In this case I switch back to the Arial font, the logic for which is built into my base classes.

I also try to make sure all objects have a consistent programming interface. Unfortunately, many of the FoxPro base classes do things a little differently. Some have a Release method, some don't. Some containers support an *Objects* collection while others have specialized ones like *Forms* or *Pages*. Some objects have Show and Hide methods while others only have a *Visible* property. I can take care of all these issues right in my base classes and save myself a lot of headache later down the road.

I think you get the idea about what kind of things belong in your set of base classes. Keep in mind that all the changes you made are subclassed into every single class you use in your project. Therefore, you should be concerned about performance. Adding 10 milliseconds to the instantiation time of a textbox might end up adding another second or two when instantiating a complex form.

Having a powerful set of base classes can add a lot to your application and make it flexible for changes later on. Nevertheless, you should be very careful with the changes you make. A little change in a base class not only can fix a system-wide bug, but it also can introduce one. Keep in mind that one small change can affect your whole application.

# Chapter 4
# Using Shrink-Wrapped Classes

**One of the main ideas of object-oriented development is to reuse classes, objects, components and frameworks. This is true for classes we create ourselves, as well as those provided by third parties. Creating reusable components is not trivial, and we'll discuss this in depth in Chapter 8. Using well-designed classes and components is relatively easy. In this chapter I'll introduce the basics of working with existing classes, as well as a great set of classes that ship with Visual FoxPro: the Fox Foundation Classes.**

## Reuse what others create

In today's world of software development, everything is moving extremely fast. At the same time, quality standards are raised constantly and more rapidly than in almost any other business. Customers expect new releases and updates more frequently and are less likely to tolerate bugs and quality leaks. New features become more complex and time-consuming to create. To make a long story short: You won't be able to do everything yourself and provide the quality expected. Not even software giants like Microsoft can. Visual Studio 6.0, for instance, shipped with a number of tools that were not developed by Microsoft, but by some third-party technology providers. And that's good! It helped to raise the quality of the package a great deal.

I encourage you to follow the same strategy. You won't be able to do it at the same level as Microsoft (by purchasing companies or entire products with all the associated rights), but you can use shrink-wrapped classes, components and frameworks. There's nothing better than cutting out weeks or months of development time by using a third-party component for $299. Sure, the component might not do exactly what you want, but chances are good that someone has created a class library that serves a similar purpose. By modifying it slightly, you might get just what you need. The beauty of this is that you can purchase a component that has been developed and tested and is proven to work. Of course, there are a number of components out there that might be quite buggy, but it's easier to evaluate components this way easier than to write bug-free code yourself.

Speaking of component quality, I often hear that people are concerned about the quality of the libraries they use. And they should be! After all, people depend on the vendor they trust. However, I believe the quality of most components is a lot better than the quality you can produce in your own classes. The reason is simple. Let's say you need a text editor in your application that allows editing text in multiple fonts, styles and colors. Writing such an editor is not a trivial task. Rather than developing such a tool in-house, where it would be one among 100—all of which had to be finished within a certain time and budget—I'd rather use an editor developed by someone who specialized in the classes and most likely spent years on this task. To investigate the example a little further, I would like to add that creating specialized or complex components might require skills that the average development team simply doesn't have. The variety of tasks that must be accomplished during a development life cycle is simply too great to be mastered by a handful of people—no matter how talented they are.

As you'll see in the next couple of sections, there is quite a difference between classes, components and frameworks. And even in these groups, the way things are done varies greatly. I'll give you an overview of different types of available class libraries and components, explain their differences, and tell you how you can customize different types of objects.

## What is available?

The objective of this chapter is not to introduce a number of class libraries, components and frameworks, but to introduce different types of reusable classes and explain how to use them. They differ in the way you can use, subclass, and modify them. The tool that was used to develop these libraries also introduces a great difference. Classes programmed in Visual FoxPro can be used very differently from others created in Visual C++, Visual J++ or other tools that can create binary objects, simply because the underlying technology is different.

Besides the difference in applied technologies, there can be great differences in the design of the classes you want to utilize. Some might be entirely self-contained, while others require the environment to be in a specific state. Yet another type of shrink-wrapped classes might represent the global environment and will simply allow you to invoke your own classes inside this framework.

As you can imagine, the approach you take when dealing with different kinds of objects varies just as much as the underlying philosophies. In the following sections I'll introduce the most important groups of shrink-wrapped classes. Note that there is no "sharp edge" between those categories. Quite the opposite is true. A framework, for instance, might be made of black box objects.

### Black box objects

Black box objects are entirely self contained, have a clear interface, do not rely on environmental settings and can live within any kind of environment or project (at least within the same programming language). Black box objects are ideal objects. They represent the main idea of object-oriented development and guarantee total reuse combined with ease of implementation. Obviously, creating black box objects isn't trivial; otherwise everybody would create them and we wouldn't need to discuss any other groups of objects. Let's investigate the markings of black box objects.

The requirement that black boxes must be self-contained, independent of other objects, and have a clear interface by themselves already sounds tough to fulfill; the more we explore the details, the more problems we encounter.

First of all, black box objects cannot depend on other objects in memory. However, objects typically require other objects—otherwise they are useless. A form-manager black box object (which could be responsible for instantiating and managing forms, for example) would be useless if there were no forms, documents or even an application. A black box object must instantiate every object it depends on. All these objects (and related objects) therefore must belong to the black box object; otherwise there'd be an external dependency and the object wouldn't be a black box object anymore. For this reason, major base objects (such as a form manager and other manager objects) hardly ever are black box objects; they're usually white box objects (described later).

The next requirement for an object to qualify as a black box object is that it doesn't have any external dependencies regarding class definitions and inheritance trees. In other words, I should be able to simply drop a black box object on my design surface without worrying about setting any class libraries or placing them in a certain directory. This is difficult to achieve with Visual FoxPro VCXes or even classes that are defined in PRGs.

Yet another important quality of black box objects is that the programmer doesn't have to know about class internals in order to use them. This requires a very careful class design. A class must provide events and hooks (see Chapter 10, "Patterns") so it is flexible and easy to modify and subclass without having to know about the internals of the class. This also guarantees that, after redesigning the black box object's internals, everything that uses the objects will still work properly because the interface doesn't need to change—therefore, all the provided hooks will continue to work.

By now, you might be wondering whether it's possible to create black box objects in real-life scenarios. Surprisingly, the answer is "yes." Good examples for widely accepted and used black box objects are ActiveX components. You can simply drop one of these controls on your design surface and you won't have to worry about the state of your environment, your path or other system settings, or any other objects the object needs, because it will take care of all these issues. Also, you don't have to worry about internals. For instance, I frequently use the Microsoft TreeView control, and subclass and modify it to my liking. To do so, I use provided events and hooks. I couldn't care less what the control does internally when the user expands one of the nodes, because there is a method that lets me hook into this event and react appropriately. Typically I would change the node's icon. Showing all the subnodes, however, is the responsibility of the object.

Another great example of black box objects are FoxPro's base classes (or at least some of them). Again, you can drop a *Custom* class on any kind of container or you can instantiate it all by itself. It has default behavior and hooks you can use. When you subclass a *Custom* class, you don't need to worry about class libraries being set and so on. FoxPro handles those issues for you. Many other Visual FoxPro base classes are black box objects as well— *CommandButtons*, for instance. They can live in any kind of container as well as by themselves. It might not make a lot of sense to instantiate a command button that can't be displayed (as would be the case if you instantiated it by itself), but it works and therefore all the requirements are fulfilled. Subclassing command buttons works great. You can change their look and feel as well as button behavior. While doing that, have you ever worried about environment settings or other things the button depends on? Well, neither have I. Have you ever worried about the Click() event disappearing in a new release of Visual FoxPro? Neither have I. It's practically guaranteed that the interface won't change, even though the FoxPro base classes have undergone major internal changes since Visual FoxPro 3.0.

As you might have noticed, all the examples of black box objects share one characteristic: They are either native to the system (base classes) or somehow registered in the environment or in the operating system, using standards supported by your development environment (ActiveX). Purists might argue that this is yet another dependency, and therefore these examples aren't real black box objects. Well, I have to grant those purists a "gotcha." Looking at the situation from this angle, there *aren't* any real black box objects. But in this case, the term "black box object" is of no use in real life. I suggest we agree that the examples above are black boxes, which will allow us to use the term, and everybody will understand what we are talking about, shall we? All right!

## White box objects

People usually are talking about *white box objects* when they say "black box objects." These objects are very well designed and encapsulated. They can live in almost any kind of environment as long as it fulfills some basic requirements. White box objects also have some external dependencies, such as inheritance structures or other objects that have to be in memory. In order to subclass and modify white box objects, you might need to know about class internals such as the method you have to overwrite or the property you need to set. White box objects don't necessarily have hooks or event methods you can use, but you can overwrite existing methods. For this reason, you need to know what those methods do and where you would put your own behavior, when to invoke the original behavior, and so forth. It also seems to be a common characteristic of white box objects that the interface and the implementation are not separated strictly. For this reason, you must be careful when changing properties because this could break some internal processes.

A typical example of a white box object is the form manager I mentioned above. You can drop it in every environment that uses regular Visual FoxPro forms that follow some basic (object) interface structures. The more complex the form manager, the more standards and rules must be set in order to make the white box object work. In the simplest form, a form manager would require top, left, height, width and visible properties as well as a standard way to instantiate and release a form. I would still call such a generic object a well-designed object. In fact, white box objects are the kind of objects we're really trying to create. Even though creating black box objects is a noble objective, they're difficult to create, and white box objects often fulfill our needs. Everything beyond white box objects can only be achieved with tremendous effort—and the result typically isn't much more useful to the developer in a single-application environment.

Most frameworks are composed of white box objects. Every framework (see the "Framework" section of this chapter) has certain rules and standards that all objects within it must follow in order to work together. That's good design, although it makes it difficult to reuse many of the complex classes outside the framework. Keep in mind that the idea of reuse is applied on a larger scale when creating frameworks. The primary target is to create a complete object system that can be reused as a whole. Reusing pieces is a secondary target.

## COM components

The term "component" is one of the most overused in object-oriented development. Often collections of loosely coupled class libraries of a generic nature are called components. However, I'll describe these kinds of components in the section titled "Class libraries." In this chapter, we'll talk about *COM components*, also known as *COMponents*.

COMponents can also be seen as binary objects. They can be created with a variety of tools such as Visual FoxPro, Visual C++, Visual J++ and even Visual Basic. As their name indicates, COMponents are based on Microsoft's COM (Component Object Model) standard. COMponents come in a variety of incarnations. Some are COM servers while others are ActiveX controls. Visual FoxPro can't create ActiveX controls but it can use them better than most other tools. One of Visual FoxPro's specialties is its introduction of inheritance for ActiveX controls.

Inheritance is not supported by Microsoft's Component Object Model. The fact that Visual FoxPro does support inheritance adds a great deal of flexibility and maintainability to ActiveX controls. For instance, you can use the Microsoft TreeView control, subclass it, change properties and methods, and even overwrite some of its predefined behavior. This is truly unique to Visual FoxPro. It allows Visual FoxPro programmers to utilize and customize more components than any non-FoxPro developer. But be aware that there are limitations to the ability to subclass due to some internal standards ActiveX controls follow. Every property or method that represents a single entity can be subclassed and overwritten at will.

However, some ActiveX controls store a lot of information in single properties or structures. An example is a toolbar ActiveX control that I use frequently. It comes with a great designer that allows creating multiple toolbars, popup menus, buttons that can be dropped in toolbars and menus, combo boxes, and more. All this information is stored internally in the control. When I create a subclass of the control and change some of the buttons or add new ones, this new information (again) is stored in one place. This is basically the same as overwriting a single property, but in this case the property contained a lot of information. The disadvantage is that not all changes made in the parent class will make it to your subclass because they are explicitly overwritten. This behavior is unfortunate and limits the ability to subclass ActiveX controls seriously. Luckily, only the most complex controls make use of this technology.

Well, because you bought this book you're probably interested in solutions, not new problems you weren't even aware of. I'll try to do my best: Whenever you use an ActiveX control's property sheet, its designer, or the interfaces it provides in the Visual Class Designer, you run the risk of storing information in complex properties and, as a result, ruining your ability to subclass properly. For this reason, I recommend defining as much as possible in source code. The toolbar control I described above is a good example. Instead of using its very good class designer, I define through source code all the toolbars, buttons and other controls it might host. The control has collections of toolbars, and I can simply call an Add() method to add new ones. The same is true for buttons and other contained controls. I can also programmatically load images. This, of course, requires that I ship all the required images with my application. Using the integrated designers, even the image's binary information is stored internally. Inheritance works fine with any kind of source code, because that source is managed by Visual FoxPro—therefore you aren't limited by the control's internal design, which is most likely not prepared for subclassing. In fact, you are not really subclassing the control itself, but rather Visual FoxPro's ActiveX container class. The result is pretty much the same, except for the scenario I described above. Obviously, defining and decorating the control programmatically is not as straightforward as using the designers. For this reason, I go this route only when I really need to.

The reason for this limitation is not within the boundaries of Visual FoxPro, but rather can be found in the specification of the COM standard and the designs of the individual ActiveX controls. Keep in mind that most creators of ActiveX controls are not even aware of the fact that Visual FoxPro supports ActiveX subclassing, or they aren't aware of the power of inheritance and don't consider it a crucial part of object-oriented programming.

As mentioned earlier, ActiveX controls are a good example of black box objects. They are very easy to use—you simply select an *OLEControl* from the Controls toolbar, drop it on a container, select a control, and *voila*, you're done. You don't have to worry about path settings, inheritance trees, and so forth. Even distribution is easy (as long as the creator of the control didn't put any traps along the deployment path). Visual FoxPro's setup wizards take care of all the issues. Now you also know the reason why I wanted to talk about COM components before discussing class libraries or frameworks—those are simply a lot harder to use.

When you decide to use an existing ActiveX control, I highly recommend that you create a subclass of the control before you start working with it. The reasons are pretty much the same as for subclassing Visual FoxPro's base classes, but there are some additional reasons. The most important one is that you can easily switch to different controls. It might not be obvious why you'd want to do that, so I'll give you a quick example: Basically with every version of Visual FoxPro, Visual Basic or (lately) Visual Studio, Microsoft has released a new version of the *Common Controls*—a collection of controls that represent standard Windows interface elements, such as the TreeView or the ListView control. Unfortunately, it turned out that different versions of these controls were not compatible with each other. So it's possible that a new version of Visual Studio could break all your forms and containers that use this control. When you try to modify such a container class, FoxPro displays an error message about an invalid or unknown control, and then it simply ignores all the code and property settings you created for these controls. In other words: Your code is gone! You now have to re-code all these classes. From my own experience, I can tell you that this is a frustrating experience. But if you had a class for those controls, you could simply make modifications to the class, and all the subclasses would be updated according to your changes.

Unfortunately, there are a couple of limitations that can ruin this relatively friendly scenario. Sometimes a class remembers the old Global Unique ID (GUID), also known as the Universal Unique ID (UUID). In this case the old version of the control might be invoked instead of the new one. This can result in a situation that's … well … a mess. Some programmers code all ActiveX classes in source code for this very reason. Most people don't even know that's possible, but it is rather simple. Here's a simple example that demonstrates how to subclass the TreeView control in source code:

```
DEFINE CLASS oleTreeView as OLEControl
    OleClass = "COMCTL.TreeCtrl"
ENDDEFINE
```

The *OleClass* property specifies the ActiveX control you want to subclass. The value is the control's name as found in the registry. The class I referenced above is stored in the following key:

```
HKEY_CLASSES_ROOT\COMCTL.TreeCtrl
```

If we explore this structure a little further, we find a sub-key called "CurVer". The default value stored in this key identifies the most current version of the TreeView control installed on the system. In my case, this is "COMCTL.TreeCtrl.2", which is the TreeView that ships with Visual Studio 6.0. You can find this key right after the tree we referenced in the registry. So

whenever I specify "COMCTL.TreeCtrl" as my *OleClass*, I'm redirected to
"COMCTL.TreeCtrl.2". In future versions, this might be "COMCTL.TreeCtrl.3". I think you
get the idea...

However, this might cause a problem. What if "COMCTL.TreeCtrl.3" is not compatible
with "COMCTL.TreeCtrl.2"? Well, your application wouldn't work anymore, but luckily you
can specify the exact version of the TreeView control you want, like so:

```
DEFINE CLASS oleTreeView as OLEControl
   OleClass = "COMCTL.TreeCtrl.2"
ENDDEFINE
```

The difficulty now is to know in advance whether future versions of this control will be
compatible with the current one. It's obvious that you can't (unless you're a good psychic, and
I'm pretty sure even they have a hard time predicting what Microsoft plans to do next
regarding the common controls). I recommend always using the most current version that's
installed on the system, but I urge you to define this in a very flexible way, so you can fix the
problem quickly if a problem emerges. If all your TreeViews are subclassed from one
TreeView class (which is the proper way to do it), this is easy. You just change the *OleClass*
property in that class, recompile, and you have your fix. If you have multiple TreeView
classes, I recommend defining the name in a header file like so:

```
* Contents of ActiveX.H...
#DEFINE REGKEY_ACTIVEX_TREEVIEW "COMCTL.TreeCtrl.2"

* Contents of your PRG file...
DEFINE CLASS oleTreeView as OLEControl
   OleClass = REGKEY_ACTIVEX_TREEVIEW
ENDDEFINE
```

This allows you to change the name in one place and fix all its occurrences with a simple
recompile. Note that the example above shows partial contents of two different files—as
indicated by the comments.

Unfortunately, there is a catch! Since Visual Studio 6.0, many controls (especially the
ones from Microsoft) require a license file whenever one tries to create or subclass ActiveX
controls in source code. Since you have Visual Studio or at least Visual FoxPro on your
computer, you have all those licenses, but when you install your application on the computer
of a customer who doesn't have Visual Studio, the instantiation of those controls will fail and
result in an error message. In this case you'll be trapped again, because you now have to
rewrite your control in visual classes. I have some applications where I changed from source
code to visual classes and back four (!) times. By now I have them all in source code, and once
again I need to rewrite them as visual classes. Needless to say, this is not a motivating
experience. Unfortunately, I don't have a good solution for this particular problem
(obviously—otherwise I wouldn't need to rewrite my own classes). I can only recommend
testing whether a simple scenario runs on a "clean machine" (a computer that doesn't have
development components or Visual Studio installed) before you decide which way to go.

Let's have a quick look at some of the settings in the registry. Every key representing an
ActiveX control has a sub-key called *CLSID*. This is the class ID. Its default value is the GUID

that identifies the class. Web pages, for instance, use this ID to reference an ActiveX control rather than its name. You can use this ID to identify required OCX files on your hard drive. Simply use the registry editor's Find feature to search all the occurrences of this ID. This will eventually lead you to a key (rather than a value) of the same name. On my machine, the path to this setting (for the TreeView) is this:

```
HKEY_LOCAL_MACHINE\Software\CLASSES\CLSID\{C74190B6-8589-11D1-B16A-
00C0F0283628}
```

This key has a sub-key called "InprocServer32". Its default value is the file name of our ActiveX control (it usually is either an OCX or a DLL file). This information can be useful if you are using a setup tool other than the one provided by Visual FoxPro, or if you simply need to know what controls you used in your application (and the files representing these controls).

### Class libraries

Class libraries are a collection of classes, in this case written in Visual FoxPro. These classes can perform a great variety of tasks, but that's not the subject of this section. Instead, I'll discuss the different kinds of class libraries as well as how to use and subclass them.

Class libraries can be delivered as VCX files, as compiled applications (APP), or as raw source code in PRG files. Each version has its advantages. VCX files are typically class libraries that provide some kind of interface, such as forms, containers or buttons. PRG files are often used for middle-tier programming (see Chapter 9). Internet applications are a good example. The PRG format is a little more difficult to handle, but it also offers some performance advantages. APP files have the advantage of being self-contained. It's easy to instantiate a class that's defined in a compiled application because you don't have to worry about path settings and so on. On the other hand, they are a little confusing to subclass and reuse. You can't just drop a class from an APP file on your form or container. The APP format has a big advantage for third-party vendors, though, because it allows them to efficiently hide source code. This is a problem for most providers. Obviously they are interested in protecting their code. Would you want to sell several hundred thousand lines of source code for $149?

No matter what flavor the class library comes in, I urge you once again to subclass all the classes you want to utilize, rather than using them directly. The reasons are the same as for FoxPro base classes and ActiveX controls.

Whenever you want to change some behavior, do it in your subclass. Never modify the existing code. If you don't do this, it will seriously limit you further down the road. Also, never store your subclasses in the same physical file as the original class. As soon as you touch the original files or code, you won't be able to use any updates or bug fixes that the creator of the original version might have for you, because those updated versions would wipe out your changes and you'd have to start over. Not a pleasant scenario, I think. Especially when you consider the simplicity of the solution: Never touch what's not yours! It always surprises me how often this simple rule is violated, and I'm amazed at the kind of trouble people get themselves into just because they don't believe the importance of this point!

## Frameworks

Frameworks are the underlying architecture of your application. They define standards that must be followed throughout the project so all the classes can work together. Many different entities form a framework. Manager classes handle interface instantiation, security issues, errors and exceptions, online help, and more. Mediator objects (see Chapter 10) handle the message flow in the application. Most frameworks have standard interface components that handle user login, document operations such as New, Open and Close, administrative tasks, and so forth.

All framework components have one thing in common: They handle tasks that are not related to the business problem. Typically those are technical issues, such as form instantiation or error handling. A couple of years ago I read that 80% to 85% of all programming tasks are concerned with technological issues rather than the problem domain. This was when I still used Microfocus COBOL—a lot has changed since then, but the majority of programmer tasks still involve resolving technical issues. Some say the current number is somewhere between 60% and 70%. My personal experience seems to back that, but I don't have an accurate source to prove it.

Sixty to 70 percent is a pretty sad number, considering that most software projects started today will go into service in the 21st century! Just imagine if we could skip that 60 to 70%! Eighteen-month projects could be done in half a year! Six-million-dollar projects could be done with $2 million and you could pocket the rest! Unfortunately this is science fiction, but reusing existing frameworks can cut your development time tremendously—perhaps in half or less. That's a pretty good reason for me to reuse frameworks, or better yet to buy frameworks from third parties. The variety of Visual FoxPro frameworks is great. All areas—from low-price application-maker type frameworks to high-price advanced object-oriented frameworks—are covered. Before you decide to go for one of the available products, make sure to evaluate what you're about to purchase, because you'll have to live with the underlying philosophy from this point on! You can create your own classes or reuse other class libraries and COM components inside the framework, but you always have to follow the basic rules the framework sets. You're also stuck with the limitations of the framework. Sure, you can always customize the framework if you have the source code (which usually is the case), but then you couldn't switch to newer versions of your framework. This basically is the first step to doing all the framework modifications yourself, from this point forward. Eventually you'll end up with your own framework again, and there you go: 60% to 70% of your work is related to technological issues again. The only difference is that you're still stuck with a framework that's not really your own and that is carried by somebody else's ideas, which you don't really like because that's why you started to modify the framework in the first place.

The kind of framework you choose depends on the kind of project you are working on. If you need to create a ready-to-go application within a couple of months and you are a one-man-show, you want a low-price framework that has a built-in application wizard that automates the most important steps and guides you through the process of creating your program. If your project is scheduled for release in 15 to 20 months, you have a development team of four people or more, and the system needs to be highly flexible, extremely powerful and must run on various platforms utilizing different kinds of interfaces and data back ends, you should look into something more advanced. More advanced frameworks are usually harder to handle, require more knowledge of object-oriented technology (but by the time you finish reading this book you should be ready for that) and you'll need quite a bit of training to fully understand what the framework does. The framework provider should also be able to send consultants if you need them. Of course, you can also expect this kind of framework to cost a pretty penny. Providers that create such specialized frameworks aren't after the mass market. They are targeting a handful of advanced projects. They also have to give a great deal of support. For this reason, such a framework couldn't possibly be cheap. But let's assume you purchased such a framework for $50,000. That sounds like a lot of money, but just estimate the costs of having half a dozen highly skilled developers working on the framework for 60% to 70% of the time during your 18-month project. And then there is always the risk that your own framework doesn't fulfill the expectations. Well, you do the math!

Once you know what kind of framework you're looking for, you'll still have a couple of competing products to choose from. Often people ask me what the perfect third-party framework would be, and I always have to give the oddest of odd answers: "It depends." But it's true! Just consider this example. Every application has a framework—the military's Desert Storm application, John Doe's record database, and standard applications such as Word, Excel or even Visual FoxPro. It should be obvious that there couldn't be a perfect framework that matches the needs of those different applications. As Visual FoxPro programmers, we usually create applications that are somehow related to databases; the differences aren't as obvious, but that doesn't mean they aren't there.

Before buying a framework, you need to evaluate its strengths and weaknesses and whether you like the way things are done. This can be a time-consuming and difficult task because you have to judge something you don't really know. Before you start playing with a framework, I recommend taking some classes on it, or at least attending demonstrations or watching a video (if such things are available). This will give you an overall idea of what the framework does—and how. From this point on, you can start to explore the product yourself. This might sound like a huge effort from a time and cost point of view, and I agree, but wouldn't you rather spend some time and money evaluating a product before you bet the future of your company on it?

Once you make a decision and start to use the framework, the rules are the same as for using class libraries. Make sure you don't change existing code. Only reuse or subclass it.

### Complimentary tools
No matter what kind of shrink-wrapped classes you use, you will always appreciate some standard tools to guide you through the basic steps of the most important tasks. This will give you a jump start and speed up time-consuming standard tasks. The variety of such tools is great. Some tools (typically frameworks) come with their own integrated development environment (IDE). Usually they have application wizards, project managers and various builders. Other products come with basic wizards. The least I'd expect are some good samples, or a catalog for the Component Gallery (see Chapter 5).

## The Fox Foundation Classes
With Visual FoxPro 6.0, Microsoft shipped a set of more than 100 classes called the "Fox Foundation Classes." The Fox Foundation Classes can be used as a class library or through the Visual FoxPro Application Wizard. The overall quality of these classes was a positive surprise

to me. I expected to find a couple of classes that would be useful for entry-level programmers, but instead I found a set of classes that were rather powerful—and I incorporated a number of them into my applications right away.

## Class overview

Unfortunately, the Fox Foundation Classes are poorly documented. For this reason, I decided to sit down and describe all the classes in a great level of detail in this book. The rest of this chapter lists all the classes in a categorized fashion. Every class has a table that lists its most important facts, including dependencies and inheritance structure. This should help you to reuse the classes more easily.

### Application

All classes in this category are designed to handle large-scale issues that occur on the application level. Among these classes are window managers, error handlers and the like.

### *Data Session Manager*

| Class | _datasession |
|---|---|
| Base class | Custom |
| Class library | _app.vcx |
| Parent class | _custom |
| Sample | ...\Samples\Vfp98\Solution\Ffc\environ.scx<br>...\Samples\Vfp98\Solution\Ffc\dsession.scx |
| Dependencies | _base.vcx , _app.h |

This class handles table manipulations and updates in various data sessions. It can be used to iterate through forms and data sessions to save or revert data. Typical scenarios are application shutdown or the now widely used "save all" functionality that saves the content of all currently open documents or forms. This class can handle free tables as well as data that is stored in a database. Of course, the class is limited by Visual FoxPro's limitations regarding transactions.

Instantiating the class is very simple, due to its self-contained nature. A simple CreateObject() or NewObject() is enough, given that the class library is in the path:

```
oDataSession = NewObject("_datasession","_app.vcx")
```

Of course, you can also drop this object in a form or container. In this case, the Data Session object is placed in the appropriate data session right away. This is good if you want to handle QueryUnload events that occur whenever a form is closed. When iterating through data sessions to handle updates globally, I recommend instantiating this object as a member object of the application object or even as an independent object inside one of the application object's methods.

For now, I'll assume that we instantiated the Session object as a stand-alone object, as in the example above. I also assume we have a couple of forms with private data sessions. We can now use the Session object to check whether data has been updated in one of the form's data sessions. To do so, we first have to define the data session we intend to use:

```
oDataSession.SetSessionID(2)
```

We can always query the previously used session ID, querying the *iSavedSessionID* property:

```
? oDataSession.iSavedSessionID
```

Now that we've specified the session, we can check whether data has been updated:

```
? oDataSession.DataChanged()
```

This method returns .T. or .F. depending on whether or not there is updated data. We can also influence the way the class checks for updated data by setting the *iDataChangedMode* property. Setting it to 0, which is the default, checks for any changes. Setting it to 1 specifies that we want to ignore fields that are not in the update fields list. Setting it to 2 specifies that we don't want to check for views that aren't set to send updates.

Once we detect a session that has modified data, we either have to decide what we want to do, or we can ask the user what he has in mind. One option would be to confirm the changes and write them to the data source. We can do this using the Update() method:

```
oDataSession.Update(.T.)
```

I pass a .T. as the parameter because that hides a dialog box that asks the user whether he wants to save his changes or not. Passing .T. as the first parameter tells the object that the user already confirmed the change. This is important in various scenarios. Of course you might want to update changes no matter what. This option is also important if you want to iterate through various data sessions and want the user to confirm his changes only once, rather than asking him for every form. Often the programmer also wants to use his own dialogs instead of the ones provided by the foundation classes. In this case you can bring up your own dialog beforehand, and pass the result as a parameter. I like to use dialogs that provide "Yes to all" and "No to all" options.

The second parameter we pass is very similar. It is a more generic flag that indicates that the update is already confirmed. This parameter also hides the dialog and confirms the update right away. If both parameters are passed, the first one has the higher priority. This is convenient if you want to write generic routines. Parameter 2 could represent an option setting or the application state, while parameter 1 represents the current user.

Additional parameters are a reference to the form the data session belongs to, which is important if more than one form shares a data session. In this case the form gets activated and also gets the focus, which means that the form is brought forward. If you don't want the form to be brought forward, you can pass a fourth parameter, which is a logical parameter that specifies whether the form should be activated. The combination of parameters 3 and 4 can be very important in scenarios with multiple top-level forms.

If we don't want to write the changes to disk, we can use the Revert() method like so:

```
aDataSession.Revert(.T.,,loForm,.F.)
```

The parameters are exactly the same as the ones supported by the Update() method.

Another significant method is DataFlush(). It ensures that all the data was written to the hard disk and didn't get stuck in some buffer. This method doesn't require any parameters.

Whenever we take action, we can check whether it succeeded using the *lSuccess* property:

```
? oDataSession.lSuccess
```

Once we are done, we should return to the original data session to make sure we leave the environment as we found it. We can use the RestoreSessionID() method:

```
oDataSession.RestoreSessionID()
```

Note that this only restores the last used session. In other words, you cannot set the session ID to more than one session (for example, when iterating through all sessions) and restore the original session afterwards. To do that, you have to remember the initial session ID, like so:

```
oDataSession = NewObject("_datasession","_app.vcx")
LOCAL lnSessionID, lnCounter
lnSessionID = oDataSession.iSavedSessionID

FOR lnCounter = 1 TO Screen.FormCount
   oDataSession.SetSessionID(Screen.Forms(lnCounter).DataSessionID)
   IF oDataSession.DataChanged()
      oDataSession.Update()
   ENDIF
ENDFOR

oDataSession.SetSessionID(lnSessionID)
```

When actions are taken, the Data Session object can optionally use transactions. We can specify that by setting the *lUseTransactions* property:

```
oDataSession.lUseTransactions = .T.
```

When a Data Session object is dropped in a form, it can be called from the QueryUnload() event. The Data Session object also has a QueryUnload() method that checks for updates and, if appropriate, confirms the changes. This is the easiest way to use this object. Here is an example:

```
oDataSession.QueryUnload()
IF oDataSession.lSuccess
   NODEFAULT
ENDIF
```

The QueryUnload() method also can be configured by a couple of parameters to specify whether the user should be asked (parameter 1) and whether the form should be activated (parameters 2 and 3).

Another method—GetActiveControlRef()—is not directly related to the data problem handled by the data session class, but it is quite useful nevertheless. It returns an object reference to the control that's currently active. Natively, Visual FoxPro already provides a reference to the active control. Unfortunately, this reference doesn't work if it is a control inside a grid object. The GetActiveControlRef() method resolves this problem. You can simply pass it the reference provided by Visual FoxPro and the method checks whether the reference is correct. If not, it returns the real active control. This can be done like so:

```
LOCAL loActiveControl
loActiveControl =
oDataSession.GetActiveControlRef(_Screen.ActiveForm.ActiveControl)
```

Like many other foundation classes, the data session class features the GetMessageBoxTitle() title. It simply returns the caption of the message boxes as it is defined in _app.h, which is located in the VFP98\FFC directory You can overwrite this method in subclasses to return a different message box caption, which will then be used by the class for all the displayed message boxes.

### Error Object

| Class | _error |
|---|---|
| Base class | Custom |
| Class library | _app.vcx |
| Parent class | _custom |
| Sample | ...\Samples\Vfp98\Solution\Ffc\error.scx |
| Dependencies | _base.vcx , _app.h |

The Error object is a generic way to handle errors that occur in objects as well as in procedural code. The object judges errors and handles them accordingly. Sometimes user interaction is required, but some errors can be handled internally or even be ignored all together. The Error object also logs all occurring errors. However, the provided behavior is rather trivial, which is not surprising, because most error handling is specific to each application. If this weren't the case, Visual FoxPro could handle those errors internally without requiring programmer interaction. For this reason, I recommend subclassing the error class to enrich it with additional behavior (see below).

The Error object can be instantiated inside certain forms, but I recommend instantiating it in the application object to make it available to the whole application. The object is easy to instantiate because it has no external dependencies that must be set beforehand. A simple NewObject() should do the trick:

```
oError = NewObject("_error","_app.vcx")
```

To invoke the Error object, it must be set as the global error handler like so:

```
ON ERROR oError.Handle(Error(),Program(),LineNo())
```

The Handle() method is responsible for handling errors. It is called with three parameters. Parameter 1 is the error number. Parameter 2 is the name of the program, procedure or method that caused the error, and parameter 3 specifies the line number on which the error occurred.

The Error object can also be invoked from within the Error() event of individual records like so:

```
PROCEDURE Error(nError, cMethod, nLine)
   oError.Handle(nError, cMethod, nLine)
ENDPROC
```

To reduce the risk of causing further errors in the Error() event, I didn't instantiate the Error object inside the event. Generally I recommend using the ON ERROR setting instead of using the Error() event, because it is more global and generally a bit easier. Also, switching to different error behavior, or passing errors to other objects is not trivial. I used to use complex error handlers that could pass on errors to other objects using the chain of responsibility pattern (see Chapter 10), but I finally switched to a simple error-handling model. Simplicity seems to be key for error handling. When an error occurs, the system already is in an unstable state, and using complex error handling mechanisms usually doesn't help, unless you're willing to put a tremendous amount of time into the error handler and handle each possible error individually in each object. This is a nearly impossible task, especially when using ActiveX components and automation servers. In my experience, using complex error handlers only introduces the risk of creating additional errors without raising the chances of handling errors dramatically.

When the Handle() method is invoked, the Error object classifies the error and tries to handle it accordingly. Obviously, the Error object can handle errors in a generic manner only. For this reason I recommend subclassing the Error object to behave properly for each application (see below). Once the error is analyzed, an error message is displayed and the user is asked for assistance (if appropriate). Also, the error is logged to a log file. The log file can be specified using the SetLog() method and the *cLogDBF* and *cLogAlias* properties like so:

```
oError.cLogDBF = "mylog.dbf"
oError.cLogAlias = "errorlog"
oError.SetLog()
```

The table name and alias also can be passed as the first and second parameter, but this is not yet documented and therefore I cannot recommend doing it this way.

If the specified error log table doesn't exist, it is created whenever the SetLog() is issued. The table is simple. It has a timestamp, a memo that has detailed information about the error, and another memo that is not used by the Error object but that can be used in subclasses for additional information.

The Error object features a DisplayErrorLog() method. By default, this brings up a simple browse, which is not very user friendly. You can change this in a subclass.

This brings us to the topic of subclassing the *Error* class. Most importantly, you need to add error-handling behavior specific to your application. There are various ways to do that. The Handle() method calls a number of additional methods that do the actual error handling and logging. I recommend overwriting or changing these additional methods rather than using the Handle() method.

The first method called is FillArrays(). This method first fills the *aErrors* array of the Error object with all possible error codes using the AError() function. The next array that gets populated is the *aErrorClass* array, which is also a member of the Error object. This array is two-dimensional. The second column is the name of the error class, while the first column holds all error numbers that belong to this specific class or group. Multiple numbers are separated by a forward slash (/). The error can then be classified by comparing the error number with the numbers in the *aErrorClass* array. If you would like to change the way errors are classified, you can simply overwrite the FillArrays() method. Typically you would do a DoDefault() first to get the original settings and then you would change some settings in the existing array.

Once the arrays are defined, the error is classified and the error class is stored in the *cCurrentClass* property. This property is used by the methods that are called next. Among them are IsFatal() and IsTrivial(). When a fatal error occurs, the application simply shuts down in an orderly fashion, trying to save as much data as possible and do some damage control. Trivial errors can be ignored. You can modify both methods to change the action taken or to change the error classes that are considered trivial or fatal. Note that both messages are called with one parameter that specifies whether an error message should be displayed. An error message will be displayed as a message box or as a wait window, depending on whether the error handler runs in an automation server (where user interaction is not possible), or in a message box in a monolithic application or interface tier. The information about whether the object is used as a server is stored in the *lServer* property. When your application is in server mode, make sure you never bring up any interface components that require user interaction.

Fatal and trivial errors are not logged in the log table, simply because trivial errors aren't worth logging, and fatal errors are so bad that logging would fail anyway, thus causing more trouble and jeopardizing damage control.

Once the error handler knows about the nature of the problem, it logs the error. But before doing so, it calls the OKToReport() method to determine whether it is okay to log the error. This method doesn't have any attached behavior. It simply returns .T., which means that all errors are logged. You can overwrite this method to set some rules about whether or not the error should be logged. To log a record, the LogErrorReport() method is called. This method displays an error message (if the object is not in server mode), makes sure the log file is available and finally utilizes the FillLogRecord() method to insert a new record and write the data to the file. You can overwrite this method if you want to log different information.

Once the error is logged, the error handler requires some help from the user. To do this, the UserHandlesError() method is invoked. Typically, the method displays a "Cancel/Ignore/Retry" type of message. Before this happens, the OKToContinue() method is queried to make sure the user can be asked. Again, this method always returns .T., but it can be overwritten to set some rules about whether the user can be asked. You can overwrite the UserHandlesError() method, or better yet, add some code to handle errors individually.

### *Object State*

| Class | _objectstate |
|---|---|
| **Base class** | Custom |
| **Class library** | _app.vcx |
| **Parent class** | _custom |
| **Sample** | ...\Samples\Vfp98\Solution\Ffc\environ.scx |
| **Dependencies** | _base.vcx , _app.h |

The Object State object can be used to restore an object's property values (the "object state"). When instantiating the Object State object, you must tell it what object to monitor. Do this by passing a reference to the object, which should be inspected when instantiating the object. In the following example, we create an Object State object that monitors changes made in the Visual FoxPro Screen object:

```
oObjectState = NewObject("_objectstate","_app.vcx",""_,_Screen)
```

Object State objects are passive observers. They don't monitor changes automatically, but they have to be notified. This is done by making changes through the Object State object using the Set() method, like so:

```
oObjectState.Set("Caption","New Screen Caption",.T.)
```

The first parameter is the name of the property we want to set, the second parameter is the new property value, and the third parameter specifies whether or not the change should be restored later on. I have to admit that I don't fully understand the reason for having a third parameter. Setting it to .F. would be just the same as setting the property directly. I can only imagine that the third parameter might be important for some very generic programs. It can't hurt to have this third parameter, but the fact that the default for parameter 3 is .F. makes the Object State object a little cumbersome to use.

When the Object State object is released from memory, it restores the initial state of the observed object. In our example, the original screen caption of the Visual FoxPro main window would be restored.

The Object State object features a number of properties and methods that allow you to influence it substantially. The *lAutomatic* property specifies whether changes should be logged and whether the original state should be restored automatically when the Object State object is destroyed. The Restore() and Save() methods can be used to manually save property values or to restore original settings. The Save() method requires the property name and value. The Restore() method optionally supports the property name as a parameter. If no parameter is passed, all properties are restored.

## System Toolbar

| Class | _systoolbars |
|---|---|
| Base class | Custom |
| Class library | _app.vcx |
| Parent class | _custom |
| Sample | ...\Samples\Vfp98\Solution\Ffc\environ.scx |
| Dependencies | _base.vcx , _app.h |

The System Toolbar object handles Visual FoxPro's internal toolbars, which can be rather annoying when testing applications because they don't go away automatically when you start your application. This object has two important methods—HideSystemToolbars() and ShowSystemToolbars(). Their purpose is straightforward. You can call them to (surprise!) show and hide the system toolbars.

The System Toolbar object also has an *lAutomatic* property. It specifies whether system toolbars are automatically hidden when the object gets created and shown when the object is destroyed. By default, this property is set to .F.

## Trace Aware Timer

| Class | _traceawaretimer |
|---|---|
| Base class | Timer |
| Class library | _app.vcx |
| Parent class | _timer |
| Sample | ...\Samples\Vfp98\Solution\Ffc\environ.scx |
| Dependencies | _base.vcx |

The Trace Aware Timer basically is a regular Visual FoxPro timer object. The difference between this and a regular timer is that this one is much easier to debug because it's aware of the Visual FoxPro debug environment. When the Trace Window is opened, the timer switches into "sleep mode," which basically means that it fires less often. You can specify how frequently it fires in the *iTraceInterval* property. The default is 10000 (10 seconds).

As you might have noticed, the Visual FoxPro debugger allows you to turn off timer events altogether. This would be the same as setting the *iTraceInterval* property to 0. However, this might not be the intended behavior if you need to debug code that is influenced by a timer, or if somebody needs to debug the timer itself.

> The Trace Aware Timer also has a property called iRegularInterval. Do not set this property directly, because it is always overwritten with the native Interval setting. For this reason you should always use the Interval property to set the standard interval for the timer.

### Window Handler

| Class | _windowhandler |
|---|---|
| **Base class** | Custom |
| **Class library** | _ui.vcx |
| **Parent class** | _custom |
| **Sample** | ...\Samples\Vfp98\Solution\Ffc\whandler.scx |
| **Dependencies** | _base.vcx, _ui.h |

The Window Handler object handles existing windows. It executes trivial tasks such as arranging windows; it does not create and manage windows as widely believed. Its most powerful method is CascadeFormInstances(), which arranges all the instantiated windows. It can be called without any parameters to arrange all existing windows, or you can pass parameters to influence what windows are rearranged and where to put them. The documentation says the first parameter is the name of the window, which should be rearranged. This is kind of a wishy-washy definition. It's really the value of the form's *Name* property. Multiple windows can have the same name, in which case all of them are rearranged. Parameter 2 is a logical parameter that specifies whether forms that are automatically centered (*AutoCenter* = .T.) should also be rearranged (.F.) or not (.T.). The default is .F., which means that all forms are arranged. Parameters 3 and 4 allow specifying the top and left properties for the first form. By default both values are 0, which means that the first form is positioned in the top-left corner of the parent form.

Besides rearranging windows, the Window Handler object also makes it easier to work with top-level forms. The GetCurrentTopFormRef() method returns an object reference to the current top-level window. If you don't use top-level windows, this method returns a reference to the _Screen object.

One of the harder tasks when using top-level windows is to provide the functionality typically defined in the Edit menu (such as Cut, Copy and Paste). Often, top-level windows don't have menus. The method InvokeMenuItemInFrame() allows you to execute these menu items programmatically. You simply need to pass the action you want to trigger as a parameter. The parameter is a string such as NEXT or PREVIOUS. Also supported are UNDO, REDO, CUT, COPY, PASTE, CLEAR, SELECTALL, FIND, FINDAGAIN and REPLACE.

Overall, this is one of the more disappointing Fox Foundation Classes.

### Automation
The Automation category features a number of classes that make it easy to deal with server applications such as Word, Excel or Graph. The problems resolved by these classes are among the most frequently encountered, at least as far as I can tell by the questions I receive. My personal favorite is the Mail Merge class (discussed later).

## Cross Tab

| Class | _xtab |
|-------|-------|
| Base class | Custom |
| Class library | _utility.vcx |
| Parent class | _custom |
| Sample | ...\Samples\Vfp98\Solution\Ffc\automate.scx |
| Dependencies | _base.vcx, vfpxtab.fxp (_GENXTAB) |

The Cross Tab object creates a cross-tab query and places the data in a cursor. A cross-tab query is a set of records in spreadsheet format, such as sales by country and month, where the months are placed on the horizontal axis (columns) and countries are displayed vertically (rows).

The Cross Tab foundation class uses the Cross Tab Wizard engine to create a cross-tab query. The Cross Tab is based on the currently selected data source. The data source must have at least three fields, one for each axis and a third for the actual content. Using the Cross Tab object is simple and straightforward:

```
oCrossTab = NewObejct("_xtab","_utility.vcx")
SELECT country, month, maxordamt FROM Sales INTO CURSOR Temp
oCrossTab.RunXTab()
```

By default, Field 1 is placed on the vertical axis (rows), Field 2 is used for the columns, and the order amount (Field 3) is used as the actual field content. You can influence this through various properties of the Cross Tab object. Here is another example:

```
oCrossTab = NewObejct("_xtab","_utility.vcx")
SELECT country, month, maxordamt FROM Sales INTO CURSOR Temp
oCrossTab.nRowField = 2
oCrossTab.nColField = 1
oCrossTab.RunXTab()
```

In this example I switched the position of the rows and columns. You could also use a different field for the data by setting the *oDataField* property. Specifying different field numbers is also important when using a data source with more than three fields.

Table 1 shows an example of the retrieved result.

*Table 1.* The first few rows and columns of a cross-tab query.

|  | January | February | March | April |
|------|---------|----------|-------|-------|
| Canada | 15,000 | 13,000 | 16,000 | 15,000 |
| Europe | 124,000 | 109,000 | 134,000 | 128,000 |
| Mexico | .NULL. | .NULL. | 6,000 | 11,000 |
| United States | 210,000 | 198,000 | 245,000 | 229,000 |

Additional properties allow you to specify details such as whether a thermometer should be displayed during creation of the result cursor (*lShowThem*), whether the name of the result file can be specified (*cOutfile*), whether one can specify that totals should be calculated (*lTotalRows*), and whether null values should be displayed as 0 or .NULL. (*lDisplayNulls*).

Subclassing this class doesn't make a lot of sense, because it just calls the Cross Tab Wizard behavior, which is defined in a program you can specify using the _GENXTAB system variable. The class itself is merely a simple wrapper that has only a couple of lines of code. If you wanted to change the underlying behavior, you have to change the program referenced by _GENXTAB.

### Graph by Record

| Class | _graphbyrec |
|---|---|
| Base class | Container |
| Class library | Utility.vcx |
| Parent class | _container |
| Sample | ...\Samples\Vfp98\Solution\Ffc\graphrec.scx |
| Dependencies | _base.vcx, _utility.h, MS Graph |

The Graph by Record object renders a graph (on a row-by-row basis) using Microsoft Graph. This foundation class has a relatively rich interface that allows the user to navigate through records, choose the kind of diagram and set some options, such as whether they want to see a legend or whether they want to plot by row. **Figure 1** shows a simple use of the Graph by Record foundation class. I simply dropped the class on a form, added a table with four numeric fields to that form, and ran it.

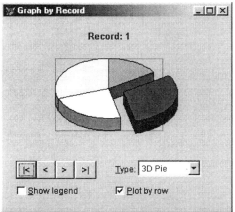

*Figure 1. The Graph by Record object rendering a 3-D pie chart using default settings.*

The rendered graph is a little rough. The caption (Record: 1) is not informative, and if the user decides to show the legend, the information isn't very useful. Luckily it's easy to define how you'd like your graph to look. The sample that ships with Visual FoxPro demonstrates this well. **Figure 2** shows the form Graphrec.scx, which is located in the FFC subdirectory of the Visual FoxPro Solutions sample. Note that this is one of those places where the Foundation

Class documentation is not only incomplete, but also wrong. The Automate.scx form does not have a Graph by Record sample.

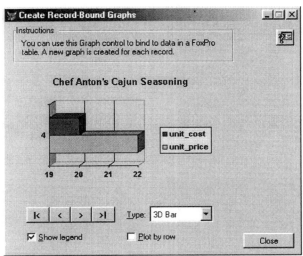

**Figure 2**. *The more sophisticated Graph by Record Solutions sample shows more useful information.*

Figure 2 shows a more informative caption than in Figure 1. This caption actually comes from the underlying data source. We simply need to specify the field name that contains this information. This can be done in the property *cGraphField*. Not only is the Figure 2 caption more informative, but the legend also contains useful information. This can be specified in the *aDataFields* array. Because array values cannot be configured through the property sheet, this has to be done in source code like so:

```
DIMENSION THIS.aDataFields[2]
THIS.aDataFields[1] = "unit_price"
THIS.aDataFields[2] = "unit_cost"
```

The *aDataFields* array allows you to define what fields should be used in the graph and in what order. This is extremely important, because in complex scenarios you don't want to display every single numeric field in the graph.

There is one less obvious thing I want to mention about Figure 2: The graph type of this diagram is initially set to "3D Column," which is a non-default setting. It can be defined through the *nChartType* property. **Table 2** shows all valid values. Please note that the values described in the VFP documentation are wrong!

***Table 2***. *Valid diagram types.*

| Value | Diagram Type | Defined in (_utility.h) |
|-------|--------------|-------------------------|
| 76 | Area | I_AREA_GRAPH |
| 78 | 3D Area | I_AREA3D_GRAPH |
| 57 | Bar | I_BAR_GRAPH |
| 60 | 3D Bar | I_BAR3D_GRAPH |
| 51 | Column | I_COLUMN_GRAPH |
| 54 | 3D Column | I_COLUMN3D_GRAPH |
| 5 | Pie | I_PIE_GRAPH |
| -4102 | 3D Pie | I_PIE3D_GRAPH |
| 4 | Line | I_LINE_GRAPH |
| -4101 | 3D Line | I_LINE3D_GRAPH |

A couple of additional properties allow you to influence the appearance of the rendered diagram. You can set these properties through the provided user interface or predefine them directly through the property sheet. Among them are *lAddLegend* and *lSeriesByRow*. You can set those properties programmatically during runtime and the graph will be refreshed immediately. This is accomplished by access and assign methods that trigger a RefreshGraph() when one of the properties changes. You can call this method at any time to refresh the contents of the graph.

So, what if the interface doesn't match the rest of your application? This is a common concern, but it's no problem at all. **Figure 3** shows essentially the same form as Figure 2 (as far as the underlying objects go), but I changed the interface somewhat. I used an ActiveX control to create a fancy toolbar (and set many of the original controls to invisible) and changed the size of the diagram to make it easier to read.

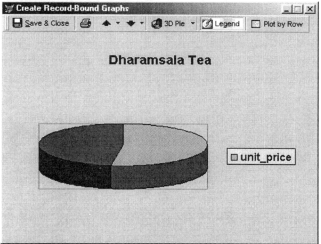

***Figure 3***. *The Graph by Record object using a different (custom) interface.*

As I mentioned above, the Graph by Record object uses Microsoft Graph to render the diagram. This is done using Automation and inplace activation. (Inplace activation is one of the oldest parts of COM/OLE. Using inplace activation, another application—such as Graph— is embedded and activated in another document, such as a Visual FoxPro form.) As with all objects of that nature, the user can double-click on the object to activate it and utilize its entire functionality. For the Microsoft Graph object, this means that the user is able to modify the underlying data as well as a number of display options, such as 3-D angle, color, and the like. **Figure 4** shows some of the possibilities.

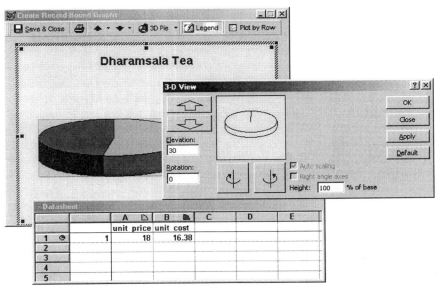

*Figure 4. The activated MS Graph object can be customized substantially.*

### Graph Object

| | |
|---|---|
| **Class** | Autograph |
| **Base class** | Custom |
| **Class library** | Autograph.vcx |
| **Parent class** | Automation |
| **Sample** | ...\Samples\Vfp98\Solution\Ffc\automate.scx |
| **Dependencies** | Automate.vcx, Automate.h, Autograph.h, MS Graph |

The Graph object provides the base functionality for communication with Microsoft Graph. This object is used by the more abstract graph objects in the Fox Foundation Classes.

### Mail Merge Object

| Class | Mailmerge |
|---|---|
| Base class | Custom |
| Class library | Mailmrge.vcx |
| Parent class | Automation |
| Sample | ...\Samples\Vfp98\Solution\Ffc\automate.scx |
| Dependencies | Automate.vcx, mailmrge.h |

Mail merge is one of the features that every programmer has to implement at one point in his career. Typically data is supposed to be sent to Microsoft Word. This is not a trivial task, and most programmers have a hard time with it, especially because Word has changed over time, and some users still have older versions that must be supported as well, and so forth.

The Mail Merge foundation class is of great help when it comes to implementing this functionality. It's easy to use, and it represents the same mechanism used by the Visual FoxPro Mail Merge Wizard. In the following example I open the Customer table, make sure the database is set properly (this is a common cause of failure for the Mail Merge object), set a couple of properties to make sure the object knows about the data I want to export, and finally I retrieve the names of all the fields and put them in the *aAutoFields* array. Now I'm ready to rock 'n' roll, which I do by calling the MakeOutput() method:

```
LOCAL loMailMerge, lnCounter
loMailMerge = NewObject("mailmerge","mailmrge.vcx")
SELECT 0
USE Customer
SET DATABASE TO TestData

* We decorate the mail merge object
loMailMerge.cAlias = Alias()
loMailMerge.cDBCTable = DBF()
loMailMerge.cDBCName = DBC()

* We retrieve information about the fields in the current table...
DIME loMailMerge.aAutoFields(FCount(),1)
FOR lnCounter = 1 TO FCount()
   loMailMerge.aAutoFields(lnCounter,1) = Field(lnCounter)
ENDFOR

* We do the merge
loMailMerge.MakeOutput()

USE
```

In this example I use the Customer table, but you could substitute any table and the code would be generic enough to handle it. When you do that, make sure the correct database is specified in the *cDBCName* property. When testing the code above, I first forgot to set the database. For this reason, the DBC() function returned a wrong database name, and the whole scenario failed, showing a very uninformative error message.

The Mail Merge class uses the specified data source by telling Word to open the specified data source using ODBC (or other mechanisms if ODBC isn't available). Based on this data source, Word creates a new mail-merge document. This document has a Mail Merge toolbar (see **Figure 5**) that allows the user to select fields and place them in a document. However, this might not be the desired result.

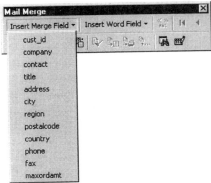

**Figure 5**. *The Mail Merge toolbar shows all the fields from a FoxPro data source.*

In many scenarios, users want to reprint mailings that they've already done, or at least use some templates. You can allow this by configuring the Mail Merge object to use an existing document and by specifying a document name like so:

```
loMailMerge.nNewDoc = 2
loMailMerge.cDocName = "C:\My Documents\MyMergeDoc.doc"
```

In this example I set the *nNewDoc* property to 2, which specifies that I want to use an existing document (setting it to 1 would specify that I wanted to create a new document). If you prefer using words instead of numbers to define whether a new or existing document should be used, you can use predefined constants defined in mailmrge.h, like so:

```
#INCLUDE mailmrge.h
loMailMerge.nNewDoc = N_EXISTING_DOC
```

In fact, this is the better way to do it if the values change in future versions. The available constants are *N_EXISTING_DOC* and *N_NEW_DOC*.

The first time the user wants to do a mail merge, he won't have an existing document. In this case, you should let him choose what kind of document he wants to create. Available are *Letter*, *Label*, *Envelope* and *Catalog*. You can specify these types through the *nTemplate* property:

```
#INCLUDE mailmrge.h
loMailMerge.nTemplate = N_FORMLETTER
loMailMerge.nTemplate = N_LABEL
loMailMerge.nTemplate = N_ENVELOPE
loMailMerge.nTemplate = N_CATALOG
```

The differences between these document types are significant. The letter creates a document for each record, while the catalog puts many records on one page. Labels and envelopes are self-explanatory.

When communicating with applications such as Word through automation, the server application might display some messages. In this case you want the dialog to look like it is one of yours. You can do so by setting the window title of all dialogs through the *cAppTitle* property.

### *Pivot Table*

| | |
|---|---|
| **Class** | Pivottable |
| **Base class** | Custom |
| **Class library** | Pivtable.vcx |
| **Parent class** | Automation |
| **Sample** | ...\Samples\Vfp98\Solution\Ffc\automate.scx |
| **Dependencies** | Automate.vcx, pivtable.h |

Pivot tables are great tools. They are interactive tables that summarize large amounts of data in a cross-tab format. Unfortunately, they are hard to create. The Pivot Table foundation class carries the burden of most of this complexity. You can rotate the table's rows and columns to see different summaries. You can also apply filters to see different pages of data, and even drill down to see the details that resulted in the displayed summary. **Figure 6** shows a simple example. Note that the fields that look like buttons can be dragged around on the document to summarize the data differently. Also, the combobox in the first row can be used to filter data.

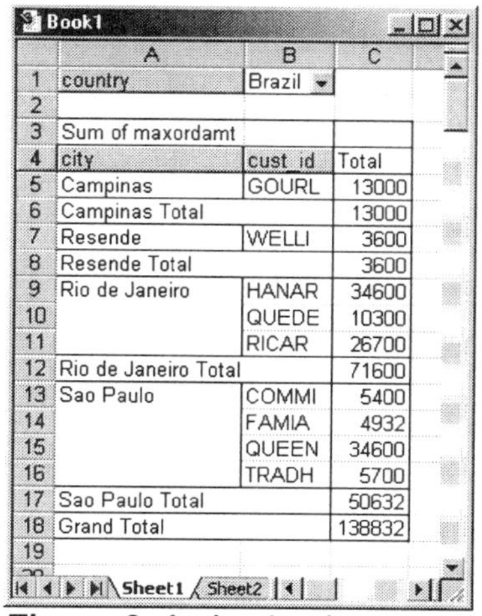

Book1

| | A | B | C |
|---|---|---|---|
| 1 | country | Brazil | |
| 2 | | | |
| 3 | Sum of maxordamt | | |
| 4 | city | cust_id | Total |
| 5 | Campinas | GOURL | 13000 |
| 6 | Campinas Total | | 13000 |
| 7 | Resende | WELLI | 3600 |
| 8 | Resende Total | | 3600 |
| 9 | Rio de Janeiro | HANAR | 34600 |
| 10 | | QUEDE | 10300 |
| 11 | | RICAR | 26700 |
| 12 | Rio de Janeiro Total | | 71600 |
| 13 | Sao Paulo | COMMI | 5400 |
| 14 | | FAMIA | 4932 |
| 15 | | QUEEN | 34600 |
| 16 | | TRADH | 5700 |
| 17 | Sao Paulo Total | | 50632 |
| 18 | Grand Total | | 138832 |
| 19 | | | |

Sheet1 Sheet2

***Figure 6****. A simple pivot table.*

Creating the pivot table in Figure 6 with the help of the Pivot Table object is relatively easy. First you need to open a data source. The name of the table, the database and the fields you want to use must be specified through the appropriate properties of the Pivot Table object.

Also, you have to specify which fields to use in the initial table and where to place them. All of this can be done like so:

```
LOCAL loPivotTable
loPivotTable = NewObject("pivottable","pivtable.vcx")
SELECT 0
USE Customer
SET DATABASE TO TestData

* Now we decorate the pivot table object...
loPivotTable.cAlias = Alias()
loPivotTable.cDBCTable = DBF()
loPivotTable.cDBCName = DBC()
DIME loPivotTable.aAutoFields(4,1)
loPivotTable.aAutoFields(1,1) = "city"
loPivotTable.aAutoFields(2,1) = "maxordamt"
loPivotTable.aAutoFields(3,1) = "country"
loPivotTable.aAutoFields(4,1) = "cust_id"
loPivotTable.cPivFldRow = "city"
loPivotTable.cPivFldData = "maxordamt"
loPivotTable.cPivFldPage = "country"

* We create the table...
loPivotTable.MakeOutput()

* We close the data
USE
```

The first couple of lines are easy to understand. I create the Pivot Table object and open the data I want to use. Then I specify the data in the object by setting the *cAlias*, *cDBCTable* and *cDBCName* properties. I'm using the DBC() function to retrieve the name of the database. If you do that, make sure the correct database is set; otherwise you will see a generic error message that doesn't really point to the problem. Next, I specify the fields I need in my table. This can be done in the *aAutoFields* array. I also specify where the fields should be positioned. *CPivFldRow* specifies the field by which the rows will be subtotaled. *CPivFldCol* would do the same thing for the columns, but I'm not using it in the example above. The *cPivFldData* property specifies the field that holds the data to be displayed. Finally, the *cPivFldPage* property is used to define a field that can be used for filtering. In pivot tables, these are usually referred to as "pages". Note that not all fields of the *aAutoFields* array show up in the pivot table initially. Nevertheless, it's very important to have them, because as I mentioned above, a pivot table is meant to be an interactive tool where the user can drag fields around and drill down to see more details.

Optionally, pivot tables can use row and column totals, activated by the properties *lHasColumnTotals* and *lHasRowTotals*. I didn't use totals in the example above. Neither did I set the application title, which is important if a message box or dialog has to be displayed. This can be specified in the *cAppTitle* property as in most of the other Automation objects.

### Data editing

The Data Editing category features all kinds of classes that provide standard functionality you will frequently need for all kinds of data manipulation. This includes issues such as taking data offline and handling data conflicts.

### *Data Edit Buttons*

| Class | Picbtns |
|---|---|
| Base class | CommandGroup |
| Class library | Wizbtns.vcx |
| Parent class | Txtbtns |
| Sample | ...\Samples\Vfp98\Solution\Ffc\dataedit.scx |
| Dependencies | Underlying framework |

This class is a set of command buttons that allow typical operations like navigation, printing, editing data and the like. The Visual FoxPro Form Wizard uses this class. Unlike the other foundation classes, the Data Edit Buttons class is stored in the Wizards directory instead of in the FFC subdirectory.

At first sight, the class looks entirely self-contained. There are no external file dependencies. However, once you take a closer look you'll recognize that this class is very specific to the forms created by the Visual FoxPro Form Wizard. Features such as Print or Edit require you to follow the standard set by the Form Wizard.

I don't have much to say about this class. If you use the Form Wizard, there isn't much you need to know. If you don't use the Form Wizard, this class isn't of much use to you unless the forms you create are the same as the ones created by the wizards. In this case I'd wonder why you aren't using the wizard...

### *Data Validation*

| Class | _datachecker |
|---|---|
| Base class | Custom |
| Class library | _datanav |
| Parent class | _custom |
| Sample | None |
| Dependencies | _base.vcx, _data.h |

The Data Validation object (a.k.a. Data Checker) can be used to check for conflicts that can occur when multiple users (or one user with multiple instances of a form or application) make changes to the same data. This class works only with buffered data (optimistic or pessimistic buffering). If a conflict is found, a message box is displayed to ask the user for help (see **Figure 7**).

Typically, this object would be invoked when the user wants to update data, such as in a Save or Navigation method. Calling the object is rather simple. Here's an example:

```
LOCAL loDataValidation
loDataValidation = NewObject("_datachecker","_datanav.vcx")
loDataChecker.HandleRecord()
```

The HandleRecord() method does all the work. It checks for conflicts and asks the user for help if there is a problem.

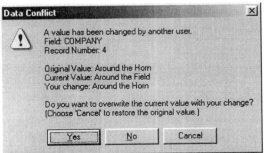

**Figure 7.** *The user is asked for help in the case of a conflict.*

I cannot think of many reasons to subclass this class. It does a great job checking data just the way it is. I might consider changing the interface from a message box to some other dialog; unfortunately, this is hard to do because a single line of code in the middle of a method brings up the message box, so the whole method must be overwritten.

### Offline Switch

| Class | _offline |
|---|---|
| Base class | Container |
| Class library | _dataquery.vcx |
| Parent class | _container |
| Sample | None |
| Dependencies | _base.vcx, _data.h, online.ico, offline.ico |

The Offline Switch toggles views from online to offline and back. Explaining the details of offline views is slightly beyond the scope of this book. The basic idea is to take offline those views (local or remote) that come across a network. A typical scenario would be a salesman who takes a view of the customer database offline so he can use it on his notebook computer even when he isn't connected to the network.

Taking views offline is relatively trivial. Taking them back online is not, because there might be conflicts. The Offline Switch object iterates through all views in the current data session and takes them offline (or online). The Offline Switch object comes with an interface. So all you have to do is drop the class on a form (see **Figure 8**).

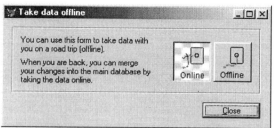

*Figure 8. This dialog allows the user to take data offline.*

### Simple Edit Buttons

| Class | Picformbtns |
|---|---|
| Base class | Container |
| Class library | Wizbtns.vcx |
| Parent class | Gridbtns |
| Sample | ...\Samples\Vfp98\Solution\Ffc\dataedit2.scx |
| Dependencies | Underlying framework, bitmaps |

The Simple Edit buttons provide some basic data editing functionality, such as Add, Edit, Delete and Print. Like the Data Edit buttons, the Simple Edit buttons are used by the Form Wizard and therefore also by applications created using the Application Wizard and Application Builder. They rely heavily on the underlying framework. **Figure 9** shows an example of the Simple Edit buttons.

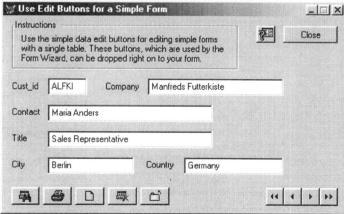

*Figure 9. Simple Edit buttons (lower left).*

## Data navigation
Every time data is stored, there must be a way to navigate that data to find records. The classes in this category cover the topic of data navigation rather well.

### Data Navigation Buttons

| Class | _datanavbtns |
|---|---|
| Base class | Container |
| Class library | _datanav.vcx |
| Parent class | _container |
| Sample | None |
| Dependencies | _base.vcx, _data.h |

The Data Navigation buttons provide a simple VCR-button interface to navigate in a data source. **Figure 10** shows an example of these buttons.

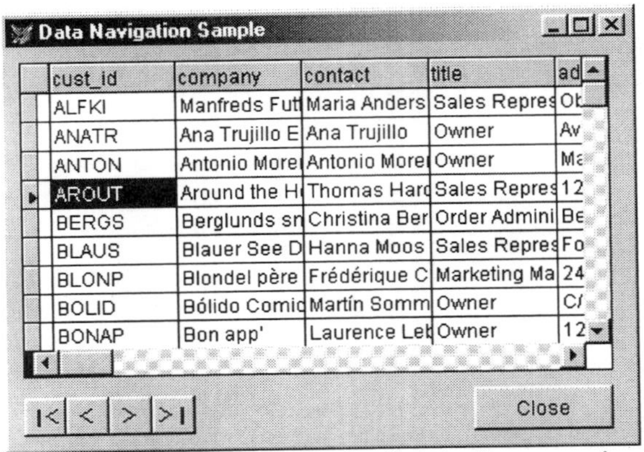

*Figure 10. The Data Navigation buttons are located in the lower left corner of the form.*

The Data Navigation buttons use the Data Checker object to check whether data has to be updated before the record pointer is moved; if so, there might be conflicts that have to be resolved.

Unlike commonly believed, the Data Navigation buttons do not utilize the Data Navigation object. This class has all the necessary behavior itself and it raises events that you can use to implement additional behavior. Before the record pointer is moved, the BeforeRecordPointerMoved() method is called. By default, this method only makes sure the correct data source is selected. The name of the data source we want to navigate is stored in a property called *SkipTable* (not *cSkipTable* as incorrectly listed by the documentation). After navigating, the RecordPointerMoved() method fires. This method makes sure the current form is refreshed properly. You can overwrite this method to add additional refresh behavior. The form in Figure 10 uses this method to make sure the record pointer movement gets displayed properly by briefly setting the focus to the grid.

Finally, the EnableDisableButtons() method is fired. This method ensures that buttons get disabled when the record pointer is at the first or the last record. The Data Navigation buttons are passive, which means that they do not recognize any record pointer movement unless it was initialized by the Data Navigation Buttons object. In Figure 10, the record pointer could also be moved if the user clicked on a row in the grid. To make sure the buttons are updated properly, we have to call the EnableDisableButtons() method from the grid's AfterRowColChange() event.

### *Data Navigation Object*

| Class | _tablenav |
|---|---|
| Base class | Custom |
| Class library | _table.vcx |
| Parent class | _table |
| Sample | ...\Samples\Vfp98\Solution\Ffc\datanav.scx |
| Dependencies | _base.vcx, _table.h |

The Data Navigation object provides the most important data navigation behavior, such as navigating to the next or previous record, as well as navigating to a specific record, which is identified by its record number. The Data Navigation object is used by many navigation buttons and other navigation interfaces.

The object has five important methods, which are GoTop(), GoPrevious(), GoNext(), GoBottom() and GoToRecord(). When using the GoToRecord() method, you have to pass the record number as a parameter. Typically, when you issue a GoNext() at the last record, or a GoPrevious() at the first one, the object will display a message. You can alter this behavior by setting the *lCycle* property to .T., which means that the record pointer will be moved to the first record when an end-of-file is encountered, and to the last record when the record pointer is at the beginning of the file.

The class has a few empty methods that you can overwrite to give some feedback. Those methods are DoBottomMessage(), DoCycleBottomMessage(), DoCycleTopMessage() and DoTopMessage(). By default, the object doesn't give any feedback when the desired navigation can't take place because the record pointer already is at the first or the last record. Using these methods, you can react properly to this event, or bring up some user interface.

After moving the record pointer successfully, a method called RefreshUIAfterChange() is invoked. This method simply issues a refresh of the current form. Overwrite this method if you need some additional refresh behavior.

### *GoTo Dialog Box*

| Class | _gotodialog |
|---|---|
| Base class | Form |
| Class library | _table.vcx |
| Parent class | _form |
| Sample | ...\Samples\Vfp98\Solution\Ffc\datanav.scx |
| Dependencies | _base.vcx, _table.h |

The GoTo dialog box is a simple dialog (form) that utilizes the Data Navigation object to navigate to a certain record, which is identified by its record number. The interface is rather simple. I've found that, for most uses, the interface must be subclassed to match one's application.

### GoTo Dialog Box Button

| Class | _gotobutton |
|---|---|
| Base class | CommandButton |
| Class library | _table2.vcx |
| Parent class | _dialogbutton |
| Sample | ...\Samples\Vfp98\Solution\Ffc\datanav.scx |
| Dependencies | _base.vcx, _table2.h, _table.vcx, _table.h |

This button is a very simple foundation class. Its whole purpose is to bring up the GoTo dialog box. Note that the GoTo dialog box is stored in another class library, which also requires a couple of additional files in order to run.

### GoTo Spinner

| Class | _goto |
|---|---|
| Base class | Container |
| Class library | _table2.vcx |
| Parent class | _container |
| Sample | None |
| Dependencies | _base.vcx |

The GoTo Spinner is very similar to the GoTo dialog box, but it is only a simple container. **Figure 11** shows this spinner in a toolbar. This object also utilizes the Data Navigation object to move the record pointer.

Using this object is rather simple. You can drop it on every form or container that has some data in its data session.

### Navigation Toolbar (Container)

| Class | _navtoolbarclass |
|---|---|
| Base class | Container |
| Class library | _table2.vcx |
| Parent class | _container |
| Sample | ...\Samples\Vfp98\Solution\Ffc\datasort.scx |
| Dependencies | _base.vcx, _table2.h |

The Navigation Toolbar object (as documented in the Visual FoxPro Foundation Class documentation) is a simple container object with a timer that can be dropped on any form. When initialized, it instantiates a navigation toolbar (documented below). You can specify a different toolbar class using the *cClass* and *cClassLib* properties. All other properties are for internal use only.

### Navigation Toolbar (Toolbar)

| Class | _tbrnavigation |
|---|---|
| Base class | Toolbar |
| Class library | _table2.vcx |
| Parent class | _toolbar |
| Sample | ...\Samples\Vfp98\Solution\Ffc\datasort.scx |
| Dependencies | _base.vcx, _table.vcx, _table.h, _table2.h, top.bmp, previous.bmp, next.bmp, bottom.bmp, sortup.bmp, sortdown.bmp, filter.bmp, find.bmp |

The Navigation Toolbar provides a simple and elegant interface for the most important data navigation features, including simple navigation, record-sorting sequences, data filtering and Find dialogs. To do so, it utilizes several other foundation classes such as the VCR Navigation Picture buttons, the GoTo Spinner, the Sort Selector, the Filter Dialog Box button and the Find Dialog Box button. Figure 11 shows an example of this toolbar.

The Navigation Toolbar container uses this toolbar by default. The toolbar can be modified through the properties and methods of the member objects as described in the individual sections about those objects.

*Figure 11. The Navigation toolbar, including the GoTo Spinner, the Sort Selector, the Filter button and the Find button.*

### Simple Picture Navigation Buttons

| Class | _nav2picbuttons |
|---|---|
| Base class | Container |
| Class library | _table2.vcx |
| Parent class | _nav2buttons |
| Sample | ...\Samples\Vfp98\Solution\Ffc\datanav.scx |
| Dependencies | _base.vcx, _table.vcx, _table.h, _table2.h, previous.bmp, next.bmp |

The Simple Picture navigation buttons are identical to the Simple Navigation buttons but they use images rather than simple characters.

### Simple Navigation Buttons

| Class | _nav2buttons |
|---|---|
| **Base class** | Container |
| **Class library** | _table2.vcx |
| **Parent class** | _container |
| **Sample** | ...\Samples\Vfp98\Solution\Ffc\datanav.scx |
| **Dependencies** | _base.vcx, _table.vcx, _table.h, _table2.h |

The Simple Navigation buttons provide a two-button interface to navigate to the previous or next record. This class utilizes the Data Navigation object. The Simple Navigation buttons can be dropped on any form or container that has some kind of data source.

The object has a method called TableNav(). It can be used to navigate to the previous or next record. The navigation direction is specified by the first parameter, which can be NEXT or PREVIOUS. The object also has an *lCycle* property. When this property is set, the value is directly passed on to the Data Navigation object.

### VCR Buttons

| Class | _nav4buttons |
|---|---|
| **Base class** | Container |
| **Class library** | _table.vcx |
| **Parent class** | _nav2buttons |
| **Sample** | ...\Samples\Vfp98\Solution\Ffc\datanav.scx |
| **Dependencies** | _base.vcx, _table.h |

The VCR buttons are very similar to the Simple Navigation buttons, but they also feature go-top and go-bottom buttons.

### VCR Picture Navigation Buttons

| Class | _nav4picbuttons |
|---|---|
| **Base class** | Container |
| **Class library** | _table2.vcx |
| **Parent class** | _nav4buttons |
| **Sample** | ...\Samples\Vfp98\Solution\Ffc\datanav.scx |
| **Dependencies** | _base.vcx, _table.h, _table.vcx, _table2.h, top.bmp, previous.bmp, next.bmp, bottom.bmp |

The VCR Picture Navigation buttons are identical to the regular VCR buttons, but they use images for each button rather than simple characters.

## Data query

For all data-handling tasks that are beyond the capabilities of simple data navigation, there are the Data Query objects. In this category you will find filter objects as well as complex conflict catchers that help to resolve problems when updating data.

### Conflict Catcher

| Class | _conflicts |
|---|---|
| Base class | Form |
| Class library | _dataquery.vcx |
| Parent class | _form |
| Sample | ...\Samples\Vfp98\Solution\Ffc\conflicts.scx |
| Dependencies | _base.vcx, _data.h |

The Conflict Catcher is a form class that represents a dialog, which can be displayed if a data conflict was found and had to be resolved by the user (see **Figure 12**).

Once the dialog is instantiated, the StartCheck() method initiates the conflict checking. This method is called automatically if the *lAutoCheck* property is set to .T. (which is the default). Once the user decides how to resolve a conflict, the class searches the next conflict until there are no more conflicts, or until the user clicks on the Close button.

By default, the selected alias is checked for conflicts. If a different alias should be checked, the *CursorAlias* property can be set to specify a different data source.

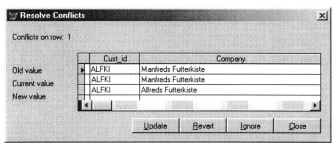

**Figure 12**. *The Conflict Catcher allows the user to choose which version of the data to select.*

You cannot change many things in subclasses. The most likely thing to change is the user interface. If you do this, make sure you use the original buttons, rather than calling methods in the parent object (form), because some of them have significant behavior attached to some of their methods.

If you want to change the way conflicts are identified, you can overwrite the NextConflict() method. This method accepts one parameter, which specifies the record number on which the method is supposed to start checking. In other words, all records before this number have already been checked. If this parameter isn't passed, you need to start checking at the current record. The rest is pretty much up to you.

### Distinct Values Combo

| Class | _cbodistinctvalues |
|---|---|
| Base class | ComboBox |
| Class library | _dataquery |
| Parent class | _combobox |
| Sample | ...\Samples\Vfp98\Solution\Ffc\datalook2.scx |
| Dependencies | _base.vcx, _data.h |

The Distinct Values combobox is much like a regular combobox, but it automatically populates the combobox's drop-down menu with the different values that can be found in the field specified as the combobox control source. So if you have a table with a field that stores country information, you can use the Distinct Values combobox to let the user enter the country information, and the combobox will automatically show all the countries that have already been referenced. See **Figure 13**.

The combobox is automatically populated in the Init() method. It is hard to repopulate the combobox once it's instantiated.

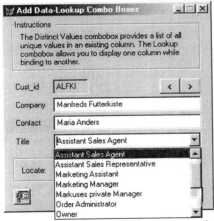

**Figure 13**. *The combobox was automatically populated from the values found in the active table.*

### Filter Dialog Box

| Class | _filterdialog |
|---|---|
| Base class | Form |
| Class library | _table.vcx |
| Parent class | _form |
| Sample | ...\Samples\Vfp98\Solution\Ffc\datasort.scx |
| Dependencies | _base.vcx, _table.h |

The Filter dialog box is a simple interface designed to create complex filter statements. To do so, the user doesn't have to know anything about SQL or dBASE syntax. **Figure 14** shows the dialog in action. The easiest way to use the dialog is to drop the Filter Dialog Box button on a form. This button will automatically bring up the Filter dialog (see below). If you do not want to use the Filter Dialog Box button, you can simply instantiate the class and make it visible.

When the class is initialized, it automatically analyzes the active filter and displays it. The class also analyzes the current data session and allows access to all the available cursors and tables. Those tables and their fields are then displayed in the Filter dialog box interface. Fields that are indexed are marked with a leading asterisk (*).

When you click OK, the full filter expression is created by the SetupFilter() method. The expression is then stored in the *cFilter* property. Once this filter is created, the button checks whether the form or object that instantiated the Filter dialog box has a special way of setting filters. To do so, the object needs to have a SetFilter() method. The source object must be passed to the Filter dialog box when initialized. Of course you could pass references to different objects. Here are some examples:

```
oFilter = NewObject("_filterdialog","_table","",THIS)
oFilter = NewObject("_filterdialog","_table","",THISFORM)
oFilter = NewObject("_filterdialog","_table","",oCustomerForm)
```

The source object can be used only if the form has a SetFilter() method. If there is no source object or that object doesn't have a SetFilter() method, the Filter dialog box sets the filter itself by issuing a SET FILTER TO command.

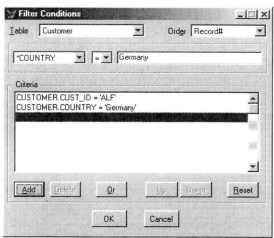

***Figure 14****. The Filter Conditions dialog box constructing a filter for all German customers whose IDs start with "ALF".*

The Filter Conditions dialog box is quite complex, so I recommend using care when subclassing it. You can change the interface by moving things around, but it is hard to replace buttons and other interface components because most controls on this form have directly attached behavior.

I mostly stay away from customizing the behavior of this class. The only thing I do quite frequently is to limit the tables or fields displayed. Limiting the number of tables is relatively easy. Let's say we have two tables in our data environment, but we want only one to show up in the Filter dialog box. The table combobox is populated in the form's Activate() event. To change the displayed tables, you can overwrite this event in a subclass like so:

```
DoDefault()
DIME THIS.aDbfs[1]
THIS.aDbfs(1) = "Customer"
THIS.cboTables.Requery()
THIS.cboTables.Value = 1
```

Of course you can set the array dimension differently to set more than one table. You might also find a need to limit the available fields. This can be done by overwriting the SetTags() method:

```
DoDefault()
DIME THIS.aFlds[2]
THIS.aFlds[1] = THIS.OnTag("CUST_ID")
THIS.aFlds[2] = THIS.OnTag("COUNTRY")
```

When this method is called, the table those fields belong to is selected, so you can display different fields based on the selected work area, like so:

```
DoDefault()
DO CASE
    CASE Alias() == "CUSTOMER"
       DIME THIS.aFlds[2]
       THIS.aFlds[1] = THIS.OnTag("CUST_ID")
       THIS.aFlds[2] = THIS.OnTag("COUNTRY")
    CASE Alias() == "EMPLOYEE"
       DIME THIS.aFlds[3]
       THIS.aFlds[1] = THIS.OnTag("EMP_ID")
       THIS.aFlds[2] = THIS.OnTag("LAST_NAME")
       THIS.aFlds[2] = THIS.OnTag("FIRST_NAME")
ENDCASE
```

The OnTag() method is a simple method that checks whether the referenced field is indexed. If so, an asterisk (*) is added to the field name.

### Filter Dialog Box Button

| Class | _filterbutton |
|---|---|
| **Base class** | CommandButton |
| **Class library** | _table2.vcx |
| **Parent class** | _dialogbutton |
| **Sample** | ...\Samples\Vfp98\Solution\Ffc\datasort.scx |
| **Dependencies** | _base.vcx, _table.vcx, _table.h, _table2.h |

The only purpose of the Filter Dialog Box button is to bring up a filter interface. This can be the Filter dialog box, the Filter Expression dialog box or your own class. The *lExprDialog* property specifies whether to use the Filter Expression dialog box (.T.) or the regular Filter dialog box (.F.). In the case of the Filter Expression dialog box, the class name is specified in the *cExprClass* property; otherwise the *cFilterClass* property specifies the class to be used. Either way, the *cClassLib* property specifies the library where the referenced class is stored. If you want to invoke your own filter class, simple specify the class name in those properties.

### Filter Expression Dialog Box

| Class | _filterexpr |
|---|---|
| **Base class** | Form |
| **Class library** | _table.vcx |
| **Parent class** | _form |
| **Sample** | ...\Samples\Vfp98\Solution\Ffc\datasort.scx |
| **Dependencies** | _base.vcx, _table.h |

The Filter Expression dialog box allows the user to set the filter; it's similar to the Filter dialog box. The major difference is that the user can directly enter the filter expression without using an expression builder interface. This form of filtering is more powerful than the Filter dialog box, but it also requires the user to be familiar with dBASE or SQL syntax. The Filter Expression dialog box interface (see **Figure 15**) also allows bringing up an expression builder. This expression builder can be either the Filter dialog box (see above) or the native FoxPro GETEXPR dialog. You can select between the two expression builders through the *lAdvanced* property. The default is .F., which brings up the Set Filter dialog box.

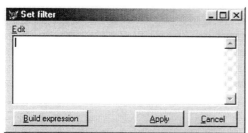

**Figure 15**. The Filter Expression dialog box. The "Build expression" button brings up an expression builder interface.

The *cFilter* property holds the current filter expression, which is essentially the same as the contents of the edit box in Figure 15. This property is not populated by the SetupFilter() method as incorrectly mentioned in the documentation. The method SetFilterOnTable() is responsible for applying the filter to the current table. This method simply issues a SET FILTER command. I often find myself replacing the Filter dialog box with the Filter Expression dialog box. In this case, I was first passing a reference to the Filter dialog box to apply a filter through my own SetFilter() method. The Filter Expression dialog box doesn't support this construction. Because I want to be able to use either one of the classes without changing the underlying source code, I overwrote the SetFilterOnTable() method to check for a calling object before executing the original behavior, like so:

```
IF VarType("THISFORM.oCaller") = "O"
   IF PEMStatus(THISFORM.oCaller,"setfilter",5)
      THISFORM.oCaller.SetFilter(THISFORM.cFilter)
   ELSE
      DoDefault()
   ENDIF
ELSE
   DoDefault()
ENDIF
```

I also added the *oCaller* property to my subclass and set this property in the Init() method if a caller object reference is passed.

The Filter Expression dialog box class also has a SetFilter() method. This method is used only when the Filter dialog box is brought up. The implementation of this method is rather simple. The passed filter expression is only stored to the *cFilter* property of the Filter Expression dialog box. The user can then make further modifications to the filter expression.

## Find Button

| Class | _findbutton |
|---|---|
| Base class | Container |
| Class library | _table.vcx |
| Parent class | _container |
| Sample | ...\Samples\Vfp98\Solution\Ffc\dataqry.scx |
| Dependencies | _base.vcx, _table.h |

The Find button represents a full-blown search engine. The Find object provides the actual search behavior. Using the Find button class is rather easy. The class has a property called *cFindString*. In a typical scenario you would provide a textbox to allow the user to specify a search string. You write the contents of this textbox to the *cFindString* property of the Find button class. Now the user can click the Find button at any time to find the first record that matched the criteria.

You can specify the searched alias through the *cAlias* property. If you don't specify an alias, the currently selected data source is searched.

When searching for a certain string, many users expect the search to be case-insensitive, or vice versa. The Find button allows you to turn on case-sensitive searching through the *lMatchCase* property. By default, the entire table is searched. This can be slow. One of the easiest ways to speed up the search process is to skip the memo files. You can set this behavior using the *lSkipMemos* property. If you want to specify the fields to be searched in a less generic fashion, you can use the SkipField() method to identify individual fields, which are not supposed to be searched. You simply pass the name of the field you want to skip as a parameter.

By default, the first occurrence of the Find string is searched. If the search expression was found, the caption of the Find button changes to "Find next". The user can click the button again to find the next occurrence of the search expression. As soon as the *cFindString* property changes, the button's caption changes back to "Find" and the behavior switches back to finding the first occurrence.

After finding the last occurrence of the search string, the search usually stops. However, the search can continue at the beginning of the table if the *lWrapAround* property is set to .T.

As mentioned above, the Find button uses the Find object's search behavior. See below for more information about the Find object.

### Find Dialog Box

| Class | _finddialog |
|---|---|
| Base class | Form |
| Class library | _table.vcx |
| Parent class | _form |
| Sample | ...\Samples\Vfp98\Solution\Ffc\dataqry.scx |
| Dependencies | _base.vcx, _table.h |

The Find dialog box provides the same functionality as the Find button, but it also provides an interface for all the provided functionality (see **Figure 16**). Just like the Find button, the Find dialog box uses the Find object to actually search data (see below for more information about the Find object). The Find dialog box features all the properties and methods of the Find button.

One of the few unique properties of the Find dialog box is *lAdvanced*. This property specifies whether the user interface allows selecting the scanned table. This property is set to .T. by default. If you set it to .F., the second combobox will be hidden and the dialog will shrink. You can set this property directly and the dialog will change instantly (this is accomplished by an assign method), or you can pass .T. or .F. to the class on Init(), which will automatically set the property.

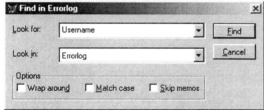

*Figure 16. The Find dialog box in advanced mode.*

Initially, the dialog has a Find and a Cancel button. Once an expression is searched and found, the caption of the Find button changes to "Find next". The user can press the button to repeat the search, or he can type a new value, which will reset the button's caption to "Find" and its behavior to finding the first occurrence of the specified expression.

When subclassing this class, I found myself changing only the interface. I imagine that some people might want to limit the tables available for searching. The easiest way to accomplish this is to set the *cAlias* property and disable the advanced mode so the user cannot select different data sources. If you want to show certain tables and hide others, you can do this in the Refresh() method of the Tables combobox. The combobox is automatically populated with all tables of the current data session. You can either execute the default behavior and remove certain tables afterwards, or you can overwrite the standard behavior altogether and replace it with your own code that populates the combobox. Note that the Refresh() method has to support one parameter, which is logical. It tells you whether or not the combobox should be repopulated. If the parameter is .F., don't repopulate the combobox. Here's some sample code that populates the combobox with two table names:

```
LPARAMETERS tlForceRefresh
IF THISFORM.lAdvanced
    IF tlForceRefresh
        THIS.Clear
        THIS.AddItem("Customer")
        THIS.AddItem("Employee")
        THIS.AddItem(SPACE(8))
    ENDIF
ENDIF
```

Note that an empty item was added at the end of the list. If the user selects this item, the currently selected work area will be searched.

This dialog is used as the default interface by the Locate button.

### Find (Findnext) Buttons

| Class | _findnextbuttons |
|---|---|
| Base class | Container |
| Class library | _table.vcx |
| Parent class | _findbutton |
| Sample | ...\Samples\Vfp98\Solution\Ffc\dataqry.scx |
| Dependencies | _base.vcx, _table.h |

The Findnext Buttons class is a subclass of the Find button, so there aren't many differences between the two. In fact, the only difference is that there is a second button with the caption of "Find next". Instead of changing the caption of a single Find button, the Findnext button is enabled when the first occurrence of the search expression is located.

### Find Object

| Class | _tablefind |
|---|---|
| **Base class** | Custom |
| **Class library** | _table.vcx |
| **Parent class** | _table |
| **Sample** | ...\Samples\Vfp98\Solution\Ffc\dataqry.scx |
| **Dependencies** | _base.vcx, _table.h |

The Find object is a behavioral object that provides functionality to locate records in a data source. The Find object is used by the other entire Find... foundation classes described in this section. It can also be used by itself.

Searching for the occurrence of a certain expression is relatively easy. Here's a simple example:

```
oFind = NewObject("_tablefind","_Table.vcx")
oFind.cFindString = "quiz"
? oFind.DoFind()
```

The DoFind() method does all the actual work. It will return .T. when it finds the Find string, and .F. if the expression couldn't be located. Note that this example requires a data source to be in use. As you can see, the expression to be searched is specified in the *cFindString* property. You can set a couple of additional properties to influence the way the object searches the data source. *LMatchCase* allows specifying (you guessed it) whether the search should be case-sensitive. *LSkipMemos* specifies whether memo fields should be searched (.F.) or whether they should be skipped (.T.). By default all memo fields are searched. When searching large data sources, this can be very slow.

Once an occurrence of the search expression is found, the property *lFindAgain* is set to .T.. This sets the object in a different mode. From now on, the DoFind() method searches the rest of the cursor rather than starting the search at the very beginning. If this is not the desired behavior, you can reset this property to .F., and the next search will also start at the beginning of the table. This is done automatically whenever a new Find string is specified, so typically you don't have to worry about it. When doing continuous searching, the user will eventually reach the end of the table. In this case the search typically stops. However, you can specify that the search should continue at the beginning of the table after encountering the end-of-file. This can be done through the *lWrapAround* property.

In the example above, I didn't specify a data source, so the object searched the current work area. However, you could also specify a different alias using the *cAlias* property.

By default, all fields in a cursor are searched. To do so, the object converts all those fields to type character (internally only, of course). As mentioned above, you can specify that all memos should be skipped, which is important for performance reasons. You can also exclude specific fields from the search using the SkipField() method. The method requires one parameter, which is the name of the field to be skipped. The class internally remembers all the fields to be searched in the *cFields* property, which is populated by the SetFields() method. This method fires every time the data source changes or fields are excluded using either the *lSkipMemos* property or the SkipField() method. The contents of the *cField* property might seem strange at first sight. Here's an example:

```
[~]+ALLTRIM(STR(XREF_ID,12,4))+[~]+TEXT+[~]
```

This defines that two fields are included in the search (XREF_ID and TEXT). If you take a closer look, you'll see that this is a valid FoxPro expression. Depending on the values of each record, the string (it is always a string!) to which this expression evaluates will be different. Here's a possible example:

```
~8.0000~Visual FoxPro quiz
```

Note that the fields are separated by tildes (~). Considering the possible complexity of the expression in *cFields*, and considering the number of times this property gets repopulated, I recommend staying away from changing the contents of this property yourself!

When a search fails (the expression cannot be located), a beep sounds and a wait window is displayed, indicating that the Find string couldn't be located. You might prefer a different kind of interface; luckily it's easy to exchange the interface. A method called ShowMessageNotFound() is responsible for the displayed message. You can simply overwrite it (ignore the default behavior) to create your own interface.

### Locate Button

| Class | _locatebutton |
|---|---|
| Base class | CommandButton |
| Class library | _table2.vcx |
| Parent class | _dialogbutton |
| Sample | ...\Samples\Vfp98\Solution\Ffc\dataqry.scx |
| Dependencies | _base.vcx, _table2.h, _table.vcx, _table.h |

The Locate button is used to instantiate a Find dialog. By default, the Locate button uses the Filter dialog box. You can specify the class you want to use through the *cClass* and *cClassLib* properties of the Locate button.

Using the Locate button is trivial. You can drop the button on any form or container. The only precondition is that the current data environment must have at least one cursor open.

### Lookup Combobox

| Class | _cbolookup |
|---|---|
| Base class | ComboBox |
| Class library | _dataquery.vcx |
| Parent class | _combobox |
| Sample | ...\Samples\Vfp98\Solution\Ffc\datalook2.scx |
| Dependencies | _base.vcx, _data.h |

The Lookup combobox is automatically populated with values from a table in the order of a certain other table field. I like to use this combobox to navigate in a data source as long as there is only a small number of records.

The Lookup combobox can be used easily. The class has four properties that specify the values of the combobox. *Display_Column* specifies the name of the field with the values to be displayed. *Lookup_Table* specifies the table the field belongs to. *Return_Column* specifies the field name, which will be used for data binding. So you could display the CustomerName field from the Customer table and bind the combobox to the CustomerID field. Additionally, you can specify a certain display order through the *Order_Column* property. The contents will then automatically be sorted according to the values of the specified field.

**Figure 17** shows the Lookup combobox in action.

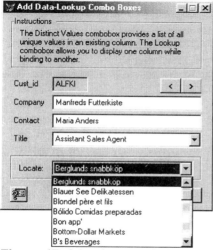

*Figure 17. A Lookup combobox is used to navigate within a small data source.*

As mentioned earlier, I like to use the Lookup combobox for navigation as long as the number of records is reasonably low (the actual number of records I consider "reasonably low" depends on field length and machine performance). However, navigational behavior is not native to the Lookup combobox. Fortunately, it is quite easy to add it in a subclass. The following code must be added to the InteractiveChange() event:

```
DODEFAULT()
LOCAL lcFieldName
lcFieldName = THIS.Return_Column
LOCATE FOR &lcFieldName = ALLTRIM(THIS.Value)
THISFORM.Refresh
```

However, I don't recommend using this class for large data sources, for simple performance and resource reasons.

## QBF (query-by-form)

| Class | _qbf |
|---|---|
| Base class | Container |
| Class library | _dataquery |
| Parent class | _container |
| Sample | ...\Samples\Vfp98\Solution\Forms\qbf.scx |
| Dependencies | _base.vcx |

Querying by Form is a quick and easy way of providing an interface to locate data. In a query-by-form scenario, a regular data entry form is used to specify an example of the data one is looking for. This sounds more complicated than it is. **Figure 18** shows an example of a typical data entry form displaying real data. To search for a certain record in this form, I can press the Enter QBF button to blank out all the fields. By doing so, I switch the form into query mode and I can now enter my search criteria. For instance, I could specify "Markus" as the first name and "Austria" as the country. To actually search for this data, I press the Query button. Then the QBF object not only locates the first record that matches my criteria, but it applies a filter based on the values I specified, so I can easily navigate all the records that match my example.

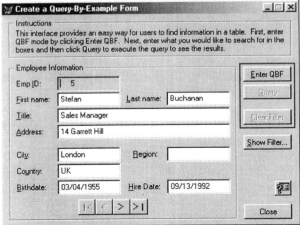

*Figure 18. A data entry form that uses the QBF object.*

It might sound as if the QBF object isn't generic, and that a lot of preconditions must be fulfilled in order to use it. Quite the opposite is true! When starting a QBF session, the object starts a transaction, appends a blank record to the current data source (which will then be used to specify the search values) and, when the Query button is pressed, a filter is automatically constructed from the specified values and applied. The transaction is then immediately rolled back to leave your data the way it was before. Because the object uses transactions, it can be used only for tables in a database. FoxPro does not support transactions for free tables.

Using the QBF object is trivial. You can drop it on any form or container containing data that is part of a FoxPro database. The object has only one property, which specifies the table name (*QBF_Table*). Setting this property is optional. If left blank, the selected work area is searched.

The object has only one custom method—ParseCondition()—which is reserved for internal use only.

### Sort Dialog Box

| Class | _sortdialog |
|---|---|
| Base class | Form |
| Class library | _table2.vcx |
| Parent class | _form |
| Sample | ...\Samples\Vfp98\Solution\Ffc\datasort.scx |
| Dependencies | _base.vcx, _table2.h, _table.vcx, _table.h |

The Sort dialog box (see **Figure 19**) allows the user to sort data in ascending or descending order based on a certain field. The class automatically analyzes the current data environment and displays a list of indexed fields. Fields that don't have an index cannot be used for sorting.

**Figure 19.** *The Sort dialog box being used to sort the Customer table.*

The class uses the Sort object (see below) to change the actual sort order. Therefore, the Sort dialog box class is rather simple. So far I haven't found many reasons to subclass this class. Making changes to the interface is trivial. Other than that, I found that I changed only the fields displayed in the Select Field combobox. This combobox is populated in the combobox's Init() event (not to be confused with the form's Init() event!). Here's an example of how the combobox can be populated with different fields:

```
IF DoDefault()
   THIS.Clear
   THIS.AddItem(C_NONE_LOC)
   THIS.AddItem("CONTACT")
   THIS.AddItem("COMPANY")
   THIS.AddItem("COUNTRY")
ELSE
   RETURN .f.
ENDIF
```

Note that I call the default behavior before I populate the combobox. This is important because there are a couple of additional settings that are initialized in the Init() event of the original combobox. Once the original behavior executes, I clear the contents of the combobox and add my own tag names. Note that the first item I add is a standard item, which allows the user to reset the sorting sequence (sorted by record number). The names I add must match the exact index tags.

The fact that the displayed index names must match the exact tag names in the database isn't very elegant. Index names might be rather cryptic, while we want to display a nice English name to the user. Changing this behavior is somewhat more difficult because you have to create a multi-column combobox like so:

```
IF DoDefault()
   THIS.Clear
   THIS.RowSourceType = 1
   THIS.ColumnCount = 2
   THIS.ColumnLines = .F.
   THIS.BoundColumn = 2
   THIS.ColumnWidths = Alltrim(Str(THIS.Width-10)) + ",0"
   THIS.RowSource = C_NONE_LOC + "," + C_NONE_LOC +;
      "," + "Contact Person" + "," + "CONTACT" +;
      "," + "Company Name" + "," + "COMPANY" +;
      "," + "Home Country" + "," + "COUNTRY"
ELSE
   RETURN .F.
ENDIF
```

First of all, I change the row source type to 1, which allows me to specify the entire source for the combobox as a single string. I believe this makes it easier to handle small, multi-column comboboxes. If you prefer another kind of row source, feel free to use it. I then set the column count to 2, disable the column lines, bind data to the second column, and set the width of the first column to the width of the entire combobox and the width of the second column to 0 in order to hide it from the user. I can now use the first column to display a nice English description, while the second column holds the actual field name, which will be bound to the *Value* property of the combobox—and that's what the class uses. Finally, all I have to do is set the row source to a string of comma-separated item values.

### Sort Dialog Box Button

| Class | _sortbutton |
|---|---|
| Base class | CommandButton |
| Class library | _table2.vcx |
| Parent class | _dialogbutton |
| Sample | ...\Samples\Vfp98\Solution\Ffc\datasort.scx |
| Dependencies | _base.vcx, _table2.h, _table.vcx, _table.h |

The Sort Dialog Box button is yet another subclass of the abstract Dialog button. Its only purpose is to instantiate a Sort dialog box. By default, the Sort Dialog Box foundation class (see above) is instantiated, but you can specify a different class through the *cClass* and *cClassLib* properties.

### *Sort Object*

| Class | _tablesort |
|---|---|
| Base class | Custom |
| Class library | _table.vcx |
| Parent class | _table |
| Sample | ...\Samples\Vfp98\Solution\Ffc\datasort.scx |
| Dependencies | _base.vcx, _table.h |

The Sort object provides the entire sort behavior utilized by the Sort... foundation classes introduced in this section. However, you can also use it by itself.

You need only one method to sort a table in a certain way: DoSort(). This method accepts four parameters, most of which are optional. Here's an example that sorts the Customer table based on the Country field:

```
USE Customer
oSort = NewObject("_tablesort","_table.vcx")
oSort.DoSort("country")
```

Note that the first parameter is the actual field name, rather than the index tag name. The object is actually smart enough to use the appropriate index tag. If there is more than one index tag for this field, the object might have a hard time finding the correct one. In this case you should specify the index tag name through parameter 3, like so:

```
oSort.DoSort(,,"mycountry")
```

If neither a field nor a tag name is passed, the Sort object checks for the current control and uses its control source for sorting.

The second parameter specifies the table alias. You need to pass it only if the table you want to sort is not the selected one. Finally, parameter 4 can be used to specify whether you want to sort descending (.T.) or ascending (.F.). You can also specify this through the *lDescending* property, which might be easier when you provide a standard user interface that uses a control such as a checkbox to specify descending order.

If you want to reset the sort order to 0 (sorted by record number), you can use the RemoveSort() method. If you want to reset a table other than the currently selected one, you have to pass the alias as a parameter.

### *Sort Selector*

| Class | _sortselect |
|---|---|
| Base class | Container |
| Class library | _table2.vcx |
| Parent class | _container |
| Sample | ...\Samples\Vfp98\Solution\Ffc\datasort.scx |
| Dependencies | _base.vcx, _table2.h, _table.vcx, _table.h |

The Sort Selector changes the sorting sequence from ascending to descending, and vice versa. The field to be sorted on is retrieved from the currently active control in the currently active form. The Sort Selector is typically used in toolbars (see **Figure 20**).

*Figure 20. The Sort Selector is typically used in toolbars.*

## SQL Pass Through

| Class | _execsp |
|---|---|
| Base class | Custom |
| Class library | _dataquery.vcx |
| Parent class | _custom |
| Sample | None |
| Dependencies | _base.vcx, _data.h |

This class is used for SQL Pass Through and can execute stored procedures on the host database. The actual connection to the server must be handled by the user. Here's an example of how you can connect to a SQL Server database:

```
hConnect = SQLCONNECT ('pubs','sa','')
```

This opens the "pubs" database and returns a handle called "hConnect". Now you can use this handle in the SQL Pass Through class. You have to configure this class on Init(). Here's an example:

```
DIME aParams[3]
aParams[1] = "'172-32-1176'"
aParams[2] = "'S'"
aParams[3] = "'E'"
oSQL=NewObject('_ExecSP', '_dataquery.vcx', '',;
    'UpdateAuthorName', hConnect, @aParams, 'tResult')
```

The first parameter that is passed to the Init() method (parameter 3 in the NewObject() function) specifies the stored procedure name. Parameter 2 is the connection handle we created before. Parameter 3 is an array of parameters that is passed to the stored procedure. This array must be passed by reference. Parameter 4 specifies the alias of the result cursor. This parameter is optional and defaults to "sqlresult".

Now that the object is configured, we can execute the stored procedure using the DoSQL() method:

```
oSQL.DoSQL()
```

Through the *IUseSQLSyntax* property, you can specify whether or not SQL Server Exec syntax should be used (default = .F.). This influences the construction of the command that is passed to SQL Server. You can also query the constructed command using the GetSQL() method. This method returns the SQL command as a string.

## Data utilities

String and array handling are quite comfortable and powerful in Visual FoxPro. However, there are a couple of details that could be handled a little better. The classes in this category attempt to fine-tune these capabilities.

### *Array Handler*

| Class | _arraylib |
|---|---|
| Base class | Custom |
| Class library | _utility.vcx |
| Parent class | _custom |
| Sample | ...\Samples\Vfp98\Solution\Ffc\arrays.scx |
| Dependencies | _base.vcx |

Visual FoxPro is rather flexible when it comes to array handling. However, I'd frequently like to have a couple of array functions that Visual FoxPro doesn't offer. Among them is scanning through an array column by column, deleting and inserting array items. The Array Handler object provides these functions.

The Array Handler should be instantiated as a generic object. Its methods can then be used like regular user-defined functions attached to an object. You simply call the methods and pass the array as well as some additional parameters to specify details about the array operation. The way these methods are called is very similar to calling array functions.

Let's look at the provided functions, the most used of which seems to be the "array scanning by column" feature. The AColScan() method implements this feature. The array and the search expression are passed as parameters like so:

```
oArray = NewObject("_arraylib","_utility.vcx")
DIMENSION aTest[3,3]
* In a real world scenario we would fill the array here...
? oArray.AColScan(@aTest,"Search Value")
```

Note that the array must be passed by reference (using the @ sign.) The internal array handling functions do not require this, but the regular FoxPro language makes it impossible to pass arrays other than by reference. As you can see, the second parameter is the search string. By default, the method scans the first column of the array unless you specify the column number like so:

```
? oArray.AColScan(@aTest,"Search Value",2)
```

The return value is the absolute position of the found item. You can also specify that you want the row number to be returned. This can be done through the third parameter:

```
? oArray.AColScan(@aTest,"Search Value",2,.T.)
```

The next method I want to introduce is DelAItem(). This method is rather trivial; it deletes an entire row from an array, just like the ADel() function. The major difference is that the array also gets redimensioned after the row is deleted. The method requires two parameters—the array (again passed by reference) and the row number you want to delete:

```
? oArray.DelAItem(@aTest, 2)
```

The Array Handler object also allows you to insert an item (similar to the AIns() function) by using the InsAItem() method. This method requires at least three parameters:

```
? oArray.InsAItem(@aTest, "Test", 2)
```

The first parameter is the array (again by reference). Parameter 2 is the value to be inserted, and parameter 3 is the number of the row after which the new item will be inserted. So in the example above, the new item will be inserted as row 3. As you can see, parameter 2 only allows passing a single value, which will be inserted into the array. In a multi-column array, this leaves us with default values for the rest of the columns. Those columns must either be populated afterwards, or we can specify that the passed value should be used for all columns. This can by done by passing a fourth parameter:

```
? oArray.InsAItem(@aTest, "Test", 2, .T.)
```

Overall, the Array Handler provides some nice functionality, but it's not like you couldn't live without it. Most important to me is the ability to scan single columns.

### String Library

| Class | _stringlib |
|---|---|
| Base class | Custom |
| Class library | _utility.vcx |
| Parent class | _custom |
| Sample | None |
| Dependencies | _base.vcx |

The String Library doesn't really deserve its name. The class has only one tiny method—TrimCRLF()—which allows you to trim leading, trailing, or leading and trailing carriage returns and line feeds. Parameter 1 is the string that you want to trim, parameter 2 specifies whether leading characters should be trimmed, and parameter 3 does the same for trailing ones:

```
cString = Chr(13) + Chr(10) +;
   Chr(13) + Chr(10)  +;
   "This is a test" +;
   Chr(13) + Chr(10)
oStringLib = NewObject("_stringlib","_utility.vcx")
cString = oStringLib.TrimCRLF(cString,.T.,.T.)
```

## Date time

Handling date-related and time-related data is crucial to most business applications. Visual FoxPro handles this data quite well. However, there are no interface components with which to enter this kind of data other than regular textboxes. The foundation classes found in this category correct this shortcoming.

### ActiveX Calendar

| Class | _olecalendar |
|---|---|
| **Base class** | OLEControl |
| **Class library** | _datetime.vcx |
| **Parent class** | _olecontrol |
| **Sample** | ...\Samples\Vfp98\Solution\Ffc\datacal.scx |
| **Dependencies** | _base.vcx, Microsoft Calendar ActiveX Control |

The ActiveX Calendar class uses the Microsoft Calendar ActiveX control to provide a nice calendar interface (see **Figure 21**). A good reason to use this class instead of the ActiveX control directly is because this class allows data binding.

You can drop the ActiveX Calendar on any form or container. The class has a property called *Date_Column*, which specifies the field that will be bound to the calendar. You can think of this property as the "ControlSource" property of this class.

Data binding with ActiveX controls is not trivial. The ActiveX Calendar class does a pretty good job binding the ActiveX control to Visual FoxPro data. However, when the control source is changed from the outside (programmatically or through another user interface component), the control might not recognize the change. In this case, you can call the RefreshDisplay() method to update the control.

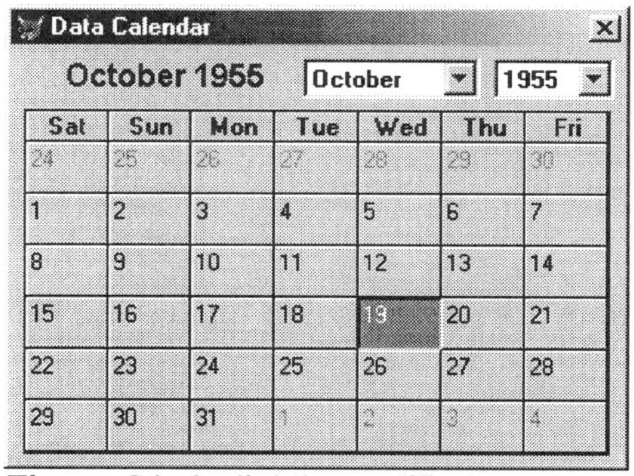

**Figure 21**. *A slightly modified version of the ActiveX Calendar control.*

### Clock

| Class | _clock |
|---|---|
| Base class | Container |
| Class library | _datetime.vcx |
| Parent class | _container |
| Sample | ...\Samples\Vfp98\Solution\Controls\Timer\clock.scx |
| Dependencies | _base.vcx |

The Clock class is a simple textbox that displays the actual time. A timer updates the display once a second. The class has a property called *TimeFormat*, which (in theory) allows you to change the time format from 12 to 24 hours. However, this did not work in the version I have (Visual FoxPro 6.0 release version). In fact, there isn't even any code that would react to settings in that property.

### Stop Watch

| Class | _stopwatch |
|---|---|
| Base class | Container |
| Class library | _datetime.vcx |
| Parent class | _container |
| Sample | ...\Samples\Vfp98\Solution\Controls\Timer\swatch.scx |
| Dependencies | _base.vcx |

The Stop Watch class provides a simple stopwatch control that can be placed on any form or container (see **Figure 22**). The Stop Watch class has three important methods: Start(), Stop() and Reset(). Their purpose is self-explanatory. The class also has a property called *ElapsedSeconds*, which you can query programmatically to check for the number of elapsed seconds.

*Figure 22. The Stop Watch class.*

### File utilities

Handling files is a necessary task in any application. Visual FoxPro provides a great number of functions to handle files, most of which are data related. But sometimes it would be nice to get a little more technical information about those files, and that's exactly what these classes do.

### *File Version*

| Class | _fileversion |
|---|---|
| **Base class** | Custom |
| **Class library** | _utility.vcx |
| **Parent class** | _custom |
| **Sample** | ...\Samples\Vfp98\Solution\WinAPI\getver.scx |
| **Dependencies** | _base.vcx, _utility.h |

The File Version object allows you to retrieve detailed information about EXE and DLL files. This information can be interesting at design time, and it is often important during runtime to make sure the proper file versions are present.

The detailed file information is stored in the aVersion() property array. To populate this array, you first have to set the *cFileName* property and call the GetVersion() method:

```
oFileVersion = NewObject("_fileversion","_utility.vcx")
oFileVersion.cFileName = Home() + "VFP6.EXE"
oFileVersion.GetVersion()
```

The created array is one-dimensional and has 15 rows. **Table 3** explains the meaning of each item. The items can be displayed using the DisplayVersion() method, which displays a message box with all the information. The user interface cannot be changed unless you overwrite the entire method.

***Table 3.*** *The contents of the aVersion() array.*

| Row | Description |
|---|---|
| 1 | Comments |
| 2 | Company name |
| 3 | File description |
| 4 | File version |
| 5 | Internal name |
| 6 | Legal copyright |
| 7 | Legal trademarks |
| 8 | Original file name |
| 9 | Private build |
| 10 | Product name |
| 11 | Product version |
| 12 | Special build |
| 13 | OLE self registration (contains "OLESelfRegister" if the file supports self-registration; otherwise contains the empty string) |
| 14 | Language (derived from the translation code) |
| 15 | Hexadecimal translation code |

### Find Files/Text

| Class | _filer |
|---|---|
| Base class | Custom |
| Class library | _utility.vcx |
| Parent class | _custom |
| Sample | ...\Samples\Vfp98\Tools\Filer\Filer.scx |
| Dependencies | _base.vcx, _utility.h, filer.dll |

The Find Files/Text foundation class is a wrapper for the Filer.dll COM object. You can use this class to search for files that have a certain name (wildcards such as * and ? are allowed) and/or files that contain a certain text string.

Using this class is straightforward. A number of properties can be used to specify search parameters, such as the text to be searched, the files you want to search, the path, and so forth. Here is an example:

```
set classlib to _utility.vcx
oFiler = NewObject("_filer","_utility.vcx")
oFiler.cFileExpression = "*.XML"
oFiler.cSearchPath = "C:\My Documents\"
oFiler.cSearchText = "Some Text"
oFiler.lIgnoreCase = .T.
oFiler.lSubFolder = .T.
nFilesFound = oFiler.Find()
```

This example searches all the XML files in "C:\My Documents\" (and all subdirectories) that contain the string "Some Text". The Find() method initiates the actual search and returns the number of files that were found. Then it starts to get a little trickier, especially because the following isn't documented in the Visual FoxPro Foundation Class documentation.

The Find() method populates a collection of files that can be referenced through the *oFiles* property. This collection has a property called *Count* that we can use to query the number of files (in case we missed the return value):

```
nFilesFound = oFiler.oFiles.Count
```

The oFiles reference doesn't have any other properties, but there is an Item() collection that can be used to access each individual item. Each item has more properties that describe each file.

```
FOR nCounter = 1 TO oFiler.oFiles.Count
    ? oFiler.oFiles.Item(nCounter).Name
ENDFOR
```

All properties and methods of the objects in the Item collection are described in **Tables 4** and **5**.

*Table 4*. *The properties of the objects in the Item collection.*

| Property | Type | Description | Example |
|---|---|---|---|
| AlternateName | C | The short name of the file if the real name exceeds the 8.3 naming convention. | ? oFiles.Item(1).AlternateName |
| Attr | N | The Windows file attributes for the file in a numeric format.<br><br>The possible values are:<br>0 = No attributes set<br>1 = Read-Only<br>2 = Hidden<br>4 = System<br>32 = Archived<br><br>More than one value can be set at a time. If the value is 6 (for instance), we have a hidden system file.<br><br>Unlike the other properties described in this table, this property is not read-only. This means that you can set file attributes using this property. | ? oFiles.Item(1).Attr<br>oFiles.Item(1).Attr = 32 |
| DateTime | N | The numeric time stamp assigned by Windows when the file is created. The integer portion of the time stamp represents the number of days since 12/30/1899, and the remainder is the fractional remainder of the day from which you can determine the time when the file was created. | ? oFiles.Item(1).DateTime |
| LastAccessTime | N | The time stamp assigned by Windows when the file was accessed the last time. | ?<br>oFiles.Item(1).LastAccessTime |
| LastWriteTime | N | The time stamp assigned by Windows when the file was modified the last time. | ? oFiles.Item(1).LastWriteTime |
| Name | C | The full file name. | ? oFiles.Item(1).Name |
| Path | C | The full path to the file. | ? oFiles.Item(1).Path |
| Size | N | File size in bytes. | ? oFiles.Item(1).Size |
| SizeHigh | N | The high 4 bytes of the file size if the file is greater than 4 gigabytes. | ? oFiles.Item(1).SizeHigh |

*Table 5*. *The methods of the object in the Item collection.*

| Name | Description | Example |
|---|---|---|
| Edit | Uses the Visual FoxPro editor to modify the file. | oFiles.Item(1).Edit() |
| Delete | Deletes the file from disk. The file is *not* placed in the Recycle Bin! | oFiles.Item(1).Delete() |

## Type Library

| Class | _typelib |
|---|---|
| Base class | Container |
| Class library | _utility.vcx |
| Parent class | _container |
| Sample | ...\Samples\Vfp98\Solution\Forms\typelib.scx |
| Dependencies | _base.vcx, _utility.h, FoxTLib ActiveX control |

The Type Library foundation class is a wrapper for the Visual FoxPro Foxtlib ActiveX control that ships with Visual FoxPro. It can be used to handle and use type library information in your applications. Type libraries host information about COM controls and servers. The Type Library foundation class is a container that hosts this ActiveX control. You can drop this container on another container such as a form. You cannot instantiate the Type Library class by itself.

To load a type library, you first specify its name and then call the GetTypeLib() method, like so:

```
oTL.TypeLibName = FullPath("wbserver.tlb")
oTL.GetTypeLib()
```

This code loads the type library, retrieves the number of type infos, stores it in the *TypeInfoCount* property, and finally loads some basic information in the *aTypeLibDocs* array. This array always has three elements: they hold information about the name, the document string, and the help file of the selected member. In the beginning, this information is specific to the entire type library; it is not member-specific.

Now that we have this information, we can explore the Type Library class further. The GetTypeInfo() method collects type information of a certain type info key. We already know how many type info keys we have (*TypeInfoCount*). When we retrieve the type information for one of those keys, the arrays *aTypeInfoDocs* and *aTypeAttr* are populated. The return value of GetTypeInfo() is 0 if everything went okay, or -1 if an error occurred. The *aTypeAttr* array is a one-dimensional array that holds information about a certain type index. **Table 6** describes the meaning of each element.

***Table 6***. The rows in the aTypeAttr *array.*

| Item | Description | Item | Description |
|---|---|---|---|
| 1 | GUID (Unique ID that identifies the server) | 9 | Number of functions |
| 2 | LocaleID | 10 | Number of variables/members |
| 3 | Reserved | 11 | Number of implemented interfaces |
| 4 | Constructor ID | 12 | Size of type's virtual function table |
| 5 | Destructor ID | 13 | Byte alignment of an instance of this type |
| 6 | Reserved | 14 | Flags |
| 7 | Instance size | 15 | Major version number |
| 8 | Type Kind | 16 | Minor version number |

Using the GetFuncDesc() method, we can also retrieve information about a specific function that is documented in the type library. This method requires passing the function index as the first parameter. It populates the *aTypeFuncDesc*, *aTypeFuncParms*, *aTypeFuncNames* and *aTypeFuncDocs* arrays as well as the *FuncNamesCount* property. The *aTypeFuncDesc* array contains information about the function (see **Table 7**), while the *aTypeFuncParms* array stores information about the function parameters.

*Table 7*. The rows in the aTypeFuncDesc *array.*

| Item | Description |
|---|---|
| 1 | ID |
| 2 | Function kind. Specifies whether the function is virtual, static, or dispatch only. Possible values: FUNC_PUREVIRTUAL = The function is accessed through the virtual function table and takes an implicit "this" pointer. FUNC_VIRTUAL = The function is accessed the same as PUREVIRTUAL, except the function has an implementation. FUNC_NONVIRTUAL = The function is accessed by static address and takes an implicit "this" pointer. FUNC_STATIC = The function is accessed by static address and does not take an implicit "this" pointer. FUNC_DISPATCH = The function can be accessed only through IDispatch. |
| 3 | Invoke kind. Specifies whether this is a property function, and if so, what kind. Possible invocation kinds: INVOKE_FUNC = The member is called using normal function invocation syntax. INVOKE_PROPERTYGET = The function is invoked using normal property access syntax. INVOKE_PROPERTYPUT = The function is invoked using property value assignment syntax. INVOKE_PROPERTYPUTREF = The function is invoked using property reference assignment syntax. |
| 4 | Specifies the function's calling convention. |
| 5 | Total number of parameters. |
| 6 | Number of optional parameters. |
| 7 | For FUNC_VIRTUAL, specifies the offset in the virtual table. |
| 8 | Count of permitted Scodes. |
| 9 | Flags. Possible flags: FUNCFLAG_FRESTRICTED (1) = The function should not be accessible from macro languages. This flag is intended for system-level functions or functions that type browsers should not display. FUNCFLAG_FSOURCE (0x02) = The function returns an object that is a source of events. FUNCFLAG_FBINDABLE (0x04) = The function supports data binding. FUNCFLAG_FDISPLAYBIND (0x10) = The function is displayed to the user as bindable; that is, the bindable flag must also be set. FUNCFLAG_FDEFAULTBIND (0x20) = The function that best represents the object. Only one function in a type info can have this attribute. FUNCFLAG_FHIDDEN (0x40) = The function should not be displayed to the user, though it exists and is bindable. |

The *aTypeFuncNames* array holds information about the function names. The *aTypeFuncDocs* array is a one-dimensional array with three elements and it's identical to the *aTypeLibDocs* array.

The Type Library object can also export the type library information to a text file using the ExportTypeLib() method. This method takes two parameters: the file name and (optional) whether or not the file should be displayed right away (.T.).

### Internet

There is no doubt that the Internet has become the driving force in the software industry. A number of new Internet-related features have been introduced in Visual FoxPro 6.0. However, public opinion still seems to be that there should have been more. Well, there are more! Just check out this category.

### Cookies Class

| Class | _cookies |
|---|---|
| Base class | Custom |
| Class library | _internet.vcx |
| Parent class | _custom |
| Sample | None |
| Dependencies | _base.vcx |

One of the standard problems on the Internet is identifying users; one resolution to this problem is to assign cookies to users. In this case, a small file is stored on the client's computer. This file basically stores an ID you can use later on to identify the user. On the server side, this ID must be stored in a table so you can figure out what ID belongs to what user. Cookies can be used only if the client's browser supports cookies and the user has turned this feature on (which should be standard, in my opinion). For more information about cookies, see Rick Strahl's book *Internet Applications with Visual FoxPro 6.0.*

### DBF-> HTML

| Class | _dbf2html |
|---|---|
| Base class | Custom |
| Class library | _internet.vcx |
| Parent class | _custom |
| Sample | ...\Samples\Vfp98\Solution\Ffc\dohtml.scx |
| Dependencies | _base.vcx |

This class creates HTML output based on a DBF file. The class is a simple wrapper for the GENHTML program, which ships with Visual FoxPro 6.0. To use the class, open a data source, instantiate the DBF->HTML object and call the GenHTML() method:

```
USE Customer
oDBF2HTML = NewObject("_dbf2html","_internet.vcx")
oDBF2HTML.GenHTML()
```

This creates an HTML file called Customer.htm, which is immediately displayed in your standard Web browser. **Figure 23** shows the created output.

By default, the class uses the current alias and creates an output file of the same name as the current table (with an HTM extension). The file is then displayed immediately, using the default Web browser. You can change this behavior through a couple of properties. The property *lUseCurrentAlias* specifies whether the currently selected alias should be used. If this property is set to .F. or no valid data source is selected, the *cSource* property specifies an alternative source. The properties *lAutoNameOutput* and *cOutFile* do the same for the created output. If the *lAutoNameOutput* property is set to .T., the output file gets the same name as the used data source (with an HTM extension). If this property is set to .F., the *cOutFile* property specifies the file name.

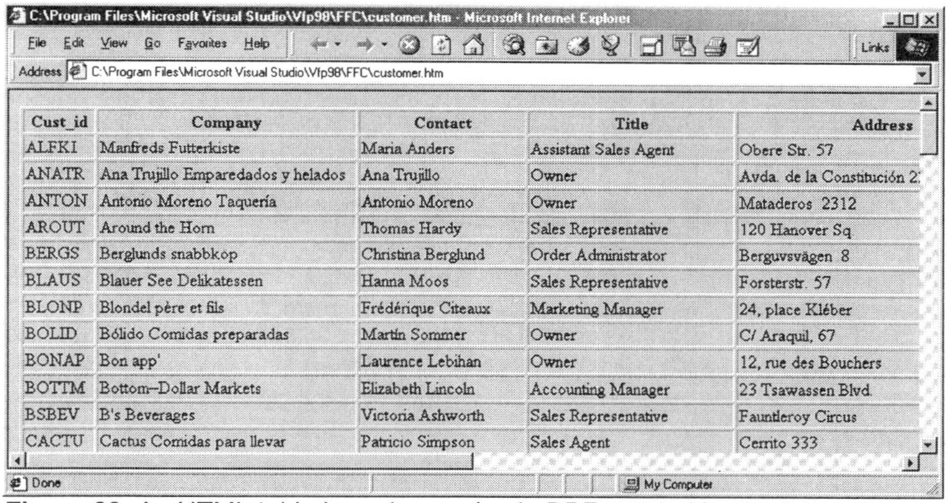


| Cust_id | Company | Contact | Title | Address |
|---|---|---|---|---|
| ALFKI | Manfreds Futterkiste | Maria Anders | Assistant Sales Agent | Obere Str. 57 |
| ANATR | Ana Trujillo Emparedados y helados | Ana Trujillo | Owner | Avda. de la Constitución 2: |
| ANTON | Antonio Moreno Taquería | Antonio Moreno | Owner | Mataderos 2312 |
| AROUT | Around the Horn | Thomas Hardy | Sales Representative | 120 Hanover Sq |
| BERGS | Berglunds snabbkop | Christina Berglund | Order Administrator | Berguvsvägen 8 |
| BLAUS | Blauer See Delikatessen | Hanna Moos | Sales Representative | Forsterstr. 57 |
| BLONP | Blondel père et fils | Frédérique Citeaux | Marketing Manager | 24, place Kléber |
| BOLID | Bólido Comidas preparadas | Martín Sommer | Owner | C/ Araquil, 67 |
| BONAP | Bon app' | Laurence Lebihan | Owner | 12, rue des Bouchers |
| BOTTM | Bottom-Dollar Markets | Elizabeth Lincoln | Accounting Manager | 23 Tsawassen Blvd. |
| BSBEV | B's Beverages | Victoria Ashworth | Sales Representative | Fauntleroy Circus |
| CACTU | Cactus Comidas para llevar | Patricio Simpson | Sales Agent | Cerrito 333 |

***Figure 23****. An HTML table based on a simple DBF created by the DBF->HTML class.*

The *nGenOutput* property specifies how (and if) the created output file should be displayed. By default, the default class browser is displayed. Figure 23 shows Internet Explorer used as the Web browser. **Table 8** explains the possible values of *nGenOutput*.

***Table 8****. Possible values for the* nGenOutput *property.*

| Value | Description |
|---|---|
| 0 | Generates an output file. The file is created and stored, but it is not displayed. |
| 1 | Generates the output file and display it using the Visual FoxPro editor using the MODIFY FILE command. |
| 2 (default) | Generates output file and displays it in the standard Web browser. |
| 3 | Generates a file and asks the user what to do with it (see **Figure 24**). |
| 4 | Generates a file and instantiates a public _oHTML object. You can make this object visible like so: `_oHTML.Show()` |
| 5 | Instantiates a public instance of the _oHTML object, but no output file is generated. |

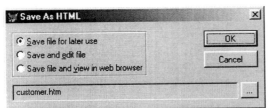

*Figure 24. The Save As HTML dialog box as used by all HTML foundation classes.*

By default, all records from the entire data source are printed, but you can limit this using the *cScope* property. This property is of type *character*. Its value is simply evaluated in the scan-loop that iterates through the table. The value could be blank, "NEXT 1", "Country = 'Austria'" or the like.

You can alter the look and feel of the table, specifying your own output styles using Genhtml.prg. The name of a certain style can be specified in the *cStyle* property. A description of this table is beyond the scope of this book.

As mentioned, the DBF->HTML class uses Genhtml.prg to create the HTML output. If you want to change the behavior of this class, you most likely have to change this program. You can specify your own genhtml program by setting the *_GENHTML* system variable. However, there are some minor features the DBF->HTML wrapper doesn't support. You can subclass the DBF->HTML class to add those features or to support your own Genhtml.prg. The only method this class has is GenHTML(). This method is relatively trivial and simple to change or overwrite.

### FRX->HTML

| Class | _frx2html |
|---|---|
| Base class | Custom |
| Class library | _internet.vcx |
| Parent class | _custom |
| Sample | ...\Samples\Vfp98\Solution\Ffc\dohtml.scx |
| Dependencies | _base.vcx |

The FRX->HTML class is essentially the same as the DBF->HTML class. The only difference is the source, which is not a DBF but an FRX report. Note that, due to essential paradigm differences, many report layout features don't convert well to HTML format.

See above (DBF->HTML) for more details.

### Hyperlink Object

| Class | _hyperlinkbase |
|---|---|
| Base class | Hyperlink |
| Class library | _hyperlink.vcx |
| Parent class | _hyperlink |
| Sample | ...\Samples\Vfp98\Solution\Ffc\hyperlnk.scx |
| Dependencies | _base.vcx |

The Hyperlink object is used by all the Hyperlink interface classes. This class provides all Web navigation functionality. It is based on the native Visual FoxPro Hyperlink class. However, it does not use the default hyperlink behavior a lot. The class first queries the standard Web browser, and if it is Internet Explorer, the browser is instantiated as a COM server to gain more control. The Hyperlink base class initially was designed for use in active documents, where it works great. However, the class can still be used in regular Visual FoxPro applications. The problem is that the Hyperlink base class fires up a new instance of the default Web browser every time the NavigateTo() method is called. This is not what most programmers want. Typically, one wants to navigate using the same instance of the Web browser. The Hyperlink object foundation class provides this behavior. However, you can still navigate using separate browser instances if you want (see below).

The Hyperlink object has two different methods that can be used to navigate to a URL. One is the native NavigateTo() method, and the other is a custom method called Follow(). The Follow() method cannot handle parameters. It simply navigates to a location specified through the object's properties (see below). The NavigateTo() method, on the other hand, can handle three parameters (*cTarget*, *cLocation* and *cFrame*). The meaning of those parameters is identical to the meaning of the properties of the same name (see below). If those parameters aren't passed, the method uses the property values instead.

Just like the regular Hyperlink base class, the Hyperlink object has GoBack() and GoForward() methods. Again, the Hyperlink object manages this behavior itself, rather than using the native Hyperlink behavior. In fact, the Hyperlink object makes these methods much more useful, because one can navigate multiple times in the same instance of the Web browser. This allows the user to build up a navigation history that can be used to go backward and forward. Using the regular Hyperlink base class, these methods don't make a lot of sense unless the object is used in an active document—there won't be a navigation history because a new browser instance is fired up on every navigation.

The Hyperlink object has several properties that allow you to influence how and where the object navigates, and it also has a property that tells the current location (*cLocationURL*). To initiate a simple navigation, set the *cTarget* property and fire the Follow() method like so:

```
oHyperlink = NewObject("_hyperlinkbase","_hyperlink.vcx")
oHyperlink.cTarget = "Http://www.eps-software.com"
oHyperlink.Follow()
```

You can also set the *cLocation* property to navigate within a certain URL. A typical example would be a "frequently asked questions" document where you want to navigate to one of the questions rather than to the top of the document. Finally, you can also specify a target frame if you already navigated to a frame-based document. Obviously, this can only work if an existing browser instance is used for navigation. By default, the Hyperlink object tries to find and use such a browser instance. However, you can also specify that you want to open a new window for navigation by setting the *lNewWindow* property to .T.

Once the navigation is complete, the URL of the current document is stored in the *cLocationURL* property.

As mentioned above, the Hyperlink object doesn't always use the default navigation behavior of the Hyperlink base class, but it uses Internet Explorer as a COM server instead (if

Internet Explorer is the default Web browser). The standard COM server class is "InternetExplorer.Application". This is specified in the *cIEClass* property. You could use this property to specify a different Web browser class. This might be important if you wanted to use a specific version of Internet Explorer. If the hyperlink object isn't able to instantiate a valid reference of the Internet Explorer COM server, it tries to do a simple shell-execute on the specified target location. This is done using the Shell Execute foundation class. As always, you can specify a different class to be used for shell-executes. You can specify a custom class through the *cShellExecuteClass* and *cShellExecuteClassLibrary* properties. More information about the Shell Execute foundation class can be found later in this chapter.

### Hyperlink Button

| Class | _hyperlinkcommandbutton |
|---|---|
| Base class | CommandButton |
| Class library | _hyperlink.vcx |
| Parent class | _commandbutton |
| Sample | ...\Samples\Vfp98\Solution\Ffc\hyperlnk.scx |
| Dependencies | _base.vcx |

The Hyperlink button is a command button that navigates to a certain URL when clicked. The button adds a bit of Internet look and feel to regular Visual FoxPro forms by using an underlined font and a special color for visited links.

The button has a *cTarget* property. Use this property to specify the URL to which you want the user to navigate. This is all you have to do to use the Hyperlink button; however, it has more functionality. You can specify (using the *cLocation* property) a certain bookmark if you want to jump to a specific location within a document. Normally the class looks for a running instance of the Web browser of your choice before it opens a new instance. If you want to open a new instance in any case, you can set the *lNewWindow* property to .T. If you want to use a specific frame of a loaded document in an existing browser instance, you can use the *cFrame* property to do so.

When the user clicks the Hyperlink button, the button remembers that the specified URL has already been visited (*lVisited* = .T.). The caption of the button is then also displayed in a different color. You can specify this color using the *nVisitedForeColor* property. This property is a numeric RGB value. You can either specify this value directly, or you can use the RGB() method to set the property.

You can even use the Hyperlink Button object to navigate within the URL history using the GoBack() and GoForward() methods. This is especially useful in scenarios where several Hyperlink objects (such as hyperlink buttons, hyperlink images or hyperlink labels) share one behavioral Hyperlink object (the Hyperlink object foundation class). To understand this, you have to know that none of the Hyperlink interface classes have any navigational behavior, but they use the Hyperlink object (see above) instead. By default, all created Hyperlink objects try to share one behavioral Hyperlink object. If you want to use a private Hyperlink object, you can specify this through the *lFormSynch* property (set it to .F. to create a private Hyperlink object). The Hyperlink button uses the Hyperlink object described above to navigate to the desired location. You can specify a different Hyperlink object by setting the *cHyperlinkClass* and *cHyperlinkClassLibrary* properties.

### Hyperlink Image

| Class | _hyperlinkimage |
|---|---|
| Base class | Image |
| Class library | _hyperlink.vcx |
| Parent class | _image |
| Sample | ...\Samples\Vfp98\Solution\Ffc\hyperlnk.scx |
| Dependencies | _base.vcx |

The Hyperlink Image class is similar to the Hyperlink button. The main difference is that the class is an image rather than a command button. Images don't have forecolors. For this reason, the Hyperlink Image class doesn't allow you to set a special forecolor for visited links. See above (Hyperlink Button) for more information.

### Hyperlink Label

| Class | _hyperlinklabel |
|---|---|
| Base class | Label |
| Class library | _hyperlink.vcx |
| Parent class | _label |
| Sample | ...\Samples\Vfp98\Solution\Ffc\hyperlnk.scx |
| Dependencies | _base.vcx |

The Hyperlink Label is essentially similar to the Hyperlink Button. As the name suggests, the base class of this class is a label rather than a command button. The Hyperlink Label class transfers Internet look and feel to Visual FoxPro forms since there is virtually no visual difference for the user. **Figure 25** shows how the hyperlink label can be used in Visual FoxPro forms. See above (Hyperlink Button) for more information.

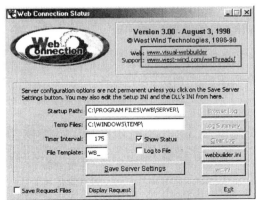

**Figure 25**. *Two hyperlink labels used in a regular Visual FoxPro form.*

## SCX->HTML

| Class | _scx2html |
|---|---|
| Base class | Custom |
| Class library | _internet.vcx |
| Parent class | _custom |
| Sample | None |
| Dependencies | _base.vcx |

The SCX->HTML foundation class is yet another wrapper for Genhtml.prg, just like the DBF->HTML and the FRX->HTML foundation classes. The only difference is the source, which now is a Visual FoxPro form (SCX) that is converted to HTML format. However, it seems that at this point the possibilities are very limited. I haven't found many forms that have converted to HTML format in an acceptable manner.

See above (DBF->HTML) for more details.

## URL Combo

| Class | _urlcombobox |
|---|---|
| Base class | Combobox |
| Class library | _internet.vcx |
| Parent class | _combobox |
| Sample | ...\Samples\Vfp98\Solution\Ffc\hyperlnk.scx |
| Dependencies | _base.vcx, _hyperlink.vcx |

The URL Combo foundation class comes in handy when you want to allow the user to navigate to a certain URL by specifying the address manually. The combobox remembers previously accessed URLs and displays them in a drop-down list. Internally, those items are stored in a DBF called Urlhstry.dbf. (You can specify a different table using the *cURLHistoryTable* property). If you don't want to keep a history, you can set the *lURLHistory* property to .F.

The URL Combo class is easy to use. You just drop it on a form, drop a button (or another control) right next to it, and call the Navigate() method of the combobox (without any parameters) in the button's Click() event. The combobox then navigates to the URL specified by the user.

To navigate, the combobox uses the Hyperlink object (see above). The Hyperlink object class is specified in the *cHyperlinkClass* and *cHyperlinkClassLibrary* properties. You can use these properties to specify your own hyperlink class if you want.

The URL Combo is essentially the same kind of object as the Address combobox of Internet Explorer. However, Internet Explorer's combobox has a nice feature that the URL Combo lacks. It automatically completes the URL as you type when it remembers one. The letters that are filled in automatically are selected immediately, so the user can continue to type if the filled-in URL is not the desired one. Luckily, it is not hard to create the same kind of behavior in a subclass of the URL Combo. You only have to add some code to the InteractiveChange() event. Here it is:

```
DoDefault()
LOCAL lnLength, lnCounter, lcValue
lcValue = Lower(Alltrim(THIS.Text))
lnLength = Len(lcValue)
FOR lnCounter = 1 TO THIS.ListCount
   IF Lower(THIS.List(lnCounter)) = lcValue
      THIS.DisplayValue = THIS.List(lnCounter)
      THIS.SelStart = lnLength
      THIS.SelLength = Len(THIS.List(lnCounter))-lnLength
      EXIT
   ENDIF
ENDFOR
```

The code actually is rather trivial. When the user changes the value of the combobox, this code iterates through the items and compares them to the current value. If they are identical (up to the length of the new value), the item is used as the current item and the inserted text is automatically selected. If the user continues to type, the selection is automatically replaced by the new characters (which is Windows-standard behavior) and the whole process starts over.

### URL Open Dialog Box

| Class | _openaddressdialog |
|---|---|
| Base class | Form |
| Class library | _internet.vcx |
| Parent class | _dialog |
| Sample | ...\Samples\Vfp98\Solution\Ffc\hyperlnk.scx |
| Dependencies | _base.vcx, _dialogs.vcx, dialogs.h, _hyperlink.vcx |

The URL Open Dialog Box is a nice interface class that allows the user to open a Web address (see **Figure 26**). It is basically the same dialog that Internet Explorer provides when the user selects the File/Open menu item. The dialog basically uses a URL Combo to allow navigation, and it also has a Browse button that brings up a regular GetFile() dialog.

*Figure 26. The URL Open Dialog Box.*

Using the class is simple—just instantiate it and make it visible. The class has only three properties you can set. One of them is *cTarget*, which stores the URL to which the user tries to navigate. Knowing this might be essential if you want to subclass this dialog. The property *lShellExecute* specifies whether the dialog should actually initialize navigation. Setting this property to .F. is useful if you want to navigate yourself. I do this frequently when I use the

Web browser ActiveX control inside Visual FoxPro. In this case I don't want this dialog to open another instance of Internet Explorer, but I still like to use the dialog.

Finally, the *cFileExt* property allows you to specify the file types that the GetFile() dialog should display. You can specify multiple values separated by a semicolon (;).

The class also can handle two parameters, which can be used to decorate the *lShellExecute* and the *cFileExt* properties. The first parameter can be used to specify that the class should not execute the navigation. In this case you are supposed to pass a .T., which sets the *lShellExecute* property to .F. This confuses me every time, but it is logical if you consider that Visual FoxPro uses .F. as a default for parameters that haven't been passed. The second parameter is directly assigned to the *cFileExt* property.

### Web Browser Control

| Class | _webbrowser4 |
| --- | --- |
| Base class | OLEControl |
| Class library | *webview.vcx (.\Gallery\_webview.vcx)* |
| Parent class | OLEControl |
| Sample | ...\Samples\Vfp98\Solution\Ffc\webvwr.scx |
| Dependencies | Microsoft Web Browser ActiveX Control |

The Web Browser Control Foundation Class is a wrapper for the Microsoft Web Browser Control (Internet Explorer control). You can use it to build your own Web browsers and to incorporate HTML functionality into your Windows applications (see **Figure 27**).

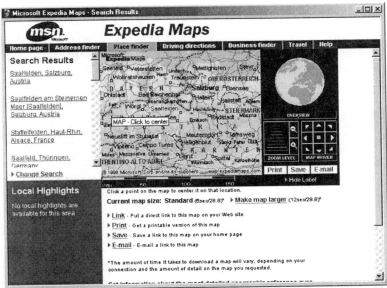

*Figure 27. Microsoft Expedia Maps incorporated into a regular Windows application using the Web Browser control.*

This class has a number of properties and methods, most of which are intuitive and self-explanatory. A great number of methods have been created to handle older versions of this control, such as Internet Explorer 3.0. At this point, this class can handle Internet Explorer versions 3.0 to 5.0.

## Menus

People expected menus to be objectified in the last couple of versions of Visual FoxPro. However, it hasn't happened yet, and even the foundation classes don't offer real object menus—but they're close.

### Navigation Shortcut Menu

| Class | _navmenu |
|---|---|
| **Base class** | Container |
| **Class library** | _table2.vcx |
| **Parent class** | _container |
| **Sample** | ...\Samples\Vfp98\Solution\Ffc\datasort.scx |
| **Dependencies** | _base.vcx, _table2.h |

The Navigation shortcut menu provides data navigation, manipulation, sorting and filtering functionality through a right-click. **Figure 28** shows an example.

*Figure 28. The Navigation shortcut menu.*

To use this shortcut menu in your own forms, simply drop the object on the form and invoke it from the RightClick() event like so (substitute your menu object name for "oNavMenu"):

```
THISFORM.oNavMenu.DoMenu()
```

The Menu object checks to see whether a valid alias is selected. This is the only precondition that must be fulfilled. If no table is selected, the menu is not displayed.

You can easily add your own menu items by overwriting the SetMenu() method like so:

```
DoDefault()
THIS.oMenu.AddMenuSeparator
THIS.oMenu.AddMenuBar("My menu bar","oTHIS.MyMethod")
```

The Navigation shortcut menu uses a regular Shortcut Menu object. The object reference to this object is called "oMenu". You can simply call the AddMenuBar() method to add a new menu item (see below). The first parameter is the caption of the new item, while the second one is a valid Visual FoxPro expression that can be evaluated and executed.

### Shortcut Menu Class

| Class | _shortcutmenu |
|---|---|
| Base class | Custom |
| Class library | _menu.vcx |
| Parent class | _custom |
| Sample | ...\Samples\Vfp98\Solution\Ffc\newmenu.scx |
| Dependencies | _base.vcx |

The Shortcut Menu foundation class makes it easy to create and manage right-click menus. The object provides a number of methods you can use to add menu items and submenus to your right-click menu. You can simply drop the shortcut menu object on your form and invoke it from the form's RightClick() event like so:

```
THISFORM.oMenu.ShowMenu()
```

In this example, we activate a menu object called "oMenu". You can activate a menu from wherever you want.

Before you can actually use your menu, you have to define all the menu items and submenus. The following example shows how to add a couple of regular menu items as well as an entire submenu to your right-click menu. The following code is located in the SetMenu() method of the Shortcut Menu object:

```
LPARAMETERS loObject
DoDefault(loObject)

LOCAL loMenu2
loMenu2= THIS.NewMenu()
loMenu2.AddMenuBar("First Record","oTHISFORM.GoTop")
loMenu2.AddMenuBar("Previous Record","oTHISFORM.GoPrevious")
loMenu2.AddMenuBar("Next Record","oTHISFORM.GoNext")
loMenu2.AddMenuBar("Last Record","oTHISFORM.GoBottom")

THIS.AddMenuBar("Navigate",loMenu2)
THIS.AddMenuSeparator()
THIS.AddMenuBar("Save","oTHISFORM.Save")
THIS.AddMenuBar("Save & New","oTHISFORM.SaveNew")
THIS.AddMenuBar("Cancel","oTHISFORM.Cancel")
THIS.AddMenuSeparator()
THIS.AddMenuBar("Refresh","oTHISFORM.Refresh")
THIS.AddMenuBar("Auto Refresh","oTHISFORM.ToggleAutoRefresh";
    ,,, THISFORM.lAutoRefresh)
```

**Figure 29** shows the resulting right-click menu. As you can see, the menu has a submenu that allows navigation. In the code above, we first create this menu by calling the NewMenu() method. This method returns an object reference to the new menu, which is basically another instance of the Shortcut Menu object. We then use the AddMenuBar() method to add new menu items. In the example above we pass two parameters. The first is the caption for the new menu item, and the second is a string that can be evaluated or executed by Visual FoxPro. So there has to be an object reference called "oTHISFORM". This object must have all methods we reference, such as GoTop(). The AddMenuBar() method can handle a number of parameters. See below for a more complete description of those parameters.

Once we've decorated the submenu with four menu items, we continue to create the regular menu by adding its first menu item, which links to the submenu we created previously. Again, we use the AddMenuBar() method to add this item, but this time the second parameter is an object reference to the submenu we created previously. Now you also know the reason why we created the submenu before we created the actual menu. Obviously we need an object reference to a valid submenu whenever we add the menu item that opens the submenu.

After creating the Navigate menu, we add a separator to add some organization to our menu. This can be done easily using the AddMenuSeparator() method. The next couple of items are added in the same manner as the ones before. Only the last one is special because it has a checkmark next to it. We added this checkmark by passing parameter 5 to the AddMenuBar() method. This parameter must be of type *logical*, and it determines whether the checkmark must be set or not. In my example, I use a property of the current form to decide whether or not I want the checkmark.

As you might have noticed (and as I have mentioned), the above example requires an object reference called "oTHISFORM". This is a reference we have to provide ourselves. A good place to do this is in the RightClick() event we already use to activate the menu. Here's the new code for this event:

```
PRIVATE oTHISFORM
oTHISFORM = THISFORM
THISFORM.oMenu.ShowMenu()
```

Note that I create the object reference as a private variable. This means that the reference is visible from now until the menu is deactivated.

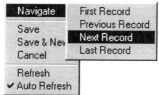

***Figure 29****. A sample right-click menu.*

Let's have a closer look at the methods of the Shortcut Menu object. You've already learned how to add menu items and separators as well as entire submenus. You've also seen how to activate the menu using the ShowMenu() method. Alternatively, we could use the

ActivateMenu() method. In fact, ShowMenu() just calls ActivateMenu() without taking any further action. Once a menu is activated, it typically gets deactivated when the user picks one of the menu items or when he clicks outside the menu boundaries. However, you can also deactivate a menu programmatically by calling the DeactivateMenu() method.

Once you've specified items for a menu, you can activate and deactivate the menu as often as you want. The same items will remain in the menu. If you want to start over, you have to clear the menu items first, by calling the ClearMenu() method.

Let's have a closer look at the methods we've already used to add items to a menu. The simpler one was AddMenuSeparator(). So far, we've called it without parameters, but you can pass a single numeric parameter that specifies the position of the separator. So if you want to add a separator between items 2 and 3 of an existing menu, you can do it like so:

```
oMenu.AddMenuSeparator(3)
```

The AddMenuBar() method, on the other hand, is a little more complex and powerful. As you've seen, menu items can be links to submenus, they can be disabled, they can have bold fonts (which typically highlight a default option) or they can have checkmarks. Let's go through the parameters one by one.

The first parameter specifies the item caption. This is a simple string. Parameter 2 defines the action to be taken when the user selects the item. This can either be a string that is a valid FoxPro expression or an object reference to a submenu (see above). Parameter 3 is a little confusing at first. It specifies additional clauses for the menu item. This is a lot easier to understand than it first sounds. Keep in mind that the Shortcut Menu object internally has to use regular DEFINE BAR commands to build the menu. The *clause* parameter allows you to add whatever you want at the end of this command. This allows you to use all the features the DEFINE BAR command supports, and that cannot be accessed through the Shortcut Menu object interface. A good example would be font settings for menu items.

Parameter 4 represents the element number. This allows you to insert menu items at a certain position. It's basically the same as the first parameter of the AddMenuSeparator() method (see above).

We've already used parameter 5. It is a logical parameter that specifies whether the item should have a checkmark (.T.) or not (.F.). You can pass a straight .T. or .F., or you can pass a variable or a property to dynamically set this property. Note that those variables are evaluated only on instantiation, so if that variable or property changes its value later on, it will not be reevaluated. If you want to have a dynamic setting, you should specify this through parameter 3 (clause).

Parameters 6 and 7 are similar—they're both logical. Parameter 6 specifies whether the item should be disabled, and parameter 7 specifies whether the parameter should use bold font. These two parameters follow the same rules as parameter 5 as far as dynamic settings go.

## Miscellaneous buttons
I can't count the number of times I've created OK and Cancel buttons among other standard buttons. In this foundation class category, you'll find a number of buttons, some performing standard tasks, others invoking foundation classes described in other sections.

### Cancel Button

| Class | _cmdCancel |
| --- | --- |
| Base class | CommandButton |
| Class library | _miscbtns.vcx |
| Parent class | _cmdOK |
| Sample | ...\Samples\Vfp98\Solution\Ffc\buttons.scx |
| Dependencies | _base.vcx |

The Cancel Button is a subclass of the OK Button (see below). There is nothing special about this button. The only difference between it and the OK Button is its caption.

### Help Button

| Class | _cmdHelp |
| --- | --- |
| Base class | CommandButton |
| Class library | _miscbtns.vcx |
| Parent class | _commandbutton |
| Sample | ...\Samples\Vfp98\Solution\Ffc\buttons.scx |
| Dependencies | _base.vcx |

This button, when clicked, displays the online help. It automatically shows the help topic that is referenced by ID in the *HelpContextID* property of this class. It works with old-fashioned help files as well as HTML Help.

### Launch Button

| Class | _cmdLaunch |
| --- | --- |
| Base class | CommandButton |
| Class library | _miscbtns.vcx |
| Parent class | _commandbutton |
| Sample | ...\Samples\Vfp98\Solution\Ffc\buttons.scx |
| Dependencies | _base.vcx |

The Launch Button executes a Visual FoxPro application (APP) or any other Windows executable (EXE) specified in the *cFileName* property. FoxPro applications are executed directly using macro evaluation, while Windows EXEs are fired up using the RUN command.

### OK Button

| Class | _cmdOK |
| --- | --- |
| Base class | CommandButton |
| Class library | _miscbtns.vcx |
| Parent class | _commandbutton |
| Sample | ...\Samples\Vfp98\Solution\Ffc\buttons.scx |
| Dependencies | _base.vcx |

The OK button is rather simple. It simply releases the current form or formset. If you want your OK button to do something special before the form is released, you have to add some code to the *Click()* event of the OK button. Here's an example:

```
THISFORM.Save()
DoDefault()
```

Note that the DoDefault() is called at the end. This makes sure that nothing is released before the custom action takes place.

### Run Form Button

| Class | _cmdRunForm |
|---|---|
| Base class | CommandButton |
| Class library | _miscbtns.vcx |
| Parent class | _commandbutton |
| Sample | ...\Samples\Vfp98\Solution\Ffc\buttons.scx |
| Dependencies | _base.vcx |

The Run Form button executes the Visual FoxPro form specified in the *cFileName* property. By default, the button's caption is set to the specified file name. The width of the button is automatically adjusted according to the length of the file name. This often ends up looking awkward. For this reason I recommend turning off this behavior by setting the *lSetCaption* property to .F.

### Run Report Button (Preview Report)

| Class | _cmdRunReport |
|---|---|
| Base class | CommandButton |
| Class library | _miscbtns.vcx |
| Parent class | _commandbutton |
| Sample | ...\Samples\Vfp98\Solution\Ffc\buttons.scx |
| Dependencies | _base.vcx, _reports.vcx, _reports.h |

The Run Report Button foundation class executes the report specified in the *cFileName* property. Similar to the Run Form Button class, this button adjusts its size and caption according to the specified file name unless you set the *lSetCaption* property to .F.

Printing a report is not as trivial as running a form or an application. For this reason, this class is slightly more complex than the two classes introduced above. The main difference is that printing a report might require an Output dialog that specifies the output media and the output format (see **Figure 30**). Many of the button's properties are used to configure this dialog.

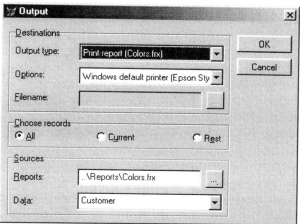

***Figure 30.*** *The Output dialog used by the Run Report button. Some of the displayed groups are optional and can be turned off.*

The *lUseOutputDialog* property specifies whether you want to display a dialog before printing. The dialog class can be specified through the *cDialogClass* and *cDialogClassLib* properties. By default, the Report Output object is used as the Print dialog (see below). Many of this object's properties are specific to this Output dialog, such as *lOutputDialogPreventScope*, *lOutputDialogPreventSource* and *lPromptForReport*. Those properties specify whether the user can change the report scope, source and layout file.

### Send Mail Buttons

| Class | _mailbtn |
|---|---|
| **Base class** | Container |
| **Class library** | _miscbtns.vcx |
| **Parent class** | _container |
| **Sample** | ...\Samples\Vfp98\Solution\Ffc\buttons.scx |
| **Dependencies** | _base.vcx, MS MAPI Session ActiveX Control, MS MAPI Message ActiveX Control |

The Send Mail Button creates a new e-mail message based on the current record and sends it using Mail Application Interface (MAPI) services. Typically, this means that Microsoft Outlook or Outlook Express is used to send the mail. The Send Mail button does not allow you to specify a receiver address or anything similar. It brings up the default mail client and requires the user to specify this information (see **Figure 31**).

The button will display an error message if there was no valid data source, or if the record pointer is at the end of the file.

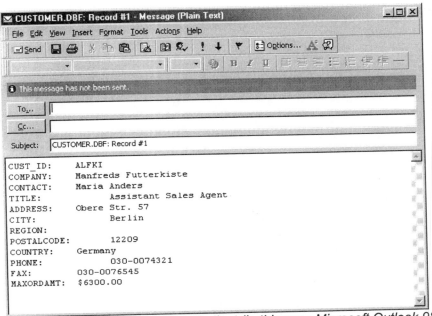

*Figure 31. The default MAPI mail client (in this case Microsoft Outlook 98) is used to send e-mail.*

Unfortunately, it is hard to use the Send Mail button for anything but sending the actual record, because the entire message is created and sent in the Click() event of the button. To change the created message, you'd have to overwrite the entire method, which means that you have to create the entire behavior yourself. You might as well create your own class.

## Miscellaneous forms

You'll find a number of forms in almost any application, such as login dialogs, message boxes, about dialogs, and so forth. If you are tired of designing those forms yourself, check out this foundation class category. You might find just what you are looking for.

### About Dialog Box

| Class | _aboutbox |
|---|---|
| Base class | Form |
| Class library | _dialogs.vcx |
| Parent class | _form |
| Sample | ...\Samples\Vfp98\Solution\Ffc\dialogs.scx |
| Dependencies | _base.vcx, registry.vcx, dialogs.h |

This class is a simple but very useful About dialog. It displays the application name as well copyright and trademark information and the name of the application's licensed user. **Figure 32** shows a slightly modified version of the About dialog box.

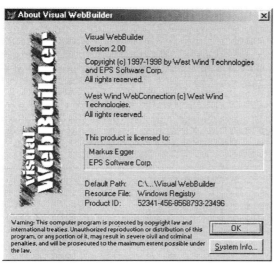

*Figure 32. A subclassed version of the About dialog box.*

One of the interesting aspects of this class is the System Info button. It uses the Registry object to display essential information about the user's system (see **Figure 33**).

You can pass a number of parameters to this class when instantiating it to set the most important display options. Here they are in sequential order: Application name, version (character), copyright, trademark and the name of the bitmap for the logo. The user information is retrieved by two methods—GetRegisteredCompany() and GetRegisteredOwner(). Overwrite these methods to provide your own user information. Simply return the information from these methods. The class will automatically use these methods to retrieve the name. Note that you are not supposed to execute the default behavior of these methods.

### Item Locator

| Class | _locateitem |
|---|---|
| Base class | Form |
| Class library | _dialogs.vcx |
| Parent class | _dialog |
| Sample | ...\Samples\Vfp98\Solution\Ffc\dialogs.scx |
| Dependencies | _base.vcx, dialogs.h |

Most business applications deal with files, but sometimes files can't be found when they are needed. In this case, we have to ask the user for his assistance to locate the file. The Locate Item dialog shown in **Figure 34** provides a nice interface to do this quickly and easily.

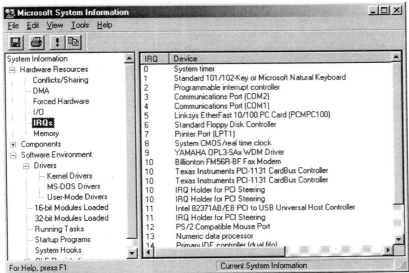

*Figure 33. The Microsoft System Information application.*

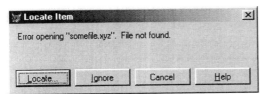

*Figure 34. The Locate Item dialog in action.*

When the user clicks the Locate button, a standard GetFile() dialog is displayed. The selected file is returned (see below). If the user clicks Ignore, the specified file name is returned. The Cancel button behaves quite differently—it returns a NULL value. In order to make the Help button work, you have to set the *HelpContextID* property of the form.

The way you have to use this class might seem a little strange at first sight, but it demonstrates a great way to resolve the old problem of returning values from a class. You first have to create a dummy object, which will be used to store the return value. Next, you create the dialog and pass the dummy object as well as the file name you are looking for to the new object. Optionally, you can pass a third parameter—a logical parameter that indicates whether a GetFile() dialog (.F.) or a GetPict() dialog (.T.) should be used. The latter allows the user to preview the image he selects.

Here's an example:

```
LOCAL loForm, loDummy
loDummy = Create("line")
loForm = NewObject("_locateitem","_dialogs","",loDummy,"somefile.xyz")

IF VarType(loForm) = "O"
  loForm.Show()
  ? loDummy.cFileName
ELSE
   RETURN
ENDIF
```

I use a line object as the dummy object because this is a lightweight class. I hate to waste resources! The last line checks for a property called *cFileName,* which has been automatically added to the dummy object. This property is used to return the selected file name. I now have to check whether the file really exists (the user could have fooled me!). If everything is fine, the application can go on with its own business.

### Keywords Dialog Box

| Class | _keywords |
|---|---|
| **Base class** | Form |
| **Class library** | _dialogs.vcx |
| **Parent class** | _dialog |
| **Sample** | ...\Samples\Vfp98\Solution\Ffc\dialogs.scx |
| **Dependencies** | _base.vcx, dialogs.h, _movers.vcx |

If you allow the user to query data by keywords, you might be interested in this dialog (see **Figure 35**). It uses a Mover object (see below) to display and select a list of keywords that are defined in a table.

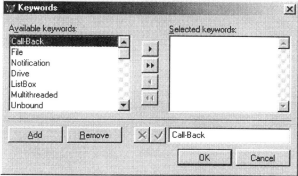

*Figure 35. The Keywords dialog using the standard Keywords table.*

By default, all keywords in the Keywords dialog box come from a default Keywords table called Keywords.dbf, which is located in the Visual FoxPro Component Gallery directory. You can specify a different table by setting the *cDBFName* property. The table structure is simple. There is only one character field called "keyword". It has a length of 30 characters, but you can make it longer if you want. As you can see in Figure 35, the user can add keywords on the fly. If you use a keywords table, the new items are automatically added and conserved for future use.

The use of the Keywords dialog box class is somewhat similar to the Item Locator class. It, too, needs a dummy object to receive the selected items. However, the implementation differs. Instead of passing the dummy object as a parameter, it must be assigned to a property once the dialog is created:

```
LOCAL loForm, loDummy
loForm = NewObject("_keywords","_dialogs")
IF VARTYPE(loForm) # "O"
  RETURN
ENDIF
loDummy = CreateObject("line")
loForm.oKeywords = loDummy
loForm.Show()
? loDummy.cKeywords
```

As you can see, the dummy object is assigned after the dialog object is created but before it is displayed. The next steps are similar to the ones taken by the Item Locator class. A new property is added to the dummy object (in this case *cKeywords*) and the selected keywords are stored to this property. Multiple values are space-delimited. This also means that keywords can't have spaces.

### Messagebox Handler

| Class | _msgbox |
|---|---|
| Base class | Custom |
| Class library | _dialogs.vcx |
| Parent class | _custom |
| Sample | None |
| Dependencies | _base.vcx |

The Messagebox Handler class is a simple wrapper for the cumbersome Visual FoxPro MessageBox() function. It allows setting properties such as *cMessage* and *cTitle* to specify the displayed text. You can also specify the messagebox type through the numeric *nType* property. The numeric value is identical to the second parameter of the MessageBox() function. Furthermore, you can specify whether a beep should sound every time a messagebox is displayed, by setting the *lBeep* property.

Once all these properties are set, you can display the messagebox using the object's Show() method. The return value of this method indicates the user's choice. It is identical to the return value of the MessageBox() function. You can also pass all the properties I listed above as parameters to the Show() method. I hardly ever pass any parameters other than the caption (parameter 1), because I think it defeats the purpose of this class.

The main advantage arises from the fact that you can redisplay a messagebox as often as you want. You can even change single parameters such as the title before you redisplay the messagebox. I usually end up instantiating the Messagebox Handler object once. The only property I usually have to change is the message. I created a subclass of the Messagebox Handler that has a couple of custom methods such as YesNo(), OK() and YesNoIgnore(). Their purpose is simple—they temporarily set the *nType* property to display the proper dialog type. This helps tremendously because I can never remember the proper type values. Here's the YesNo() method's code.

```
LPARAMETERS lcCaption
LOCAL lnOldType, llRetVal
lnOldType = THIS.nType
THIS.nType = 36     && Yes/No buttons, question mark icon
llRetVal = IIF(THIS.Show(lcCaption)=6,.T.,.F.)
THIS.nType = lnOldType
RETURN llRetVal
```

As you can see, this method not only uses a default item type, but it also returns a simple .T. or .F. instead of a numeric code, because this is yet another code I can never remember.
The other methods are essentially similar.

### *Password Dialog Box*

| Class | _login |
|---|---|
| Base class | Form |
| Class library | _dialogs.vcx |
| Parent class | _form |
| Sample | ...\Samples\Vfp98\Solution\Ffc\dialogs.scx |
| Dependencies | _base.vcx, dialogs.h |

The Password dialog box provides a simple login screen (see **Figure 36**). To use it, you must have a table with user names and passwords. The dialog will then tell you whether the user specified a name and a matching password. Obviously, you have to tell the dialog what table and what fields to use. You can do this by setting a couple of properties:

```
LOCAL loForm, loDummy
loForm = NewObject("_login","_dialogs")
IF VARTYPE(loForm) # "O"
  RETURN
ENDIF
loDummy = CreateObject("line")
loForm.oPassword = loDummy
loForm.cDBFName = "..\..\data\employee.dbf"
loForm.cTable = "employee"
loForm.cFieldName = "last_name"
loForm.cPassword = "first_name"
loForm.Setup()
loForm.Show(1)
? loDummy.lValidPassword
```

In this example, I first create the Password Dialog object. I then create a dummy object that will be used to store the return value. This dummy object must be assigned to the *oPassword* property of the Dialog object. Next I specify the table name and its alias. This is done through the *cDBFName* and *cTable* properties (the documentation has these wrong!). I also specify the user name field (*cFieldName*) and the password field (*cPassword*). Finally, I have to call the Setup() method to decorate the object before I display it.

***Figure 36***. *A simple login screen.*

Once the dialog is closed, the dummy object has a new property that has been added on the fly. The property is called *lValidPassword*, and it's a logical property that indicates whether the user knew the matching password. It's up to the programmer to take appropriate action at this point.

### Splash Screen

| Class | _splash |
|---|---|
| **Base class** | Form |
| **Class library** | _dialogs.vcx |
| **Parent class** | _form |
| **Sample** | ...\Samples\Vfp98\Solution\Ffc\dialogs.scx |
| **Dependencies** | _base.vcx |

The Splash Screen foundation class provides a form that can be displayed for a certain time when the application starts up. This form typically displays an image and the application name (see **Figure 37**). The duration the form is displayed can be specified through the *nDuration* property (in seconds). By default, the splash screen is displayed for three seconds. That's a good setting for most applications. It gives the user enough time to read everything but it doesn't bother him later on when he's already seen it. I recommend using this default setting.

You can set the background image and the application title in a subclass, or simply before the screen is set visible, like so:

```
LOCAL loForm
loForm = NewObject("_splash","_dialogs")
loForm.Picture = "myapp.bmp"
loForm.label1.Caption = "My Great Application 1.0"
loForm.nDuration = 5
loForm.Show()
```

*Figure 37*. *A sample splash screen.*

As you can see, this class is relatively simple. Unfortunately, it has a weakness: The delay from clicking an application icon until the splash screen comes up (if you display it right away) is relatively long, because it takes a while to instantiate Visual FoxPro (even in the runtime version). Fortunately, there is another way to display a simple splash screen. Visual FoxPro 6.0 allows you to specify a splash screen image as a startup parameter. This native Visual FoxPro 6.0 feature has nothing to do with the Fox Foundation Classes. However, I thought it was worth mentioning anyway. The startup parameter must be specified like so:

```
"C:\Program Files\My Application\MyAppp.exe" -bMyApp.bmp
```

This parameter would be specified in Start menu shortcuts. Typically, the Visual FoxPro Setup Wizard would create it. The special part is the "-b" parameter, followed by the name of the bitmap file name (no space between the "-b" parameter and the file name!).

## Movers
Mover dialogs are used to select a number of items from a list of available items. This sounds like a common thing to you? Well, it is. I couldn't think of any business application I've worked on that didn't have a kind of Mover dialog. Surprisingly, the quality of these dialogs is often poor, but the classes you find in this category should put an end to this misery.

### Field Mover

| Class | _fieldmover |
|---|---|
| Base class | Container |
| Class library | _movers.vcx |
| Parent class | _supermover |
| Sample | ...\Samples\Vfp98\Solution\Ffc\movers.scx |
| Dependencies | _base.vcx, _movers.h |

The Field Mover class is a Super Mover class (see below) that's automatically populated with the field names of the current data source (see **Figure 38**). Using this Mover object is simple. You drop it on a form that has some kind of data source, which will be used to automatically populate the listboxes. The user then selects the fields he wants. Once he's done, you can use the GetSelections() method to query the selected fields and do what you want with them.

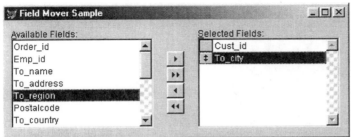

*Figure 38. A Field Mover sample that's automatically populated with the fields of the Orders table.*

The Field Mover class has a greater number of newly defined properties and methods. However, this doesn't mean that it's harder to use. Quite the opposite is true. The *AutoInit* property specifies whether the class should be automatically populated on instantiation (default is .T.). You might not want this if you load your data later on. In this case, you'd have to call the InitData() method to initialize the mover. Alternatively, you can also use the GetTableData() method to initialize the Mover object. Normally, the current data source is used to populate the mover. However, you can also specify a certain data source using the *CurrentAlias* property.

By default, all fields are displayed in the left-hand listbox, but you can also specify to skip memo fields (*SkipMemo* = .T.) and to skip the general fields (*SkipGeneral* = .T.).

The *MultiTable* property is rather confusing at first. It allows specifying whether selections can come from multiple tables. At first I was under the impression that this would allow displaying fields from multiple tables in the right-hand listbox. However, this is not the case. The *MultiTable* property simply specifies whether the selected items listbox (the right-hand listbox) should be cleared when the left-hand listbox is repopulated. Setting this property to .T. keeps the selected items, even when the left-hand listbox is repopulated.

See below (Super Mover) for more information about other features of this listbox.

## Mover

| Class | _mover |
|---|---|
| Base class | Container |
| Class library | _movers.vcx |
| Parent class | _container |
| Sample | None |
| Dependencies | _base.vcx, _movers.h |

The Mover foundation class is the base for all FFC mover classes. It provides a simple interface with two listboxes and two command buttons to add and remove items from the right-hand listbox (see **Figure 39**). The available items are displayed in the left-hand listbox.

When an item is added to the right-hand listbox, it is removed from the left-hand one so the user can't select items twice.

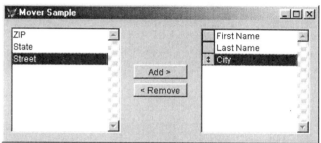

***Figure 39**. The most basic mover provided by the foundation classes.*

The class has special methods to populate the listboxes: InitChoices() for the left-hand listbox and InitSelections() for the right-hand one. Each of these methods expects a one-dimensional array of items passed by reference like so:

```
LOCAL laChoices(6,1)
laChoices(1,1) = "First Name"
laChoices(2,1) = "Last Name"
laChoices(3,1) = "Street"
laChoices(4,1) = "City"
laChoices(5,1) = "State"
laChoices(6,1) = "ZIP"
THIS.InitChoices(@laChoices)
```

The above code should be placed in the Init() event of the mover object. It populates the choices (left-hand) listbox. The same code would also work for the selections (right-hand) listbox. In this case, you would need to call the InitSelections() method instead. Normally, the arrays you used to populate the listboxes are copied to internal arrays that serve as the control source for each listbox. Those arrays are called *aChoices(1,1)* and *aSelections(1,1)*. You could modify and read these arrays later on. If you don't want to use these arrays, you can set the *UseArrays* property to .F., which means that the specified items are added using the listbox's AddItem() method.

Once the user has made his selection, you need a way to somehow query the selected fields. This is provided through the GetSelections() method. Again, this method expects an array passed by reference. This array is populated with all selected items. Here's an example:

```
LOCAL laItems(1), lnCounter
THIS.GetSelections(@laItems)
FOR lnCounter = 1 TO Alen(laItems,1)
   ? laItems(lnCounter)
ENDFOR
```

The Mover class is a container that has a couple of member objects. The class has all the knowledge to resize and reposition all member objects according to the size of the container.

However, there is no automatic mechanism that triggers this resizing algorithm. This is due to the fact that movers are typically used in dialogs that can't be resized. I recommend triggering the resizing algorithm in the Init() of the form like so:

```
THISFORM.oMover.SizeToContainer()
```

As you can see, the resizing method is called SizeToContainer(). You can also send the above message from the Resize() event of the Mover object, in case your dialog is resizable.

### Sort Mover

| Class | _sortmover |
|---|---|
| Base class | Container |
| Class library | _movers.vcx |
| Parent class | _mover |
| Sample | ...\Samples\Vfp98\Solution\Ffc\movers.scx |
| Dependencies | _base.vcx, _movers.h |

The Sort Mover is a special mover class that is automatically populated with field and tag names of a table or cursor (see **Figure 40**). It lets the user choose which fields to use for sorting, in what order, and whether the general sorting sequence should be ascending or descending.

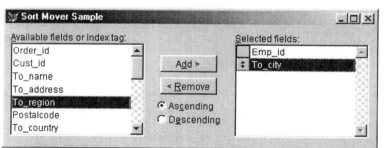

*Figure 40. The Sort Mover being used to re-sort the contents of the Tastrade orders table.*

This class does not provide the actual sorting logic. It merely provides a simple way to populate the Mover dialog with fields and tags from a certain data source. Populating the mover is simple. You set the data source in the *CurrentAlias* property and fire the UpdateMover() method like so:

```
THIS.CurrentAlias = "orders"
THIS.UpdateMover()
```

This will populate the left-hand listbox with all field names of the order table. Optionally, you can also display all the index tag names by setting the *ShowTags* property to .T. Index tags are displayed with a trailing asterisk (*). That's also how they appear in the selected-items array.

Like the Super Mover (see below), you can specify a maximum number of selected items in the *MaxFields* property. However, there is no property that allows setting the message that's displayed if the user selects more fields than allowed. You'd have to change this message through the _mover.h include file.

See above (Mover class) for general information about movers.

### Super Mover

| Class | _supermover |
|---|---|
| Base class | Container |
| Class library | _movers.vcx |
| Parent class | _mover |
| Sample | ...\Samples\Vfp98\Solution\Ffc\movers.scx |
| Dependencies | _base.vcx, _movers.h |

The Super Mover foundation class is a direct subclass of the Mover foundation class (see above). It has graphical add/remove buttons as well as "add all" and "remove all" buttons (see **Figure 41**).

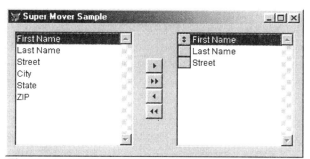

*Figure 41.* An advanced Super Mover dialog.

The Super Mover also allows you to specify a maximum number of items (*MaxItems* property) and a message (*MaxMessage* property) that's displayed when the user tries to select more items than you allow.

See above (Mover class) for more information.

### Table Mover

| Class | _tablemover |
|---|---|
| Base class | Container |
| Class library | _movers.vcx |
| Parent class | _fieldmover |
| Sample | ...\Samples\Vfp98\Solution\Ffc\movers.scx |
| Dependencies | _base.vcx, _movers.h |

The Table Mover is a special kind of field mover that provides an interface to select a data source (see **Figure 42**). Using this object is simple. The class is intelligent enough to analyze the current data environment.

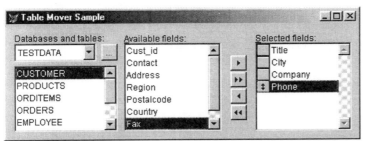

**Figure 42**. *A Table Mover object is complex and intelligent, yet easy to use.*

A couple of properties allow you to specify whether certain data source types should appear in the dialog. The *AllowQuery* property can be used to specify whether queries should be displayed. *AllowViews* does the same (you guessed it) for views. Another property can be used to influence the way views are treated: *ViewNoData*. If you set this property to .F., the class retrieves the view's data before it uses it. Typically you don't need to do that, so the default of this property is .T.

See above (Field Mover) for more information about this class.

## Multimedia

"Multimedia" is a buzzword that has an almost nostalgic flair by now. Nevertheless, it hasn't yet found its way to Visual FoxPro. One might argue that Visual FoxPro is used to create business applications and therefore, multimedia isn't really important. However, I don't agree. Sounds and videos are used all over the place. AVI files are used for all kinds of animations such as in the File Copy Progress dialog provided by Windows Explorer. I can think of a hundred places where I'd like to use such animations in my application.

The two classes I introduce in this category provide all the functionality you need to introduce the flair of multimedia to your applications.

### Sound Player

| Class | _soundplayer |
|---|---|
| Base class | Container |
| Class library | _multimedia.vcx |
| Parent class | _container |
| Sample | ...\Samples\Vfp98\Solution\Forms\mci_play.scx |
| Dependencies | _base.vcx |

The Sound Player foundation class can be used to play sound files such as AVI and MDI. The Sound Player class achieves this by making Windows API calls rather than using any ActiveX controls.

Playing sounds has been made easy with this class. All sound-playing features are accessible through a handful of properties and methods. To play a sound file, simply drop this class on a form (or any other kind of container) and set the *cFileName* property. When instantiated, the sound player object automatically plays the specified sound file until it is destroyed or until somebody triggers a PauseSound() or CloseSound() message. The sound file is automatically played, because the *lAutoOpen* and the *lAutoPlay* properties are set to .T. by default. The first property defines that the specified sound file is automatically opened on Init(). The second property makes sure the sound file is automatically played when loaded. If you set the *lAutoOpen* property to .F., you have to open the file manually using the OpenSound() method. If *lAutoPlay* is still set to .T., the sound will automatically be played after opening the file. If it is set to .F., you also have to trigger the playing manually by sending a PlaySound() method. Once a sound is played, it repeats endlessly, because this is the default setting specified in the *AutoRepeat* property. Again, you can set this property to .F. to play the sound only once. At any time while a sound is being played, you can pause it by sending a PausePlay() message. This can be useful when you want to change the actual play position. You can set the position using the SetPosition() method, which uses parameters of "Start", "End", or a position in milliseconds (still passed as a character string). You can resume playing at any time by issuing the PlaySound() message. Once you are done playing a sound, you can close the sound file using the CloseSound() method, or simply by destroying the Sound Player object.

The Sound Player even provides data binding. You can use the *ControlSource* property to specify a data source that holds the file name of the sound file. This file name is used internally, just like the *cFileName* property.

When an error occurs, the Sound Player class displays a message box with the exact error details. This message box is displayed in the ShowMCIError() method. You can overwrite this method to provide your own error handling or error-display algorithms. The properties *MCIError* and *MCIErrorString* provide information about the nature of the error.

### Video Player

| Class | _videoplayer |
|---|---|
| Base class | Container |
| Class library | _multimedia.vcx |
| Parent class | _container |
| Sample | ...\Samples\Vfp98\Solution\Forms\mci_play.scx |
| Dependencies | _base.vcx |

The Video Player works much like the Sound Player, with the exception that it plays videos rather than sounds. The Video Player object has almost the exact same set of methods and properties, but some of the names have been altered to say "Video" instead of "Sound."

Initially, I wondered how to define where the video should be displayed. After browsing the source code, I figured that the Video Player (which is a container class) is set invisible on startup. However, this container is still used to determine the size of the video. Now here is the weird part: The video is always displayed in the currently active window at the size of the Video Player container. When I was experimenting with this class, I used the command window a lot to trigger individual messages, with the result that the video was displayed inside the Visual FoxPro command window. Whether this is a bug or not, I don't know. You can use it to instantiate the Video Player once, but display the video in different windows. On the other hand, this might lead to rather weird bugs where videos show up in windows that don't have anything to do with the video. Unfortunately, it's beyond my knowledge whether this behavior will change in the future, since the Video Player class is almost undocumented.

## Reporting
Output is the most important part of a business application. People don't key in megabytes of data because it's so much fun to do. They spend all that time in order to get valuable output. The classes in this category should help you provide better output.

### Output Object

| Class | _output |
|---|---|
| Base class | Container |
| Class library | _reports.vcx |
| Parent class | _container |
| Sample | ...\Samples\Vfp98\Solution\Ffc\output.scx |
| Dependencies | _base.vcx, _reports.h |

The Output object is a wrapper for the Visual FoxPro REPORT FORM command and a couple of other output options. The basic idea is simple. You instantiate the Output object, specify the report you want to print in the *cReport* property, define the output destination (such as the screen or a printer) in the *cDestination* property, and additional options in the *cOptions* property. The report is printed when you send an Output() message to the Output object. The beauty of the Output object comes into play as soon as you have to print a report more than once with different settings, or when you try to print different reports with the same settings.

As mentioned above, the *cReport* property is used to specify the report file. The report file can either be an FRX report, or an LBX label. The *cDestination* property specifies where to print. The *aDestinations()* array lists all possible output destinations. The default destinations are listed in **Table 9**. Depending on the current destination, you can set output options (see **Table 10**) in the *cOption* property. Again, all possible options are listed in the *aOptions()* array. Once you've set these properties, you can print your report by calling the Output() method like so:

```
oReport = NewObject("_output","_reports.vcx")
oReport.cReport = "MyReport.frx"
oReport.cDestination = "SCREEN"
oReport.cOption = "GRAPHICAL"
oReport.Output()
```

In this example, we print a screen preview in graphical format. This is a more flexible version of the following line of code:

```
REPORT FORM MyReport.frx PREVIEW
```

When looking at this simple line of code, it might seem easier to do it the old, non-objectified way. However, you give up a whole lot of flexibility this way. Let me give you an example. Let's assume the oReport object from the example above is still in memory. We could now print this report in HTML format and display it in Internet Explorer like so:

```
oReport.cDestination = "HTMLFILE"
oReport.cOption = "WEBVIEW"
oReport.Output
```

Note that we didn't have to reset the report file. The object remembered this setting and allowed us to print the same report multiple times. In fact, we could create a subclass of the Output object, specify a certain report right in the class, and then set only the destination.

***Table 9***. *Possible output destinations.*

| Destination | Description |
|---|---|
| PRINTREPORT | Prints a report on paper. |
| PRINTLIST | Prints a text preview as shown in **Figure 43**. |
| SCREEN | Prints a screen preview of the report. |
| TEXTFILE | Creates an output text file in regular ASCII format. |
| PRINTFILE | Creates an output image representing the data sent to the printer in printer-specific format. The file could be copied to the printer later on. |
| EXPORT | Exports a table. |
| HTMLFILE | Creates an output file in HTML format. |

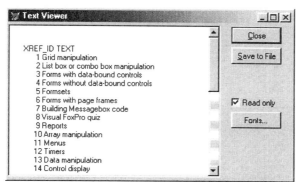

***Figure 43***. *Any Visual FoxPro data source can be used for text output with the "LIST" option.*

So far you've seen only printed report files, but as the name of the object suggests, it's a more generic output handler that can do more than printing reports. The Output handler can also use practically any Visual FoxPro data source and create output, either using a browse window, a text display window (Figure 43) or an HTML file that may or may not be displayed immediately in Internet Explorer.

*Table 10. Available options for certain destinations.*

| Option | Available for destinations | Description |
|---|---|---|
| ASC | EXPORT | Exports table to file in ASCII format. |
| ASCII | SCREEN | Prints a screen preview in ASCII format. |
| BROWSE | SCREEN | Creates a screen preview in the form of a browse window. |
| CSV | EXPORT | Exports table to file in comma-separated-value format. |
| DIF | EXPORT | Exports table to file in VisiCalc DIF (data interchange format) format. |
| FILEONLY | HTMLFILE | Creates an HTML output file but doesn't display it. |
| FOX2X | EXPORT | Exports table to file in FoxPro 2.x format. |
| FOXPLUS | EXPORT | Exports table to file in FoxBase+ format. |
| GRAPHICAL | SCREEN | Prints a screen preview using the graphical Visual FoxPro report engine. |
| LIST | SCREEN | Displays a screen preview using a special text view window (see Figure 43). |
| SDF | EXPORT | Exports table to file in system data format. |
| SETVFPDEFAULT | PRINTREPORT, PRINTLIST, PRINTFILE | Creates a printed report and asks the user for a printer. |
| VFPDEFAULT | PRINTREPORT, PRINTLIST, PRINTFILE | Creates a printed report on the VFP default printer (as specified in the *cVFPPrinterName* property). |
| VIEWSOURCE | HTMLFILE | Creates an HTML output file and displays its source code. |
| WEBVIEW | HTMLFILE | Creates an HTML output file and displays it using Internet Explorer. |
| WINDEFAULT | PRINTREPORT, PRINTLIST, PRINTFILE | Creates a printed report on the Windows default printer. |
| WK1 | EXPORT | Exports table to file in Lotus 1-2-3 (version 2.x) format. |
| WRK | EXPORT | Exports table to file in Lotus Symphony (version 1.10) format. |
| XL5 | EXPORT | Exports table to file in Excel (version 5.0 and higher) format. |
| XLS | EXPORT | Exports table to file in Excel (up to version 4.0) format. |

You can also use any kind of data source and export it in a number of standard formats (see Table 10). To do so, you set the destination to "EXPORT" and the option to your preferred export format. The data source is specified in the *cAlias* property. You have to open the data source yourself. Only the Output object uses it. When you create an output file (HTML output, or exported data), you can set the name of the destination file using the *cTextFile* property.

You can limit the number of records to be used for any kind of output by setting a scope in the *cScope* property. The scope has to be a valid Visual FoxPro expression. For special output options that handle data directly (such as "BROWSE" or "LIST"), you can also specify the fields you want to display. You can do this using the *cFieldList* property, which specifies a list of fields in comma-separated format.

The _GENHTML program handles any kind of HTML output created by the Output object. It allows you to specify various settings such as a special HTML class or an HTML style. You can set those options through the *cHTMLClass* and *cHTMLStyleID* properties.

In addition to the output behavior settings, the Output object features a couple of properties that are used to specify how an interface to this object could look, even though the Output object doesn't have an interface. (The Output control described below is a standard interface for the Output object.) One of these properties is *cDisplayFontName*, which specifies the font for all controls used in an interface. The *aDestinations()* and *aOptions()* arrays can be used as a source for drop-down lists. If you do that, you can specify whether you want to add the name of the source file to the drop-down list using the *lAddSourceNameToDropdown* property. Quite handy is the *lPreventSourceChanges* property, which sets the *cReport* and *cAlias* properties to read-only. However, I'm not sure that these properties should be in this class. I think this breaks the rules of encapsulation because we have properties belonging to an interface in a behavioral object.

### Output Control

| Class | _outputchoices |
|---|---|
| **Base class** | Container |
| **Class library** | _reports.vcx |
| **Parent class** | _output |
| **Sample** | ...\Samples\Vfp98\Solution\Ffc\output.scx |
| **Dependencies** | _base.vcx, _reports.h |

The Output Control is a direct subclass of the Output object (see above). It provides an interface for the most important options, such as the destination, print options and the file name if the destination requires an output file. The Output Control class doesn't have custom properties or methods.

The Output dialog box (see below) uses this object to give the user intuitive access to the most important settings (see Figure 30).

### Output Dialog Box

| Class | _outputdialog |
|---|---|
| **Base class** | Form |
| **Class library** | _reports.vcx |
| **Parent class** | _form |
| **Sample** | ...\Samples\Vfp98\Solution\Ffc\output.scx |
| **Dependencies** | _base.vcx, _reports.h |

The Output dialog box represents a standard interface for any kind of output operation. Figure 30 shows an example of this dialog.

The dialog has a large number of properties and methods that make it appear quite complex. Fortunately, it isn't. You must set only a few properties in order to use this dialog. In fact, you don't have to set any properties at all. In this case, the user is asked for all the missing information, such as an FRX file or another kind of data source. However, I don't recommend doing this because the chances to introduce problems are too great. Here's an example:

```
oReport = NewObject("_outputdialog","_reports.vcx")
oReport.cReport = "MyReport.frx"
oReport.lPreventSourceChanges = .T.
oReport.Show
```

The second line defines an FRX file as the source. I also specify that I don't want the user to change the source. Finally, the example displays the dialog shown in **Figure 44**. Compare this dialog to Figure 30 to see the changes caused by setting the *lPreventSourceChanges* property to .T.

*Figure 44. The Output dialog configured to hide the source selection controls (compare to Figure 30).*

All properties you set in the Output dialog box object are default settings that will be used for the output operation later on. Most of these properties are similar to the ones I described for the Output object, because the dialog's properties are used to set the properties of the Output object (which is used by this dialog to create output).

I found it useful to subclass this object, mainly to change its look and feel. If you do that, make sure you understand that the object automatically resizes the dialog when certain properties are set (as in the example above). Those changes are usually triggered by the assign methods of those properties. If you change the dialog's dimensions or the layout of the controls, you also have to change those methods so they can handle your dialog.

### Text Preview

| Class | _showtext |
|---|---|
| **Base class** | Form |
| **Class library** | _reports.vcx |
| **Parent class** | _form |
| **Sample** | ...\Samples\Vfp98\Solution\Ffc\output.scx |
| **Dependencies** | _base.vcx, _reports.h |

This class is a simple text editor that allows you to open, edit and save text files. It is always displayed in a fixed font. The main purpose of Text Preview is to provide a controllable preview window for text files. This class is used by the Output object to display screen previews in "LIST" format (see Figure 43).

You can load a text file simply by setting the *cSourceFile* property like so:

```
oText = NewObject("_showtext","_reports.vcx")
oText.cSourceFile = "ReadMe.txt"
oText.Show
```

It takes a while to get used to loading the text by setting a property. The Text Preview class uses an assign method to do that.

The class has a number of properties and methods, but you can't influence much because almost all of them are reserved for internal use only. The only other property I found useful is *cTargetFile*. It specifies the file name in which the text will be saved if the user clicks the Save button. Unfortunately, there isn't a good way to trigger the Save method other than to fire the Save button's Click() method manually like so:

```
oText.cmdSave.Click()
```

If no destination file was specified, the class asks the user for a new file name using the standard Save As dialog.

### System utilities

Until recently, Visual FoxPro programmers pretty much lived in their own little world. But this is changing. Systems become more integrated and applications must communicate with the operating system and other applications. Typically this isn't trivial, which is why most Visual FoxPro developers tried to stay away from this kind of programming. Using the classes introduced in this category, this is no longer a valid statement. System programming just became very easy. Try it out one day!

### *Application Registry*

| Class | Filereg |
|---|---|
| Base class | Custom |
| Class library | Registry.vcx |
| Parent class | Registry |
| Sample | ...\Samples\Vfp98\Solution\winapi\regfile.scx |
| Dependencies | Registry.h |

The Application Registry object provides easy access to application-specific settings in the Windows registry. This class has three important methods: GetAppPath(), GetApplication(), and GetLatestVersion().

First of all, we have the GetAppPath() method. It retrieves the path of an application associated with a certain file extension. An example would be Microsoft Word as the application associated to the DOC extension. The GetAppPath() method requires four parameters. Two of them are passed by reference to be populated with the return values. Here's an example:

```
LOCAL loReg, lcKey, lcApplication, lnErrorCode
loReg = NewObject("filereg","registry.vcx")
lnErrorCode = loReg.GetAppPath("DOC",@lcKey,@lcAppliaction,.F.)
IF lnErrorCode = 0
    ? lcKey
    ? lcApplication
ENDIF
```

This example retrieves the registry key and the application path for the application associated with the DOC extension. The return value of the GetAppPath() method is an error code. If it is 0, everything went fine. Otherwise, the returned error code is a Windows API error code.

The example above prints the following two lines when I run it on my computer with the current configuration:

```
Word.Document.8
"C:\Program Files\Microsoft Office\Office\Winword.exe" /n
```

The first line is the registry key value. One could use this value to instantiate the application as a server. The second line tells how to start the server as a regular application. As you can see, I pass .F. as the fourth parameter. This specifies that I don't want to see the application path as the COM server uses it. In other words, this is the path to the stand-alone executable. If I wanted to see the path to the EXE used by the server version, I could pass a .T. as the fourth parameter, which would return the following path:

```
C:\PROGRA~1\MICROS~1\OFFICE\Winword.exe
```

As you can see, the result is very similar (and possibly even confusing in this example), but I can assure you that the object actually reads two entirely different registration keys. On some occasions, the two values can be totally different, especially in scenarios where the server features are provided by a different application than the stand-alone features.

The second interesting method of the Application Registry object is GetApplication(). In fact, we've already seen how this method works, because it is utilized by the GetAppPath() method. It retrieves the application path according to a registry key. Here's an example:

```
LOCAL loReg, lcApplication, lnErrorCode
loReg = NewObject("filereg","registry.vcx")
lnErrorCode = loReg.GetApplication("Word.Document.8",@lcAppliaction,.F.)
IF lnErrorCode = 0
    ? lcApplication
ENDIF
```

Again, the return value is placed in a parameter we pass by reference. This time, parameter 3 is used to specify whether we want the stand-alone or the server path. As for the GetAppPath() method, the return value is a Windows API error code.

The third method of interest is GetLatestVersion(). It is very handy when you need to figure out which version of an application is installed on your system. For instance, if I know I want to use a server class called "Word.Document" I can figure out the current version of it like so:

```
LOCAL loReg, lcKey, lcApplication, lnErrorCode
loReg = NewObject("filereg","registry.vcx")
lnErrorCode = loReg.GetLatestVersion("Word.Document",@lcKey,@lcAppliaction,.F.)
IF lnErrorCode = 0
   ? lcKey
   ? lcApplication
ENDIF
```

This example would produce the following output:

```
Word.Document.8
"C:\Program Files\Microsoft Office\Office\Winword.exe" /n
```

This is very similar to the result of the GetAppPath() example. The main difference is that we didn't start out with a certain file extension, but with a specific class name.

### INI Access

| Class | Oldinireg |
|---|---|
| Base class | Custom |
| Class library | Registry.vcx |
| Parent class | Registry |
| Sample | None |
| Dependencies | Registry.h |

INI files are somewhat out of fashion. Too many people preach about using the Windows registry instead (and I have to admit I'm one of them). However, there are a couple of scenarios where you still have to use old-fashioned INI files. This might be the case when you have to modify older (or even newer) applications. Let's just assume we need to maintain multiple INI files that are virtually identical. This is hard to do using the registry. The INI Access foundation class makes dealing with INI files very easy.

The INI Access class has two important methods: GetINIEntry() and WriteINIEntry(). Both methods require four parameters: the value (passed by reference to the GetINIEntry() method), the section (all INI files are organized in sections), the actual entry name, and the name of the INI file. Here's one section of the Win.ini file that I found in my Windows directory:

```
[Devices]
Symantec WinFax Starter Edition=OLFAXDRV,LPT1:
EPSON Stylus 400=EPIDRV10,\\EPS-NT\Epson400
```

Obviously this is a very small section of a huge INI file. Here's how I can read a specific setting:

```
LOCAL lcValue, loINI, lnError
loINI = NewObject("oldinireg","registry.vcx")
lnError = loINI.GetINIEntry(@lcValue,"Devices","EPSON Stylus
400","C:\Windows\win.ini")
IF lnError = 0
    ? lcValue
ENDIF
```

Again, the method returns a Windows API error code. The actual value is returned in the first parameter, which is passed by reference.

Writing a value to an INI file works in a similar fashion. Here's an example:

```
LOCAL loINI, lnError
loINI = NewObject("oldinireg","registry.vcx")
lnError = loINI.WriteINIEntry("EPIDRV10,\\NTS\Epson400",;
    "Devices","EPSON Stylus 400","C:\Windows\win.ini")
IF lnError = 0
    MessageBox("Value set successfully.")
ENDIF
```

## ODBC Registry

| Class | Odbcreg |
|---|---|
| Base class | Custom |
| Class library | Registry.vcx |
| Parent class | Registry |
| Sample | ...\Samples\Vfp98\Solution\winapi\odbcreg.scx |
| Dependencies | Registry.h |

When dealing with ODBC data sources, it is helpful to know what's available. The ODBC Registry object allows you to query all available ODBC data sources. Once you have those data sources, you can query all the options for each individual source.

Let's start out with the GetODBCDrvrs() method, which queries all available ODBC data sources and places them in an array that's passed by reference as the first parameter. This should be done like so:

```
LOCAL laDrivers(1), loODBCReg, lnCounter
loODBCReg = NewObject("odbcreg","registry.vcx")
loODBCReg.GetODBCDrvrs(@laDrivers,.F.)
FOR lnCounter = 1 TO Alen(laDrivers,1)
    ? laDrivers(lnCounter)
ENDFOR
```

There are two different arrays this method can create, depending on the second parameter you pass. The version above creates a one-dimensional array with the names of all drivers (parameter 2 is .F.). Here's an example for the contents of this array:

```
Microsoft Access Driver (*.mdb)
Microsoft dBase Driver (*.dbf)
Microsoft Excel Driver (*.xls)
Microsoft FoxPro Driver (*.dbf)
Microsoft Text Driver (*.txt; *.csv)
SQL Server
Microsoft Visual FoxPro Driver
Microsoft ODBC for Oracle
```

The second version creates a two-dimensional array that lists the driver names as well as the data source name. Here's an example (the columns are separated by commas):

```
MS Access 97 Database, Microsoft Access Driver (*.mdb)
dBASE Files, Microsoft dBase Driver (*.dbf)
Excel Files, Microsoft Excel Driver (*.xls)
FoxPro Files, Microsoft FoxPro Driver (*.dbf)
Text Files, Microsoft Text Driver (*.txt; *.csv)
Visual FoxPro Tables, Microsoft Visual FoxPro Driver
Visual FoxPro Database, Microsoft Visual FoxPro Driver
VLPSQL, SQL Server
```

Once you retrieve driver names, you can enumerate the driver options using the EnumODBCDrvrs() method. This method, once again, populates an array that's passed by reference. The array is two-dimensional. The first column represents the option setting name, while the second column holds the current value. The number of the retrieved options as well as the individual options vary from driver to driver. Here's an example of using this method:

```
LOCAL laOptions(1), loODBCReg, lnCounter
loODBCReg = NewObject("odbcreg","registry.vcx")
loODBCReg.EnumODBCDrvrs(@laOptions," Microsoft Visual FoxPro Driver")
FOR lnCounter = 1 TO Alen(laOptions,1)
   ? laOptions(lnCounter,1) + ", " + laOptions(lnCounter,2)
ENDFOR
```

Yet another method is similar to the one we've just discussed: EnumODBCData(). This method creates the same array as the EnumODBCDrvrs() method, with the difference that you have to specify a data name instead of a driver name. To me, this seems to be somewhat easier than dealing with the driver name because some of those are quite cryptic. The method must be called like so:

```
loODBCReg.EnumODBCData(@laOptions," Visual FoxPro Database")
```

## Registry Access

| Class | Registry |
|---|---|
| **Base class** | Custom |
| **Class library** | Registry.vcx |
| **Parent class** | Custom (base class) |
| **Sample** | ...\Samples\Vfp98\Solution\winapi\regfox.scx |
| **Dependencies** | Registry.h |

The Registry Access class provides access to the Windows registry in general (who would have guessed it?). Let's go through its methods one by one.

One of the first things I ever did with the registry was reading key values. This can be accomplished using the GetRegKey() method like so:

```
LOCAL loRegistry, lcValue, lnError
loRegistry = NewObject("registry","registry.vcx")
lnError = loRegistry.GetRegKey("ResWidth",@lcValue,;
   "Software\Microsoft\VisualFoxPro\6.0\Options",;
   HKEY_CURRENT_USER)
IF lnError = 0
   ? lcValue
ENDIF
```

The first parameter identifies the value we want to read, in this case "ResWidth". Parameter 2 is passed by reference and will be populated with the key value we are asking for. Parameter 3 is the path to our key and parameter 4 is the root key. In my example I use "HKEY_LOCAL_USER", which is a predefined value (defined in Registry.h). The method returns an error code. Zero (0) means that everything went fine, and all other values are Windows API error codes.

Now that we know how to read values from the registry, we also want to be able to change them and write new values to the registry. This can be accomplished using the SetRegKey() method. The parameters passed to this method are identical to the ones passed to the GetRegKey() method, with the obvious exception that the value is the value to be set and not the value to be retrieved. For this reason, there is no need to pass parameter 2 by reference. Here's an example:

```
lnError = loRegistry.SetRegKey("ResWidth","1600",;
   "Software\Microsoft\VisualFoxPro\6.0\Options",;
   HKEY_CURRENT_USER)
```

Note that the value I set is a character value even though it seems that the "ResWidth" setting would be numeric. However, the Registry object can handle only string values.

Creating new values is easy. You simple use the SetRegKey() method and specify a value name that doesn't yet exist. The Registry Access object then automatically creates that new value for us. If you just tried that and now have a registry value you didn't really want, you can delete it using the DeleteKeyValue() method like so:

```
lnError = loRegistry.DeleteKeyValue("MyValue",;
   "Software\Microsoft\VisualFoxPro\6.0\Options",;
   HKEY_CURRENT_USER)
```

The methods I described so far are usually sufficient to handle the registry. However, there is more to come. The EnumOptions() method allows you to enumerate all the values and subkeys located under a certain key. The method takes four parameters.

Here's an example:

```
LOCAL laOptions(1)
lnError = loRegistry.DeleteKeyValue(@laOptions,;
  "Software\Microsoft\VisualFoxPro\6.0\Options",;
  HKEY_CURRENT_USER,.F.)
```

Parameter 4 specifies whether you want to query all the options (.F.) or all the subkeys (.T.). In the first scenario, a two-dimensional array is created that holds all the options (column 1) and all the values (column 2). If you're looking for all the subkeys, the resulting array will be one-dimensional, holding simply the key names.

### Shell Execute

| Class | _shellexecute |
|---|---|
| Base class | Custom |
| Class library | _environ.vcx |
| Parent class | _custom |
| Sample | ...\Samples\Vfp98\Solution\ole\buttons.scx |
| Dependencies | _base.vcx |

Often the programmer has to manage and handle files that don't belong to his application—Word documents, for instance. Wouldn't it be nice if you could simply open the application associated with this document to edit the actual document? Well, with this class you can.

The Shell Execute class has only one method and it's surprisingly simple to use. In most cases you have to pass only a single parameter, which is the name of the document you want the user to edit. This can be done like so:

```
oShellExecute = NewObject("_shellexecute","_environ.vcx")
oShellExecute.ShellExecute("MyDocument.doc")
```

The ShellExecute() method returns an error code that takes a while to get used to. Codes higher than 32 tell you that everything worked fine. Codes below 32 indicate an error (the documentation lists all the possible error codes).

There are two additional parameters you can pass to the ShellExecute() method: Parameter 2 specifies the default path the application will start in. Parameter 3 allows you to specify additional operations. Unfortunately, this parameter is virtually undocumented and I haven't yet encountered a use for it.

### Text formatting

Traditionally, text formatting isn't a strength of Visual FoxPro. The Text Formatting foundation classes try to add a little more flexibility in this area. Results seem to be moderate.

### Font Combobox

| Class | _cbofontname |
|---|---|
| Base class | ComboBox |
| Class library | _format.vcx |
| Parent class | _combobox |
| Sample | ...\Samples\Vfp98\Solution\Toolbars\format.scx |
| Dependencies | _base.vcx |

The Font Combobox foundation class is a relatively trivial class. It simply lists the names of all the fonts that are installed on the system. The class doesn't have any special methods or properties. To react to user selections. you have to use the regular methods and events such as InteractiveChange().

### Fontsize Combobox

| Class | _cbofontsize |
|---|---|
| Base class | ComboBox |
| Class library | _format.vcx |
| Parent class | _combobox |
| Sample | ...\Samples\Vfp98\Solution\Toolbars\format.scx |
| Dependencies | _base.vcx |

The Fontsize combobox goes along well with the Font combobox described above. It displays all the available font sizes for a certain font. This class has two custom properties (*nLargestFont* and *nSmallestFont*) that are used to define the range in fontsize. You can also use the FillList() method to automatically set the available fontsizes for a certain font. The font name must be passed as a parameter like so:

```
THISFORM.cboFontSize.FillList("Arial")
```

If you use the Fontsize combobox and the Font combobox in combination, you should call the FillList() method from the Font combobox's InteractiveChange() method.

### Format Toolbar

| Class | _tbrediting |
|---|---|
| Base class | Toolbar |
| Class library | _format.vcx |
| Parent class | _toolbar |
| Sample | ...\Samples\Vfp98\Solution\Toolbars\format.scx |
| Dependencies | _base.vcx |

The Format Toolbar foundation class is a toolbar similar to those found in many applications. It provides standard formatting options such as choosing fonts and font sizes, changing font style to bold, italic and underlined, and choosing different colors. The class uses other foundation classes such as the Font combobox and the Fontsize combobox. **Figure 45** shows how this toolbar looks in an undocked position.

**Figure 45.** *A standard formatting toolbar as used by many applications.*

The toolbar automatically applies the chosen settings to either the active control in the active form, or to all controls in the active form. Which one of those options is true can be specified through the *nAppliesTo* property (1=current control; 3=all controls).

### RTF Controls

| Class | _rtfcontrols |
|---|---|
| Base class | Container |
| Class library | _format.vcx |
| Parent class | _container |
| Sample | ...\Samples\Vfp98\Solution\Toolbars\format.scx |
| Dependencies | _base.vcx |

This container class looks somewhat similar to the Format Toolbar described above. It uses the Font combobox and the Fontsize combobox as well as buttons for bold and italic fonts. However, no behavior is attached to any of these controls, so you have to add it yourself.

### User interface
The user interface is a very important part of your application. After all, it's the only part people will ever see. The classes in this category are meant to help you create better interfaces.

### Get File and Directory

| Class | _folder |
|---|---|
| Base class | Container |
| Class library | _controls.vcx |
| Parent class | Container (base class) |
| Sample | ...\Samples\Vfp98\Solution\Ffc\getproject.scx |
| Dependencies | None |

This class is not meant to be used in applications designed for end users. It has been created for developer tools where the user/programmer is required to create new projects.

## MouseOver Effects

| Class | _mouseoverfx |
|---|---|
| Base class | Custom |
| Class library | _ui.vcx |
| Parent class | _custom |
| Sample | ...\Samples\Vfp98\Solution\Ffc\mousefx.scx |
| Dependencies | _base.vcx |

The MouseOver Effects class allows you to create objects that behave similarly to "hot activate" buttons as used in the Office 97-style toolbars. Those buttons are flat, and the typical 3-D effect appears only when the mouse hovers above the object. If you want to use the MouseOver Effects object for command buttons, you need to use a little trick. Instead of using a real button, you simply create an image. The button's 3-D border is actually drawn manually by the MouseOver Effects object.

To draw a temporary 3-D border around an object (you can draw it around any object, not just buttons), you simply call the HighlightMe() method and pass a reference to the current object like so:

```
THISFORM.oMouseOverEffects.HighlightMe(THIS)
```

This code should be executed in the MouseOver() event of the object you want to highlight.

The object has a number of properties that can be used to influence the look and feel of the temporary border. You can set the border width through the *nHighlightWidth* property. By default it is set to 2, but I recommend setting it to 1, which makes your object look more like the typical Office 97 objects. You can also specify the shadow color as well as the highlight color through the *iHighlightColor* and *iShadowColor* properties. Finally, you can set a margin using *nMargin*, so there is a little space between your object and the temporary 3-D border.

## Resize Object

| Class | _resizable |
|---|---|
| Base class | Custom |
| Class library | _controls.vcx |
| Parent class | _custom |
| Sample | ...\Samples\Vfp98\Solution\Forms\cresize.scx |
| Dependencies | _base.vcx |

The Resize Object class automatically adjusts object sizes when a form is resized. Similar to most automatic resizing classes, the Resize Object does a sub-optimal job. There simply isn't a generic way to resize Visual FoxPro forms because there is no resize information in any of the objects. So the Resize object has to do all of this by itself, and the best it can do is make some educated guesses. Actually, those guesses aren't that impressive. However, making things more advanced would be extremely difficult and hardly worth the effort. Creating individual resizing algorithms is much easier.

The Resize object is invoked from the Resize() event of a form. You simply call the AdjustControls() method of the Resize object and hope for the best.

### *Thermometer*

| Class | _thermometer |
|---|---|
| **Base class** | Form |
| **Class library** | _therm.vcx |
| **Parent class** | Form (base class) |
| **Sample** | ...\Samples\Vfp98\Solution\Ffc\therm.scx |
| **Dependencies** | None |

The Thermometer class displays a progress bar as shown in **Figure 46**. It can be used to inform the user about the progress of long tasks. Using this class is trivial—simply instantiate it and display it. On instantiation you pass the caption of the thermometer, which will be displayed in the first line of the dialog. Later on, during the process, you send Update() messages to the thermometer to display the current state. Once you are done, you send a Complete() message and you're done. Here's a simple example:

```
LOCAL loTherm
loTherm = NewObject("_thermomenter","_therm.vcx","","My Application")
loTherm.Show()
SELECT Customer
loTherm.iBasis = Recc()
LOCATE
SCAN
    loTherm.Update(Recn(),"Scanning record #" + Trans(Recn()))
    * More code goes here...
ENDSCAN
loTherm.Complete()
```

In this example, I use the Thermometer to display progress while I'm scanning the Customer table. Normally, the basis of all calculations is 100, representing 100%. This means that a value of 50 passed to the Update() method actually represents 50%. However, the basis can be set to a different value. If it were set to 200, for instance, a value of 50 passed to the Update() method would represent 25% (because 50 is 25% of 200). In the example above, I set the basis to the number of records. The basis can be defined through the *iBasis* property. In the scan loop, I constantly update the thermometer by calling the Update() method. I simply pass the current record number as the first parameter. Because I've set the basis, the thermometer automatically calculates the correct percentage. I also pass a message to be displayed, which will actually appear in the second line of the dialog (see Figure 46).

***Figure 46***. *A thermometer informs the user about the progress of an operation.*

Once I'm done scanning the customer table, I send a Complete() method, and the thermometer goes out of scope and disappears.

## Conclusion

Before I started to investigate the Fox Foundation Classes, I was under the impression they were designed to be used by beginners only (mainly in conjunction with the Application Wizard). Boy, was I wrong! It turns out that these are a solid set of classes that do help beginners to get started, but a major part of this collection of classes has been designed for the advanced developer. Many of the classes cover high-level scenarios and can be helpful even in the daily life of a professional FoxPro guru. I highly recommend investigating the Fox Foundation Classes; I've already incorporated many of them into my own framework.

# Chapter 5
# OOP Standard Tools

**Handling source code and other resources for object-oriented projects is more complicated than managing code for procedural applications. For this reason, you need a solid set of tools to help navigate through code to find the dependencies. Visual FoxPro has some excellent tools to accomplish these tasks. Among them are the Class Browser and the Component Gallery.**

## The Class Browser

The Class Browser is my favorite tool that ships with Visual FoxPro. In fact, I like it so much that I use it more often than the Visual FoxPro command window.

The Visual FoxPro Class Browser is used to manage visual classes and visual class libraries. One of the few things it cannot do is handle source code classes stored in PRG files. It is written entirely in native Visual FoxPro code and therefore, once instantiated, it is a regular FoxPro object sitting in memory. Many of the Class Browser objects' internals are exposed and can be easily manipulated, customized, extended and automated. This ensures that the Class Browser can fulfill the needs of every programmer.

### Basic functionality

**Figure 1** shows the new Visual FoxPro 6.0 Class Browser. The look and feel has changed slightly from Visual FoxPro 5.0. The new browser looks cleaner, more colorful, and overall more modern. The top portion of the window contains the toolbar, which has a reduced number of items to make the browser easier and more efficient to use. In return, the shortcut menu now contains more items. I'll discuss some of these items (that are not documented in depth elsewhere) in more detail shortly.

The two main panels of the browser show the classes (typically in hierarchical mode so you can see the inheritance structure) and all their properties, methods and other details. At the bottom you see some additional information about the class in plain English, or some comments you've added to your class.

The main area of the Class Browser is a lot more flexible and informative now. It has slider bars so you can resize each panel, and the right-hand panel has some nice icons to indicate the type and visibility of each property, method or member object. Until now, some cryptic special characters that came straight out of the VCX file (see below) indicated these details. Now, the Class Browser uses standard Visual Studio icons for properties and methods.

By default, the Class Browser displays only properties and methods that are exposed, and methods that have some code attached. I prefer to see some more information, like new defined methods that are still empty, or protected and hidden properties and methods. The shortcut (right-click) menu allows you to display this information. One nice feature of the Class Browser is that it remembers all the settings and other things you change, so you only need to activate the protected and hidden properties and methods once. The browser stores all this information in Browser.dbf. As you'll see later, you can also use this DBF for your own needs.

Most of the items in the Class Browser toolbar are well documented in the online help and in the regular documentation. However, almost every single button holds a little secret that I'd like to share with you. I'll do this in a logical order rather than going through the toolbar from left to right. **Figure 2** shows the toolbar and a short description of its important items. Take note that not every button holds special features. In this case I won't discuss them. The Visual FoxPro documentation does a nice job explaining them.

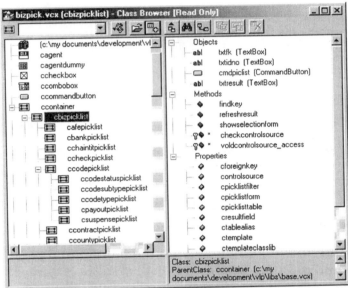

*Figure 1. The new Visual FoxPro 6.0 Class Browser.*

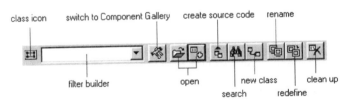

*Figure 2. The Class Browser toolbar.*

## Opening libraries

Opening class libraries is the most trivial and most common task you will perform. When you start the Class Browser, it opens modeless and without any content. This is different from what used to happen in Visual FoxPro 5.0, where the browser always asked for a library on startup. This behavior became inappropriate for reasons you'll discover shortly.

The browser can open a variety of different files, starting (of course) with visual class libraries. It can also handle forms, since their structure is identical to the VCX structure. In addition, you can browse applications, type libraries, ActiveX controls and even DLL files.

The browser has two different buttons to open libraries. The first one (from left to right) is used to open libraries exclusively. This means that all opened libraries will be closed before a new one is opened. The second button opens an additional library and leaves the one that's already there so you can view the contents of multiple libraries at once. This is very useful, especially since inheritance typically spans multiple class libraries.

So far, everything has been quite intuitive, but there's more! You can also right-click on both open buttons to see a list of the most recently used class libraries. The number of items in this list seems to grow with every (service) release of Visual FoxPro. In my current version I counted 32 items. It makes sense to keep a long list of recently used libraries because programmers modify many libraries during a typical project. This list of 32 items should be long enough to hold all the libraries you normally use, and it's the quickest way to open a class library. Now you also know why the browser doesn't ask for a library on startup anymore. It's simply quicker to select one from the right-click menu.

There is one more way to open a class library, which I use quite frequently. Often I need to look at a class whose parent class is stored in another class library (indicated by a little chevron as displayed in **Figure 3**). If this library isn't open, I can't see the class. I could click the Open button and select the library where the class is stored. But to do so I'd have to know the name and the location of the library, which is hard to remember in large projects. But there's an easier way to get to that library. Simply right-click on the class and choose "Select parent class." The browser will open the correct library and set the focus on the parent class of the previously selected class.

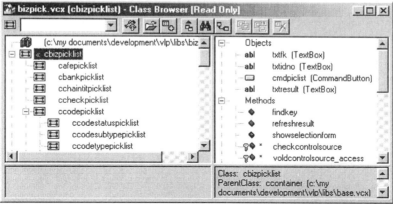

*Figure 3*. The class cbizpicklist *has a parent class that's stored in a different library, which is indicated by the leading chevron.*

## Renaming items

The Class Browser allows you to rename classes as well as properties and methods. The ability to rename properties and methods is a rather unique feature. To do so, simply select the item you want to rename, and either press the Rename button or select Rename from the right-click menu.

Renaming items is an important but dangerous feature. If you rename a class, you could break inheritance structures forever. Let's say you rename a class that has a subclass in another class library. The subclass refers to its parent class only by name. So if that name changes, the subclass loses its parent and cannot be instantiated or modified. If this happens, you have to rename the parent class back to the original name. However, this can be tricky! You might have new subclasses that rely on the new name. Or maybe you renamed the class because the name was mistyped. In this case it might be hard to remember the original name. The only way out of this situation is to redefine (see below) the now broken subclass, if the browser can even open and display the class library.

The Class Browser has continually been improved to find subclasses that can be influenced by a renamed class. In the latest version, it is fairly safe to rename a class if all subclasses from different libraries are opened at the same time. In this case, the browser iterates through all involved classes and updates the relation. Unfortunately, this doesn't work with source code. For this reason it's very dangerous to rename methods and properties. All source code references to these items will be broken after renaming them. For instance, if you refer to MyFavoriteMethod() in your Init() code and you change the name of the method to MyMostFavoriteMethod, your code will error out. You can use Visual FoxPro's Find feature to locate references in code and make the changes there.

## Redefining classes

To "redefine a class" means to change the class's parent class, which is easy to do in source code. Simply go to the class definition and change the AS clause. With visual classes, however, this is a whole different story. The Class Browser is basically the only tool that can redefine these classes.

Redefining classes is useful for many different reasons. You might want to add one more layer of subclassing to your inheritance structure. If you have Class A and a subclass of it called Class B, you could simply add a layer in between by creating another subclass of Class A called Class C, and by redefining Class B to be a child of Class C. Or you might have a bug in your structure or a misconception in your design. In all these cases, redefining classes can be very helpful. You can also redefine forms. If you want to create a Visual FoxPro form of a certain class, you can either specify the class in the Options dialog or add an additional clause in the CREATE FORM command. Both methods are rather cumbersome, so I prefer to create a default form—later on, I'll open it in the Class Browser and redefine it. Not really straightforward, but at least better than the other methods.

Unfortunately, redefining classes is very dangerous. To explain why, I'll walk you through a small sample. Let's say we created a *MovieTheater* class for our movie theater example that I use throughout the book. It is a subclass of the abstract class *Theater*. In this class we have a method called Perform(). This method is empty, but we have several hundred lines of code in this method of the *MovieTheater* class. Now we decide to redefine this class to be a subclass of our generic *Screen* class. This class doesn't have a Perform() method. The next time we open our *MovieTheater* class, FoxPro checks its internal list of all defined methods and properties, and figures that no Perform() method is supposed to be in this class. For this reason FoxPro assumes that the code is outdated, and removes the whole method permanently from our class. Not exactly the results we expected!

In Visual FoxPro 6.0, the Redefine feature is a lot easier to use than in previous versions. You now get a nice dialog (see **Figure 4**) that allows you to pick a class rather than to enter the class name and its location manually. It also allows redefining directly to the class's base class and even switching to another base class. I'll discuss this feature in more detail later.

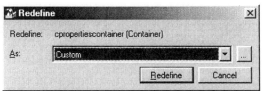

*Figure 4*. *The new Redefine dialog allows you to choose different base classes. Using its Browse (...) button, you can navigate to the regular class selection dialog, rather than having to remember the class name.*

### Switching to different base classes

Different Visual FoxPro base classes can be very similar—Custom and Container classes, for instance, or TextBoxes and EditBoxes. In fact, sometimes I wish these classes would be the same with just a couple of additional properties—like a *ScrollBars* property for TextBoxes or a *Visible* property for Custom classes. But because they are different I often need to change to an entirely different base class. Let's say you change a field in your database from a regular text field to a memo. You now have to change all classes that refer to this field from TextBoxes to EditBoxes. Or maybe you've based a lot of invisible composite classes on the base class *Custom*. This is perfectly fine until you want one part of this class to be visible. Now you really need a Container.

Obviously, only a handful of base classes are interchangeable. Redefining a *Grid* to be a *Line* or vice versa wouldn't be a great idea. The Class Browser only allows you to redefine classes to which it can securely convert. But you still need to be careful with this feature. It's powerful but it needs an experienced programmer to be tamed.

To change to a different base class, you can either pick a different base class directly from the drop-down list, or you can select another user-defined class from the class selection dialog. In this case you have even more flexibility because you can basically redefine to every base class you want. The Class Browser gives only a sloppy warning message indicating the possible problems you could get yourself into. So be aware of the fact that you carry all responsibility for this operation! I recommend trying such operations on backup copies of your class libraries so you can easily recover older versions in the event of a problem.

### Cleaning up class libraries

Visual class libraries tend to grow extremely large. When you modify a class and save it, Visual FoxPro deletes the old copy of the class and appends a new one at the end of the VCX file. This is due to the structure of the VCX file and the way classes are stored. When a class is modified, even small changes can cause major rearrangements in the class library. For this reason, it is safer to append a new copy at the end of the file. The old copy remains there, marked as deleted. (See below for more information about the structure of the VCX file and how classes are stored.) If you create a large composite class and modify it 10 times (even if changes are minor), the VCX becomes 10 times larger than necessary. Even very small class libraries can end up being several megabytes in size because of all the "hot air" they contain.

The clean-up feature of the Class Browser is a great way to remove all outdated copies of your classes. All you have to do is open a library, click the Clean-up button and the browser will take care of the rest. It amazes me every time I use this feature. It is not unusual for several-megabyte class libraries to shrink to a handy 50 or 100 KB.

## The class icon

The class icon is probably the most overlooked element of the Class Browser. At the same time, it has more hidden functionality than any other item in the toolbar. Let's start by examining one of its simpler features.

### Changing the icon

When you right-click on the Class Browser icon, the File Selection dialog appears so you can select a new image file. The image file will then be used in the Class Browser as well as in the Form Controls toolbar, instead of the standard icon for each individual base class. You can right-click again to switch to another icon. If you press Cancel in the File Selection dialog, the browser asks whether you want to cancel only the current operation, or if you want to revert to the standard icon for the base class of the selected class. This is almost like a two-step undo. It is the only way to revert to the default icon.

### Drag and Drop

The main reason why the class icon is so important is its drag-and-drop functionality. I'm still not certain whether I have discovered all the different options, but I will try to give you a good overview of the possibilities.

The standard drag-and-drop action is to drag the icon and drop it on the Visual FoxPro screen. In this case, the Class Browser creates an instance of the class you dropped. If you dropped a form class on the screen, the class will be created using NewObject(). You can also see the instance in the right-hand panel of the Class Browser as shown in **Figure 5**. If the dropped class needs a hosting container (such as a command button), the class will be instantiated inside the Visual FoxPro screen using AddObject(). Such an object is not a stand-alone object and cannot be detected by the Class Browser. For this reason, it will not show up as an instance in the details panel. This is sometimes…well…confusing.

When you drag and drop to the screen, the Class Browser ignores all errors that occur during instantiation. All later errors that occur when you use this object will still be fired. The fact that the errors are ignored is important for bench testing. ("Bench testing" is a technique that allows testing single components without instantiating and invoking the entire system. This also includes ignoring certain errors and dependencies.) Typically, all your classes will be part of a larger object system, and therefore will depend on other objects during construction. For this reason, many errors can occur when instantiating the class. But those errors might not be relevant at that time because you might want to test something totally different.

On the other hand, this behavior can also hide bugs. Very often I create a class, test it directly from the Class Browser, and later on I discover some problems during instantiation that were hidden by the browser. Fortunately, you can tell the browser not to ignore errors. Simply press the Ctrl key while dragging and dropping.

Often it is interesting to know what the browser actually does when you instantiate a class by dragging and dropping. You can see the appropriate code when you drag and drop to the command window. In this case, the code will be placed in the command queue and will be executed right away. Usually it is your responsibility to make the new instance visible by either setting the *Visible* property or calling the Show() method.

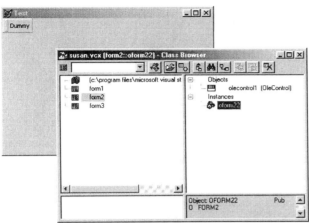

**Figure 5**. *The Class Browser and the form we instantiated by dragging and dropping. The new instance is also listed in the details (right-hand) panel of the browser.*

You can drag and drop not only on Visual FoxPro desktop standard objects, such as the screen or the command window, but also to any kind of existing container object in memory. If you have a form, for instance, you can simply add a button to it by dropping a button class on the form. Keep in mind that even objects you modify are "alive" and fully functional. So if you edit a form, you can drag and drop classes from the Class Browser onto it, because there is no difference between a final instance and a class or form that is being modified. When you drop on a modified class, the Class Browser acts as a builder that replaces the Form Controls toolbar. I prefer to use the browser over the toolbar because it is a lot easier to find classes in the browser. Also, you can start multiple instances of the browser or open multiple libraries in one browser window.

A word about multiple instances: If you are running multiple instances of the browser, you can drag and drop from one instance to another. By default, the browser moves a class from the library displayed in one browser to the library displayed in another. When doing so, the Class Browser also redefines all dependencies and inheritance structures in all class libraries that are opened in both instances. It's important to maintain a working inheritance structure because moving the class influences all its subclasses.

Again, you can press the Ctrl key during the drag-and-drop operation, and the Class Browser will copy the class instead of moving it. Usually this is the safer choice, but you have to come back and clean up afterwards (unless the class libraries involved in the drag-and-drop operation belong to entirely different projects).

## Creating source code

When I first started using Visual FoxPro and visual classes as well as forms, it bothered me that I could never see the entire source code in one piece. In FoxPro 2.x, I created screens and generated source code, and I could then read the code and learn from it. In Visual FoxPro this capability was lost. Or was it? Actually, it wasn't! The Class Browser can create source code for all visual classes and forms.

To view the code for a specific class, select the class in the browser and click the View Class Code button. The browser creates a file called Viewcode.prg, which shows the exact code for your class. There are some limitations, though. Subclassed ActiveX controls, for instance, don't show much information when viewed in source code. But overall, this feature is quite useful. You can also create code for an entire class library. To do so, select the library (at the very top of the list) instead of a specific class.

A new feature was added to the browser in Visual FoxPro 6.0. If you right-click on the View Class Code button, you get a view of the class code that looks almost the same as the created PRG file. But if you take a closer look, you will discover that you're looking at an HTML file displayed using Internet Explorer within Visual FoxPro. It also includes some syntax coloring, although it is not as complete as Visual FoxPro's internal syntax coloring. The HTML preview is useful for anyone who wants to publish source code in technical articles, or also for documentation purposes. To save the created HTML, simply right-click on the code window, select "View Source," and save the file under a name of your choice.

## Different ways to start the Class Browser

The easiest way to start the Class Browser is to select it from the Tools menu. However, there are other ways as well—for instance, you can use the "_Browser" system variable:

```
DO (_BROWSER)
```

This is especially useful if you want to pass parameters to the browser. The Class Browser is very flexible when it comes to receiving parameters. One possibility is to pass a numeric parameter:

```
DO (_BROWSER) WITH 0
```

When you pass 0, the Class Browser installs itself in the menu if it isn't already there. It seems that this has been accepted as a standard throughout the FoxPro world. Many tools do the same if called with 0 as the first parameter.

However, the first parameter can also be of type *character*. In this case, the browser expects the name of the class library to open on startup. Optionally, you can pass a second parameter, which is the name of the initially selected class and member, separated by a period:

```
DO (_BROWSER) WITH "SAMPLES\VFP98\CLASSES\BUTTONS.VCX","vcr.recordpointermoved"
```

This will open one of the sample classes that ships with Visual FoxPro and will select the *vcr* class and one of its methods, called *recordpointermoved.* Typically you wouldn't specify all of this just to open a class, but many tools that use the Class Browser use this syntax.

When you start the Class Browser from the Tools menu, it first looks at the current environment. If you are currently modifying a class, the browser will open with this exact class selected.

Usually, I start the browser without any classes opened by default. I then right-click the Open button and select the class library I want to work on. However, if you always work on the same class, you can also specify this as your default file. To do so, open the desired class library and call the SetDefaultFile() method of the browser like so:

```
_oBrowser.SetDefaultFile()
```

_oBrowser is a reference to the currently active Class Browser instance. (See below for more details.) The SetDefaultFile() method registers your current library as the default library. If you want to register more than one library, open another one and call the method again, with.T. as a parameter. To remove a library from the list of default libraries, use the ResetDefaultFile() method the same way you use the SetDefaultFile() method.

## Customizing and extending the Class Browser

One of the greatest strengths of the Class Browser is its flexibility and customizability. I think it's fair to say that the browser has set new standards in this area. In order to customize the browser, you need to know how it works internally and what its object model looks like.

### Class Browser internals

As mentioned before, the Class Browser—once instantiated—is just a regular Visual FoxPro object. There is an exposed reference to the browser at all times, called _oBrowser. This reference points to the active instance of the browser if you have multiple instances running at the same time. Knowing this reference, it is relatively simple to start customizing the browser. Here's a little example:

```
_oBrowser.Caption = "My very own class browser"
```

As you can see, the caption of the browser changes. In the same manner, you can customize almost everything in the Class Browser. Let's say you don't like the tooltip text of the Open button. You can change it like so:

```
_oBrowser.cmdOpen.ToolTipText = "Exclusive Open"
```

How did I know the name of the Open button? Well, there are a couple of ways to explore the internal object structure of the browser. One is to use the debugger and to explore the _oBrowser reference in the Watch window. This will show all exposed objects and properties. You cannot cheat your way through as easily to find the exposed methods because the debugger doesn't show them. Fortunately, the internals of the Class Browser are documented quite well in the online help.

One internal method I use quite a lot is SetFont(). It sets the font for the Class Browser and all the windows and dialogs it will use. (The new browser also exposes this functionality through the right-click menu.) Here's how you call it:

```
_oBrowser.SetFont( "Comic Sans MS", "24" )
```

Additional parameters for font style are available as well. Another nice example is the ExportClass() method, which returns the code for the currently selected class or class library. This is the programmatic interface to the "View Class Code" feature. Calling this method rather than pressing the button is a bit more flexible. First of all, the method returns the created code, so you can simply assign it to a variable and work with it. Also, you can pass a couple of parameters, so you can decide whether the created code is displayed in a window (parameter 1 set to .T.) or you can pass a file name (parameter 2) to save the source in a file. Here's how:

```
_oBrowser.ExportClass(.F.,"test.prg")
```

One of the more useful methods is AddFile(), which allows you to programmatically open a class library. We will use this in one of our demo add-ins. Also quite useful are ModifyClass(), NewFile(), OpenFile(), and others. I could go on for pages and pages listing all the exposed methods, but I think the documentation does a nice job of that. I will stop at this point and demonstrate more methods when we create some sample add-ins (see below).

Just as important as the exposed methods are the exposed properties. Most of them hold some information about the currently selected class or class library. _oBrowser.cAlias, for instance, holds the alias name of the currently viewed library. You could use it to programmatically select the file and work with it, as in the following example:

```
SELECT (_oBrowser.cAlias)
WAIT WINDOW User
```

This displays the contents of the user field of the current class in a wait window. Another property I like (and use) a lot is *aClassList*. It is an array that holds a lot of important information about the currently displayed class tree. This array is used internally to build that tree and to easily reference the displayed information. You can find the exact structure of this array in the Visual FoxPro documentation.

Again, all the properties are documented quite nicely, so there is no need to reprint this information in this book. I encourage you to read the Class Browser topics in the online help.

Let's have another look at the member objects of the browser. I've already shown a simple example that demonstrates how to change a property of any member object you want. Now let's continue with this thought and explore what that means. Because the positioning properties (such as *left* and *top*) are just regular properties, you can start to rearrange objects in the browser. You can set them invisible, or enable and disable them as you like. In fact, you can add your own buttons (or other objects) to add new functionality or replace existing ones (as you'll see shortly). Just play a little bit with these possibilities and you'll realize the true power of this architecture.

### Browser.dbf

A lot of things you do in the Class Browser, like moving it around on the screen or changing the font, will appear the same way the next time you start the browser. All of these settings are stored in a regular DBF file called Browser.dbf, located in the Visual FoxPro home directory. You can open it like so:

```
USE Home() + "browser.dbf"
```

There are two different types of records in this DBF, identified by the Type field. One is *PREFW*, which can be a user preference, a recently used file, or any kind of other item the browser remembers the next time it gets called. The second type is *ADDIN*, which identifies a Class Browser plug-in. I'll discuss this topic further later.

The interesting part is that the Class Browser ignores all records that are not of type *PREFW* or *ADDIN*. This means that you can use it for your own purposes if you create new types. I do this often with all kinds of tools I write. Instead of giving every single one its own resource file, I reuse Browser.dbf. However, be careful doing this, because this DBF might not exist. Browser.dbf gets created when the Class Browser is started for the first time. If you give away a tool to a programmer who doesn't use the Class Browser (shame on him!), it could happen that Browser.dbf doesn't exist. In this case I simply start the browser programmatically and release it right away. Showing the Class Browser for a brief moment might look a little weird to the user, but it surely does the trick. The other option would be to create Browser.dbf yourself, but I don't recommend that, for a very simple reason: The structure might be extended in future versions, and in this case you would have created an invalid version.

Often I'm asked why one would use Browser.dbf rather than the registry. There are a couple of good reasons: First of all, it is rather easy to use; secondly, the registry is not a good place to store record-oriented data. In other words, it is relatively easy to write some settings to the registry, but it is hard to store data that requires tabular structures as found in any FoxPro table. It's also a good idea to use the browser if you require the use of memo fields, which are practically non-existent in the registry.

**Table 1** shows the structure of Browser.dbf. Take note that this file is used by the Class Browser and the Component Gallery (see below). In Table 1, I also describe the fields that are used by the Component Gallery. Columns 5 and 6 indicate the fields used by each tool.

*Table 1*. The structure of Browser.dbf.

| Field Name | Type | Description | Example | Browser | Gallery |
|---|---|---|---|---|---|
| Platform | C(8) | The value of this field is always "WINDOWS" because Visual FoxPro is no longer a cross-platform tool. However, if the record type is "ADDIN", this field is blank. | WINDOWS | ☑ | ☑ |
| Type | C(12) | This field defines the type of the record. It is usually either "PREFW" or "ADDIN". Records with other type values are ignored. | PREFW, ADDIN | ☑ | ☑ |
| ID | C(12) | The ID further identifies the record type. "FORMINFO" records are used by the gallery and by the browser to store form preferences. "BROWSER" records contain default settings for the Class Browser. In this case, the Properties field contains more information about the settings. If the ID is "METHOD", the record defines a Class Browser add-in that is tied to a particular event or method. If the value of this field is "MENU", the record describes an add-in that shows up in the menu. | FORMINFO, BROWSER, METHOD, MENU | ☑ | ☑ |

**Table 1**, *continued*

| Field Name | Type | Description | Example | Browser | Gallery |
|---|---|---|---|---|---|
| Default | L | Logical true for the default Component Gallery catalog. | .F. | | ☑ |
| Global | L | Logical true for global Component Gallery catalogs. | .T. | | ☑ |
| Backup | L | When this field is set to True, the catalog or class library is automatically copied to a \backup subfolder. | .T. | ☑ | ☑ |
| Name | Memo | The file name that relates to this record. This could be a class library (or any other kind of file the browser can open) or a component catalog. If the current record describes an add-in, this field has the name of the add-in. | Genrepox.vcx Test.app Object Metrics Add-In | ☑ | ☑ |
| Desc | Memo | The Component Gallery uses this field to store the description of a registered catalog. | Visual GenRepoX Catalog | | ☑ |
| Method | Memo | Contains the name of a method an add-in is tied to. If the value of this field is "*", the add-in will fire for every method. | INIT cmdOpen.Click * | ☑ | ☑ |
| Properties | Memo | Used by the Class Browser to store preferences. | this.lRunFileDefault = .F. this.lAddFileDefault = .F. this.lAutoLabelEdit = .T. this.lAdvancedEditing = .T. | ☑ | |
| Script | Memo | Internal use by the Component Gallery. | | | ☑ |
| Program | Memo | This field contains the name of the add-in program to call. | Pbrowser.prg | ☑ | ☑ |
| ClassLib | Memo | If an add-in is a visual class, this field contains the name of the class library. | Loc.vcx | ☑ | ☑ |
| ClassName | Memo | If an add-in is a visual class, this field contains the name of the class. | CCountCodeLines | ☑ | ☑ |
| FileFilter | Memo | Used for Class Browser add-ins that apply only to certain files. | Genrepox.vcx | ☑ | |

***Table 1***, *continued*

| Field Name | Type | Description | Example | Browser | Gallery |
|---|---|---|---|---|---|
| DispMode | N(1,0) | The window state for the browser or gallery form. This setting is stored on a per-file basis. | 1 | ☑ | ☑ |
| Top | N(6,0) | The stored top coordinate of the browser/gallery window. | 30 | ☑ | ☑ |
| Left | N(6,0) | The stored left coordinate of the browser/gallery window. | 15 | ☑ | ☑ |
| Height | N(6,0) | The stored height of the browser/gallery window. | 500 | ☑ | ☑ |
| Width | N(6,0) | The stored width of the browser/gallery window. | 400 | ☑ | ☑ |
| Height1 | N(6,0) | Stores the height of the description pane in the Class Browser. | 50 | ☑ | |
| Width1 | N(6,0) | Stores the width of the description pane in the Class Browser. | 200 | ☑ | |
| Height2 | N(6,0) | Stores the height of the description pane in the Component Gallery. | | | ☑ |
| Width2 | N(6,0) | Stores the width of the description pane in the Component Gallery. | | | ☑ |
| WindowStat | N(1,0) | Window state of the gallery/browser window (0=normal, 1=minimized, 2=maximized). | 0 | ☑ | ☑ |
| Protected | L | Specifies whether the Class Browser shows protected properties and methods. | .T. | ☑ | |
| Empty | L | Specifies whether the Class Browser shows empty methods. | .F. | ☑ | |
| Hidden | L | Specifies whether the Class Browser shows hidden properties and methods. | .T. | ☑ | |
| DescBoxes | L | Specifies whether the description panels should be displayed. | .T. | ☑ | ☑ |
| AutoExpand | L | Specifies whether the treeviews should be expanded automatically. | .T. | ☑ | ☑ |
| PushPin | L | Specifies whether the browser/gallery window should be always on top. | .F. | ☑ | ☑ |
| PCBrowser | L | Specifies whether the browser should display the parent class toolbar. | .F. | ☑ | |

*Table 1*, continued

| Field Name | Type | Description | Example | Browser | Gallery |
|---|---|---|---|---|---|
| ViewMode | N(1,0) | Stores the gallery display view mode (1-4). | | | ☑ |
| FontInfo | Memo | Stores information about the selected font. | MS Sans Serif,8, | ☑ | ☑ |
| FormCount | N(4,0) | Stores the number of instances open for a specific file in the browser/gallery. | | ☑ | ☑ |
| Updated | T | Date and time the record was last updated. | 09/03/1998 03:34:52 PM | ☑ | ☑ |
| Comment | Memo | Unused. Reserved for comments the user wants to enter directly. | I have to… | | |
| User1 | Memo | Unused. Reserved for user extensions. | *:EXTEND… | | |
| User2 | Memo | Unused. Reserved for user extensions. | *:EXTEND… | | |
| User3 | Memo | Unused. Reserved for user extensions. | *:EXTEND… | | |
| User4 | Memo | Unused. Reserved for user extensions. | *:EXTEND… | | |

## Creating add-ins

You've now seen how to customize the browser. Unfortunately, all the changes we've made so far were temporary and were initiated from the command window. Once we closed the browser and reopened it, our changes were gone. Fortunately, the browser features a mechanism called "AddIns" that allows you to permanently customize it. Let's have a look at a simple example. Earlier I showed one line of code that temporarily changed the tooltip text of the Open button. Here is the code that accomplishes the same thing permanently. Put this code in a file called Sample1.prg:

```
LPARAMETERS loBrowser
loBrowser.cmdOpen.ToolTipText = "Exclusive Open"
```

This is the most basic add-in you can write. Every add-in has to accept one parameter, which is a reference to the browser. You can use this reference instead of _oBrowser, which is more reliable because you could have multiple browser instances.

Now, the question is how to call this add-in. First of all, you have to tell the browser that it exists. Do so using the AddIn() method:

```
_oBrowser.AddIn("Change ToolTipText","sample1.prg")
```

To register an add-in, the AddIn() method requires at least two parameters. The first one is the name of the add-in, and the second is the code or class that has to be executed. Add-ins can be PRGs, FXPs, SCXes, APPs, and EXEs. The only requirement they have to fulfill is to accept one parameter.

Okay, you've now registered the add-in in the Class Browser, so now you can call it by right-clicking on the browser, selecting "Add-ins…" and then selecting the "Change

ToolTipText" add-in from the menu. Now, when you move the mouse over the Open button, you'll see the changed caption. You can also close the browser, restart it, open the menu again to select the add-in, and you'll end up with the same tooltip text. That's a lot better than what we had before, but it still isn't perfect. It would be much better to have the change occur automatically—which is possible. The browser allows you to associate an add-in to a certain event, so if you link the add-in to the Init() event, it gets called every time the browser starts. You can do this as follows:

```
_oBrowser.AddIn("Change ToolTipText","sample1.prg","INIT")
```

Now you can close the browser and restart it, and the tooltip text will change right away. Excellent! Also, the add-in won't be displayed in the menu anymore because it is triggered automatically. If you'd like to see the add-in in the menu as well, you'd have to register it twice. But as you can see from this example, is usually doesn't make sense to do so.

You can link add-ins to almost any event and method throughout the Class Browser and all its member objects. Let's say (I know it doesn't make a lot of sense, but bear with me) you want to change the tooltip text after you've opened one library. To do so, you could link your add-in to the Click event of the Open button, like so:

```
_oBrowser.AddIn("Change ToolTipText","sample1.prg","cmdOpen.Click")
```

You can pass other parameters to the AddIn() method. You can create add-ins for specific files only, and even for specific platforms, even though this is outdated by now.

Since our sample add-in isn't very useful, you might have already wondered how to get rid of it. This is quite easy:

```
_oBrowser.AddIn("Change ToolTipText",.NULL.)
```

Now that you know the basics about add-ins, you can start to write your first useful one. Often I would like to see the source code for my classes when browsing through them, without clicking the Export button every time. The following code is stored in Showcode.prg. It adds buttons and an editbox to the browser to display the code:

```
LPARAMETERS loBrowser
* We add the checkbox
loBrowser.AddObject("chkSourceCode","cSourceCodeActive")
loBrowser.chkSourceCode.Top = loBrowser.cmdOpen.Top
loBrowser.chkSourceCode.Height = loBrowser.cmdOpen.Height
loBrowser.chkSourceCode.Left = loBrowser.cmdCleanup.Left +
loBrowser.cmdCleanup.Width + 5
loBrowser.chkSourceCode.Visible = .T.

* We add the editbox
loBrowser.AddObject("edtSourceCode","cSourceCodeDisplay")

RETURN
```

```
DEFINE CLASS cSourceCodeActive AS CheckBox
   Style = 1            && Graphical checkbox
   Caption = "Source"  && An image would be nicer...
   Width = 50
   Value = .F.

   FUNCTION InteractiveChange
      thisform.edtSourceCode.Visible = THIS.Value
   ENDFUNC
ENDDEFINE

DEFINE CLASS cSourceCodeDisplay as EditBox
   ReadOnly = .T.

   FUNCTION Visible_Assign (llNewVal)
      IF VarType(llNewVal) = "L"
         IF llNewVal
            this.Left = THISFORM.oleMembers.Left
            this.Width = THISFORM.oleMembers.Width
            thisform.oleMembers.Height = (THISFORM.oleMembers.Height/2) - 2
            thisform.txtMembers3d.Height = THISFORM.oleMembers.Height
            this.Height = THISFORM.oleMembers.Height
            this.Top = THISFORM.oleMembers.Top + THISFORM.oleMembers.Height + 4
         ELSE
            thisform.oleMembers.Height = THISFORM.oleClassList.Height
            thisform.txtMembers3d.Height = THISFORM.oleMembers.Height
         ENDIF
      ENDIF
      this.Visible = llNewVal
   ENDFUNC
ENDDEFINE
```

This code is rather simple. Only a couple of lines hold real functionality—the rest is cosmetic. When the add-in is executed, we first add a checkbox object to the browser window. The class for this checkbox is called *cSourceCodeActive* and is defined further down in Listing 5-1. The checkbox is graphical, so it looks like a button that can be pressed or released. Its dimensions are calculated relative to the other buttons in the browser window. This checkbox will be used later on to enable and disable the preview mode.

Once we have this checkbox, we add the editbox that will be used to show the code. The editbox is an instance of the class *cSourceCodeDisplay* that's defined in the code as well. It is read-only because it wouldn't make sense to edit the displayed code. There is some fancy coding in this editbox. The *Visible* property has an Assign method. Every time the editbox is set visible, we verify its dimensions and also have to correct the dimensions of the Details treeview to make space for the new window element. When the editbox is hidden, we adjust the size of the treeview to fill the entire right-hand panel. Whether or not the editbox is visible will be determined by the checkbox we added earlier.

Now we have to register this add-in with the Class Browser. We want this to happen every time the browser starts, so we'll register this add-in with the INIT event:

```
_oBrowser.AddIn("ShowCode","showcode.prg","INIT")
```

So now we have a checkbox and an editbox that we can toggle on and off, but we still need some code to refresh the contents of the editbox. The following code does all the work. It retrieves the source code and puts it in the editbox. It is stored in Showcode.prg:

```
LPARAMETERS loBrowser
IF Type("loBrowser.edtSourceCode.Visible") = "L"
   IF loBrowser.edtSourceCode.Visible
      loBrowser.edtSourceCode.Value = loBrowser.ExportClass()
   ENDIF
ENDIF
```

The single function of this code is to check whether the editbox is visible. If so, it retrieves some source code from the Class Browser and puts it in the editbox. The only thing that's left to do now is to register the add-in. We don't want it to fire when the browser starts—only every time the user selects a new class. The RefreshMembers() method fires at exactly the right time for our needs. So we register our second add-in like this:

```
_oBrowser.AddIn("ShowCode","showcode2.prg","REFRESHMEMBERS")
```

You might wonder how I knew about this special method. Well, it's quite simple. The browser has a property called *lAddInTrace*. If this property is set to .T., all the events and methods that could have an add-in are listed on the screen as soon as they fire. This is a great way to figure out where to put your code.

**Figure 6** shows the result: the browser with a new button in the toolbar and the editbox beneath the Details treeview.

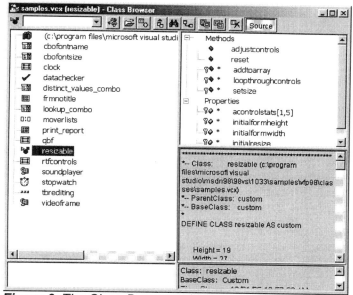

*Figure 6*. *The Class Browser with the new button in the toolbar and the source code preview panel.*

This add-in looks pretty professional already, but it still isn't of commercial quality. If the user resizes the browser window, for instance, the add-in doesn't react properly. So we'd have to create another add-in for the resize. There are a couple of little similar problems, but I'm sure with the knowledge you've gathered by now, you can figure them out for yourself (if the add-in isn't good enough for your own use).

### A sample add-in: object metrics

In Chapter 11 I'll introduce *object metrics*, a great way to measure the progress and quality of your application. The problem with object metrics is that there aren't many tools that help you to measure your application. Many metrics are based on classes, and a lot of them are somehow based on lines of code (even though the number of lines of code itself isn't very useful). The following code shows an add-in that counts the lines of code in the selected class:

```
LPARAMETERS loBrowser

IF Empty(loBrowser.cClass)
   * The user needs to select a class
   MESSAGEBOX("Please select a class first.",16,"Object Metrics")
   RETURN
ENDIF

SELECT (loBrowser.cAlias)
LOCAL lcCode, lnCounter, lcLine

* 1 = total lines, 2 = code lines, 3 = remarks, 4 = number of methods
LOCAL laLOC(4)
laLOC = 0
lcCode = Properties + Chr(13) + Methods

_MLINE = 0
laLOC(1) = MemLines(lcCode)
FOR lnCounter = 1 TO laLOC(1)
   lcLine = MLine(lcCode,1,_MLINE)

   * We check if this line has any code at all
   IF NOT Empty(lcLine) AND NOT lcLine = "ENDPROC"
      laLOC(2) = laLOC(2) + 1
   ENDIF

   * We check if this is a remark
   IF Chr(38)+Chr(38) $ lcLine OR Alltrim(lcLine) = "*"
      laLOC(3) = laLOC(3) + 1
   ENDIF

   * We check if this is a new method
   IF lcLine = "PROCEDURE"
      laLOC(4) = laLOC(4) + 1
   ENDIF
ENDFOR

* We assemble the message…
LOCAL lcMessage
lcMessage = "Lines of code in the current class:"+Chr(13)+Chr(13)
lcMessage = lcMessage + "Total lines: "+Alltrim(Str(laLOC(1)))+Chr(13)
lcMessage = lcMessage + "Lines with code: "+Alltrim(Str(laLOC(2)))+" ("+;
   Alltrim(Str((laLOC(2)/(laLOC(1)/100)))) +"%)"+Chr(13)
```

```
lcMessage = lcMessage + "Lines with comments: "+Alltrim(Str(laLOC(3)))+" ("+;
   Alltrim(Str((laLOC(3)/(laLOC(1)/100)))) +"%)"+Chr(13)+Chr(13)
lcMessage = lcMessage + "Number of methods: "+Alltrim(Str(laLOC(4)))+Chr(13)
lcMessage = lcMessage + "Average total lines per method: "+;
   Alltrim(Str(laLOC(1)/laLOC(4)))+Chr(13)
lcMessage = lcMessage + "Average lines with code per method: "+;
   Alltrim(Str(laLOC(2)/laLOC(4)))+Chr(13)
lcMessage = lcMessage + "Average lines with comments per method: "+;
   Alltrim(Str(laLOC(3)/laLOC(4)))+Chr(13)

* We display the message...
MESSAGEBOX(lcMessage,64,"Object Metrics")
```

This add-in iterates through all lines of code for each class, and counts and analyzes them according to rules described in Chapter 11. The result is a message box with the information about the actual class (see **Figure 7**). In a real-world scenario, it might also make sense to store the result in a table to have metrics for all the classes in your project. Making those changes would be trivial.

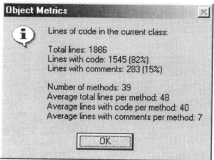

*Figure 7. The result window of the Object Metrics add-in.*

### A sample add-in: the PowerBrowser

The PowerBrowser is a public domain add-in. At the time I wrote this, it was only available for Visual FoxPro 5.0, but I plan to update it for Visual FoxPro 6.0 in the near future. By the time you read this, you should be able to download a new version from the Developer's Download Files at www.hentzenwerke.com. Future updates will be available from my Web site at www.eps-software.com.

The PowerBrowser adds a number of features to the Visual FoxPro Class Browser. Some of them have been implemented in the new version and some are still useful today. For obvious reasons I'll concentrate on the second group of features. If you still use Visual FoxPro 5.0 and you are interested in the other features, you can find full documentation at www.eps-software.com.

Almost everything the PowerBrowser does happens within the regular browser window. **Figure 8** shows the PowerBrowser window. Take note that this image shows the Visual FoxPro 5.0 Class Browser, but the PowerBrowser rearranged most of the items and added some icons, so it looks much like the new Class Browser.

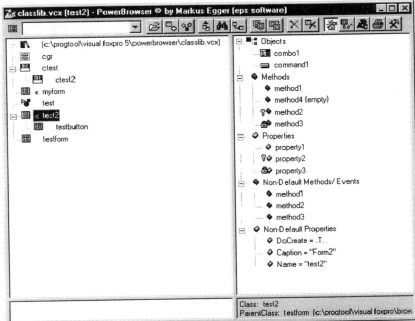

*Figure 8. The Visual FoxPro 5.0 Class Browser with the PowerBrowser add-in.*

As you can see, the PowerBrowser adds a number of new items to the toolbar. **Figure 9** highlights the new items. The details treeview also contains a couple of new nodes, like *Non-Default Methods/Events* and *Non-Default Properties*. These were added by hooking into the RefreshMembers() method. Every time the browser is refreshed, the add-in iterates through the Methods and Properties fields to find those methods and properties, as well as the property values.

Sets        Power Redefine        Different Views

*Figure 9. The Class Browser toolbar with the new items.*

The first new feature in the toolbar is the Set Manager. A set is a group of class libraries that belong together or are typically modified together. **Figure 10** shows the Set Manager dialog, which allows you to open and define sets of class libraries. In addition, the auto-open feature allows you to open all files with a certain extension in a given directory. All features have been implemented using the original File Open methods of the Class Browser. Once a set is defined, it is stored in Browser.dbf. This is a good example of alternative ways to use this resource table.

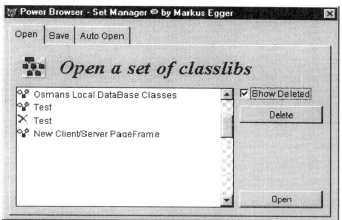

*Figure 10. The Set Manager dialog.*

The next feature is the Power Redefine, which lost some of its importance with the new Class Browser in Visual FoxPro 6.0. Nevertheless, this is a very good example of a browser add-in. First of all, the original button was moved off the screen and replaced by a Redefine button that looks basically the same as the old one, but it behaves differently. When the user clicks this button, a menu is displayed that allows the user to choose between the Power Redefine and the original Redefine. If the user selects the original one, the Click() method of the original Redefine button (now invisible) gets called. When the user selects Power Redefine, a dialog window appears, which allows the user to select a new parent class for the currently selected class. One difficulty with the cloned Redefine button is that the original one gets enabled and disabled based on certain settings and selected classes in the browser. Of course, the new button has to be enabled and disabled as well, but the browser doesn't know about the new button. Therefore, we have to deal with this issue ourselves. I accomplished this task using an active observer (see Chapter 10). This observer is a timer that fires twice each second and checks the enabled status of the original Redefine button and applies it to the new one.

Finally, there is a group of buttons that switch the browser to an entirely different mode. When the first button is clicked, the browser is in standard mode. The second button switches the browser into low-level VCX mode (see **Figure 11**), which allows you to modify the actual class library low level directly in the VCX. The third button switches the browser into source-code mode (see **Figure 12**), which allows you to modify the methods of the current class without opening the Visual Class Designer. Each method is displayed in a separate page in a pageframe. The fourth button allows you to print information about the current class (see **Figure 13**). This feature is important for documentation. Finally, there is the Tools view, which simply launches a couple of wizards that are additional tools, but not browser add-ins.

These five different views are implemented using a pageframe. The buttons in the toolbar are a graphical option group that switches to different pages. This is a very simple way to display views 2 through 5. Of course, the original items of the Class Browser cannot be moved into a page. For this reason they have to be hidden individually every time you switch to a different mode.

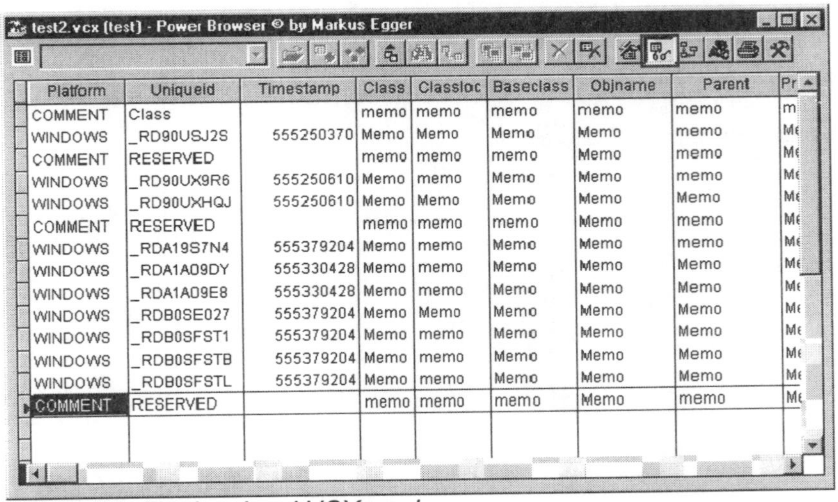

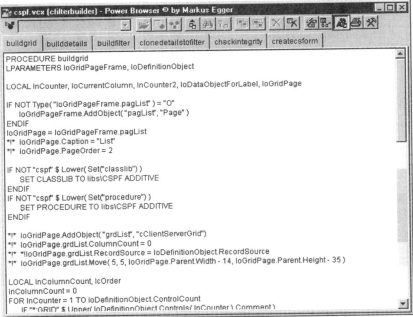

*Figure 11. The low-level VCX mode.*

*Figure 12. Editing source code in the Class Browser.*

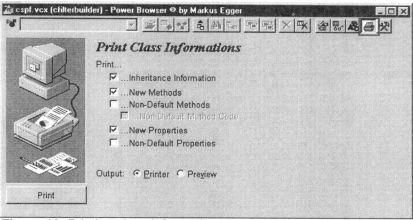

*Figure 13*. Printing class information.

# What's the deal with the VCX file?

Visual FoxPro stores all its visual classes in a file with the extension .VCX. Actually, it stores its classes in two files: The VCX and the VCT, which is a familiar combination for FoxPro programmers. Really and truly, those two files are DBF and FPT files. So you could open the VCX with a regular USE command and BROWSE through the records like so:

```
USE Base.vcx
BROWSE
```

This is useful when you want to make certain kinds of changes (like correcting typos that point 50 classes to the wrong parent class) or to fix broken VCX files (yes, it can happen). Also, there are special fields that are just there for the programmer so he can extend the VCX (see below).

## The VCX structure

The VCX structure is relatively simple. Most of the information is stored in a handful of memo fields, mostly in plain English. Some of the memo fields have binary information (like compiled code or OLE information). The VCX (visual class libraries) file structure is identical to the SCX (forms) file structure.

Later in this section, I'll describe how this structure is used in different scenarios to store classes. **Table 2** describes the basic structure and the meaning of the fields.

*Table 2*. The VCX/SCX structure.

| Field Name | Type | Description | Example |
|---|---|---|---|
| Platform | C (8) | VCX/SCX—Used to specify the platform where this object is used. In single platform VCXes, there is one record per object. In multi-platform environments (Windows and Mac, for instance), there will be one record per platform. In this case, both records that describe the same object share the same unique ID.<br><br>Records that aren't platform-specific are usually listed as "COMMENT". Also, the header record (the very first record) is marked as a "COMMENT".<br>Visual FoxPro isn't a cross-platform tool anymore (once upon a time, FoxPro was available on DOS, Windows, Macintosh and UNIX platforms, but now it is Windows only). Therefore, this field exists only for compatibility reasons. | WINDOWS |
| UniqueID | C (10) | VCX/SCX—Unique ID for classes and objects. Records that describe the same object for different platforms share the same unique ID. Records that don't describe a class or object don't have unique IDs; instead, they have special keywords that describe the record type. The header record (record number 1), for instance, has the keyword "Class".<br><br>SCX—These files have the keyword "Screen" in the header record, instead of "Class". | _QVW1055YU |
| TimeStamp | N (10) | VCX/SCX—Contains the date of creation (or last modification) of this particular record in an encoded format. Records that don't describe a class or object have TIMESTAMP=0. | 498761340 |
| Class | Memo | VCX/SCX—Defines the parent class if the current record is a class. If the current record describes a member object, this field defines the class for the object.<br><br>Note: The class name is always in lowercase. | mycommandbutton |
| ClassLoc | Memo | VCX/SCX—The relative path to the class library that contains the class referenced in the "Class" field. If the class is a Visual FoxPro base class, this field is empty. | ..\libs\test.vcx |
| BaseClass | Memo | VCX/SCX—Contains the name of the Visual FoxPro base class that is the root of the current class (or object). | commandbutton |
| ObjName | Memo | VCX/SCX—Defines the name of the current class or member object. | cmdOkButton |
| Parent | Memo | VCX/SCX—Defines the parent object of the current object. This field is used only if the current record describes a member object. Otherwise it is empty. | form1 |

*Table 2, continued*

| Field Name | Type | Description | Example |
|---|---|---|---|
| Properties | Memo | VCX/SCX—Contains a list of all overwritten and new defined properties and their values.<br><br>Note: This field is used to store the values of the properties. It is not used to define new properties. | Height = 22<br>Width = 69<br>FontSize = 8<br>Caption = "OK"<br>Name = "cmdok" |
| Protected | Memo | VCX/SCX—Contains a list of all properties and methods that are protected or hidden. If a property or method is hidden, its name is followed by a caret (^). | scAlias<br>slUpdated^<br>scCodeWord |
| Methods | Memo | VCX/SCX—Contains the source code for all methods of the current class or object. If the current record describes a subclass of a subclassed composite class that has overwritten methods for member objects (pseudo subclassing), this field might also contain code for one of the member objects of the current class. (See below for more information about pseudo subclassing and how this is stored in VCX files.)<br><br>Note: After code changes in this field, the VCX has to be recompiled. Otherwise, results are unpredictable. | PROCEDURE Click<br>this.Save()<br>thisform.Release()<br>ENDPROC<br>PROCEDURE Save<br>wait window "Save"<br>ENDPROC |
| ObjCode | Memo | VCX/SCX—Stores the compiled version of the code in the Methods field. | |
| Ole | Memo | VCX/SCX—Contains binary information about OLE and ActiveX classes and objects. | |
| Ole2 | Memo | VCX/SCX—Contains binary information about OLE and ActiveX classes and objects. | |
| Reserved1 | Memo | VCX—Used to define the beginning of a new class definition. If the current record is the beginning of a new class definition, this field contains the word "Class". Otherwise, it is empty.<br><br>SCX—Not used. | Class |
| Reserved2 | Memo | VCX/SCX—Contains the number of records that define the actual class. If the class has member objects, each member object has its own record in addition to the actual class record. The actual class record is counted as well as all the records for the member objects. So if the number is 2, this indicates a container with one member object. If the actual class doesn't have any member objects, the value of this field is 1. | 2 |
| Reserved3 | Memo | VCX—Contains a list of all new defined properties and methods as well as a short description. The description is separated from the property/method name by a space. Array properties have a leading caret (^). Methods begin with an asterisk (*).<br><br>SCX—Not used. | ScAlias<br>snResult<br>slUpdated<br>^saMyArray<br>*MyMethod |

*Table 2*, *continued*

| Field Name | Type | Description | Example |
|---|---|---|---|
| Reserved4 | Memo | VCX—The relative path and file name for a bitmap that will be displayed in the Form Controls toolbar.<br><br>SCX—Not used. | ..\bmps\ok.bmp |
| Reserved5 | Memo | VCX—The relative path and file name for a bitmap that will be displayed in the Class Browser.<br><br>SCX—Not used. | ..\bmps\ok.bmp |
| Reserved6 | Memo | VCX/SCX—Defines the scale mode (Pixels/Foxels) for the current class or object. | Pixels |
| Reserved7 | Memo | VCX/SCX—Contains the description of the current class or object. This description can be defined in the Class Information dialog, or in the Class Browser. | This class saves the current form. |
| Reserved8 | Memo | VCX/SCX—If the current record describes a class, this field contains the relative path and the file name of a header file. If the current record is a member object and NoInit is selected in the Class Information dialog, the value of this field is "NOINIT". | ..\vfp\foxpro.h NOINIT |
| User | Memo | VCX/SCX—Not used by Visual FoxPro. Available for the user/programmer to extend the VCX structure. | *:GenX |

## How Visual FoxPro stores visual classes

Now you know the basic structure of a visual class library, but this isn't quite enough to understand VCXes. Every class library has a number of records, most of which define classes; others hold additional information about the library in general.

The first record of every VCX is the so-called "header record." This record gets added as soon as class libraries (including empty ones) are created. It specifies whether the current file is a class library (VCX) or a form (SCX). If it is a class library, the UniqueID is "class"; otherwise it is "screen". In addition, the Reserved1 field contains some information about the version of the class library, but this is all relatively trivial.

Once you start to add classes to a library, it gets a bit more complex. Let's start with a subclass of the Visual FoxPro base class *Custom*. This is a simple case, because custom classes don't have member objects (at least not in the visual editor). For this reason, a single record can describe this class. Refer to Table 1 to see the values of each field. Because we created a subclass of a Visual FoxPro base class, the name of the parent class is the same as the name of the base class, and the name of the class library is empty. By the way, this information is always stored in lowercase. The only other detail worth explaining is the Reserved2 field, which contains the number of records that describe the class. In this case it would be 1. This seems obvious, but a lot of people get confused for a couple of reasons. First of all, everybody seems to think that the Reserved2 field contains the number of records describing member objects. This is incorrect. The actual class record itself gets counted as well. The second reason for the confusion is a comment record that gets added after the class definition. A lot of people seem to think that this record should be counted as well, and therefore, the number in Reserved2 should be 2. This is incorrect, too, because the comment record is optional. If you created a low-level visual class by directly hacking the VCX, you wouldn't have to worry about the comment record. But the first time this class was modified using the Visual Class Designer, Visual FoxPro would add this record automatically.

Let's have a look at a composite class. As an example, we'll use a form class that has an OK button as a member object. Two records can describe this construction: one for the form class and the other for the member object (the button). Still, this construction is very simple. All properties and methods belonging to the form will be stored in the first record, and all the ones belonging to the button will go in the second record. Some information will be defined in the first record only, like the scalemode (pixels or foxels) because they are valid for the whole class. However, don't confuse this information the *ScaleMode* property.

Let's take a closer look at the Methods memo. As mentioned before, this field holds the source code for all methods we create. To allow FoxPro to differentiate between different snippets, a simple solution is applied: Every method gets an additional PROCEDURE and ENDPROC line, as in the following example:

```
PROCEDURE Click
wait window "Test"
ENDPROC
PROCEDURE Destroy
wait window "Destroy"
ENDPROC
```

When you modify this code in the Visual Class Designer, Visual FoxPro does not show those two lines. The example above only has two lines of code in the Visual Class Designer.

The properties are stored in an even simpler fashion—one line per property. Here are the contents of the form record:

```
DoCreate = .T.
Caption = "Form2"
Name = "test"
```

And here we have the contents of the member object's (the button's) Property field:

```
Top = 84
Left = 120
Height = 23
Width = 70
Caption = "\<OK"
Name = "cmdOK"
```

All properties start with capital letters because they are internal properties defined by the base class. As soon as you use user-defined properties, they will be in lowercase to make it easy to differentiate.

Once we subclass our composite class, it gets a little more complex. A single record can describe the new class, even though it has the button as a member object. The definition of the member object is inherited from the parent class. This, of course, introduces some difficulties when changing properties or adding source code (pseudo subclassing), since we don't have a record in which to store these properties. The only alternative is to store this information with the container record. In this case, we have to identify the object the property or method belongs to.

The Method field from above would look like this in a subclass:

```
PROCEDURE Command1.Click
wait window "Click"
ENDPROC
PROCEDURE Command1.Destroy
wait window "Destroy"
ENDPROC
```

The same is true for the properties. Here is the Properties field of the container record:

```
DoCreate = .T.
Name = "test2"
Command1.Name = "Command1"
```

I should mention some exceptions and special cases, which are all related to special types of container classes and objects. PageFrames are a perfect example. Even though a PageFrame is a combination of multiple objects (the PageFrame itself as well as each Page), it is stored as one record in the VCX. FoxPro simply knows the number of page objects because the PageFrame has a *PageCount* property. This has a couple of disadvantages—one is that Visual FoxPro always uses the Page base class to add new pages. Special page classes can only be added manually outside the Visual Class Editor. The same is true for other containers, such as CommandGroups and OptionGroups.

You could explore the previous example even further by adding subclasses and additional member objects, but you wouldn't be learning anything new. The class definitions would grow larger and more complex, but they would still follow the rules discussed above.

Knowing about the VCX file is important for various reasons. This is true for all programmers, not only for third-party tool providers and other people who might be interested in writing Class Browser add-ins. Class libraries can be damaged due to various reasons— when this happens, you can lose months of work. But often a library can be fixed easily if you know about the VCX structure. It often happens that there is a problem when saving a class— the old copy of the class might already be deleted but the new version is not yet saved. It appears that the class simply disappeared, but it is still there, marked as deleted. If you know about the VCX structure you can simply open the library and recover at least an old version of your class.

Sometimes you might want to do a large number of similar tasks in your class libraries. Let's say you discover that you used the wrong parent class for a whole set of classes. Redefining every single one of them in the Class Browser can be cumbersome. It is a lot easier to open the VCX and change one or two fields in all influenced records, using a REPLACE ALL command with a FOR condition.

## Compiling a class library

When you modify code and close a code snippet of a visual class, Visual FoxPro compiles that code right away and stores it in the ObjCode field of the VCX, while the source code gets stored in the Methods field. Those two fields need to be synchronized at all times. When you modify the Methods field directly, opening the VCX like a DBF, you need to make sure that those changes get compiled. Otherwise you will find the funniest results when modifying the class the next time, such as code from other snippets appearing in wrong methods, or old code reappearing and the like. To compile the changes, use the COMPILE CLASSLIB command, like so:

```
COMPILE CLASSLIB MyClassLib.vcx
```

This works fine when you have full control over the library, but you need to be careful if you manipulate the source code using a Class Browser add-in. Compiling the class usually isn't possible because the browser is using the file. For this reason you need to close the library, compile it, and reopen it.

## Cleaning up class libraries

It is essential to clean up your class libraries. They tend to grow huge, even though their real contents might be tiny. This is due to the fact that every time you modify a class, Visual FoxPro marks the old records in the VCX as deleted and adds new records at the bottom.

Cleaning up a class library is simple. You can open the VCX exclusively and do a simple PACK. This works well in most scenarios. However, I recommend using the Cleanup feature of the Class Browser (see above).

## How to protect your source code in a VCX

The source code for all methods of a class is stored in the Methods field of the VCX. When this code is modified, Visual FoxPro compiles it right away and stores the compiled version in the Objcode field. This is the only version of the code that Visual FoxPro needs to instantiate the class and execute its methods. So when you want to give away a VCX library without giving away your source code, you can simply delete the contents of the Methods field, but make sure you do this on a copy of the original library. Otherwise you won't be able to modify the classes in this library anymore.

# The Component Gallery

The Component Gallery is a new tool in Visual FoxPro 6.0. It's a companion of the Class Browser. Both share the same display surface (see **Figure 14**) and you can toggle between the two. The Component Gallery is a very powerful shortcut and hyperlink manager. I like to think of it as my "mission control center for application development." In the past we had many different tools that helped to manage the different kinds of events that occurred when creating an application. The most generic was the Project Manager. It can handle all kinds of items and bind them together in one application, but it has a number of limitations. First of all, the Project Manager can handle only a handful of items properly—classes, forms, programs, menus, and the like. The Project Manager ties specific behavior to all these items. Unfortunately, in modern projects there are a number of items the Project Manager is not aware of—items like multimedia files, HTML documents, Office documents, ActiveX controls, and others. Of course you could enhance the Project Manager to handle these items as well, but this is not the point. The point is that the list of component types that make up a project is constantly growing. A tool as static as the Project Manager simply isn't flexible enough.

The second big limitation of the Project Manager is that it (obviously) handles a single project at a time. This is fine because that's the Project Manager's purpose. But the world is not that simple. Usually you have to deal with more than one project during your programming career, and ideally (this is one of the main ideas behind object-oriented programming) you can reuse components across projects. For this reason, you need a tool that is not "production oriented," not "results oriented" like the Project Manager (its whole functionality is targeted to build the final result, which is an EXE). A production-oriented tool helps to manage all components in the typical way a programmer uses them every day, rather than focusing on compiling them into the final product.

When creating applications, you must accomplish many more tasks than just modifying classes and source code and compiling an application. Among them are component installation, invoking wizards and builders, reading documentation, searching the Internet, creating documentation, and more. Until now, the only tool FoxPro offered to accomplish these tasks was the System menu, which was not very flexible. Imagine the following situation: You buy a framework from a third party. You install the framework on your system and you begin to explore what you've just purchased. To do so you can either read the manuals (which, as we know, is something no programmer does), or you can explore the contents of your hard drive using the Windows Explorer, the Visual FoxPro Class Browser or similar tools. The framework might even have a menu that can be installed, or a startup program that provides a simple interface to the most important features. This interface might be a dialog that allows you to start an Application Wizard or open existing projects. You might even get an overview of the provided classes and libraries if you want to reuse only certain components.

In any case, this kind of approach is cumbersome unless the provider of your framework spent a tremendous amount of time creating the interface. The Component Gallery offers a better way to accomplish these tasks. The provider of the framework could simply create a Component Gallery catalog (which is basically a library of links) that contains all of this functionality. The catalog could have a Start node that contains links to the most important tools and features, as well as some documentation (like "Getting Started"). The user could double-click those items to start wizards and other tools, and the contents of the node could be dynamic to provide links to the most recently used projects. In other nodes of the catalog, there might be links to all components, in case they should be reused as single components rather than as a framework. The programmer could then simply drag and drop those components into the Visual Class Designer or the Project Manager. Often, reusing a component is not as easy as dragging and dropping the item. Other components might be required, so they also would have to be added to the container object. In this case, instantiating the class wouldn't be enough.

Without the Component Gallery, the programmer would run into an error, have to read the documentation, and a couple of hours later he might be able to make the construction work. With the Component Gallery, the catalog provider can simply associate additional actions to the drag-and-drop operation to make sure all preconditions are satisfied. This could mean that other objects are added, or that some documentation is displayed to tell the programmer what to do if the task cannot be automated. One example is a component I wrote a little while ago. It uses the Microsoft Agent ActiveX control to provide Office Assistant-like help in Visual FoxPro applications. My component is a simple wrapper that makes it easy to handle the Microsoft Agent Server. Of course, the Microsoft Agent control has to be installed on the system for the wrapper to work. Using the Component Gallery, a message could be displayed if the control is not installed on the system, telling the user that he has to install this control. In addition, this message has a hyperlink to Microsoft's Web site, so people can go there and download the necessary software.

Speaking of setup, a Component Gallery catalog could also have a node containing all necessary installation items, as well as those for a clean uninstall.

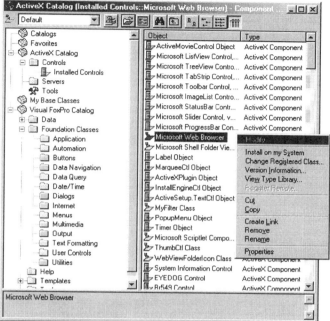

***Figure 14****. The Component Gallery.*

## Basic functionality

The Component Gallery looks much like the Windows Explorer. It has a treeview panel on the left-hand side that displays all catalogs with their nodes. On the right, there is a panel of shortcuts and hyperlinks for the selected node. At the bottom, a description for each item is displayed. At the top of the window, there is a toolbar just like in the Class Browser. **Figure 15** explains the items of the toolbar.

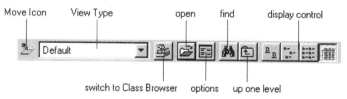

***Figure 15****. The Component Gallery toolbar.*

Just as in the Class Browser, the Move icon can be used to drag and drop items to the screen, a design surface or the Project Manager. You can also right-click it to change the icon. The View Type combobox allows users to switch to different views. (See below for more information about Component Gallery views.) The Open button leads you to an unconventional Open dialog, which is similar to the Open dialog of Internet Explorer, rather than the regular Windows Open dialog (see **Figure 16**). It has a drop-down combobox with a list of all registered catalogs. If you want to register a new catalog you can simply click the Browse button, select a file, select "Add catalog to current default view" and click the Open button. You can also right-click the Open button of the Component Gallery to get a list of recently used catalogs.

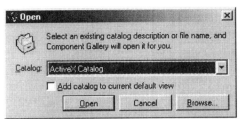

*Figure 16*. The Open dialog of the Component Gallery.

The Options dialog has three tabs. The options on the Standard tab (see **Figure 17**) are self-explanatory. The only item that might be confusing is "Advanced editing enabled." If you select this check box, the Component Gallery's Options and Properties dialogs will contain advanced features.

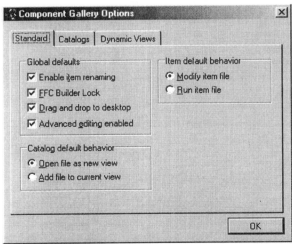

*Figure 17*. The Standard tab of the Component Gallery Options dialog.

The Catalogs tab allows you to define the list of catalogs (see **Figure 18**), which is displayed in the Open dialog. Each catalog can be defined as global and/or default. Global catalogs are always open, no matter what other catalogs are currently opened. This is handy for a catalog containing your most standard components, and also for special catalogs such as Favorites, which ships with Visual FoxPro 6.0. Default catalogs are opened initially when the Component Gallery is started. Unlike global catalogs, these catalogs will be closed when others are opened.

For some reason, neither default nor global catalogs are opened when you switch from the Class Browser into Component Gallery mode. I personally don't like this behavior, but I'm told it is by design.

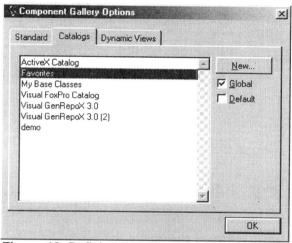

*Figure 18. Defining and managing catalogs in the Options dialog.*

The Dynamic Views tab shows a list of all custom views (see **Figure 19**). From here, you can create, modify and delete custom dynamic views.

Finally, the Component Gallery's Find button provides a powerful interface for locating certain components. Surprisingly, the Component Gallery uses dynamic views to search. The results are stored as dynamic views, and the search criteria can be reused and modified.

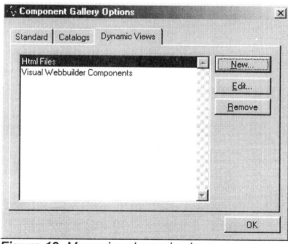

*Figure 19. Managing dynamic views.*

## Creating dynamic views

Dynamic views limit the number of items displayed in the Component Gallery, based on certain search criteria that are evaluated every time you apply a view. You define dynamic views either through the Options dialog or through the Find feature of the Component Gallery. **Figure 20** shows the dialog used to define dynamic views.

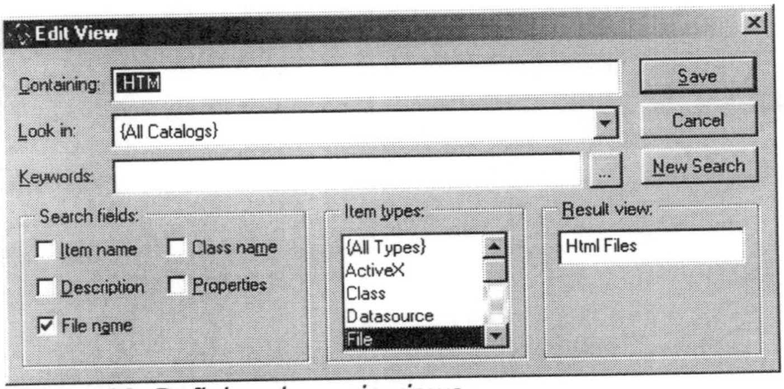

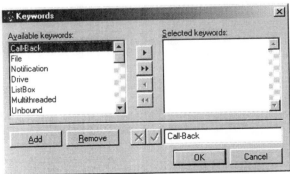

*Figure 20. Defining dynamic views.*

Figure 20 shows a dynamic view that displays only the files with HTM extensions. You can also specify multiple search strings separated by commas. I specified that all catalogs should be included. Because I checked only for certain file extensions, I limited the search fields to the file name; I could have selected additional items, but this would slow down the process. Also, because I want to see only files, I limit the search to items of the type *File*. The result view is called *Html Files*.

The beauty of dynamic views is that I can now add many HTML files to any catalog, and they will show up in this dynamic view because the specified criteria are constantly reevaluated.

You can also search for certain keywords using the keyword entry field. Each Component Gallery item can have specific keywords assigned. The Component Gallery features a special keyword-selection dialog (see **Figure 21**), which guarantees that you can find existing keywords quickly and easily. You can also add new keywords to the predefined list.

*Figure 21. Selecting and managing keywords.*

## Working with existing catalogs

Catalogs can be used in a number of different ways, depending on what the creator of the catalog wants to implement. Therefore, it is hard to come up with a generic explanation of how to use these catalogs. Nevertheless, most catalogs (and their items) share common features. Typically, all actions associated with catalog items can be accessed through the items' right-click menus. Double-clicking the items also triggers one of those actions (usually the first one in the list). In addition, you can move items via dragging and dropping, in order to add them to projects, forms and container classes. To do so, either use the Move icon (in the top-left corner of the Component Gallery) or drag the item in the listview. In the latter case, OLE Drag and Drop is utilized. The Visual FoxPro online documentation contains a list of all drag-and-drop actions associated with the default items.

## Creating catalogs

 To fully understand the power of the Component Gallery, you have to create a catalog by yourself. I'll guide you through this process step by step. As an example, I'll use Visual GenRepoX, a public-domain tool I wrote to extend the functionality of the Visual FoxPro report writer. This tool is included with the Developer's Download Files at www.hentzenwerke.com, and future updates will be available from my Web site, www.eps-software.com. One problem with GenRepoX is that it has no real interface because everything happens programmatically. For this reason, many people have trouble getting started. The Component Gallery can help guide you through the tool. Not only is this an easy way for GenRepoX newcomers to learn, but it also allows experts to explore the whole GenRepoX functionality.

The first step is to create a new catalog file. Simply open the Component Gallery's Options dialog, click the Catalogs tab (page 2) and click New. Next, specify a file name (catalogs are regular DBF files), and *voila* . . . you're done.

The new catalog's name is the file name you specified. Typically you'll want to specify a descriptive and informative name. You can change the name by renaming the catalog item or modifying the item's properties (see **Figure 22**).

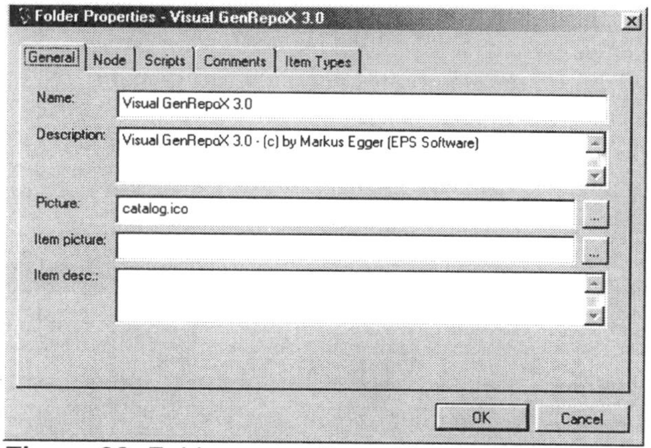

*Figure 22. Folder properties of the topmost node of the new catalog.*

The variety of options in each property sheet is discussed below. For now, we are only interested in changing some options in the General tab. Here we can change the name, the description and the picture for the catalog. Note that the caption of the dialog is "Folder Properties", even though we are looking at the catalog properties. I'm told this is by design. However, note that this property dialog is essentially different from the property dialogs of the subfolders.

The next step is to create a couple of folders in the catalog. I would like to have folders for the *Classes and Programs* belonging to Visual GenRepoX, a folder for *Documentation*, another for *Samples*, yet another for the *GenRepoX Wizards*, and finally a folder that allows the user to browse the Web (*EPS on the Web*). To create a new folder, right-click the Details panel, select New Item, and then select Folder (see **Figure 23**). All folders listed above are relatively simple to create. You only have to change their captions, descriptions and icons.

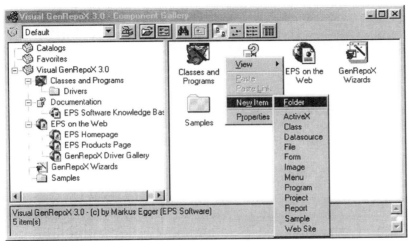

*Figure 23. Creating a new folder.*

Now let's add some items to the folders, starting with Classes and Programs. **Figure 24** shows the desired contents of this folder. Basically, this is a summary view of the most important Visual GenRepoX components, which are GenRepoX.prg, an object wrapper for regular Visual FoxPro reports, a subclass of this report wrapper that contains all GenRepoX functionality, and a driver base class, which can be subclassed to create new drivers. There is another folder for existing drivers. Creating these items is straightforward. Right-click in the Details panel and select the kind of item you want to create.

This first folder already demonstrates some of the strengths of the Component Gallery. The created folder provides an overview of the most important Visual GenRepoX components. Without the Component Gallery, you'd have to search through the Visual GenRepoX class library where you'd find a dozen classes, two-thirds of which cannot be used or modified by the user. Then you'd have to find the GenRepoX.prg, which is somewhere on the hard drive. Finally, there are several class libraries with various drivers. Using the Component Gallery is a lot easier. The created catalog shows only the important items, and all of them are in one place.

But not only does the Component Gallery show all those items, it also allows you to work with them. The gallery is aware of the different kinds of items it shows, and automatically provides appropriate actions for those items when the user double-clicks or right-clicks on the item. If you go back to Figure 23, you'll see a list of items the Component Gallery is aware of. You can extend this list with your own items if you're missing one. I'll demonstrate this later, using the example of a special GenRepoX report.

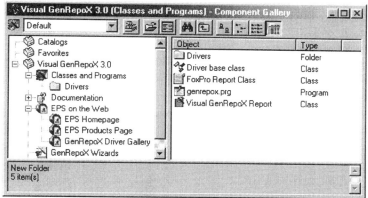

*Figure 24. The contents of the Classes and Programs folder.*

### Dynamic folders

So far you've created only simple folders by adding items manually, but the Component Gallery also allows special kinds of folders, called *dynamic folders*. These folders can be direct links to a directory on the hard drive (see **Figure 25**), or even to a location on the Internet (see **Figure 26**).

When using dynamic folders to point to a directory on the hard drive, Windows Explorer is utilized to display the contents of the folder inside the Component Gallery.

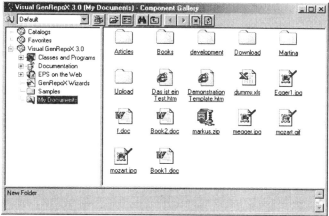

*Figure 25. A dynamic folder pointing to C:\My Documents.*

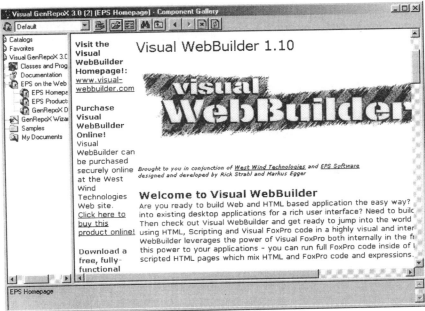

***Figure 26.*** *A dynamic folder pointing to the Internet.*

To create a dynamic folder, you simply set the *Dynamic Folder* property in the Node tab of the folder's Properties dialog (see **Figure 27**). You can specify an Internet address (such as http://www.eps-software.com) or a directory on your hard drive (such as C:\My Documents).

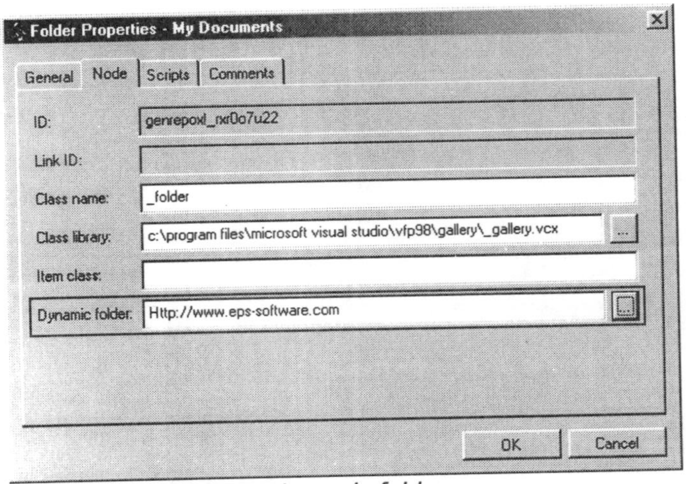

***Figure 27.*** *Creating a dynamic folder.*

Now you also know how I created the links to the EPS Web page. I simply created dynamic folders that show the contents of my Web site. There is another way to do this: Instead of a dynamic folder, you could create a Web item. The difference is that dynamic folders are displayed in the Component Gallery, while Web items open an instance of Internet Explorer to display the desired Web page.

## Creating links

Typically, a catalog shows the same item in more than one node. An example would be the Checkbox driver in the Visual GenRepoX catalog. (This example ships with Visual GenRepoX 3.0 in the Samples folder.) This is a useful driver, so it should also be in the Drivers folder. Creating the item twice wouldn't be a good solution because this would make the catalog hard to maintain. The better way is to create a link. To do this, first create the item for the Checkbox driver in the Drivers folder. Then right-click the item and select Create Link. The link is created in the current folder and looks just like the original item. The only hint that the item is a link is its name. Also, when you look in the Properties dialog of this new item (the linked one), all properties but the name are read-only.

You can now drag and drop the link into any folder you want.

## Understanding item types

The strength of the Component Gallery is its flexibility, which is based on the great variety of different items the gallery can handle. The default list of items already handles the most important item types. However, you might want to introduce your own items. A good example is the Visual GenRepoX catalog created above. Even though Visual GenRepoX reports are regular FoxPro reports, they have to be executed slightly differently in order to allow GenRepoX to handle things differently and to extend the report writer's functionality. For this reason, you have to create a special item type that has the ability to execute those special reports. Later I'll explain how to do that, but before you can create our own items, you should understand how the Component Gallery handles item types.

### How item types are handled

For every item displayed in the listview or treeview panel of the Component Gallery, the gallery internally instantiates another object representing the item's behavior. This object is responsible for managing the user interaction and for triggering and executing possible actions. For each item type, the Component Gallery uses a different class. These classes are stored in Vfpglry.vcx, located in the *Home()* + '\gallery' directory. The source code for these classes, as well as the source code for a generic item class (which is the parent class of all other items), ship with Visual FoxPro. You can modify these items, or better yet, subclass them to provide your own functionality.

When you add an item to a catalog, you first select the item type, which also predefines the class the gallery is supposed to use. You can change this setting in the Node tab of the item's properties (see **Figure 28**). This way you could set up another item type that the gallery supports but that isn't exposed through the standard interface (see below), or you could invoke your own classes if you want different or new behavior (see below).

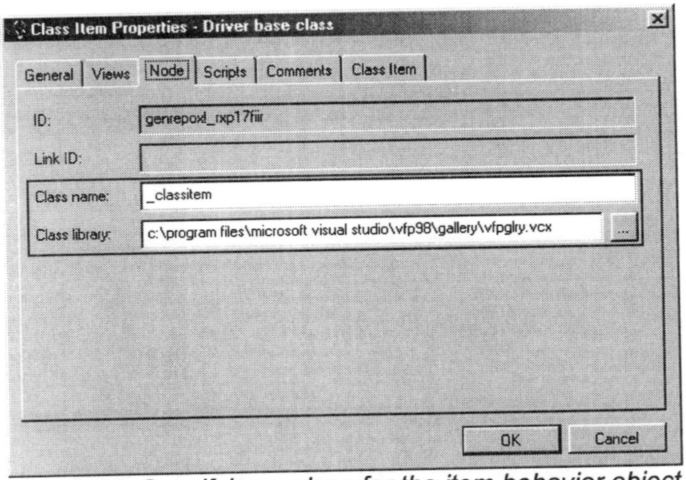

*Figure 28. Specifying a class for the item behavior object.*

When you double-click, right-click or drag and drop an item, the call is passed on to the underlying behavior object, which then decides what to do. This includes standard behavior like modifying or executing an item, as well as defining the right-click menu and executing complex tasks such as invoking wizards and the like. Many standard items share behavior that is coded in a shared behavioral object. You can call this object rather than executing actions directly in each individual object. You can also reference and use this object in your own behavioral objects (see below).

### Standard items

The Component Gallery supports a number of standard items, only a handful of which are exposed through the interface. **Table 3** lists all items stored in the Vfpglry.vcx and the _gallery.vcx class libraries. You can use these items in different ways: You can specify the class name in the Properties dialog of each item (Figure 28), you can add new item types to the standard interface (see below), and you can subclass the existing items to create new behavior.

*Table 3. Standard items that ship with Visual FoxPro 6.0.*

| Item class | Class library | Parent class | Description |
|---|---|---|---|
| _activexfolder | Vfpglry.vcx | _folder | Used for folders only. A folder based on this item type automatically displays all ActiveX controls installed on the system. |
| _activexitem | Vfpglry.vcx | _item | Used for ActiveX items, including ActiveX controls (OCX) as well as other COM servers (EXE/DLL). |
| _catalogitem | Vfpglry.vcx | _item | Allows you to link to other catalogs. |
| _classitem | Vfpglry.vcx | _item | Used for every Visual FoxPro class item. The class can be stored in a VCX or a PRG. |
| _dataitem | Vfpglry.vcx | _item | Used for any Visual FoxPro data source, including database containers (DBC), tables (DBF), and all kinds of views. |

*Table 3, continued*

| _fileitem | Vfpglry.vcx | _item | Every file can be managed through the Component Gallery using this item type. The Component Gallery reads the registry for more information about each particular item type and how to handle it. |
|---|---|---|---|
| _folder | _gallery.vcx | _item | A generic folder item. Subclass this class when you want to create your own folder class. |
| _formitem | Vfpglry.vcx | _item | Handles Visual FoxPro forms (SCX). |
| _imageitem | Vfpglry.vcx | _fileitem | A special kind of file item that handles all kinds of image files. |
| _item | _gallery.vcx | _item | All other item classes are subclassed from this class. Use this class as a parent class when you want to create your own item behavior classes. |
| _menuitem | Vfpglry.vcx | _item | Manages Visual FoxPro menus (MNX). |
| _node | _gallery.vcx | _item | Generic class used as a base for all kinds of items and folders. |
| _programitem | Vfpglry.vcx | _item | Handles all kinds of Visual FoxPro program files such as PRGs and header files (H). |
| _projectitem | Vfpglry.vcx | _item | Used to manage Visual FoxPro projects. |
| _reportitem | Vfpglry.vcx | _item | Used to manage Visual FoxPro labels (LBX) and reports (FRX). |
| _sampleitem | Vfpglry.vcx | _item | Can be used to run executable Visual FoxPro files such as EXEs, APPs, FXPs, PRGs, SCXs, FRXs and more. |
| _shareditem | Vfpglry.vcx | _item | Has some generic behavior that is called from various other items. |
| _sounditem | Vfpglry.vcx | _fileitem | A special kind of file item that handles sound files in WAV or RMI format. |
| _templateitem | Vfpglry.vcx | _item | Used to execute wizards. |
| _urlitem | Vfpglry.vcx | _item | Handles the navigation to all kinds of Web addresses that Internet Explorer can handle. This includes Web sites, HTML documents, Visual FoxPro active documents, Active Server Pages and more. The URL can be on the World Wide Web as well an on an intranet environment and even on your local hard drive. The URL also can be a directory name. In this case the result is a Windows Explorer-like view. |
| _videoitem | Vfpglry.vcx | _fileitem | A special kind of file item that handles video clips in AVI format. |

It is important to understand three basic item classes, which are *_node*, *_item*, and *_folder*. The *_node* class is the most basic and defines the common behavior of all kinds of items, whether items or folders. The *_item* class is a subclass of *_node*, and the *_folder* class is a subclass of *_item*. **Tables 4** and **5** explain the *_node* class.

*Table 4. Properties of the _node class.*

| Property | Description |
|---|---|
| _cVersion | Contains some version information. |
| AItemIndexes[x] | If the item is a folder, this array contains the indexes of all sub-items. There is a collection of items in the gallery. You can use the indexes in this array to reference all the active items. |
| Builder | Used at design time only. It can define builders and extended builders (BuilderD) to be used with this item. |
| BuilderX | Used at design time only. It can define builders and extended builders (BuilderD) to be used with this item. |
| cAlias | Alias of the catalog cursor for an item or folder. |
| cCatalog | The file name of the current catalog. |
| cCatalogpath | Full path of the current catalog. |
| cClass | Default class used for all sub-items. |
| cClasslib | Class library that contains the definition of the current class. |
| cClassname | Class used for the current item. |
| cClick | Allows you to define an alternative method that handles the Click event. To redirect the call to a Test() method, set this property to oTHIS.Test(). |
| cComment | Comment as stored in the catalog. |
| cDblclick | Allows you to define an alternative method that handles the double-click event. |
| cDesc | Item description. |
| cDragdrop | Allows you to define an alternative method that handles the DragDrop event. |
| cDragdrop2 | Allows to define an alternative method that handles the Drop event of the class icon onto some target object. |
| cFilename | Name of the currently referenced file. |
| cFolderpicture | Bitmap or icon used for the current folder (if the item is a folder). |
| cId | Unique ID that identifies the catalog and the item. |
| cId2 | Catalog ID. |
| cItemclass | Class used for the behavior object. |
| cItemclasslibrary | Class library containing the class for the behavior object. |
| cItemtpdesc | Alternative item types for certain files (redirect). |
| cItemtype | Display name of the current item type. |
| cKeypress | Allows you to define an alternative method to handle the KeyPress event. |
| cKeywords | Keywords that identify the current item. |
| cLink | Optional ID that links the current item to another item. |
| cObjecttype | Item type. |
| cOledragdrop | Allows you to define an alternative method to handle the OLEDragDrop event. |
| cOledragover | Allows you to define an alternative method to handle the OLEDragOver event. |
| cParent | String that describes the parent object (folder). |
| cPicture | Item image (icon or bitmap). |
| cProperties | Property settings specified in the scripts. |
| cRightclick | Allows you to define an alternative method to handle the right-click event. |
| cScript | Script source of the current item. |
| cScriptmethod | Internal. |
| cSourcealias | Alias of the table that defines the current item. |

**Table 4**, *continued*

| Property | Description |
|---|---|
| cSourcecatalog | File name and path of the current catalog. |
| cSourcecatalogpath | Path of the current catalog. |
| cStatusbartext | Text displayed in the status bar. |
| cTarget | Internal. |
| cText | Item text. |
| cTooltiptext | The item's tooltip text. |
| cType | Specifies whether the current node is an item or a folder. |
| cTypedesc | Specifies the type description text for all child items/folders of a folder. |
| cUser | Specifies the user text for an item/folder (unused by the gallery). |
| cViews | Specifies the views list for an item/folder. |
| enabled | Indicates whether the item is enabled (.T./.F.). |
| lCatalog | Indicates whether the current item is a catalog. |
| lDeleted | Indicates whether the current item has been deleted. |
| lDynamic | Indicates whether the current item is a dynamic folder. |
| lFolder | Indicates whether the current item is a folder. |
| lFolderitem | Indicates whether the current item is a folder item. |
| lFullpath | Specifies if various file name properties for an item/folder are automatically full pathed. |
| lGetfileaddress | Specifies if the file name is a file addresss. |
| lObject | Specifies if the current item is type OBJECT. |
| lRelease | Specifies that the item's Release method has been executed. |
| lRuncodemode | Specifies that the item is currently in the RunCode() method mode. |
| lScriptmode | Specifies that the item is currently in the RunScript() method mode. |
| lView | Specifies that the item is type VIEW. |
| nIndex | Index of this item. |
| nItemcount | Number of sub-items. |
| nItemindex | Specifies the item index of the item in the TreeView/ListView object. |
| nNodeindex | Specifies the node index of the item in the TreeView/ListView object. |
| nRecno | Absolute record number in the current catalog table. |
| nSourcerecno | Internally assigned record n umber (stored as regular data in the catalog table). |
| oAction | Reference to an object that is delegated to for all actions such as Click, DblClick, etc.  You can hook a custom object that has these methods to oAction of an item, and the events for that item will be delegated to the oAction object. |
| oControl | Specifies the TreeView or ListView parent object of the item node object. |
| oFolder | Reference to the folder this item belongs to. |
| oHost | Reference to the Component Gallery. |
| oLink | If the object is a link, this is a reference to the real item. |
| oNode | Reference to the TreeView or ListView node object for the item. |
| oObject | Object reference to a VFP object used for objects of type OBJECT. |
| oParent | Reference to the parent object (parent folder). |
| oRecord | Specifies the SCATTER NAME object from the catalog cursor table record for the item. |

**Table 4**, *continued*

| Property | Description |
|---|---|
| oShortcutmenu | Reference to the shortcut menu definition. |
| oSource | Specifies an object source reference during a drag-and-drop operation. |
| oTarget | Specifies an object target reference during a drag-and-drop operation. |
| tUpdated | Date and time when the item was last updated. |
| visible | Specifies whether the current item is visible. |
| vResult | Used internally by the gallery for returning variant return values from method calls. |

**Table 5**. *Methods of the* _node *class.*

| Method | Parameters | Description |
|---|---|---|
| Click | | Method that handles click events. |
| DblClick | | Method that handles double-click events. |
| DragDrop | oSource, nXCoord, nYCoord | Method that handles drag-and-drop events. |
| DragDrop2 | oSource, nXCoord, nYCoord | Method that handles the target drop event from dragging the class icon to a target. |
| FullPath | tcFileName, lcNewFileName | Returns a full path of a file name relative to the item's catalog folder location. |
| GetFile | tcFileExt, tlAutoExtDialog | Returns a file name from a user dialog. |
| GetFileAddress | TlNoShellExecute, tcFileExt | Returns a URL from a user dialog. |
| InitProperties | | Internal. |
| KeyPress | nKeyCode, nShiftAltCtrl | Method that handles keypress events. |
| NewInstance | | Returns a new instance of an object based on the same class of the object (new _Item, new _Folder). |
| Properties | | Can be called to programmatically display the property sheet. |
| ReadProperties | | Reads the properties from the catalog Properties memo field into the *cProperties* property and sets the relative properties. |
| Refresh | | Handles refresh events. |
| RefreshFolderPicture | | Refreshes the folder image. |
| RefreshPicture | | Refreshes the item's image. |
| Release | | Handles release events. |
| ReleaseObjects | | Releases all object references for a node object. |
| Remove | tlConfirm, tlNoRefresh | Handles remove events. |
| RightClick | | Handles right-click events. |
| RunCode | TcCode | Executes a code snippet. |
| RunScript | TvItem | Executes a Visual FoxPro script. |
| ScriptHook | TcProgram | Specifies a script hook program to be specified when running a script. |
| SetProperties | TcProperties | Sets properties specified in the *cProperties* property to their associated values. |
| WriteProperties | TlUpdateSource, tlAutoAdd | Writes the various item properties to the catalog Properties memo field. |

Beyond the basic functionality the _node_ class provides, the _item_ class has some specialized behavior for all kinds of items (including folders). You should subclass this class rather than the _node_ class if you want to create a new item type. **Tables 6** and **7** explain this class.

**Table 6.** Properties of the _item_ class.

| Property | Description |
|---|---|
| cFormclasslibrary | Specifies the form class library. |
| cItemtypedesc | Specifies the item type description. |
| cMethod | Specifies the method to edit when opening the Class Designer for a class item. |
| cRightclickmenu | Specifies a program to run for the right-click menu event. |
| lAutosetmenu | Specifies that the code in SetMenu is automatically used to initialize the right-click shortcut menu for an item. |
| lDefaultmenu | Specifies whether default menu items such as Cut, Copy and Paste should be displayed. |
| lModify | Specifies whether the current item can be modified from within the Component Gallery. |
| lNewmenu | Specifies whether the default menu has a "New" item. |
| lPastemenus | Specifies whether the default menu has a "Paste" item. |
| lPropertiesmenu | Specifies whether the default menu has a "Properties" item. |
| lRightclickmenu | Specifies whether the current item has a shortcut menu. |
| lWebview | Specifies whether the current item requires Internet Explorer to display some dynamic content. If this is the case, the Component Gallery changes significantly. The standard toolbar buttons are replaced by typical browser buttons such as Refresh, Stop Loading, and Back. |

**Table 7.** Methods of the _item_ class.

| Method | Parameters | Description |
|---|---|---|
| About | | Displays an about dialog for an item (optional). |
| AddDefaultMenu | ToObject | Adds a default shortcut menu to the current item. |
| AddMenuBar | tcPrompt, tcOnSelection, tcClauses, tnElementNumber, tlMark, tlDisabled, tlBold | Adds a menu bar to an existing shortcut menu. |
| AddMenuSeparator | TnElementNumber | Adds a menu separator to the existing shortcut menu. |
| AddPasteMenus | toObject, toMenuObject | Adds Paste menu items to the current shortcut menu. |
| AddPropertiesMenu | toObject, toMenuObject | Adds the Properties item to the current shortcut menu. |
| AfterLabelEdit | cancel, newstring | Fires when the user finishes editing a label. |
| ClearMenu | | Deletes the current menu definition. |
| Copy | | Copies the current object. |
| CreateLink | | Creates a link to the current object. |
| Cut | | Cuts the current object. |
| Disable | | Disables the current object. |

*Table 7, continued*

| Method | Parameters | Description |
|---|---|---|
| Enable | | Enables the current object. |
| Help | | Activates the help for the current object. |
| Hide | | Hides the current object. |
| Modify | | Starts the appropriate editor for the current item if the item can be modified. |
| NewMenu | | Creates a new shortcut menu. |
| OLECompleteDrag | oControl, nEffect | Handles the OLECompleteDrag event. |
| OLEDragDrop | oControl, oDataObject, nEffect, nButton, nShift, nXCoord, nYCoord | Handles the OLEDragDrop event. |
| OLEDragOver | oControl, oDataObject, nEffect, nButton, nShift, nXCoord, nYCoord, nState | Handles the OLEDragOver event. |
| OLEGiveFeedBack | oControl, nEffect, defaultcursors | Handles the OLEGiveFeedBack event. |
| OLESetData | oControl, oDataObject, eFormat | Handles the OLESetData event. |
| OLEStartDrag | oControl, oDataObject, nEffect | Handles the OLEStartDrag event. |
| Open | | Method to open an item (defined at item type level). |
| Paste | | Pastes the item that is currently in the clipboard. |
| PasteLink | | Pastes the link that is currently in the clipboard. |
| QuickView | | Activates the quick view for the current item. |
| Rename | | Starts an item-rename operation. |
| Run | | Executes items. |
| SetFocus | | Handles the SetFocus event. |
| SetMenu | | Sets the shortcut menu items for an item. |
| Show | NStyle | Handles the Show event. |
| ShowMenu | | Activates the shortcut menu for the current item. |
| UpOneLevel | | Navigates to the parent item (folder). |

Folders are special item types. The default folder class is _folder_, which is a subclass of the _item_ class. This class has some highly specialized behavior for folders. **Tables 8** and **9** explain these special item types.

*Table 8. Properties of the _folder class.*

| Property | Description |
|---|---|
| cFolderType | The information stored in this property gives an indication of special folder types, such as dynamic folders that can point to an Internet URL. In this case the value of this property would be "web". |
| lSearchSubdirectories | Specifies that the dynamic folder will search all subdirectories, which will create a sub-dynamic folder for each subdirectory found. This is optional and might slow down the refreshing of the gallery. |
| lSortOnCleanup | Specifies whether a folder should be sorted when the user issues a "Cleanup catalog". |

**Table 9.** Methods of the _folder class.

| Method | Parameters | Description |
|---|---|---|
| Backup | TcFileName | Creates a backup of the selected catalog if the current folder is the main catalog folder. |
| Cleanup | tlNoRefresh, tlIgnoreErrors | Executes a cleanup of the current catalog. This includes packing the table and reordering items. This method executes only if the current folder is the main catalog folder. |
| Find | | Displays the Find dialog. |
| GetFolderType | | Gives an indication about special folder types, such as dynamic folders that can reference a URL on the Internet (return value is "web"). |
| InitDBCFolder | | Initialize the DBC folder of a dynamic project folder. |
| InitFileFolder | | Initialize the files of a dynamic folder. |
| InitFolder | | Initialize a dynamic folder. |
| InitPJXFolder | | Initialize the PJX folder of a dynamic folder. |
| InitVCXFolder | | Initialize the VCX folder of a dynamic project folder. |
| Restore | TcFileName | Restores the current catalog from an earlier created backup. This method executes only if the current folder is the main catalog folder. |

### Creating new items

As an example, I want to use my Visual GenRepoX catalog again. I'd like to add some sample reports to the Samples folder. Of course, those reports aren't regular Visual FoxPro reports. Visual GenRepoX has to be invoked before the report can be previewed. All other report functionality, like modifying a report, is the same as with regular Visual FoxPro reports. For this reason, I simply subclass the _reportitem class. I call the new class cGenRepoXReportItem. The _reportitem class has a Run() method, which is the method that needs to be changed. In fact, I'll get rid of the original behavior altogether and overwrite it with the following code:

```
** Overwrite the default behavior...
LOCAL lcCommand
lcCommand = ["REPORT FORM "]+Alltrim(THIS.cFileName)+[" PREVIEW]
GenRepoX(lcCommand)
```

Instead of executing the report directly, I route the call through the GenRepoX wrapper. For simplicity's sake, I call the GenRepoX *function* instead of the GenRepoX *object*, even though this would be the proper way now. After all, I want to show you how the Component Gallery works—not how to properly invoke GenRepoX.

I can now add a report item and specify this class as an item class. When I right-click such an item and select Preview from the shortcut menu, the new method fires and GenRepoX gets called. Quite simple, isn't it?

The next step is to modify the menu, because we want to give the user a clue that we are doing something different. Here's the code:

```
LPARAMETERS toObject

IF NOT _item::SetMenu(toObject)
  RETURN .F.
ENDIF
IF !THIS.oShared.CheckItem(THIS)
  RETURN .F.
ENDIF

this.AddMenuBar("Modify","oTHIS.Modify()",,,,,!this.oHost.lRunFileDefault)
this.AddMenuBar("Preview
GenRepoX)","oTHIS.Run()",,,,,this.oHost.lRunFileDefault)
```

First of all, I am executing inherited behavior. Note that I'm not using DoDefault(), but the scope resolution operator. I do this because I don't want to inherit the items defined in the _reportitem_ class. However, all menu items should be defined generically in the _item_ class. For this reason, I skip the direct parent class and go one step higher. In the next step, I check whether the current item can be handled by the shared item because I still want to let the shared item handle standard tasks such as modifying the class. You might wonder why I knew I had to do this. Well, I actually didn't. I just looked it up in the _reportitem_ class and figured it must be there for a reason.

Finally, it's time to add an item to the shortcut menu. I simply used the AddMenuBar() method. The first parameter is the caption. Parameter two defines the action that occurs when the item is selected. When a right-click menu is created, the gallery stores a reference to the active object in a public reference called *oTHIS*. So with oTHIS.Modify() and oTHIS.Run() we send messages to the current object. And remember that I changed the code in the Run() method. So this is how this method gets called.

The final parameter is a little confusing. It defines whether the added menu item should be displayed in boldface. In the Component Gallery options, the user can specify the default item action (either *modify* or *run*). Our menu should show the default action in boldface. So the first thing I have to do is figure out the option setting, which is stored in the gallery itself. I always have a reference to the gallery called *oHost*. The actual setting is stored in a property called *lRunFileDefault*. This setting is simply passed to the AddMenuBar() method.

By now you know how to modify behavior and how to set items in the menu. You also know how to link those items to a certain method, so you could easily create new methods and add menu items that call those methods. With this knowledge, you're limited only by your creativity.

### Adding item types

By default, the Component Gallery supports only a dozen item types, but you'll often want to add new ones. You might want to add items and change the underlying classes to get different behavior, or maybe create a catalog that deals with non-default behavior, like the Visual GenRepoX catalog. In this case, it is much more comfortable to add new item types.

Adding new item types is done per catalog. You can do it through the Properties dialog of the main catalog node (see **Figure 29**).

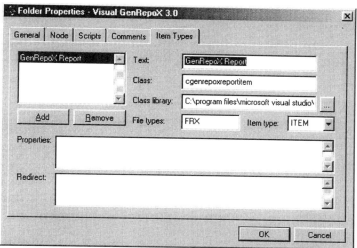

***Figure 29***. *Adding item types.*

When creating a new item type, you need to specify an item type name, a class and a class library to be used for the behavior object, and whether the new item is a folder or a regular item. Optionally, you can specify properties and alternative item types (redirect). Items often need certain properties that the user can change, which you can specify in the Properties edit box. In the previous example, we could add a property that allows setting the file name:

```
Report file name,cFileName
```

When the user adds a new GenRepoX report item, he can now open the item's properties and see another page that allows him to specify the item name. I'll discuss this topic in more detail later.

We can also specify alternative item classes in the current dialog. Let's say the user incorrectly selects a DOC file as a GenRepoX item. We could redirect this item to a regular file item like so:

```
DOC=_fileitem
```

Once a new item type is added, it is available in the right-click menu as well as in the treeview (see **Figure 30**). But remember that items are defined per catalog. It sometimes gets confusing when you open multiple catalogs and one catalog supports items that are unsupported by the other.

## Folder and item properties
Each item and folder in the Component Gallery has a Properties dialog that allows you to modify and customize the behavior, look and feel of each item. For most items, the property sheets will vary in appearance due to the flexibility of each item. I'll give you an overview of

the most important items and their different property sheets. I'll also explain how to customize the items and their property sheets.

The property sheets I describe here are advanced property sheets. You can activate advanced property sheets in the Component Gallery's Options dialog (Advanced editing enabled). If you don't activate this feature, the property sheets will have significantly fewer items.

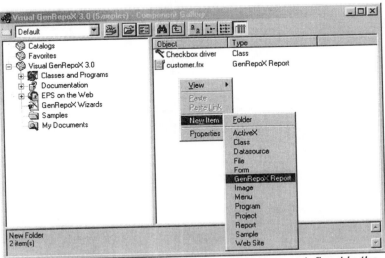

*Figure 30. The "GenRepoX Report" item that was defined in the Visual GenRepoX catalog.*

## Catalog properties

**Figure 31** shows the General tab of a sample catalog property sheet. On this tab, you can define the most basic properties such as the catalog name and a short description, as well as an item for the catalog. The catalog's property sheet is a specialized form of a folder property sheet. Take note that the specified name is used for the topmost node as well as for the whole catalog (in the Open dialog, for instance). The General tab allows you to specify two additional properties—the item picture and an item description. These settings are used for items within the current catalog that don't have specific icons and descriptions assigned.

On the Node tab of the property sheet (see **Figure 32**), you can specify some internals for the catalog node. The ID is the automatically created name of the actual node. This property is always read-only. The *Class name* and *Class library* properties allow you to specify the class to be used internally (see above). The *Item* class is a standard class for all items that don't have a defined class. Finally, the *Dynamic folder* property defines the location of a dynamic folder (see above).

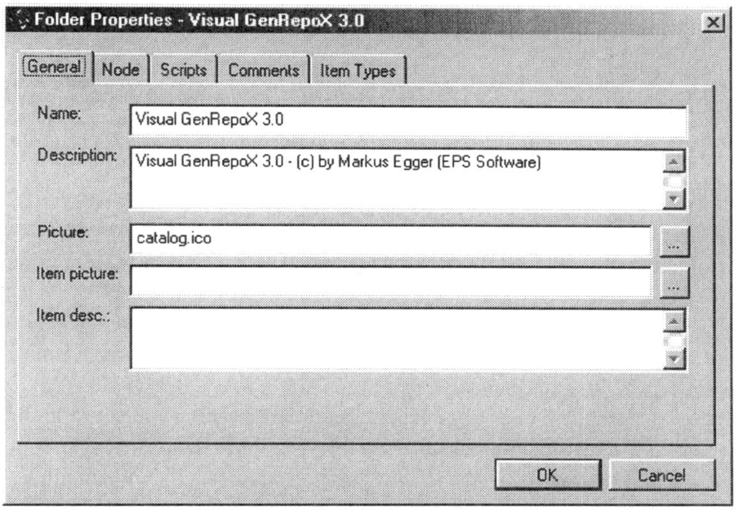

*Figure 31. The General tab of the catalog property sheet.*

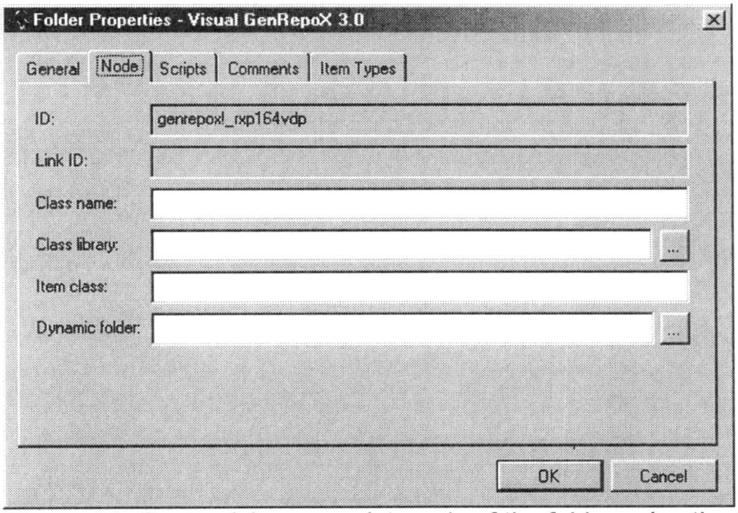

*Figure 32. Customizing some internals of the folder using the Node tab.*

The Scripts tab is used to maintain scripts and property settings. This topic is discussed below. On the Comments tab, you can add personal comments and modify the contents of the User field of the catalog. Finally, there is the Item Types tab, which is used to add custom item types to a catalog (see above).

### Folder properties

Folder properties are similar to catalog properties. The major difference is that they do not have an Item Types tab. Also, properties such as the folder name have less impact than the catalog properties because they only define local names.

### Item properties

Item property sheets are also similar to folder and catalog property sheets, but they have some additional tabs and omit some generic settings. On the first tab, you can set properties for the name, description and item image. Sub-item images and descriptions can't have properties because items (unlike folders) can't have sub-items.

The first new tab is Views, which allows you to influence how an item is displayed and how it can be found. You can specify a list of keywords, which can then be used in the Search dialog to define dynamic views based on one or more keywords. The View settings are a bit confusing at first, but helpful nevertheless. The Visual FoxPro standard catalog has a good example for View settings. It has a Dialogs folder that contains an About Dialog item. Now let's assume the user wants to use the "Class By Type" view. In this case, the About dialog should be listed as a form. This can be accomplished with the following setting in the *Views* property:

```
Class By Type=Forms
```

The Node tab is a simplified version of the Node tab in the folder and catalog properties. It allows you to specify classes for the current item, but not for sub-items. The Script and Comments tabs are identical to the ones in the folder and catalog properties.

In addition, there typically is one more tab that has some properties specific to the current item. Class items have properties that show the base class, class locations, and so on. URL items have the Web address and so forth. This special property tab can be customized if you create special items that have some properties that need to be set by the user. See below for more information about custom properties.

### Creating custom properties

Often you will want your users to set some properties. The GenRepoX example is a perfect example. In the special GenRepoX report item, we overwrote the Run() method to execute a GenRepoX report by calling the GenRepoX method. However, there might be a need to execute a GenRepoX report directly without invoking GenRepoX. People like to do that to see whether a report can still be executed without GenRepoX. For this reason I decided to create a new property called *lUseGenRepoX* in the *cGenRepoXReportItem* class. Now I need to register this property with the Component Gallery so it will be displayed in the Properties dialog. I can do this two different ways: One allows the user to remove the definition, and the other is done internally and can't be removed from the property sheet by the user.

First I'll describe the secure way of registering the property, which prevents the user from removing it. To do this, I have to open the catalog like a regular DBF and manually add a record (see below for an explanation of the table structure). The Type field must be "CLASS". The ID is simply a unique value. The next couple of fields remain blank. The TypeDesc has to be "ITEM" because I want to create new properties for an item. It could also be "FOLDER" if I wanted to create folder properties. The magic actually happens in the Properties field. Here's what I added there:

```
Use GenRepoX to preview,lUseGenRepoX
Copies,nCopies
```

The first value up to the comma is the text that will be displayed. After the comma, I specify the property name. In this example I created a second property that specifies how many copies should be printed by default. The gallery allows you to specify as many properties as you want, separating them with a carriage return. Note that the properties are of different types—the first is logical and the second is numeric. The Component Gallery handles different property types automatically.

Now there is only one thing left to connect this record to a specific class. We do this in the Class and ClassLib fields, where we specify the appropriate name. In this example, the class name would be *cGenRepoXReportItem* and the library is the name of the VCX file we've chosen to store our class. **Figure 33** illustrates our property sheet.

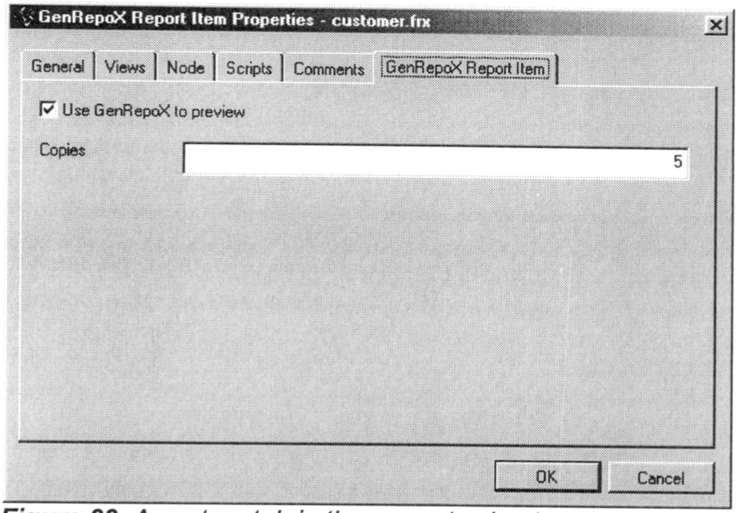

*Figure 33. A custom tab in the property sheet.*

Properties also can be specified in the Item Type tab of the catalog properties (see above). You simply specify some descriptive text and the name of the property. If the behavior object doesn't have the specified property, the property definition is ignored (unlike in the internal descriptions where this would cause an error). Note that this works only for newly defined items. Properties for internal objects can only be defined low level in the catalog DBF.

Once I allow the user to set certain properties, I can react to them in the Run() method (or other methods) of my special report class like so:

```
LOCAL lcCommand
lcCommand = ["REPORT FORM "]+Alltrim(THIS.cFileName)+[" PREVIEW]

IF THIS.lUseGenRepoX
  GenRepoX(lcCommand)
ELSE
  &lcCommand
ENDIF
```

In this example I support only one of the two properties, but I think you get the idea.

## Scripting
You might need to customize some properties or some behavior, but if the change is small (or located only at one place) you might not want to create a new class. In this case you can utilize the Component Gallery's scripting capabilities. You can define scripts on the Scripts tab of an item's property sheet (see **Figure 34**). This tab allows two different types of scripts. One allows setting properties (you guessed it: this is the edit box with the caption "Properties:"), and the other allows creating entire FoxPro functions. Properties are set one by one. You can specify as many property settings as you want, separating them with a carriage return (new line). I could set my *lUseGenRepoX* property like so:

```
lUseGenRepoX = .F.
```

This would set to .F. the behavior's *lUseGenRepoX* property (which normally defaults to .T.). Without the script, I always had to go to the property sheet to set this property before I printed. You can access every public property of the current behavior object. The gallery simply adds the defined property expression to the object name and evaluates it. Remember that each behavior object also has links to other objects, such as the parent node, the host (which is the Component Gallery itself), and so forth. So you could easily set properties of the Component Gallery like so:

```
oHost.BackColor = 255
```

This would set the Component Gallery's back color to red, as soon as the behavior object gets instantiated (which happens as soon as the user looks at a folder that contains the item with the script). This can be very useful to interact with add-ins that you might have created for the gallery (see below).

Properties can also be used to redirect method calls. To use the user-defined Test() method to handle the Click event, you could redirect it like so:

```
CClick="oTHIS.Test()"
```

For simple tasks, you can also use a Visual FoxPro script, which is a regular Visual FoxPro function. You can use all kinds of structures, such as IF and CASE statements. The only limitation is that you cannot define sub-structures like other function or class definitions. Unlike regular Visual FoxPro code, scripts are not compiled; instead, they are executed and interpreted line by line, similar to Visual Basic or Java scripts.

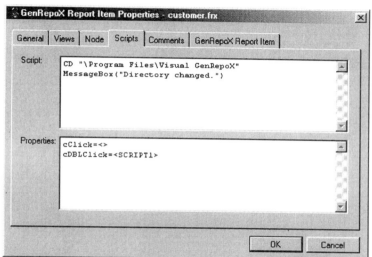

*Figure 34. A simple script and two redirected method calls.*

But *whll an your code?*

To call a script, you have to redirect a method call, similar to the last example, but instead of setting a method name you would specify a script call in the properties:

```
CClick=<>
```

Because no ID was specified between the brackets, the script specified in the current item is executed. Let's say we want to use the script to set the default to a certain directory every time the user clicks an item. We would create a script similar to the following:

```
CD "\Program Files\Visual GenRepoX"
MessageBox("Directory changed.")
```

**Figure 34** shows how this is specified in the property sheet. Take note that you can specify only one script in a property sheet. If you wanted to create another script for a different event, you'd have to add another record to the component catalog—something you could only do low-level in the DBF file. Additional script records have the type SCRIPT, a unique item ID that will be used to reference the script, and the actual script in the Script field. Let's assume you created a script record with the ID *SCRIPT1*. You would call this script with the following setting in the properties:

```
CRightClick=<SCRIPT1>
```

Take note that redirecting methods overwrites the default behavior assigned to a certain event. The above example redirects the right-click event. This means that the default behavior (like the shortcut menu) is now disabled. Unfortunately, there is no equivalent of DoDefault() in scripts or other redirected methods.

### Add-ins

Like the Class Browser, the Component Gallery itself can be customized through add-ins. I explained add-ins in detail in the Class Browser section. However, I'd still like to give you a simple example of a Component Gallery add-in. I would like to add a button to the gallery that scans the current folder for GenRepoX report items and executes all of them. Here is the code that does that:

```
LPARAMETERS loGallery
loGallery.AddObject("cmdGenRepoX","cPrintReportsButton")
RETURN

DEFINE CLASS cPrintReportsButton AS CommandButton
    FontName = "MS Sans Serif"
    FontSize = 8
    Height = 23
    Width = 100
    Caption = "GenRepoX Exec."
    Visible = .F.

    FUNCTION Visible_Assign (llNewVal)
        IF Type("llNewVal") = "L" AND llNewVal AND NOT THIS.Visible = llNewVal
            * The button is set visible
            THIS.Top = THISFORM.chkDetailsView.Top
            THIS.Left = THISFORM.chkDetailsView.Left + ;
                THISFORM.chkDetailsView.Width + 5
        ENDIF
        THIS.Visible = llNewVal
    ENDFUNC

    FUNCTION Click
        LOCAL lnCounter
        FOR lnCounter = 1 TO ALen(THISFORM.oFolder.aItemIndexes,1)
            IF "genrepox" $ ;
                THISFORM.aItemList(THISFORM.oFolder.aItemIndexes(lnCounter)).Class
                THISFORM.aItemList(THISFORM.oFolder.aItemIndexes(lnCounter)).Run
            ENDIF
        ENDFOR
    ENDFUNC
ENDDEFINE
```

The code has to be stored in a PRG file. For now, I'll assume you stored it in a file called Grxaddin.prg. You can now run the Component Gallery and register the add-in like so:

```
_oBrowser.AddIn("GenRepoX Execute","grxaddin.prg","INIT")
```

Note that the reference to the gallery is still called *_oBrowser*. That's because the gallery and the browser share underlying architecture as well as the interface. I would like to see a second object reference called *_oGallery*, but apparently nobody else thought of this before. If you would like such a reference, too, you can create a simple add-in that defines a public variable called *_oGallery* and turns it into an object reference pointing to *_oBrowser*. This add-in needs to be called in the Activate event of the gallery.

When the add-in is executed, the new button gets instantiated. However, the button is invisible at first because I don't want it to show up unless a GenRepoX item is displayed. For this reason I have the GenRepoX item activate the button. To do that, I could either code something in the Init() method of the GenRepoX behavior class, or I can create a little script (actually a property setting) that sets the *Visible* property of the button to .T. This can be done in the property sheet of any GenRepoX item, like so:

```
oHost.cmdGenRepoX.Visible = .T.
```

When the button is set visible, an assign method fires and handles the positioning of the button according to other items in the gallery.

When the button is clicked, I iterate through the current items, check if they have "genrepox" in their class names, and if so, I fire the item's Run() method to execute the report. Iterating through the active items is simple. The gallery has an object reference called *oFolder*, which is a reference to the currently selected folder. This folder object has an array of item numbers that are members of the folder. We can use these numbers to reference items in the gallery's *aItemList* collection. This collection has a reference to all the behavioral objects the gallery has instantiated so far. Take note that there could be items from other folders as well, because the gallery creates behavior objects as soon as a folder is browsed, but no longer removes them for performance reasons. Once we have a reference to the items in the selected folder, we can check their *Class* property to see whether the item is related to GenRepoX.

### The gallery's object model

The internal object model of the Component Gallery is quite rich. Full documentation of the internal object model is beyond the scope of this book. Please refer to the Visual FoxPro documentation. However, I would still like to give you an overview of the most important references and properties of the Component Gallery (see **Table 10**). You can access those properties either from add-ins or through the *_oBrowser* object reference (yes, the reference to the gallery is also *_oBrowser*, since the two tools share one interface).

### Catalog file structure

Component Gallery catalogs are regular Visual FoxPro tables (DBF). Most content in a catalog can be edited through the Component Gallery's interface. However, some data (such as custom property sheets or scripts) have to be defined as low level in the DBF. Also, there are other reasons for editing the file directly: corrupt content, or mass updates that can be done with a REPLACE ALL...FOR statement. **Table 11** explains the structure of catalog tables.

The Component Gallery has a default catalog—Vfpglry.dbf—that it opens when the gallery is called from the menu. This catalog has references to catalogs and other items. All items displayed by default are somehow references from the default catalog.

*Table 10.* The most important properties and references of the Component Gallery.

| Property/Reference | Description |
|---|---|
| aFolderlist | Collection of all displayed folders. |
| aItemlist | Collection of all items the browser displays and has displayed (they are not removed once they are displayed). |
| cCatalog | Contains the name of the currently selected catalog file. |
| cDefaultcatalog | Stores the name of the default catalog file. |
| cDefaultcatalogclasslibrary | Stores the name of the default class library for catalog items. |
| cDefaultcatalogpath | Contains the name of the default Component Gallery path. |
| cFolderclass | Default folder class name. |
| cItemclass | Default item class name. |
| cViewtype | Currently active view type. |
| cWebbrowserclass | Class used for dynamic folders (Internet and directories). |
| cWebbrowserclasslibrary | Class library that stores the class for the Web browser view. |
| lBrowser | This property is set to .T. if the gallery runs in browser mode. This is important for add-ins. |
| lFFCbuilderlock | Specifies whether the Fox Foundation Class builder lock is on. |
| nFoldercount | Number of opened folders. |
| nFolderlistindex | Index of the currently selected folder. |
| nItemcount | Number of items. |
| nItemlistindex | Index of the currently selected item. |
| oCatalog | Reference to the active catalog. |
| oFolder | Reference to the current folder. |
| oItem | Reference to the current item. |
| oItemshortcutmenu | Reference to the shortcut menu (and the menu settings) of the current item. |

*Table 11.* The structure of catalog tables.

| Field | Type | Description | Example |
|---|---|---|---|
| Type | C(12) | Specifies the kind of item represented by the current record. | ITEM, FOLDER, CLASS, SCRIPT |
| ID | C(12) | Unique identifier for each record. | Clireg, _gfr445g5 |
| Parent | Memo | Specifies the parent folder of the current item. Used to build the hierarchical view the gallery uses. | Clireg, _gfr445g5 |
| Link | Memo | Identifier of a linked item. A link identifier is composed of the catalog name and the item ID. | Activex!treeview, genrepox!_dgj8342 |
| Text | Memo | Item name that will be displayed in the listview and the treeview. | About Dialog, Documentation, My Documents |
| TypeDesc | Memo | Additional description text for each item of a folder. This text is inherited by all child items/folders of a folder. | Double-click these items to execute. |
| Desc | Memo | The text that will appear in the description area. | This component can be used to… |
| Properties | Memo | Contains all properties that are set in the Script tab of the item property sheet. | cbaseclass=container lUseGenRepoX = .F. |

**Table 11**, *continued*

| Field | Type | Description | Example |
|-------|------|-------------|---------|
| FileName | Memo | The file name where the referenced item is stored. If the item is a class, this field contains the name of the class library. If the item is a URL, it is stored here. | (HOME()+"ffc\\_dialogs.vcx") GenRepoX.vcx http://www.eps-software.com |
| Class | Memo | If the referenced item is a class, it is stored here. Note that there needs to be a reference to the library as well, which is stored in the filename field. | _aboutbox cCheckBoxDriver |
| Picture | Memo | Picture (icon or bitmap) for non-folder items. If the current record is a folder, this field specifies the standard icon for all sub-items. | File.ico (HOME()+"gallery\\class.ico") |
| FolderPict | Memo | Picture (icon or bitmap) used for folders. If the item uses the standard icon, this field is empty. | dfldr.ico (HOME()+"genrepox\\grxreport.ico") |
| Script | Memo | Visual FoxPro script. | cVBRFile = GETFILE("VBR") cCliReg = oTHIS.cFIleName<br><br>IF !FILE(m.cCliReg)<br>    RETURN .F.<br>ENDIF<br><br>IF EMPTY(m.cVBRFile) OR UPPER(JUSTEXT(m.cVBRFile)) #"VBR"<br>    RETURN .F.<br>ENDIF<br><br>oTHIS.Runcode([RUN /N &cCliReg. "&cVBRFile." – NOLOGO]) |
| ClassLib | Memo | Class library where the class definition for the behavior object is stored. | (HOME()+"gallery\\_gallery.ico") (HOME()+"genrepox\\grxreport.ico") |
| ClassName | Memo | Class used for the behavior object. The ClassLib field specifies the library for that class. | _folder _activexfolder |
| ItemClass | Memo | The default class used for all items within a folder. Used only in folder items. | _activexitem _reportitem |
| ItemTPDesc | Memo | Contains information about alternate file items for particular file types if the current item is a generic file item. | BMP=_imageitem ICO=_imageiem WAV=_sounditem DBF=_dataitem |
| Views | Memo | Specifies special settings for certain views. | Class By Type=Forms |
| Keywords | Memo | Specifies a list of keywords that can be used to identify and search the component. | Class |
| SRCAlias | Memo | Specifies the source alias of the catalog table the item originated from. | Catalog1 |

*Table 11*, *continued*

| Field | Type | Description | Example |
|---|---|---|---|
| SRCRecNo | N(6,0) | Specifies the source record number of the catalog table where the item originated from. | 3 |
| Updated | T | Information about the date and time of the last update through the gallery's interfaces. This field is for internal use only. | 09/03/1998 11:57:00 AM |
| Comment | Memo | Can be used to store comments. | Need to finish this… |
| User | Memo | Reserved for user extensions. The Component Gallery does not use this field. | *:EXTENSION |

## Browser.dbf

As a close relative of the Class Browser, the Component Gallery also uses the browser table to store metadata. In the section about the Class Browser, I described the structure of Browser.dbf (see Table 1). The rules of using Browser.dbf in combination with the Component Gallery are the same as for the Class Browser.

# Conclusion

Managing the development process is essential for successful object-oriented applications. The bigger a project, the harder it is to manage the development process. When you reach a level where you want to reuse code across projects (which should be the ultimate target of every object-oriented development effort), it seems impossible if you don't have the proper tools.

People often tell me that they spend a lot of time learning to use object-oriented technology, but they don't experience the level of desired success when it comes to code reuse. Typically, my first question is whether they do any object modeling or other kinds of designs. The answer to this question is often "No," which isolates the problem right there. Sometimes the answer is "Yes," but components still cannot be reused successfully. When analyzing the problem further, I often discover that the problem is a lack of process or management for reusing classes. No tools are utilized. Classes are simply copied into new directories, dropped into new projects, and sometimes even changed to fit new needs, making it impossible to use the newer versions of those classes in future versions of existing projects. This entirely defeats the purpose of object-oriented programming. Simply using tools such as the Class Browser and (even more important) the Component Gallery can solve most of these problems.

# Chapter 6
# Good Habits

**Writing applications that follow the rules of object orientation is one thing. Writing them properly in a clean and elegant fashion is another. This chapter discusses coding techniques that a lot of people (including myself) consider "good habits." All of them are meant to be suggestions rather than rules. You should, however, remember that good code always approaches the same task in the same manner each time. Decide which guidelines you want to conform to, but then make sure that you do.**

## Coding standards

Coding standards and naming conventions are topics that are treated religiously rather than objectively. However, most people (including myself) find them very useful. Naming conventions are supposed to make source code easier to read, easier to maintain and easier to debug.

I do not intend to re-specify all the details of standards such as Hungarian Notation. Instead I'll focus on conventions concerned with object technology.

The notations I present here are based on standards used by Microsoft as well as many other companies, including Flash Creative Management. Yair Alan Griver described similar standards in his *Visual FoxPro 3.0 Codebook*. The wide acceptance of these standards is one of their great strengths. Nevertheless, programmers can still alter these standards to make them match their own needs. I added a couple of variations to these standards that serve my needs very well. Regardless, one of the advantages of standards is the fact that everybody knows them. Altered standards that seem to have some advantages might not work that well after all, since they can cause major confusion that outweighs all the gained advantages.

I'd like to discuss the original standards suggested by Microsoft and Flash Creative Management, as well as some of my own variations. You can decide for yourself whether or not these variations make sense or if you feel it's smarter to stick with the original version.

### Object naming conventions

The original conventions suggest that all objects have to be named according to a single scheme. This scheme is based on notations used in other languages like Visual Basic. It suggests that every object name should have a three-letter prefix that specifies the base class.

It seems that very few people actually stick to this convention; they differentiate between two different groups of object names instead. One uses the three-letter prefix while the other one is more along the lines of variable naming conventions that I'll discuss in a moment.

### Contained objects

Contained objects have a clearly defined ownership—they belong to the objects that contain them. Often, these objects are composed using instance programming and pseudo-subclassing. Usually, they are created during design time (early composition), using drag and drop in the class designer. Sometimes they are assembled at runtime (late composition), usually due to some implementation issues like using classes that can't be modified in the Visual Class Designer. Contained objects are always members of other objects and cannot exist by themselves.

This is the kind of object name that uses the three-letter prefix to indicate the base class. The prefix is always lowercase, while the actual name begins with an uppercase character. The name doesn't contain underscores. If the name is a composition of multiple words, each word starts with an uppercase character. Here is a list of all prefixes used for object bases on FoxPro classes:

| FoxPro class | Prefix | Example |
|---|---|---|
| ActiveDocument | acd | acdInvoiceApplet |
| CheckBox | chk | chkItemIsActive |
| Column (Grid-Column) | col or grc | colCustomerName grcLineItemNumber |
| ComboBox | cbo or cmb | cobLanguagecmbCustomerGroup |
| CommandButton | cmd | cmdApply |
| Container | cnt | cntCustomerInfo |
| Control | ctl | ctlAddressField |
| Custom | cus | cusBehavior |
| EditBox | edt or txt | EdtMemo txtComment |
| Form | frm, doc or dlg | frmCustomer docContract dlgOpenTable |
| FormSet | frs | frsPayroll |
| Grid | grd | grdLineItems |
| Header (Grid-Header) | grh or hea | grhCaption heaDescription |
| Hyperlink | hyp or lnk | hypEMailAddress lnkHomePage |
| Image | img or pic | imgWizard picLogo |
| Label | lbl | lblName |
| Line | lin | linHorizontal |
| ListBox | lst | lstStyles |
| OLEControl (ActiveX Control) | ole or acx | oleTreeView acxListView |
| OLEBoundControl | ole or olb | oleQuickTime olbEmbeddedObject |
| OptionButton | opt | optYes |
| OptionGroup | ogr or opg | ogrOutput opgDestination |
| Page | pag | pagStep1 |
| PageFrame | pgf | pgfWizard |
| ProjectHook | pjh | pjhVisualWebBuilderProject |
| Separator | sep | sepDocument |
| Shape | shp | shpRectangle |
| Spinner | spn | spnPercentage |
| TextBox | txt | txtName |
| Timer | tmr | tmrObserver |
| Toolbar | tbr | tbrNavigation |

Keep in mind that these conventions are meant to be helpful, not a burden. For this reason, some of the prefixes aren't used very often. *ProjectHooks*, for instance, are usually used at design time only. Unless you are creating a tool you want to give away, you probably won't want to bother with these conventions. Some objects like the *separator* simply don't do a whole lot; for this reason, many people don't even go through the hassle of defining a name. That's fine.

The only personal variation I added is the *txt* prefix for edit boxes. Even though this prefix is already used for regular text boxes, I found that I often end up replacing edit boxes with text boxes or vice versa. The special naming convention for the edit boxes became a major hassle because I had to go through all my code and replace the name. After all, edit boxes are just specialized text boxes that allow longer text.

### Stand-alone objects

The second group of objects are stand-alone objects. Most of the contained objects are used for the user interface. For this reason, there are more stand-alone objects than contained ones. Stand-alone objects are created using CreateObject() or NewObject() functions rather than by .AddObject() or .NewObject() methods. Typically, the ownership of these objects is not clearly defined. An object can create a reference to an existing object and keep it alive even though the previous owner has already released it.

Naming of stand-alone objects is very similar to naming variables. They have a scope and a type, which is always "o." Keep in mind that references to stand-alone objects are just variables. The other issues attached to stand-alone objects are discussed in the "Variable naming conventions" section.

Names for stand-alone objects are always chosen in source code, just as you define variable names.

## Class naming conventions

Just as we have naming conventions for objects, we also have conventions for the classes they are based on. Unlike the conventions for object naming, these conventions are simple and straightforward. Typically, classes have a lowercase, one-letter prefix indicating whether a class is concrete or abstract.

| Class type | Prefix | Example |
|---|---|---|
| Abstract | a | aDialog |
| Concrete | c | cPrintDialog |

Originally, people used "c" to indicate a class. This doesn't make a whole lot of sense, though, because classes can be easily identified as such. Therefore, no special indication is needed. Whether a class is abstract or concrete is valuable information. There is no other simple way to specify that a class is abstract, which makes this simple naming convention a powerful and elegant solution.

## Variable naming conventions

This topic is not entirely related to object-oriented technology, but since object references are just variables with fancy names, I have a good excuse to discuss variable naming conventions as well.

Variables typically have a two-letter lowercase prefix that indicates their scope and type. Each word of the actual name starts with an uppercase letter. No underscores are used.

| Scope | Prefix | Example |
|---|---|---|
| Public (Global) | <none> *or* g | gcUserName<br>oApplication |
| Private | p | pcHTMLOutput |
| Local | l | lcLine |
| Parameter | t, p *or* l | tcItemId<br>lcCustomerId<br>pcCustomerName |
| Property (Attribute) | <none> *or* a | Customer.cName<br>Invoice.acItemId |

The scope is quite straightforward. One of my variations is to use an "l" or "p" for parameters instead of the "t". I don't think the "t" adds a whole lot, but it hides the actual scope. In Visual FoxPro, parameters can be private or local. It wasn't like that in FoxPro 2.x since there were no local variables. However, the "t" is a dinosaur brought over from the old days and it takes away the information that "l" or "p" provides.

Object references are treated a little differently than regular variables. Whenever they are public (global), the notation doesn't require a scope, so you'll see oApp, but not goApp. Why? Well, I don't know, but it doesn't seem to hurt anything since global object references are the only variables that don't have a scope.

Another special case is properties. Their scope is automatically determined by the object they belong to. Some people add an "a" for "attribute" (that's what C++ people call properties). I don't have a problem with that, but I don't see a real advantage either. Others use an "s" for "static," because properties fulfill the requirements for a static variable, at least when it comes to object lifetime and visibility. I don't agree with that, since this is only true when the property is protected; a property is not just a regular variable after all. Also, there is no such a thing as a "static property." FoxPro doesn't support that, but I still try to avoid the confusion—who knows what new features Visual FoxPro 7.0 will have? The same is true for real static variables. I do like the idea of adding the visibility to the property names, though. This has saved me many times from trying to access a property that was protected and therefore not visible. The following table demonstrates these prefixes:

| Scope | Prefix | Example |
|---|---|---|
| Public (Global) | g | THISFORMSET.gnToolbars |
| Protected | p | THIS.pcUserName |
| Hidden | h | THIS.hcPassword |

The following is a list of all variable types used in Visual FoxPro:

| Type | Prefix | Example |
|---|---|---|
| Array | a | laItems(1,1) |
| Character | c | GcUserName |
| Collection | a *or* e | laForms(1,1) |
| | | peForms(1,1) |
| Currency | y | lyPrice |
| Date | d | LdLastModified |
| DateTime | t | ltTimestamp |
| Double | b | pbValue |
| Float | f | lfTotal |
| General | g | lgVideo |
| Integer | i | liCounter |
| Logical | l | llActive |
| Memo | m | pmComments |
| Numeric | n | lnLineNumber |
| Object | o | oApplication |
| Variant | v | lvReturnValue |

These variables are pretty straightforward. The only one that requires some extra explanation is the collection. Collections are either treated like regular arrays, or they use the letter "e". I guess this was the only letter of the word "collection" that wasn't taken by another variable type. I don't see a real advantage to using the "e" instead of the simpler and more intuitive "a". Array collections aren't real collections anyway, so it doesn't really matter.

## Field naming conventions

There is no special naming convention for table fields. It's obvious that fields can't really have a scope, since they're always visible throughout the current data session. Indicating the scope in the field name would be pointless. Not quite as obvious is the reason for dropping the field type. Let's discuss that in a little more detail.

One reason for adding the type to variables is the fact that FoxPro treats all variables as "semi-variants." Variables do have a certain type, but you can change that type simply by assigning a new value. This is powerful, but also dangerous. The naming convention makes it obvious if somebody assigns a value of the wrong type to a variable.

Fields, on the other hand, aren't variants. Therefore, the danger of assigning an invalid value isn't as great; and even if it happens, you'll get an error message right away. This helps to avoid hard-to-find bugs and anomalies, and the naming convention isn't really necessary.

One might argue that the field type is still a helpful hint, especially when scattering data to objects, and I have to agree. But hey! Nobody says you can't add the type in your field names if you want to.

## Method naming conventions

For some mystical reason, nobody so far has come up with naming conventions for methods. There would be some good reasons to do so. Methods have return values of certain types. They also request a specific number of parameters—some by value and others by reference. We have to figure out all these issues by ourselves. However, I have to admit that it would be pretty weird to pack all this information into a naming convention, but adding the visibility and the return type couldn't hurt.

The following tables show some suggestions:

| Scope | Prefix | Example |
|---|---|---|
| Public (Global) | g *or* none | THISFORMSET.glRefreshToolbars()<br>THISFORM.cGetOriginalCaption() |
| Protected | p | THIS.pcGetName() |
| Hidden | h | THIS.hlValidatePassword() |

The return type of a method is very similar to its variable type. However, there are some differences in the details, mostly because not every field type can be a return type as well.

| Return Type | Prefix | Example |
|---|---|---|
| Character | c | THIS.gcGetUserName() |
| Currency | y | THIS.pyGetPrice() |
| Date | d | THIS.hdGetLastModifiedDate() |
| DateTime | t | oApplication,gtGetTimestamp() |
| Logical | l | loInvoice.plIsActive() |
| Memo | m *or* c | THIS.pmGetComments()<br>loHTML.gcGetOutput() |
| None | x *or* none | loMail.SendMail<br>oApplication.xRefreshAllForms() |
| Numeric | n | THIS.gnGetCurrentLineNumber()<br>goDataService.gpGetRecord() |
| Object | o | |
| Variant | v | THISFORM.txtPhone.gvGetNumber() |

Methods that are visible throughout an application and don't have a return value are about as close as you can get to defining your own commands in Visual FoxPro. Whenever I create a method that does something I'd really like to see as a native Visual FoxPro command, I don't add any prefixes to it.

A note about parentheses: I don't add them, because I don't think using them with methods adds a whole lot. The danger of confusing methods and properties is minimal, especially when using proper naming conventions. The only scenario where methods could be confused with properties is when they are used to assign a value to another variable or property, as in the following example:

```
lcCaption = THISFORM.Caption
lcCaption = THISFORM.GetCaption()
```

The first line refers to a property and the second one calls a method. In this case, the parentheses are required anyway. In all the other scenarios, it's obvious whether the code represents a property or a method.

Keep in mind that this is not part of the original conventions. However, I don't see a good reason to use naming conventions for properties and variables but not for methods.

# Other conventions

There are a number of other conventions that we haven't discussed. Some are concerned with coding style, others with table naming, and so on. Other conventions take an approach that's quite different from the Hungarian Notation I discussed in this chapter.

This book is not the place to discuss all of these. Other people have done an outstanding job doing that, so I decided to stick to the topic and talk about object-oriented programming instead.

### Advantages and disadvantages of naming conventions

As mentioned above, the question of whether one wants to use naming conventions or not is rather religious and hardly ever objective. As a believer, I'm in danger of treating the topic the same way, but I'll still try to look at the downsides from an objective point of view.

One concern with using naming conventions is that one might lose the advantage of alphabetically sorted lists. Properties that have a prefix will not show up sorted correctly in property sheets and in the Class Browser. I don't see a major problem with that, especially since user-defined properties are always at the bottom of the list anyway, and therefore aren't sorted properly. I guess everyone has to decide for himself whether this is a disadvantage or not. If it bothers him, I have to grant him a point.

Another concern is the readability of source code. My opinion is that prefixes don't affect readability very much. It might take a little time to get used to it, but then it shouldn't be an issue anymore. The information you can get out of the prefix should outweigh the disadvantages by far. But again: If one doesn't like it, I couldn't argue with him. After all, this is all based on personal opinion.

As with most techniques described in this book, the advantages don't come for free if you just blindly follow the guidelines. The actual naming of variables, properties and methods is at least equally important as following the actual notation. The variable name "lnX", for instance, is a lot worse than using "Counter", even though the latter doesn't follow the naming convention. The obvious solution would be to use "lnCounter", which combines the standard with an intuitive name.

Other examples are even more obvious. Using "lnLine" and "lcLine" is a good one. I use these often, especially when iterating through lines of a memo field.

Sometimes, a name that seems to be intuitive is not as obvious as it first seems. Let's consider "Number," for instance. How could we know if "TelephoneNumber" is numeric or alphanumeric? What about "CustomerNumber"? Using "lcTelephoneNumber" and "lnCustomerNumber" instead clarifies the situation.

Hungarian Notation also makes debugging a lot easier. If you treat properties and memvars as if they were not variants and all of a sudden "lnCount" is character, you have valuable information about what's gone wrong.

### Naming conventions in interfaces

Naming conventions should not be used in programming interfaces provided for other programmers. Imagine using a third-party class library that uses a naming convention you are not familiar with. This could end up being a major disaster, since you start mixing different conventions and therefore lose the advantages of either one. It's far better to use a component that doesn't use any conventions at all. In this case you lose the advantage of conventions in that component, but it doesn't hurt your own conventions. If not having the convention is a problem for you, you could always create a wrapper that uses your conventions.

Take the Visual FoxPro base classes, for example. None of them follows Hungarian Notation, even though Microsoft promotes that idea in the Visual FoxPro documentation. Keep in mind that all those conventions are just suggestions. Forcing someone to use a notation he doesn't like does more damage than good.

# Design standards

Coding standards are concerned with a very small-scale standard. Nonetheless, object-oriented systems also require some larger-scale standards. Techniques like polymorphism or components make sense only if they match the general design.

Very often I hear people comparing object-oriented technology to electronic parts. As a former electronics student (I chickened out and majored in business instead), I can agree with that. However, the analogy of electronic parts doesn't work well, either, unless they match the overall design. Have you ever tried to push a Pentium II processor in a 68000 socket? Not a good example? Then try using a simple transistor with something that provides the wrong voltage. Get the idea?

Ideas like components and code reuse are wonderful, but no matter how generic and self-contained a class is, you won't be able to use it unless you somehow manage to make it match your standards. Very often, you can accomplish this using wrapper classes. However, this works only if the component has been designed properly and follows a well-defined interface.

Unfortunately, design standards are not as straightforward as coding standards. There are no clear rules to follow or standards you could simply reuse. You'll have to work out your own standards. These standards should be concerned with naming classes and methods, as well as behavior ownership issues and so on.

Whenever you create objects that do similar things, make sure you give the same name to the methods that perform the same functions. Don't call one of the methods Execute(), another one Build() and a third one Do(). Pick one of them—it doesn't matter which one. When you create different classes that play together, make sure you keep some consistency with behavior ownership. Let's say you have an *InvoiceLogic* object and an *InvoiceInterface* object. Decide up front which one of these objects should be responsible for saving the invoice. If you create a *CustomerLogic* and a *CustomerInterface* later on, stick to this decision. It doesn't matter which one of these objects gets the behavior, as long as the *Logic* or the *Interface* gets the behavior for any item.

You also have to find a common notation for the design phase. I recommend using the UML notation. However, I won't go into the details here because I devoted Section 3 of this book to object design and UML.

# Class hierarchies

Creating proper class hierarchies is both a science and an art—there is no easy recipe. People say a good portion of it is experience. I'm sure this doesn't sound very good to you. After all, you bought this book to learn these kind of things rather than going through the painful process of gaining experience. Fortunately, some basic rules and good habits can provide at least a starting point.

First, make sure you create your own set of base classes and derive all your own classes from them. Try to categorize your classes. For instance, create a *DialogForm* class and a *DocumentForm* class that are subclasses of your own form class. This way you can build a simple class hierarchy that will provide some flexibility. Once you become more experienced, you can go back and change a couple of things, which shouldn't be too hard if you followed these basic rules.

Don't be afraid to redesign! Every software project will go through a certain amount of redesign and rewriting. That's fine! Analyze your classes on a regular basis. Check for methods and properties you create. You might find that a lot of classes you derived from one parent class have the same newly defined method or property, in which case it's time to move the class to the parent class rather than defining it separately in every subclass. You might discover classes that have a lot of similarities but that are in different inheritance branches. In this case it might be time to redesign the class hierarchy. This can be a lot of work, but usually it's worth doing.

# Documenting

Documentation is a very important part of an application. In fact, it's so important that a lot of European countries require software companies to document their applications by law. I do not favor laws that try to over-regulate and micro-manage, but I can see the reasons for having such regulations. Software is useless unless its features are documented and people know how to use them.

There are three different kinds of documentation: end-user documentation, maintenance documentation and internal documentation. I'll focus on the last one, since this is a book for programmers, but don't overlook the importance of the other two types.

As a consultant, documenting my work is a very important task. I usually help people, write some code, move on to the next project and leave the customer with the code I wrote. The only way to keep this customer happy is to make sure he understands that code so he can use it. Reading and understanding somebody else's code is not trivial, especially when the person wrote the code to do something you couldn't accomplish yourself.

A lot has been written about documenting a programmer's work. I'll try to bring up some new thoughts, rather than repeat what has been written a hundred times.

## Comment lines in source code

This is the simplest way of documentation, as well as one of the most effective. It is very informal, too, which means that there is no real process to follow. It's your own decision where to put comment lines and how to describe the code they document. Comments that are valuable for one programmer might be useless for another.

A common way of thinking about it is to comment as much as possible. This is a good start. Nevertheless, the quality of the comments is even more important. Creating a method called "Save" in the "Invoices" class and adding a comment like "This method saves the invoice" doesn't do a lot of good. A comment like this is much more useful: "This method varies from the inherited save behavior because it also saves related line items."

I also like to add more information to my comment lines. Typically, FoxPro comments start with an asterisk (*). I usually add a second character to indicate different kinds of comments. Two asterisks indicate a regular comment:

```
** We search for the party related to the invoice
SELECT Parties
LOCATE FOR PartyId = Invoice.PartyId
```

Sometimes, I try to fix bugs or make changes to existing code, but I don't want to delete the old code right away, so I can go back to older versions in case of an error. In this case I use curly brackets:

```
*{ 06/01/1998 - Changed by Markus
*{ The following line was changed because of
*{ problems due to different field-lengths
*{ LOCATE FOR PartyId = Invoice.PartyId
*{ 06/01/1998 - End of changes
LOCATE FOR Alltrim(PartyId) == Alltrim(Invoice.PartyId)
```

I have to admit that I simplify this every now and then, and put the *{ only in front of the original line. C'mon, what do you expect? Nobody is perfect…

One of my personal favorites is the remark about suboptimal or incomplete code, as in the following example:

```
*! I have to add some error handling in case the customer wasn't found
LOCATE FOR Alltrim(PartyId) == Alltrim(Invoice.PartyId)
```

This is a very easy and efficient way to mark parts of code that need more work. I can simply search for every occurrence of "*!" later on. Before I did that, I often wrote code that wasn't quite polished, since it had some loose ends that had to be tied up, but I simply couldn't remember where all those ends were. Now I know what areas need more work, and I also know when I'm finished, which eliminates that weird feeling in my stomach whenever I release a product.

I use a couple other tags as well. Not all of them are generic enough to be used by everyone, but using them as a model you can come up with some tags that you find useful. However, there is one final example I would like to share:

```
DEFINE CLASS cInvoice AS cItem
   PROCEDURE AddItem( lcItemId )
   *= AddItem( cItemId )
   *= This function allows you to add a new item to the invoice object
   *= It requires one character parameter which specifies
   *= the item that should be added.

   …code goes here…

ENDDEFINE
```

This tag allows you to add formal documentation to the source code. I use a utility that scans my source code, takes these tags and automatically puts them in a Word document, which eventually becomes the manual. This makes it easier to keep the manual up to date, because I can run this utility repeatedly to update existing documentation.

### Automated comments

The shortcut menu in the Visual FoxPro editor allows you to comment and uncomment single lines or whole code blocks with one mouse click. The standard comments FoxPro creates start with *!* as in the following example:

```
*!* These lines have been commented by FoxPro
*!* WAIT WINDOW "Hello World!"
```

As you can see, I use this same notation for code segments that aren't finished and need more work. Fortunately, you can change the way FoxPro indicates comments by adding a simple (but undocumented) entry in the Registry, shown in **Figure 1**.

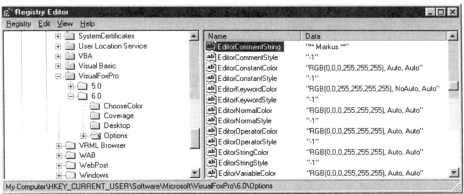

**Figure 1**. *You can change the way FoxPro comments code by adding this entry in the Registry.*

All you have to do is add a new string value in the key listed below. The value will be inserted in your code whenever you choose *comment* in the editor's shortcut menu. Here are the names of the string value and the key:

```
Key: HKEY_CURRENT_USER\Software\Microsoft\VisualFoxPro\6.0\Options
String Value: EditorCommentString
```

## Description fields

If you use the Visual Class Designer, you can use description fields to document classes, methods and properties. You can define these comments when creating new methods or properties, as shown in **Figure 2**.

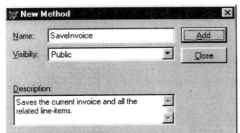

*Figure 2. Using the Description field to document a new method.*

Once created, the description can be modified in the Edit Property/Method dialog, shown in **Figure 3**.

| Name | Type | Access | Assign | Visibility |
|------|------|--------|--------|------------|
| Height | P | No | No | Public |
| HideDoc | M | | | Public |
| Init | M | | | Public |
| Name | P | No | No | Public |
| Parent | P | No | No | Public |
| ParentClass | P | No | No | Public |
| ReadExpression | M | | | Public |
| ReadMethod | M | | | Public |
| ResetToDefault | M | | | Public |
| Run | M | | | Public |
| SaveAsClass | M | | | Public |
| ShowDoc | M | | | Public |
| Tag | P | No | No | Public |
| Width | P | No | No | Public |
| WriteExpression | M | | | Public |
| WriteMethod | M | | | Public |
| **saveinvoice** | **M** | | | **Public** |

Property/Method Name:
saveinvoice

Description
Saves an invoice and al the related line-items.

Visibility: Public

New Property   New Method   Remove

Apply   Close

*Figure 3. Modify the description using the Edit Property/Method dialog.*

Unfortunately, you aren't prompted for a description when a new class is created, so you need to enter this documentation in the Class Info dialog, as shown in **Figure 4**.

As discussed earlier, you can also use the Class Browser to edit the description. This is the way I prefer, since the browser allows you to edit all the different descriptions in one place. Furthermore, it seems to be a lot quicker to enter the descriptions in the browser than to use the dialogs that require you to press Apply every time.

I made it a rule for myself to always add a description to properties and methods, no matter what. The same is true for classes. It seems to be an easy task that has a big impact and a lot of advantages.

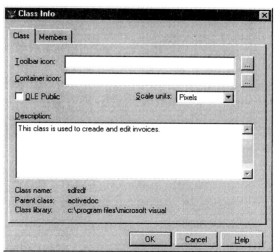

*Figure 4*. *Enter the description of the new class in the Class Info dialog.*

## Formal documentation

Formal documentation can be done in many different ways, but using Word seems to be the most common. I like Word because its OLE interface is relatively simple and straightforward, which makes it easy to create and update documentation automatically. I use source code parsers that look for special comment tags, and also a Class Browser add-in, which creates a Word document that describes class structures as well as methods and properties.

Another great way to create documentation for object-oriented applications is by using Microsoft Visual Modeler or Rational Rose. I'll discuss this option in more detail in Part 3 of this book (especially in Chapter 17).

Another issue to consider is the format in which to save your formal documentation. The simple way is to use regular Word documents. Typically, these documents are collected in binders that collect dust on a shelf, and are already outdated at the time of printing, which means they're useless. For this reason I favor something a little more up-to-date, such as online HTML files. These documents are relatively easy to create using conventional tools such as Word. They also make it easy to convert existing documentation from Word to HTML, and allow you to provide your users with up-to-the-minute changes in your documentation.

You might consider creating a tool that starts automatically every night, collects information from class libraries and source code, exports it to Word, saves it as HTML, and uploads it to a Web server. In addition, you could send automated e-mail to inform team members about changes. Hey, wait a minute … this sounds pretty cool … maybe I could …

# Chapter 7
# Evaluating Risks and Benefits

**By now, we've reached the point where most OOP books end. We've seen all the important concepts and we've also seen how all of this flows into FoxPro. With this know-how, we should be able to evaluate the risks and benefits to make a wise decision: whether or not our next project should be based on object-oriented technology.**

## Benefits

Since I'm a very optimistic person, I'll start out with the benefits. However, I want you to understand that all those benefits are based on properly applying object-oriented technology. None of them comes for free just because you use an object-oriented language.

### Faster development

The obvious benefit of object-oriented programming is faster development. Fast development is based on a couple of techniques. One of them is *rapid prototyping*. This technique is especially important for Visual FoxPro programmers because it's one of the strengths of the product. Another fast-development-technique is *reuse*. There are different kinds of reuse. *Code reuse* is the most obvious and most popular one. However, *design reuse* is usually just as important. As a consultant, I often help customers get started with an entirely new project. Very often I reuse a certain framework design that I've had for the last couple of years, but I hardly ever reuse the actual implementation. I have reused this design successfully on a number of projects. Over time, myself and others spent about 8,000 man-hours to design this framework. The time spent to actually implement this design in all the projects together is roughly 3,000 hours. Reusing only small parts of the implementation keeps the system young. I hardly ever use code that's old and outdated. Adjusting the design to match new technologies is a lot easier than adjusting an existing implementation. Nevertheless, it still cuts a major part of development time as the numbers demonstrate.

Unfortunately, creating reusable design and reusable code is not trivial. For this reason, I will talk about this issue in great detail in Chapter 8.

A further promising technique for improving development speed is using components. They can be class libraries that you can use and subclass, or they might be compiled components you can use as ActiveX controls or as COM components. Components have been around for quite a while, but they've just become popular. Their popularity is based on new technology like Microsoft's ActiveX and COM/DCOM standard.

Despite all these techniques, I'm not suggesting that starting your first project in OOP will be faster than going the procedural way. None of the benefits I discussed in the previous paragraphs comes for free. In fact, they are hard to achieve and require extra work.

If you count the number of lines and compare that to the time it took to write those lines, you will find that code is written faster in non-object-oriented projects. That's not unusual. Object-oriented projects are hard to manage because it's very hard to measure their progress. (That's why I devoted a chapter to this topic.) Object-oriented projects don't grow in a linear fashion like procedural ones. This makes them appear slow in the beginning. Later on, things speed up but they slow down again in the end. Don't be fooled by these slightly different dynamics of software development.

Understanding object-oriented technology is crucial for gaining an advantage in development speed. Don't get frustrated when things don't seem to work out right away. After mastering the learning curve, you'll be paid back for all the trouble you went through.

## Higher quality

When applying techniques like reuse or implementing existing components, you might be able to drastically increase application quality. Not only is it faster to reuse classes from another project, but a class that worked fine somewhere else is also likely to work fine in the current scenario.

However, this requires following the rules of object-oriented programming. A class that isn't properly encapsulated and self-contained might work in one scenario but not in another. Not only can you take advantage of bug-free components, but you might also end up trapped with bugs or design flaws caused by improper use of object-oriented technology.

Object-oriented technology itself does not guarantee better code quality. Creating high-quality code is still the responsibility of the programmer and not the environment he uses. It's just as easy to write a bad object-oriented program as it was to write a bad procedural one. In fact, bad OOP code tends to be even worse than bad procedural code, because code is spread over many different classes and places. This not only makes it hard to find bad code, it also makes it hard to figure out *why* code is bad, since you never see the overall picture. However, writing high-quality programs seems to be easier in an object-oriented world, at least for those who know what they're doing.

After all, in many highly complex projects, the difference between good and bad is being able to finish the project at all. In the modern and fast-moving world of computer programs, it seems almost impossible to create complex applications without applying object-oriented technology.

## Easier maintenance

Easier maintenance is partly based on higher quality. If the application has fewer defects, it will be easier to maintain. Detecting and fixing defects becomes easier due to the modular architecture of the system. Object-oriented programs are usually better organized because most parts of an application are stored in some kind of library. Libraries typically host a certain group of behavior. This makes it easy to spot where certain defects can be fixed.

However, techniques like inheritance and aggregation may also make it easier to find code that's responsible for possibly buggy behavior.

A typical problem in procedural systems is that one fix usually causes two new bugs. Thanks to the self-contained nature of object-oriented technology, fixes are less likely to break other things. Of course, one might still break code within each class, but the consequences are usually less critical and easier to fix than the defects that might exist throughout the whole system.

An important point when trying to create an easy-to-maintain application is documentation. An object-oriented application that is well documented is much easier to maintain than a well-documented procedural program. However, a poorly documented one will be more difficult to handle than an undocumented procedural application. Inheritance, aggregation and messaging can make it hard to see how things work together, for reasons we discussed earlier.

## Reduced cost

The first three benefits result in a fourth benefit: reduced cost.

It's obvious that creating better code that's easier to maintain and can be built in less time must save some money as well. However, keep in mind that none of the three advantages we discussed earlier comes for free. Especially in your first project, where you don't have a lot of classes that can be reused, savings might be little. In fact, you might find yourself spending more money and more time on your first object-oriented project than it would have taken doing it the procedural way. This is not unusual. You have to consider your first object-oriented project as a learning experience and an investment in the future. Don't get frustrated if you don't see the advantages right away. Back home in Austria we have a saying: "Good things take time." This seems to be more true for object-oriented technology than for anything else. Keep in mind: Unless you are willing to do a little extra work and create reusable classes, you might not be able to take advantage of the cost benefits at all.

Using ready-to-go, third-party class libraries and frameworks helps to save some money (and time, but that's the same thing) as well. Even if you might not have the experience to create reusable components right away, other people do. With procedural systems, your problem is that you're stuck with other people's ideas. Somebody might have a tool or code that does almost what you want, but not quite. Changing this product might be just as expensive as creating a new one. However, with object-oriented technology, you can subclass the original components and make all the changes you need. The result is a custom program for the fraction of the cost of creating a new one.

Another way to be more cost efficient is to sell more copies of your product. If you are a tool or component provider, object technology might help you a great deal to sell your products. We already discussed the reasons: Because people will find more components that match their needs if they can modify them a little bit, it is easier to find customers that might have a use for your component.

## Increased scalability

Scalability is one of the biggest issues when creating modern software.

Scalability is concerned with application size, the amount of traffic an application can handle, the size of the database that can be managed, and the speed the application maintains when moved from a small scale to a larger one.

Object technology itself is a great tool to create scalable applications. The modularized nature makes it easy to deploy single components over multiple machines. When upsizing a small-scale application, you might face some serious problems that may force you to rewrite. A typical example would be a system using native FoxPro data that has to be migrated to a client/server system. In this scenario, you most likely have to rewrite the part of the application that handles the data. However, rewriting object-oriented software and removing bottlenecks is usually a lot easier than rewriting procedural programs. In a typical scenario, you only have to rewrite a couple of data handling classes or maybe just some methods. As long as the interface remains the same, the rest of the system remains untouched.

New technologies like Component Object Model (COM) components and Distributed COM (DCOM) make it easier to deploy applications over multiple computers. Microsoft Transaction Server (MTS) is doing a great job when it comes to component-based applications. These technologies promise truly fascinating possibilities and make Visual FoxPro 6.0 a great new product.

## Better information structures and complexity management

As mentioned earlier, object-oriented applications are better organized than procedural ones. You just can't help but put your classes in libraries and break the application into pieces. Huge and complex tasks are mastered in little steps. Modern and highly complex tasks can hardly be accomplished efficiently in one monolithic step.

This also helps for team development and for testing. Each component, class or method can be tested on its own, possibly even outside the whole system. Clearly defined interfaces allow you to monitor whether the resulting output is according to all specifications and therefore correct. One of the main problems with testing is that the test team can only feed input to the application and monitor the output. Testers have little knowledge about what's going on internally. And even if they did, they couldn't see it. Output might look proper, even if there are serious internal problems. This might be caused by other objects that interact with the tested one, or by preventive programming techniques inside the object that might hide bugs. Even if output looks incorrect, it might be hard to locate the source of the problem. The smaller the pieces are that we can test, the easier it is to spot and fix defects.

Computers may be able to handle extremely complex and huge scenarios, but humans cannot. After all, it's still the programmer who has to make sure his algorithms work. If they become so complex that he has a hard time understanding them himself, code quality will decrease and bugs are unavoidable and hard to fix. Creating many little methods, each just a few lines long and simple to understand, helps to accomplish greater tasks.

## Increased adaptability

The best application is useless if it doesn't match the current needs of the users. In the fast-moving and constantly changing modern business world, it's extremely important to be able to change an application quickly and painlessly.

Object-oriented technology makes it easy to make system-wide changes or to add entirely new objects that were never part of the original design. Clearly defined interfaces and standards, as well as the use of object-oriented design patterns, make it possible to plug in new objects without running into many related changes. In procedural systems, scenarios like these are real nightmares, extremely expensive and a serious quality concern.

## Better mapping to the problem domain

Everyone *thinks* that object-oriented programming is terribly abstract. In fact, if you go into a room filled with programmers and say "You know, you really have to think in abstract terms when you do object-oriented programming," you would probably get a universal nodding of heads. If you think about it, that's not the way it is. Procedural applications are the most abstract way to create computer programs that I can think of. Objects, on the other hand, reflect the real-world problem in a more realistic fashion—they just do it in a different way.

When creating computer programs, the majority of time and effort goes toward solving technical problems, rather than the business problems the application is meant to solve. This, of course, is a horrible, inefficient scenario. Everything that helps to get away from this technical point of view will help us to be more productive. Object-oriented technology is at least one step toward this goal.

This advantage is a big one for FoxPro programmers. Most xBase programmers aren't technical people. Many have been businessmen that weren't satisfied with the applications they were given and decided to create their own ones. Therefore, they aren't interested in solving technical problems at all. Object-oriented programming will help these people more than anyone else.

# Concerns

As always, there is no such thing as a free lunch. There are some disadvantages to OOP as well. Most of them are concerned with applying the technology properly, mastering the learning curve, and making the switch to the new paradigm. This last seems to be the major disadvantage. However, object-oriented technology itself is not perfect. There are some downsides attached to the technology that you should be aware of.

## Need for standards

Object orientation is a relatively young and steadily developed technology. For this reason, we face a lack of standards. Many systems are still monolithic and hard to link to other environments. However, Microsoft's COM and ActiveX technologies promise some solutions. There are other standards as well, like CORBA for instance, but since they aren't supported by Visual FoxPro, they aren't important to us.

Even COM lacks some features that are crucial for object-oriented programming. Inheritance is one example. However, Visual FoxPro deals better with this problem than any other language I know. It's the only tool that introduces OLE subclassing, which allows you to modify ActiveX controls and apply the rules of programming by exception. Note that this doesn't work for other COM components. (ActiveX is only one of many possible implementations of the COM standard.)

In addition to these global standards, you also need to develop your own. The old saying "Any standard is better than no standard" comes to mind, and I have to agree. Standards are crucial to creating reusable classes and components. Whether or not you want to use a standard like Hungarian Notation, or implement certain patterns, is up to you. No matter which way you want to go, make sure you stick to it. Otherwise, objects won't be able to communicate with each other.

## Speed of execution

Objects add overhead to an application. Technologies like inheritance or composition add even more. This results in a speed disadvantage compared to procedural programs. For example, in order to instantiate a program, Visual FoxPro has to go up the inheritance tree to check for a member that needs to be inherited.

However, most modern languages (including Visual FoxPro) are highly optimized to deal with these scenarios. Most concerns with the speed of object-oriented technology are remains of early measurements and observations, which are outdated today. Nevertheless, slight speed penalties will always be the result of the richer set of features that object-oriented technology offers.

## Availability of qualified personnel

Although object-oriented programming has been around for some time, it hasn't been widely accepted until recently. This leaves us with a lack of qualified personnel.

The most obvious aspect is the shortage of good object-oriented programmers. However, since object-oriented technology requires a totally different way of doing things, managers and other people involved in a project need to understand this new technology as well. As mentioned above, the dynamics of object-oriented projects are very different from procedural ones. Projects don't grow in a linear fashion. I've worked on many projects that went through crises created by the project manager just because he didn't understand the technology or had wrong expectations.

Training people is extremely important. Unfortunately, the road from procedural programming to real object-oriented development is rather long. Often, sending people to a training class isn't quite enough to make them go through an entire paradigm shift. And making the paradigm shift is required to successfully undertake object-oriented projects. For your first projects, I strongly recommend hiring a consultant or employee who is an expert with object technology. A consultant can guide you through that process and allow everyone to catch up and learn new ways of doing things, which is better than painfully discovering them yourselves or never realizing the advantages.

## Costs of conversion

Converting existing procedural applications to object-oriented technology isn't cheap. Costs can result from rewriting and converting the actual application as well as from training people, buying new tools, and replacing outdated components.

Training people will be the biggest initial cost. This includes actual classes and hiring consultants, as well as a likely initial loss of productivity.

Once this hurdle is overcome, you will face creating a base set of classes and components. In this phase, you might encounter a good amount of useless code and classes that have to be replaced later. In many cases, big parts of the system will have to be redesigned as a result of trying to take a procedural path through the jungle of object-oriented technology.

Finally, you face the actual rewrite of the existing application. In the FoxPro world, one typically ends up rewriting the interface. It's often possible to reuse existing code in the methods of behavioral objects. However, it seems that in many cases it turns out to be cheaper to rewrite the whole application in a truly object-oriented fashion, than to convert the old code.

## Support for large-scale modularity

Objects do an excellent job of encapsulating functionality and hiding behavior from the outside world on a small-scale level. However, this doesn't work as well on a larger scale. You can combine objects into larger modules using composition, but the basic principles of hiding information and providing clean interfaces are hard to follow, and rules are broken back and forth. External objects are able to access the internals of composite objects in ways they couldn't on smaller scale objects, and even if one manages to hide this information, interfaces become huge and cluttered.

Microsoft's COM components try to resolve this problem. However, they usually don't hide internals properly, and on top of that, they lack some object-oriented features, as discussed above.

## Learning curve

There is no doubt that the learning curve is steep. The path between initially understanding object-oriented technology to applying it in real-life projects is long and rocky.

Object-oriented programming is not just about learning a couple of new features. It is about doing things in a totally different way. This paradigm shift cannot be overcome within a couple of days or weeks. You must remember that Visual FoxPro is a hybrid language. It allows you to apply object-oriented technology while continuing to go the procedural way. Unfortunately, semi-object-oriented programs usually lack many advantages that truly object-oriented systems offer, but they still introduce some of the overhead, the leaning curve and possible performance disadvantages.

Don't expect that simply using object-oriented technology without fully understanding it will give you all the advantages you've heard about. If you want to go the object-oriented route, go it all the way! Once you master the learning curve, you'll discover a whole new world of programming. Object-oriented technology makes programming a lot easier, but only for those who know what they're doing. And that's what we're going to spend the rest of the book talking about.

# Section 2
# Advanced Object-Oriented Programming

# Chapter 8
# The Bigger Picture

**In Part 1 of this book, I explained the basic ideas of object-oriented programming. I introduced the most important tools, presented a set of ready-made classes, and even taught you how to behave well in the world of objects. However, all of the wisdom I've presented so far has been geared to a very granular level. Now I'll explain how to create large object systems and entire object-oriented applications.**

## This isn't all about subclassing buttons, is it?

Typically, when one talks about object-oriented programming, he uses the example of a button, a textbox, a label or another visual base class offered by Visual FoxPro. The explanation usually includes some font definition (or definition of another visual property) and how to subclass or change the property globally later on. And those examples are pretty good. In fact, they make it easy to understand the general ideas and they explain a real-life use. After all, inheritance and object-based programming are great for all interface issues. However, this alone would not cause the major development shift toward one technology as object-oriented programming has.

You're thinking there's got to be more—and there is! Unfortunately, explaining the bigger picture without skipping a number of steps isn't trivial. That's why this step is one of the most difficult when learning object-oriented application development. Most people understand the general principles. Still, many are not able to construct an entire object-oriented application. In this chapter we'll explore larger objects, see how things come together to form an application, and also learn how to create reusable code.

## Creating behavioral objects

Behavioral objects are the first and easiest step toward larger, more advanced object systems. Behavioral objects are the workhorses of the application. They have no visible appearance. Other objects that call the behavioral object handle all user interface issues. Behavioral objects can handle entire logical areas (such as credit card transactions) or just very specialized tasks. This depends on the architecture you choose—there is no right or wrong.

Behavioral objects are the object counterpart of functions and function libraries in the procedural world. As with all objects, they have attached data (variables or properties) that greatly enhances the number of options and possibilities you have.

Behavioral objects appear in a variety of incarnations. They can be manager objects that handle data access, forms, menus or other technical parts of the application. They can also be business logic objects that enforce business rules. Middle tiers are built entirely of behavioral objects (see Chapter 9). This means that a great part of every application is made of behavioral objects (typically one-third or more).

If you wanted to follow the COM Automation idea, you'd typically create behavioral objects and compile them into COM components that could be instantiated from every COM client. This is an easy way to reuse objects, although it isn't the most powerful (see below for more information about reusable objects).

A typical behavioral object is a data manager that handles all data retrieval or modification. I use such an object in all of my applications. In fact, I have an individual data manager for each one of my tables and views. Of course I don't start from scratch every time, but I have an abstract data manager class. In typical scenarios, I subclass this class and change a couple of properties to specify the table name (in plain-vanilla FoxPro tables), primary key fields and a couple of other options. The data manager objects have a couple of key methods. Because I subclass all manager objects from one abstract manager class, the interface is the same for all data manager classes. **Figure 1** gives a brief overview of my data manager architecture.

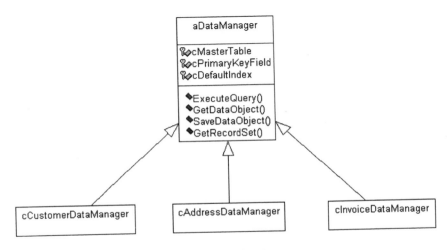

*Figure 1*. A simple data manager architecture.

This figure shows a generic data manager class with a number of properties and methods. The class also has three subclasses (see Chapter 12 for a more detailed explanation of the notation). Of course, all those classes inherit all methods and properties.

In a regular scenario I don't have to change more than a couple of properties, but if I need a more customized version for one of my tables, I can always overwrite or extend the existing methods. I can even add new ones, but I try to stay away from this kind of change unless the new method is used only internally. New public methods would redefine the interface and therefore defeat all attempts to create a clean interface that can be used in a polymorphic environment.

The functionality of the data manager object shouldn't be addressed in this chapter because it doesn't have anything to do with behavioral objects. Behavioral objects are just an implementation detail of this particular class. However, I still want to mention a couple of things so you can understand the power behind this architecture. The properties you see in Figure 1 (which represent only a fraction of my data manager's properties) define what table I want to use, what the primary key field is and what I want to use as the default sort order. The object's featured methods are there to access data. The ExecuteQuery() method runs a regular SQL select statement. If I don't pass any parameters, I get a cursor that contains all the fields and records of the referenced table. Here's an example of how this method can be used:

```
oCustomerData.Query()           EXECUTE QUERY()
oInvoiceData.Query()
oCustomerData.Query("* WHERE NAME='A'")
```

As you can see, it doesn't matter what object I talk to. The query method behaves the same way no matter whether I query customer or invoice data. In fact, all I have to do is instantiate the objects and use them because all properties have already been set in the class.

The other methods of the data manager object work differently. Instead of dealing with cursors, they use data objects that are instantiated by the manager object. This kind of architecture is somewhat different from what most people would expect in Visual FoxPro, but then again, this particular implementation detail isn't the topic of this chapter. For now, all you need to know is that GetDataObject() returns an object that has no methods and one property for each field in the data source. The property's values are the same as the values in each field. The method requires the value of the primary key field of the desired record to be passed as a parameter like so:

```
loData = oCustomerData.GetDataObject("XHUYKIF1")
```

Other methods help me deal with the primary key value.

Once I have the data object I can hand it over to other objects, I can modify the field (property) values through various interfaces, and I can finally save the changes using the SaveDataObject() method like so:

```
oCustomerData.SaveDataObject( loData )
```

Again, notice that I don't need any knowledge specific to the current data source. This is important, because it means I can create generic classes that use this object. I need only one data entry form class, for instance. I will need to create subclasses of this class, but the modifications in each class will be minor. To save the modified data, I simply use a data object that's a member of the form and hand it over to the data manager object, no matter what the data source is or what particular interface class is currently in use.

As mentioned above, I use this approach to handle local data, but as we all know, in today's world we need to deal with other data sources such as SQL Server or ADO. Fortunately, the current architecture works great with these kinds of data sources. **Figure 2** shows how I extended my class hierarchy to handle these scenarios.

As you can see, I added another layer of abstract manager classes—one for every data source I want to handle. Each of those classes has a subclass for every table I'm using. Most of the work will be done in the second layer, which defines the individual data managers for the various data sources. The topmost class in the hierarchy (*aDataManager*) is used only to define the interface. It has all the properties and methods but no code attached to it. In the second layer, there are very few new properties, methods or objects. (Exceptions might be some methods on the SQL Server object that handles connections, but then again, those methods are used only internally so they don't clutter the interface.)

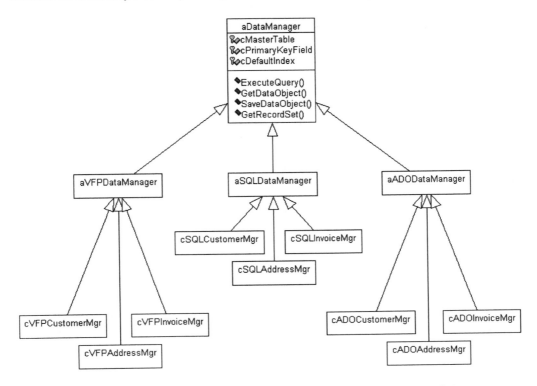

*Figure 2. The revised data manager architecture that handles different data sources.*

   The second layer contains all the code. The code used in this layer is essentially different for all classes because they handle very different data sources. However, the interface is the same in all the classes, and the objects and cursors they create are identical. This is where the power of this architecture comes from. I can exchange the data manager objects, and everything else will remain the same. In fact, the rest of the application won't even notice that a different back end is utilized. As you can imagine, this kind of design is extremely easy to extend and to modify as long as the object interface remains the same.

   This is only one example of a behavioral object. The idea behind it is rather simple, which is how it is with most behavioral objects. They help you to break large and complex behavior into small, well-defined and easy-to-manage pieces. Let's have a look at how those pieces come together.

## How everything comes together

Advanced object-oriented applications are composed of a well-thought-out web of behavioral objects that retrieve data from some kind of database and use interface objects to display the information to the user. Some of the objects handle business logic while others deal with technical issues. The objects that handle technical issues are usually referred to as "the framework."

Even people familiar with object-oriented development tend to think that applying object-oriented techniques automatically gives you the ability to plug all kinds of objects together. Nothing could be further from the truth. Objects have to be well organized to interact with each other. **Figure 3** demonstrates the object interaction in my framework.

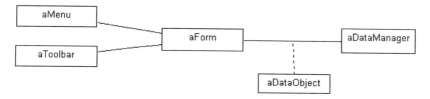

**Figure 3**. *A rough overview of a part of my framework.*

In this scenario, a form communicates with a data manager to retrieve a data object. The form may also talk to the data manager to save the data object. The user—either through the form itself, or through a menu or toolbar—usually initiates saving the object. In this case, the menu (or toolbar) simply communicates with the form, which then communicates with the data manager. All objects must follow strict communication guidelines. The menu needs to know about the interface of the form. So does the toolbar. The form needs to know about the interface of the data manager and it has to know how to handle the data object. Objects that don't know these things and don't follow the guidelines set by my framework objects will be hard to reuse (see below for more information about object reuse).

As you can imagine, a number of additional objects will be involved in setting up this kind of scenario. All forms must be managed; the same is true for toolbars and menus. **Figure 4** shows some more detail.

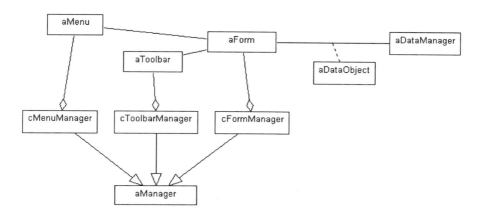

**Figure 4**. *A more detailed framework overview.*

My abstract manager class ensures that all manager objects have a standardized interface. Figure 4 also shows three individual manager classes that control the forms, menus and toolbars.

The concept of behavioral objects that communicate with each other through clearly defined interfaces can be found all over advanced-object systems. I could continue to reveal more details about my framework example, but this would bring us into the area of object modeling, which is covered in Section 3 of this book.

# Creating reusable objects

Reuse is the ultimate goal of any object-oriented development effort. Unfortunately, it is also hard to achieve. Contrary to popular belief, reuse does not come "for free" with object-oriented development. Objects and classes must be created with reuse as one of the major goals. Beyond basic architectural challenges, reusable objects also need to fulfill organizational needs. Where should classes be stored? What dependencies will you encounter if a class is reused? How many additional classes will you have to include in your new application just to reuse this cool progress bar class?

## Reuse—a fairytale?

To make a long story short: Reuse is hard to achieve. In fact, it's so hard that even people who apply object-oriented techniques successfully, fail to reuse existing code. Over time, so many attempts to reuse code failed, that people started to doubt the possibility of reuse. In fact, reuse came to be considered a fairytale.

I don't agree.

In my experience, reuse is possible as long as you start reuse at design time (see Chapters 14 and 15). You need to make reuse one of your major design goals. In fact, by coding in Visual FoxPro you've already started to reuse; using the Visual FoxPro base classes is reuse in its purest form. As you can imagine, the Microsoft Visual FoxPro team spent a lot of time designing reusable base classes. You'll have to be equally committed to reuse as the Fox team was (and is). But before you learn how to create reusable objects, you need to know the pitfalls. Let's take a look at the reasons why attempts to create reusable code fail.

The most common reason for reuse failure is lack of a good design. Classes that are created (and methods that are added) as the need arises are unlikely to have a clean interface and to fulfill the needs of other applications. When programmers take this approach, they're in danger of navigating themselves into dead ends and facing the need to redesign. But are projects that don't allow programmers to design what they planned to do, likely to allow redesign? I doubt it. For this reason, they apply workarounds rather than looking for proper resolutions to problems, which clutters the interface even more. In fact, it typically ties different objects together. Internals that used to be encapsulated get exposed so other objects can bypass the object's interface to compensate for shortcomings in the design. All kinds of direct object interactions that don't happen with clear and well-defined interfaces is the number 1 reuse killer.

"So what's the fuss?" you say. "If I simply follow all the design guidelines described in Part 3 of this book, I'll end up with reusable code." Unfortunately, even well-designed object systems don't guarantee reuse because there are a number of logistical issues concerning your implementation. Recently, I tried to reuse a behavioral class that was part of an object system that was designed to be reused (and it fact it had been reused successfully in a number of applications). Unfortunately, this attempt to reuse what was reused before failed, because the system didn't allow reusing this particular class without reusing others that were stored in the same library. Other classes in those libraries had their own dependencies, so whenever I tried to compile the application I would fail due to missing components. I tried to resolve the situation by adding those additional libraries and classes to the project, but as you can imagine, all those libraries had yet another set of dependencies, and so forth. In the end I would have had to reuse an entire application to reuse the class I really wanted when I started out. Still, I could have made this scenario work by reprogramming the desired component. I didn't do that, but I copied the class into a separate library to get rid of all the additional dependencies. That did the trick for a moment, but it didn't accomplish my ultimate goal, which was to reuse a data management component in the administrative tool of a larger application. It worked fine in the first version, but as soon as I changed the component in the main application, I had to go back to the administrator tool and make those changes there as well. In the long term, I didn't even achieve half of what I originally intended.

Now let's assume we didn't fall into either one of those traps. This should open the door for successful reuse. But what actually is "successful reuse"? Whether or not you'll be able to reuse components successfully depends greatly on your expectations. If you build small components (such as the Fox Foundation Classes described in Chapter 4), you might be able to reuse a large percentage of your code. However, applications are also built of much larger classes, and reusing those is much more difficult. When you create a framework, you should be able to design it so you can reuse all of it quite easily, but it might be impossible to reuse only one of the components. The data manager object described above will be very hard to reuse in different frameworks unless they adjust to the way the manager object does things. Does that mean I wasn't successful in creating reusable objects? I don't think so. When I designed this framework, I never expected those classes to be reusable individually. The most important point is that I save myself about 40% development time by reusing the framework together.

So now that you've learned about the most common reuse traps, you can have a look at how to do things the right way.

## Application-internal reuse

People usually envision reusing code in various applications. However, the first step is to reuse code within a single application. In the first sections of this chapter I introduced a couple of classes that are designed for application-internal reuse (data managers, for instance). I believe that application-internal reuse accounts for more saved time than any other kind of reuse.

Reuse within one application is much easier to achieve than cross-application reuse because you don't face organizational issues. The key is to design clean interfaces and to abstract behavior properly so other classes can easily inherit from the class you want to reuse. The data manager classes at the beginning of this chapter are a good example of application-internal reuse.

## Cross-application reuse

Cross-application reuse is the ultimate level of reuse. You create components once and reuse them in all your applications from then on. On top of the time you save, you get the advantage of updating all your applications at once or fixing bugs globally.

The easiest form of cross-application reuse is COM components. You simply instantiate a specific component in a COM client application without worrying about anything but the component's name and interface. In fact, this form of cross-application reuse is no more difficult than application-internal reuse. Not only is this the easiest way to reuse code across applications, but it also is one of the few ways to reuse it across various development environments. Unfortunately, there are some limitations to COM components. Most importantly, there is no inheritance or subclassing.

Another incarnation of reusable COM components is ActiveX controls. As we know, Visual FoxPro can't create ActiveX controls but it can use them. In fact, it can use ActiveX controls better than most other tools especially because Visual FoxPro introduces inheritance, which is a truly unique feature for binary components.

The most powerful form of reuse is code reuse on the class level. This kind of reuse provides access to all of Visual FoxPro's object features, including inheritance, pseudo-subclassing and instance programming. Unfortunately, this is also the most difficult version of reuse because you have to face all the issues at once, including object interface design, implementation logistics and more. This means that besides designing your application architecture, you also have to spend a good amount of time on designing your implementation. I generally try to separate framework classes from individual classes so the framework is easy to update. I also try to keep my class libraries small. This reduces the number of classes I reuse unwillingly along with others. A good guideline is to put all classes that depend on each other in one class library. If you can't do that (which is often the case when dealing with complex classes), you should add asserts (the new ASSERT command) that inform the programmer about all the dependencies, so if he forgets something and an error arises, the class will explain what is needed.

## What if components get updated?

The time you save building applications with reusable classes or components is essential, but the advantages of reuse don't stop there. In my opinion, one of the most important points about reuse is that you can update your classes and all your applications will be able to take advantage of them immediately. This applies to bug fixes as well as new features. Obviously, you have to be extremely careful not to change the interface of your objects—otherwise you could break your applications severely in a matter of minutes.

This reminds me that I should discuss acceptable interface changes. When I say "Don't change the interface," I'm referring to the existing interface, because it usually isn't a problem to enhance an interface. This means that you can easily add new methods and new behavior. You can even add to existing methods. New parameters, for instance, aren't a problem as long as they are optional. The return value (or the produced result in general) can also change, as long as it doesn't change when the method is called in the original way. In other words: The result should change only when the passed parameters change. This ensures that other applications that use the class but aren't aware of the changes will see the same result as before.

It might make you nervous to know that changes in one application will change other applications that use the same code. This drives me crazy, but it's good to know there are tools to help with this scenario. Microsoft Visual SourceSafe is one of them. It allows you to share components and to pin down a certain version of a component for a specific project. This means that a particular project won't get the updated version of a class before you explicitly say so.

A scenario you should avoid is to copy classes into separate class libraries, even if you don't change the code. This might give you some short-term advantages, but you wouldn't be able to update your application easily.

If you do all your work in a single environment, you can leave shared class libraries in one directory for all your projects. However, this might not always be possible. In my case, for instance, doing consulting work for different companies, I have to keep copies of my framework (or other classes) in special directories (typically at the customer's site or on a secure Web server). This is not a problem as long as I don't touch those copies. I always have one directory—and one directory only—where I keep the version that I modify. I then deploy new versions to all projects that need updating at that point. The projects I'm not working on remain with the pinned-down version of those components until I make changes (I use SourceSafe in all my projects).

## Reusing components that don't match your architecture

You are likely to face situations where you need to reuse components that aren't designed for reuse. In this case you can use a *wrapper*, which is a class that is designed to match your architecture. This class then talks to the component you want to reuse in a way the component understands. The wrapper essentially acts as a translator or adapter.

I've already described a wrapper in this chapter. One of the data manager objects I used in my example dealt with ADO data. ADO is object-based data that can be used as a COM component. However, when I started to create my framework, ADO wasn't yet invented. When the need arose to use ADO, I created the wrapper class that translated the ADO methods and properties into something my framework could use.

Wrappers can be implemented in a variety of ways. A wrapper can just be aware of the class it handles, or it can contain and fully control that object. Either way, all the wrapper does is receive messages and translate them into something the object understands. The messages are then passed on to the object you want to reuse. The result is then translated back into something your system can understand. Finally, the result is passed back to the system that doesn't even know it just talked to a component that speaks a different language.

In the ADO example, this would mean that the ExecuteQuery() method is translated into a plain Execute() method that the ADO connection object can understand. The resulting recordset is then converted into a regular Visual FoxPro cursor.

# Conclusion

We've made the transition from the basic concepts of object-oriented programming to the development of complex object systems. Of course, the wisdom in this chapter is only a fraction of what it takes to create advanced object systems. I'll spend the rest of the book explaining further issues and solutions as well as proper techniques of object design.

# Chapter 9
# Three-Tiered Development

**Lately there's been a lot of hype about three-tiered development. The main idea is to split applications into different layers—the interface, the business logic and the data back end. Many people tout three-tiered development as the best thing since sliced bread. While it can't cure world hunger, it definitely helps me a great deal in my development efforts.**

## A brief introduction

Every application has some kind of user interface, attached business logic and data back end. Of course, each part can have a different appearance. The interface might be a regular windows interface, a Web page, a voice interface or even an automated process or script. The data might be stored in Visual FoxPro tables, in SQL Server databases, in XML files or any other kind of storage. The business logic might be compiled into an EXE or some kind of COM component. None of these pieces are specific to three-tiered architecture. You'll find them in any kind of business application, whether it be a modern component-based Windows application or an old mainframe monster.

A modern software development approach has to be a lot more flexible and powerful than in past days. Changes must be implemented more quickly, cheaply and at a higher quality. Applications are no longer monolithic. Data sources such as ADO, SQL Server and XML must be used in addition to regular Visual FoxPro data. Different interfaces must be used, including HTML, Windows interfaces and more exotic ones (at least for Visual FoxPro developers) such as Windows CE. Even if you can do everything using FoxPro data and a regular Windows interface, your app might need to talk to other components such as Microsoft Office. On top of that, you will definitely need flexibility so you can quickly change parts of an interface or the business logic without worrying about overall project quality or going through an enormous amount of work.

The three-tiered model is designed to reduce design complexities and increase the application developer's flexibility in creating, maintaining, and redeploying applications on different platforms.

In the three-tiered approach, the interface, business logic and database layers are kept separate. This can be done in various ways. All components are compiled separately in COM components and EXEs, or the classes are simply kept in different libraries and inheritance trees, but they are still compiled into one EXE, possibly using a monolithic Visual FoxPro approach. The key is that the layers talk to each other *only* through a defined API and are *not* linked in any other way. This means that, at any time, you can modify, change, or even replace a tier, and—assuming that you continue to write to the same inter-tier API—keep the entire system working. The independence that you gain is the key to this approach. The rest of this chapter is dedicated to explaining, supporting, defending, and preaching about this idea.

## The model-view-controller approach

Like many things in object-oriented development, the three-tiered architecture isn't really new. Many of the traditional object-oriented languages such as Smalltalk have been using this approach for quite a while. It was (and is) known as the "model-view-controller" design, where the "model" is the data, the "view" is the interface and the "controller" is the business logic. The Unified Modeling Language (UML—see Chapter 12) replaced this terminology with the terms "user services," "business services" and "data services."

# Better than sliced bread: sliced applications

Conceptually, the idea of three-tiered development is simple: You take your regular applications and slice them in three layers. Interface elements belong in the interface layer. Business rules, logic, and data validation belong in the middle tier, and the data store is in the data layer. While this sounds easy, it's a significant change of view for the "traditional" FoxPro developer. Because we have always had data controls that are "intimate" with the data, we have always been able to design interfaces that directly access data in our tables and, with the VALID clause, do validation in the interface. The "one-tier" model (or one and a half if you want to argue about editing memory variables instead of the table) was the natural way to go and, with FoxPro, worked quite well.

Well, Visual FoxPro is now playing in a larger arena and, if you want to structure applications to play the new game, you are going to have to move away from the old ways of doing things. You cannot put your logic into the Valid event of a field in a form. Neither can you directly bind fields to data. You can't even have these parts in the same composite object. Fortunately, all this complies with most of the principles of proper object-oriented design. Rather than using a part of the interface to validate entries, you would call out to a behavioral object. Data would be bound to the interface through well-defined object interfaces. The actual implementation can vary greatly, depending on whether you create COM components or a monolithic Visual FoxPro application (see below).

The most difficult part of three-tiered development is following the rule of keeping the three tiers separate. The interface and business logic components are especially hard to separate. It's tempting to add some code to one of the controls in a form rather than creating another method in a behavioral object that does all the calculations. Unfortunately, as soon as you take such a shortcut, you break your entire three-tiered model. This will set you back to the prior level of software development. Self-control (if you are developing an application by yourself) and code reviews (in team development scenarios) are key. In most areas of development, you can get away with bending the rules every now and then. This is not true for three-tiered architecture. Bend the rules once and you'll lose all the advantages but still carry all the burdens.

# Three-tiered internally

When you hear the term "three-tiered", you might immediately think of an application that is compiled in various COM components that talk to some back-end server (possibly on a network) to retrieve data and a number of different interfaces to interact with the user. COM, ADO (or ODBC) and MTS (Microsoft Transaction Server) are the key technologies that make these scenarios work. Most of these things seem strange and unnatural to Visual FoxPro developers who are used to a straightforward way of making things happen.

However, this is only one of the possible scenarios. Another approach is to stick to Visual FoxPro (or any other environment) and compile all the tiers into one EXE. The main advantage of three-tiered development is the flexibility and ease of maintenance you gain. The fact that you have to recompile your application in order to switch components, interfaces or data sources isn't usually a big problem. After all, compiling takes only a couple of minutes, even for large projects. The fact that you can change interfaces or data sources in a matter of minutes, on the other hand, weighs heavily.

I often reuse a certain framework for my consulting customers. This framework follows a strict three-tiered approach. When I initially designed the framework, nobody was interested in this kind of architecture (not the FoxPro or Visual Studio world, anyway). Important technologies such as ADO and MTS weren't even planned at that time. For this reason, I designed my three-tiered application using only Visual FoxPro technology. In other words, this application was a monolithic Visual FoxPro application, yet it was strictly three-tiered.

Over time, as new technologies emerged, I enhanced my framework. Now I can use it to create COM components that are called from Visual Basic or Active Server Pages as well. However, I often use the old approach simply because the majority of applications still run in a regular Windows network environment and scalability is not a major issue. (Visual FoxPro still is pretty fast at handling data (whether it is FoxPro tables or SQL Server databases.)

Let me introduce some basic ideas behind my framework.

One of the main design goals was to use different data sources without changing any of the business logic or interface components. Another requirement was to use different interfaces (at this point, mainly Windows and plain HTML interfaces). On top of that, I wanted to be able to switch the business logic layer, mainly to make sure I could handle multi-lingual and (more importantly) multi-cultural issues as well as adjustments to serve different branches of the targeted businesses. This requirement was relatively trivial, yet most three-tiered applications don't handle that very well. Usually only the interface and the data source can be switched, but the logic remains the same. (I guess by now you get the idea that I don't particularly like this approach.)

## Handling the data

In order to handle the data generically, I use controller objects. (This term wasn't chosen very wisely. "Model" or "DataService" would have been more appropriate.) An abstract controller defines the object interfaces, and there are subclasses for each of the data back ends I want to talk to. Originally, the framework was designed to handle Visual FoxPro and SQL Server data. Now it handles Oracle as well as ADO.

To get to data, you can use the controller's query methods, which can create regular Visual FoxPro cursors as well as objectified data (see below). The way I talk to the controllers never changes. The controller serves as a translator between my attempts to retrieve data and the language spoken by each specific back end.

It might surprise you that the controller objects are part of the back end (data layer). Typically, the data back end simply is a collection of data in a standardized format such as SQL Server, FoxPro tables or XML. However, there is no reason why you couldn't create objects that belong to the data layer. Many of today's products such as SQL Server and ADO represent the object part of the data layer. My controller objects simply add another layer of abstraction to this scenario, thus making it more generic.

When Microsoft first released ADO, I was concerned that the additional layer I built would be redundant, but this concern proved wrong. Today, I still talk to SQL Server directly using SQL Pass Through (mainly for performance reasons) and not ADO. I also use XML data sources directly (using the ActiveX control provided by Microsoft). And what if I use plain Visual FoxPro data? Should I retrieve that through ADO? I don't think so! So far I have been satisfied with this additional layer, and I would redesign it in the same manner without hesitation.

## Creating the interface
In most three-tiered applications, the interface is the driving force that invokes business logic, which then retrieves the data. However, this is limiting because the interface decides what kind of business logic to invoke, which automatically defines what data to use. This would be fine in scenarios where my main concern is reusing components in different interfaces or applications, but as mentioned above, not only do I want to reuse middle-tier components (business logic), I also want to be able to exchange these components in a flexible manner. If I were to use the interface to invoke those objects, I would need to change every interface after I introduced new middle-tier classes.

This scenario didn't work for me, so I created special objects that are responsible for launching the interface. These objects are my "UserService" objects. Again, I have an abstract user service object that I subclass into a user service object for every interface I want to support. Initially, the interface would be either a regular Visual FoxPro Windows interface or an HTML-based approach. By now I've enhanced this so any kind of COM component can require interface operations.

The user service object provides a number of standard operations, such as loading some data for editing (single items) or displaying a list. Any user service object can be decorated, so it talks to a controller to retrieve the correct data. Depending on whether I'm using a regular Windows interface or another component, the user service either launches a form or creates HTML that will eventually travel across the wire. Launching a form is trivial. Creating HTML pages is somewhat more complex. Basically, the HTML user service object requests data, merges it into HTML templates and sends it out. Initially, the system was designed to work with the West Wind WebConnection (www.west-wind.com) and Visual WebBuilder (www.visual-webbuilder.com). Now I've enhanced it so it can serve as a COM component that's called from Active Server Pages or any kind of other COM client that can handle HTML. Once the user modifies the data, the request hits the Web server again and the user service object gets involved. The user service collects all the data in the page, reassembles regular Visual FoxPro data, and hands it back to the rest of the application—which doesn't even know what kind of interface was utilized.

Both the regular VFP user service and the HTML user service actively create a user interface. In the case of an HTML interface, additional rules are attached in order to reduce traffic. In the case of a Visual FoxPro user service, the interface directly calls the business logic layer to validate and handle data. The HTML user service does this as well, but only when the user submits data. This is the final and most important data validation step. All validation that is done right in the Web page (using scripts) is very basic and doesn't cover complex business rules. That's fine. The main purpose here is to eliminate stupid problems such as submitting an empty form. Whether the data that has been submitted actually makes sense is hardly ever validated in the page itself. This helps to reduce the number of hits and total traffic.

In the case of the COM user service, things work slightly differently. This user service doesn't create an interface, but it does create a composite object that contains all data to be used in the interface, and it has some very basic business rules that are implemented through access and assign methods. This object is then sent through COM channels, and it's the responsibility of the client to create the actual interface. This way, I can use any COM client (such as Visual Basic) to provide the interface.

The user service objects are configured at compile time. I have a couple of compiler directives (#DEFINE) that specify what kind of user service object I want to use. The user service objects don't get to decide what kind of controller or logic object will get involved. To load customer data, for instance, the user service object would simply invoke the customer controller. Whether this controller is subclassed from the VFP controller class, the ADO controller class, or any other controller, is defined elsewhere (see below). The same is true for the business logic. The user interface would simply invoke a "tax-calculation object." The class this object is made of depends on a number of settings, such as the country the application is used in, or the country/state you are dealing with. These things can be configured at compile time as well as during runtime, depending on the kind of business logic you need to invoke (see below).

## Invoking the business logic

Creating the business logic layer isn't quite as straightforward as creating the other two layers. The business logic layer is responsible for getting data from the data layer, presenting it to the interface, receiving edits, validating them against business rules, and then sending the results back to the data layer.

Creating abstract parent classes is difficult because you'll encounter various different needs. You could create an abstract logic base class that had a number of standard methods, but you would soon discover that those methods would hardly ever match your needs. And that's fine. After all, the business logic is what programming is all about. Our target must be to reduce the effort it takes to resolve technical issues, but the business logic often will be coded individually.

However, polymorphism will be important within certain kinds of business logic objects. You should create an abstract class for all your tax-calculation objects, for instance. This will allow you to exchange different objects without changing the rest of your system. Another typical example would be an object that validates whether addresses were entered correctly. Depending on the country you are in, different rules will apply, so you should create different classes for each country, all subclassed of one abstract parent class to keep the interface persistent. However, it isn't that important for the tax-calculation and the address-verification objects to share the same interface. What are the chances you will rip out the "U.S. tax-calculation" object from your invoicing module and replace it with the "European-address-verification" object? Not very high, I would say, unless you want to check whether the invoice total coincidentally is a valid ZIP code, or something like that.

This leaves us with the dilemma of not having a clear approach to invoking the business logic. For this reason I decided to introduce yet another set of abstract classes that are used to create instances of business logic. All they do is return object references to the business logic object that's appropriate for the current use. There would be one of those objects for each of the logic objects I have. For instance, a tax-calculation business service object would have a GetHandle() method that retrieves or creates a reference to a business logic object and returns it. From this point on, I would directly talk to the business logic object rather than the business service object.

The way the business service object decides what logic object to invoke varies greatly. In the tax-calculation scenario, many decisions might be made at runtime. Depending on where the customer is located, different objects will be invoked. However, there might also be some configurations that happen at compile time. When I create a U.S. version, an entirely different set of logic objects will be compiled into the product than when I create a European version. After all, when shipping something from the U.S. to Germany, the tax will be calculated differently than when shipping from Austria to Germany, even though the destination country is the same.

## Compiling one EXE

By now you know the ideas behind the three tiers, but you have yet to explore how the entire application is compiled. In many scenarios, the user interface is the part that contains or invokes the rest of the application. As mentioned above, I don't like this approach. I like to use an object that works as a launch pad and coordinator for all other tiers. This is my application object. It asks the user service object to provide a starting point (the main window, or the home page) and it is used to define application-global settings such as what objects are to be utilized. This removes a lot of responsibility from the interface layer. Note that this object doesn't have a lot of code. It would not handle the instantiation of interface objects, for example, but it would have a property (or something similar) that would tell us whether the current interface is Windows-based or Web-based.

## Displaying and manipulating data

One of the most difficult parts of three-tiered development is transferring data from the back end to the interface. It's easy to run a query in the data service object (controller), but how do you get that cursor into a form's data session? Well, there are a number of different approaches. I like to use objectified data. In other words, I create a data object representing a record (or many data objects representing a record set). The objects have only properties, and each property represents a field in a table. The objects are created by the controller and handed over to all kinds of interface components. The user service object is responsible for handing the object to a form, merging the object into an HTML template, or creating a composite object if a COM client makes a request. This approach works fine for single records or small record sets (up to a couple of hundred records). However, it doesn't work very well for large data sets. In this case, performance won't be all that great, and resources will run out quickly. Also, Visual FoxPro grids cannot use these kinds of record sets as the data source.

Another approach is to use the controller objects to create regular Visual FoxPro cursors in the data session of a certain form (or other interface component). To do so, the controller has to switch data sessions before a cursor is created and before data has to be saved. In this case, you need to be very careful resetting the data session. If the controller fails to restore initial settings, the entire application is likely to get confused and to malfunction. Data objects are a much safer approach, so I try to stay away from the "session hopper" scenario wherever possible.

As a general tip, I recommend not using grids for data entry. Interfaces that use grids are very hard to implement in other interfaces such as HTML. I use grids almost exclusively for display purposes.

## Class and inheritance hierarchies

You've probably heard it a hundred times by now: "Never use the Visual FoxPro base classes! Create your own set of classes, put them in a library called Base.vcx and base all your other classes and controls on this set."

This is still true in three-tiered applications, but you shouldn't use this approach in all tiers. If you want to stick to this approach, keep separate sets of base classes for each tier. In other words, create the libraries "user service base.vcx", "data service base.vcx" and "business logic base.vcx". Make sure you never base classes in different tiers on base classes belonging to another tier. This will tie the tiers together, which moves you closer to single-tiered development again.

Obviously not all base classes are required in each tier. Most of Visual FoxPro's base classes are interface related. You don't need those classes anywhere but in the "user service base.vcx". Typically, the middle-tier and the back-end classes are all based on *Custom*. Sometimes you might see classes such as "line" or "separator," because those classes are resource-friendly (unlike the heavy *Custom* class). However, those classes never become visible.

In Visual FoxPro, every class must be based on a Visual FoxPro base class. You cannot start from scratch. However, this is what most people mean to do when creating middle-tier or back-end objects. So let's just assume for a minute that we could start out with a brand-new class. We would create abstract classes, create concrete subclasses, and so forth. We would have many different inheritance trees starting from scratch. We would have a tax-calculation tree, we would have an address-verification tree, and so forth. What do those trees have in common? Nothing! They all are independent classes. Now let's go back to the real Visual FoxPro world, where we can't start from scratch but have to base everything on the *Custom* base class instead. What would those trees have in common, other than the fact that Visual FoxPro forced them to use an unnecessary parent class? Not a bit more than the classes in the example above! So does it make sense to create a set of base classes for the logic layer and the back end? I doubt it. In fact, it will make it harder to reuse those components because they always rely on some parent classes that you have to drag over into other projects. These projects might use their own set of base classes for the middle and back-end tiers. You can now redefine your classes (making it impossible to reuse updated versions of that class) so they use the new set of base classes, or you can maintain multiple sets of base classes, which would defeat the purpose of the concept altogether. And then again, what would be the benefit in this situation? I don't know. So I recommend creating your own set of base classes for the interface tier only.

## Exposed tiers

Let's return to the scenario of three-tiered development using COM components. In this case, you would design your application in a similar fashion as described above. In some regards, it's even simpler to create COM components than an EXE. You aren't in danger of breaking the rules of three-tiered development, because you simply can't. Reusing components is much easier because you don't have to worry about dependencies. Creating clean class hierarchies is also easier because you're dealing with various projects, which reduces the risk of creating unwanted relationships. Creating good object interfaces comes quite naturally, because there is no way to talk to a COM component other than through its interface. You aren't in danger of cheating (which might happen unknowingly, but with the same complications nevertheless).

Unfortunately, a number of issues are quite a bit harder to resolve in the world of COM components than in a regular Visual FoxPro application. How do you display the data, for instance? Again, single records aren't a problem, because you can always create a data object, but there is no way to switch into some other component's data session. That's where ADO comes in. ADO handles all data as objects, which can be passed through COM channels from the back end through the middle tier into the interface.

The great advantage of COM-based three-tiered applications is language independence. You can create a data-specific component in Visual FoxPro, another one that does a lot of calculations in Visual C++, a third one in Visual J++ and yet another one in Visual Basic. Even though you might not want to do that right away, you always have the option to switch to different components later on. If you switch to Visual FoxPro from Visual Basic, for instance, and aren't quite familiar with the environment, you can create a performance-critical data-retrieval component in Visual FoxPro, and other components that aren't so critical in Visual Basic (the tool you're familiar with). Later, when the application grows and performance becomes critical in other parts, you can easily trade single components for faster ones.

COM-based, three-tier applications often run on servers, whether Web servers or just intranet servers. In these scenarios, one powerful computer does almost all the work. When you have a large number of users, a large number of hits, or both, you need to make sure your application scales well. This isn't a trivial task in monolithic Visual FoxPro applications. Visual FoxPro is fast, no doubt, but once a certain amount of traffic occurs, there isn't much you can do. There's no intrinsic multithreading, no load balancing, basically nothing you can do other than coding your own pool manager (good luck!). When your application is based on COM components, this becomes much easier. You can simply let Microsoft Transaction Server handle your components, and it will make sure enough resources are available. All you need to do is register your component, and MTS will manage all calls to it. This includes component instantiation, which is handled entirely by MTS to ensure there are enough resources and component instances. Essentially MTS is a very advanced pool manager.

However, there is more to MTS than just scalability. "Transaction" is its middle name, which indicates that MTS is a transaction manager system as well. In fact, it allows you to span transactions over multiple components, no matter what language they are written in. In this case, things don't happen automatically anymore, but you have to design your COM components specifically for MTS. This isn't rocket science, but it is beyond the scope of this book. If you are interested in MTS, visit my Web site (www.eps-software.com) where I keep a list of recommended reading and a number of MTS articles.

## Conclusion

Three-tiered development isn't as difficult as many people would have you believe. The easiest way to get started is to create a small prototype that handles some dummy data. Try to keep the data in different databases and create different interfaces, following the rules outlined in this chapter. Once you are more comfortable with this approach, you can try to create different logic components that can be swapped (static at first, and dynamic later on). You will soon realize the advantages of this approach, and I promise you, once you get used to the slightly different way of doing things (and the handful of complications), you won't want to go back to the old way. In fact, single-tiered applications now seem like source-code chaos to me. Three-tiered design helped me to raise the quality of my code tremendously—not only because of the obvious advantages I laid out in this chapter. Many design questions, such as what classes should be based on your own set of base classes, will become easy to answer once you take this well-organized approach.

# Chapter 10
# Patterns

**Among the first of the advanced object topics that made it into the Visual FoxPro world were object-oriented design patterns. The concept of patterns was initially pushed by Erich Gamma and has been widely accepted throughout object-oriented development environments. Steven Black has been one of the pattern pioneers of the Visual FoxPro community. I had the privilege of working with Steven on a project during the Visual FoxPro 3.0 beta phase, when he first started investigating patterns while other "gurus" were still trying to figure out basic object-oriented development.**

## An overview

This fortunate coincidence got me immediately involved with patterns as well. In fact, thanks to Steven, I started using patterns in my daily development shortly after making my first steps in Visual FoxPro, long before Visual FoxPro 3.0 was actually released.

Before I started working on this chapter, I sat down to think about what I was going to write. All of a sudden, patterns came to mind—a remote topic I hadn't dealt with in a long time. Fortunately, this feeling didn't last long because I realized that the only reason patterns seemed remote was the fact that I hadn't written an article or given a talk on the subject in quite a while. However, I still use patterns on a daily basis. Now that I think of it, just a couple of hours ago I implemented a perfect "strategy" pattern in combination with a "bridge" pattern. But these things now come so naturally that I don't even realize I'm using them.

You might not be familiar with the two pattern names I mentioned above, but once you read this chapter, things should be a lot clearer. In fact, if you were familiar with those particular patterns, you would have a pretty good idea of what I did.

In this chapter, I'll introduce the basic ideas behind object-oriented design patterns. I'll also give you a couple of actual pattern examples, such as the two I mentioned above. Note that this chapter is not meant to replace a pattern catalog; it only gives some quick examples in a less detailed fashion. Pattern catalogs are usually quite a bit bigger than the one you are holding. They introduce a huge number of patterns in a language-independent fashion. Every pattern is explored in a great level of detail, typically including case studies of known uses, diagrams, code samples and other useful information.

Erich Gamma's book (*Design Patterns, Elements of Reusable Object-Oriented Software,* ISBN 0-201-63361-2, Gamma, Helm, Johnson, Vlissides) is the classical example of a patterns catalog. Every serious object-oriented developer should have a copy of this book on his desk. When I worked with Steven Black, he always bought a copy of this book for every programmer on the team. I picked up the same habit and continue to do the same. It has always worked out well, improving overall product quality and cutting a good chunk of time off our meetings.

While Erich Gamma's book was one of the first to pick up the topic of patterns, there are now an incredible number of books that have the word "pattern" in their titles. Some of them are good, but a lot of them seem to be looking for the "quick buck." Check out my Web page (www.eps-software.com) for an up-to-date list of recommended reading.

## What exactly is an "object-oriented design pattern"?

A pattern is an abstract solution to a standard problem "class." When creating object-oriented applications, you'll notice that many problems seem to occur on a regular basis. In fact, this isn't a characteristic of object-oriented development. One issue that comes up in almost every application is the requirement of writing data to files. The solution is simple. You open a file, write the data and close the file. This three-step process is a perfect example of a design pattern. It isn't object-oriented, nor is it very sophisticated, but it's a real pattern nevertheless.

If you've used FoxPro 2.x, you might have used another pattern: the Foundation Read. This pattern solved the problem of applications shutting down automatically after startup. I could continue to list examples of patterns you might have used, but I think you get the idea. Patterns are everywhere!

Object-oriented design patterns are specific to object-oriented development. Due to the widely accepted ideas of reuse, encapsulation and polymorphism, patterns make more sense in the object-oriented world than anywhere else. Instead of reusing code, we are simply reusing design that is known to work. This has obvious advantages. We don't have to come up with new solutions all the time. We also don't have to think of all possible complications because somebody else has already taken care of that.

## Our first pattern

A simple object-oriented design pattern is the "strategy" pattern. This pattern describes how one object uses various strategy objects to achieve a task. For instance, an invoicing module could use a number of tax-calculation objects to calculate taxes depending on the location of the customer. We could create all the required logic in one object that knows about all kinds of taxes that apply in the area of the customer. However, this would be inflexible, hard to maintain and hard to extend if new taxes had to be added, new areas included, or if the laws changed. For this reason, we could create a number of different tax-calculation objects. Depending on the area the customer lives in, a different object could be invoked.

Note that I haven't yet talked about the actual implementation of this pattern. That's fine. In fact, patterns aren't concerned at all with implementation because they're language independent. Later in this chapter I'll give you some implementation examples, which should be considered only as additional information.

## One common terminology

Patterns not only give us guidance, but they also provide a terminology that allows us to "talk objects" more efficiently. How important is it to use this terminology? Does it make things harder than necessary? To answer these questions I'd like to give you an example of pattern terminology. As mentioned above, patterns can be found in object-oriented design as well as in other areas of development and even outside the programming world. In fact, we use pattern terminology in our daily lives.

If I tell you "I have an elevator in my office," this statement is quite clear. By using the word "elevator," I'm able to give you an accurate description of a piece of equipment that I use all the time. If I couldn't use the term "elevator," I'd have a hard time giving you a good description. I would say something like, "My office has a metal box that runs up and down on a cable and it can transport people from one floor to the other." However, this still wouldn't be as accurate as the earlier statement. In fact, it might not even be true. After all, I'm not quite sure whether that elevator runs on a cable or on a rail. Also, the way you would imagine this "metal box" might be quite different from what it really is. I could describe its appearance in more detail, but then I'd be giving you a specific description of my elevator and you might wrongly assume that all elevators look like mine.

In the end, I would have delivered a complicated description, possibly giving you some wrong impressions, and I only wanted to tell you that I'm too lazy to take the stairs so I had an elevator installed.

How much easier was it to use the pattern term "elevator" rather than the description? I'd say quite a bit. Did it make the language unnatural and unnecessarily complex? I don't think so. In my opinion, the opposite is true, but it required you to know the meaning of the word "elevator." The same is true in the field of object-oriented design.

By the way: Did you notice that the statement "I have an elevator in my office" didn't tell you any details about my specific elevator, yet it was sufficient and more effective than the exact description? That's a very important observation. When talking about patterns, you're not concerned with implementation details. There is no need to tell you that my elevator has a total capacity of eight people, it has a wooden interior with mirrors, and nice elevator music plays at all times. Equally, I wouldn't care how you implemented the strategy pattern in your application. You could create visual classes or plain source code. You could use a case statement to decide what object to use, or you could use precompiler statements. I couldn't care less, but the use of the strategy pattern is an important design milestone I care very much about.

The detailed information might be useful, but it would detract from my initial statement and therefore make it less clear, a consequence that might be fine when making small talk, but fatal when doing object-oriented design.

## Some examples

As I mentioned before, this book is not meant to be a pattern catalog. The level of detail I reveal below isn't quite as high as in a pattern catalog, and the examples aren't as well organized. I also give a couple of Visual FoxPro implementation examples that you wouldn't find in a catalog. These should help you to see how other patterns found in catalogs can be used in Visual FoxPro.

Most examples I use here can be found in Erich Gamma's book and other catalogs in similar form.

### Adapter pattern

An adapter is used to convert an object's interface into another interface that is expected by other objects. This is useful when you want to reuse an incompatible object in your system.

Consider the movie theater example. We used a screen class with methods that we needed to maintain a screen. Later in our example, we took over another theater that had a well-organized software system, and we wanted to incorporate the screen manager classes of that system. As expected, those screen manager classes weren't compatible with ours. However, we could still use those classes if we wrote an adapter. **Figure 1** shows the general idea.

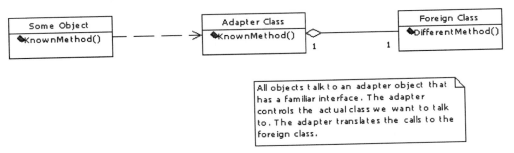

*Figure 1. The basic idea of an adapter.*

Note that an adapter doesn't house a lot of functionality. It simply translates the messages and some of the parameters that travel along. The following code shows an example of our screen class, a foreign screen class and an adapter.

```
DEFINE CLASS OurScreen AS Custom
    PROTECTED lLightsOn
    lLightsOn = .F.

    FUNCTION ToggleLights
        * Code to toggle the lights
    ENDFUNC

    FUNCTION StartMovie( lcMovieTitle )
        * Code that turns on the projector
        * and starts the movie specified in the parameter
    ENDFUNC

    FUNCTION StopMovie
        * Code that turns off the projector
    ENDFUNC
ENDDEFINE

DEFINE CLASS OtherScreen AS Custom
    PROTECTED cCurrentMovie
    cCurrentMovie = ""

    FUNCTION TurnOnLights
        * Code that turns on the lights
    ENDFUNC

    FUNCTION TurnOffLights
        * Code that turns off the lights
    ENDFUNC

    FUNCTION SpecifyMovie( lcMovieTitle )
        * Specifies the current movie in cCurrentMovie
    ENDFUNC
```

```
    FUNCTION StartProjector
      * Starts the current movie as specified in cCurrentMovie
    ENDFUNC

    FUNCTION StopProjector
      * Stops the projector (and the movie)
    ENDFUNC
ENDDEFINE

DEFINE CLASS ScreenAdapter AS OurScreen
    PROTECTED oForeignObject

    FUNCTION Init
      THIS.oForeignObject = CreateObject("OtherScreen")
    ENDFUNC

    FUNCTION ToggleLights
      IF THIS.lLightsOn
        THIS.lLightsOn = .F.
        RETURN THIS.oForeignObject.TurnOffLights()
      ELSE
        THIS.lLightsOn = .T.
        RETURN THIS.oForeignObject.TurnOnLights()
      ENDIF
    ENDFUNC

    FUNCTION StartMovie( lcMovieTitle )
      IF THIS.oForeignObject.SpecifyMovie( lcMovieTitle )
        RETURN THIS.oForeignObject.StartProjector()
      ELSE
        RETURN .F.
      ENDIF
    ENDFUNC

    FUNCTION StopMovie
      RETURN THIS.oForeignObject.StopProjector()
    ENDFUNC
ENDDEFINE
```

As you can see, the real classes (*OurScreen* and *OtherScreen*) lack some detail to keep the example simple. The adapter class (*ScreenAdapter*) is fully implemented and functional.

The adapter class is a subclass of my internal class, but this may or may not be the case in all situations. I like to do it this way because it ensures the interface is compatible and always up to date. However, you could also create a separate class. In many scenarios, the adapter wouldn't be a direct subclass of the real class, but those two classes would share a common abstract parent class. **Figure 2** shows examples of different hierarchies an adapter might use.

As you can see, the adapter automatically creates an instance of the class that is supposed to be used. It keeps a reference to this class internally (*oForeignObject* in my example). This is important, because it ensures that I can instantiate the adapter in the same way as other objects, which is essential if I want to use the adapted class as if it were an internal one.

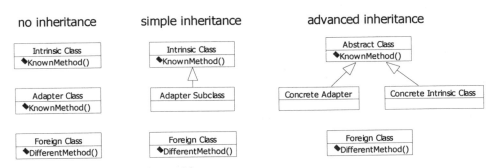

*Figure 2. Possible class hierarchies.*

Some of the calls are straightforward. The StopMovie() method, for instance, simply transfers the call to StopProjector(). The incompatibility was minimal in this case, caused by a different method name. Other things might be a little harder, such as the ToggleLights() method. Our class uses the approach of toggling lights on and off every time we use the method, while the foreign screen class has specific methods to turn the lights on and off. For this reason, the current status must be evaluated before the call is made to the two different methods. We also need to keep track of the current light status.

The StartMovie() message needs to be translated into multiple messages because we simply pass the movie name as a parameter in our class, while in the foreign class one method is used to set the movie and another one to start it. Of course, the adapter also needs to check whether the calls were successful.

Note that the adapter also takes care of the return value. Often you'll be able to simply return the value sent by the adapted class, but sometimes you'll have to translate this value or take care of multiple values at a time, as in the StartMovie() method that translates to two separate methods in the foreign class.

Like many patterns, this pattern is also known by other names (such as "wrapper" and "translator"). This somewhat defeats the purpose, but it isn't as big a deal as it might seem.

## Observer pattern

An observer is an object that observes some objects and notifies others if changes occur. Observer objects are typically used to keep objects synchronous.

Awhile back, when I created the PowerBrowser (a Class Browser add-in), one of the things I did was to replace the Class Browser's Redefine button. The original button was enabled and disabled by the browser depending on the selected class. Obviously, the browser couldn't have known about my new button, so the new button always stayed enabled. This caused serious trouble if the user clicked on the button when the wrong class was selected. The solution to the problem was to use an object that observed the original button (which was still there but invisible) and—if the enabled status changed—did the same for my button. I implemented this observer as a timer that checks the status twice a second.

There are two different kinds of observers: active observers (see **Figure 3**) and passive observers (see **Figure 4**).

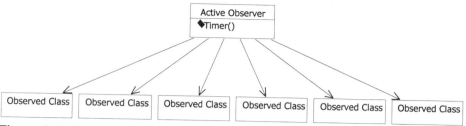

*Figure 3*. *Active observer diagram.*

Active observers (or "pop observers") actively monitor the status of other objects. In Visual FoxPro, they are usually implemented as timers. The major advantage of active observers is that other objects don't have to know they are observed (for this reason, active observers are sometimes referred to as "voyeurs"). My Class Browser example is a typical use of active observers. Typically they are used to enhance a system that wasn't designed to be easily enhanced, and to overcome design shortcomings.

The disadvantage of active observers is that they need resources and can be costly in terms of performance. Fortunately, observing tasks is usually very simple, so this disadvantage doesn't hurt too much.

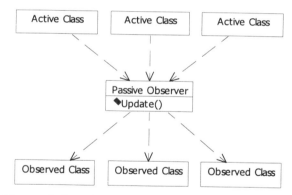

*Figure 4*. *Passive observer diagram.*

Passive observers have to be notified by other objects about changes. These kinds of observers are usually used in large scenarios where a lot of objects must be kept synchronous. In this case, it is hard for every object to know about every other object that has to be updated. Let's assume we have 10 such objects. If every object only needs to know about one method of each other object, that's a grand total of 90 messages that can be sent. If we add one more object to this scenario, every other object has to be notified of the change and modified so it can handle this new object. When we add an 11th object, 10 messages must be added to the existing objects. The larger the scenario gets, the more objects have to be changed and the larger (and more confusing) the number of messages.

The alternative is to use an observer object. Every time an object changes its status, it notifies the observer. The observer knows about all the other objects. If we add another object, we only have to add one method call to the observer, rather than 10 as in the previous scenario.

A passive observer is a specialized version of a mediator (yet another pattern). Mediators are used to handle messaging between a large number of objects. This is essentially very similar to the behavior of a push observer. The difference is that mediators can handle all kinds of messages, while passive observers are specifically used to handle an object's state.

## Strategy pattern

The strategy pattern defines a family of algorithms, encapsulates each one of them in a separate object, and makes them interchangeable. Other objects that talk to this construction would not be able to see the difference in the behavioral object that is invoked.

Earlier in this chapter I used this pattern as an example that calculates taxes in different parts of the country. In fact, I used the strategy pattern in a lot of examples throughout the book without mentioning it.

**Figure 5** documents the general idea behind the strategy pattern.

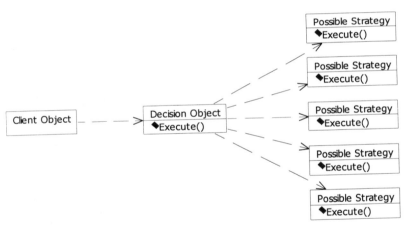

*Figure 5. Strategy pattern overview.*

In short, there is an object that needs some kind of behavior (such as an invoice object that needs the ability to calculate taxes), some algorithm that decides what kind of behavioral object is invoked, and finally, a set of behavioral objects, one of which will be utilized.

Implementations of the strategy pattern vary greatly. In small scenarios, the object that requires some behavior actually makes the decision of what object to invoke (see **Figure 6**). However, this architecture takes away many advantages of this pattern, mainly because this object must be changed in order to enhance the number of invoked algorithms. I generally do not recommend this approach (even though I sometimes use it myself in very small scenarios).

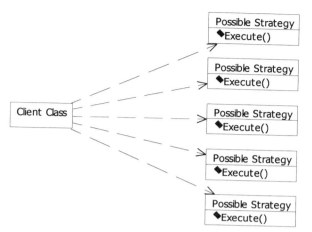

*Figure 6*. *The caller decides what strategy will be implemented.*

Another version of the strategy pattern is to use three separate objects (see **Figure 7**). In this case, the caller talks to a decision object that decides what behavioral object to invoke. The decision object typically returns an object reference. All further messaging does not involve the decision object.

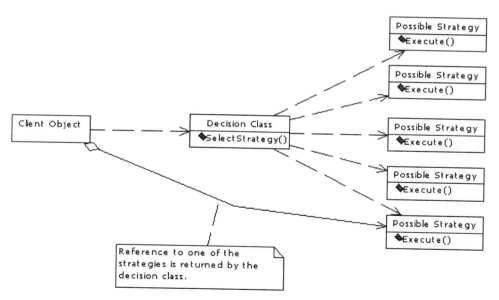

*Figure 7*. *A separate object decides what strategy to use and returns a reference to the strategy to the client class.*

I prefer this architecture because it offers the most advantages. Additional behavioral objects can be added easily because changes have to be made only in the decision object. This is much easier than the earlier approach in which we also needed to change only one object, but this object was much larger and therefore more complex. We can also exchange the decision object for another one. This is very important if we want to take our tax-calculation example to an international level. The decision object would be responsible for deciding what calculation object to involve. In other words, taxes we have to charge a U.S. customer are very different than taxes we have to charge if we ship to Germany. However, this also depends on our current location. If we ship from Austria to Germany, the situation might be very different from shipping from the U.S. to Germany. For this reason, we need to be able to swap out the decision object as well (possibly at compile time).

The architecture documented in Figure 7 can also be seen as a "double-strategy" pattern (even though this is not an official term).

A third possible version is to make all the behavioral objects members of the decision object. In this case the use of the strategy pattern is not obvious, because to the outside it looks like one object is used. **Figure 8** demonstrates this concept.

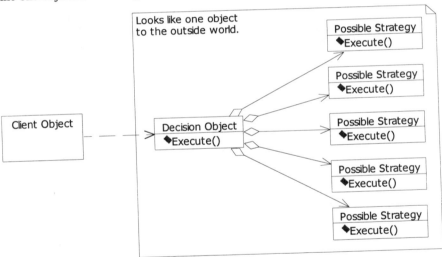

*Figure 8. The decision object is a container that owns all possible strategies. To the client object, the construction looks like a single behavioral object.*

This version is harder to maintain than the three-object architecture, but it's easier to use from the client's point of view because all messaging goes through the decision object. This means that the caller doesn't retrieve a reference to the actual behavioral object and therefore needs no knowledge about it. You can use this approach quite easily if you want to add strategies to an existing component.

The strategy pattern is also known as the "policy" pattern.

## Template method pattern

A template method pattern is a very small-scale pattern. I include it here so you can see that patterns occur on all scales, beginning at the method level and going all the way up to the framework.

The template method pattern describes a way of organizing a method to overcome problems that occur due to the static nature of inheritance. The main idea is to specify a skeleton of an algorithm that is split into several steps (methods) rather than keeping the code in only one method. Consider the following code:

```
DEFINE CLASS Class1 AS Custom
    FUNCTION Execute
        MessageBox("Step 1")
        MessageBox("Step 2")
        MessageBox("Step 3")
    ENDFUNC
ENDDEFINE

DEFINE CLASS Class2a AS Class1
    FUNCTION Execute
        MessageBox("Before Step 1")
        DoDefault()
    ENDFUNC
ENDDEFINE

DEFINE CLASS Class2b AS Class1
    FUNCTION Execute
        DoDefault()
        MessageBox("After Step 1")
    ENDFUNC
ENDDEFINE
```

In this example, a simple method (Execute) displays three message boxes. In the two subclasses, we display a message box before invoking the original method (class2a) and after the default code is fired (class2b). So far so good, but what if we want to add another message box between the first and the second one? We couldn't do that unless we overwrite the original method. This might not seem like a big deal in this example, but keep in mind that in a real-life scenario we wouldn't have three message boxes—we'd have a large number of lines of code.

The following code behaves exactly the same, but it gives us more flexibility in the subclasses:

```
DEFINE CLASS Class1 AS Custom
    FUNCTION Execute
        THIS.Step1
        THIS.Step2
        THIS.Step3
    ENDFUNC

    FUNCTION Step1
        MessageBox("Step 1")
    ENDFUNC
```

```
   FUNCTION Step2
      MessageBox("Step 2")
   ENDFUNC
   FUNCTION Step3
      MessageBox("Step 3")
   ENDFUNC
ENDDEFINE

DEFINE CLASS Class2 AS Class1
   FUNCTION Step1
      DoDefault()
      MessageBox("After Step 1")
   ENDFUNC
ENDDEFINE
```

As you can see, we can now make more detailed subclass adjustments because we can add code in the middle of a process.

In this example, the number of lines of code grew a lot, which gives us an incorrect perspective because every single method would have much more code. So all we really did was add the three lines that call the steps.

Another advantage of using this code is that we can reorganize how the steps are called:

```
DEFINE CLASS Class1 AS Custom
   FUNCTION Execute
      THIS.Step1
      THIS.Step2
      THIS.Step3
   ENDFUNC

   FUNCTION Step1
      MessageBox("Step 1")
   ENDFUNC
   FUNCTION Step2
      MessageBox("Step 2")
   ENDFUNC
   FUNCTION Step3
      MessageBox("Step 3")
   ENDFUNC
ENDDEFINE

DEFINE CLASS Class2 AS Class1
   FUNCTION Execute
      THIS.Step1
      THIS.Step3    && We call this one first...
      THIS.Step2
   ENDFUNC
ENDDEFINE
```

In this example, we had to overwrite (rewrite) the Execute method in the subclass. However, this was not a big deal because template methods don't grow very large (no more than 10 or 15 lines depending on the number of steps). Also, we didn't rewrite any real behavior.

# Conclusion

Using patterns is straightforward and natural. Whether you know it or not, you've already been using patterns in your applications. I recommend familiarizing yourself with more patterns, which will make it easier for you to implement patterns that are known to work, rather than constantly reinventing them. It will also make it much easier to communicate with other programmers or members of your team.

# Chapter 11
# Object Metrics

**Object metrics is one of the most overlooked topics in the Visual FoxPro world. To me, it is extremely important and it's a constant companion on my journeys through the world of objects.**

## The importance of metrics

Metrics, or measuring the progress of a project, is essential for several reasons. Imagine taking a car trip with a three-year-old who says, "How long before we get to Grandma's house?" without knowing where you started, how far away your mother's place is, or how fast you are traveling. Well, management, customers, and even programmers are like that three-year-old. They need to know how things are progressing. While it's possible to just "dive in" to a project, it's impossible to manage it properly. You have to start with some idea of what's involved, how fast you are moving, and how much is left to do if you are going to professionally manage a software development project. This is where metrics come in. They provide a framework to evaluate your progress.

The only way to get information about the amount of work remaining is to measure progress. Unfortunately, this is a non-trivial task in object-oriented projects. Object-oriented applications grow in a non-linear fashion; they behave more like living organisms. Like trees, perhaps. They grow from the inside out and at all branches equally. This makes it difficult to measure their progress and to explain it in an easily understandable way for people who are not directly involved in the development process, like managers and customers.

But metrics not only help to plan the schedule. They also tell you about some characteristics of an application and how well object-oriented (and other) principles are applied. Are programmers using inheritance properly? Did they abstract the scenario nicely? Are they putting comments in the source code? Are the created components reusable, or are there too many dependencies that make classes inflexible?

Metrics need to be standardized to provide valuable, objective information. Metrics should not be influenced by somebody's personal coding style. If applied incorrectly, metrics can be frustrating and bad for the morale of the troops because they can spread negativism. All metrics described in this book are suggestions, not rules. Based on the type of project you are working on, some metrics might be more important than others. In general, you should be more concerned with quality metrics than with those measuring quantity. Also, only certain quantity measurements are useful for scheduling, but most of them should only be used to get a better profile of your application—and further on, to find indicators for possible quality threats.

## Automated measuring

Without the proper tools, it's difficult to apply object metrics—not only because it's hard to count lines of code, classes and other important items, but also because the retrieved results are valuable only if they are up to date at all times. Unfortunately, I don't know of any standard tools that would help you to accomplish all necessary tasks. As mentioned above, the FoxPro world hasn't cared about metrics too much in the past. Luckily, it is not too hard to write such tools yourself. As an example, in Chapter 5 I introduced a simple Class Browser add-in that counts lines of code and other things.

To measure your application properly, you need different kinds of tools. You need tools that analyze source code to count lines of code or the number of classes. This usually is the most important kind of measuring tool you will need. However, you'll require other tools and mechanisms to accomplish special goals. To count object instances, for example, you will need a runtime mechanism that writes to a log file every time an object gets instantiated. Typically, there are no generic tools for these tasks. For the previous example, I recommend writing a simple method or function that gets called from the constructor of all of your base classes. As a parameter, I would pass the name of the instantiated class as well as the object name, and maybe some additional information such as the name of the parent object. Here is a simple class that handles instance counting:

```
DEFINE CLASS cInstanceCounter AS Custom
    FUNCTION Init
        * We ZAP our instance log table without asking
        LOCAL lnOldSelect, lcOldSafety
        lnOldSelect = Select()
        lcOldSafety = Set("safety")
        SET SAFETY OFF
        SELECT 0
        USE InstanceLog EXCLUSIVE
        ZAP
        USE
        SET SAFETY &lcOldSafety
        SELECT (lnOldSelect)
        RETURN
    ENDFUNC

    FUNCTION LogInstance (lcClass, lcObject, lcParentObject)
        * This method logs every instantiated class
        LOCAL lnOldSelect
        lnOldSelect = Select()
        SELECT 0
        USE InstanceLog
        APPEND BLANK
        REPLACE TimeStamp WITH DateTime()
        REPLACE Class WITH lcClass
        REPLACE Object WITH lcObject
        REPLACE Parent WITH lcParentObject
        USE
        SELECT (lnOldSelect)
        RETURN
    ENDFUNC
ENDDEFINE
```

This class should be instantiated when the application starts—typically it would be in Main.prg. The constructor of the class opens the log file and deletes all records in it. This allows you to start with a clean log file every time. If you want to count class instances over a longer period, you might not want to do that; instead, you might add some kind of start pointer so you could easily tell where the application was started when you analyze the log file. This is crucial to know, because instance counts are meaningful only when they're tied to a single run.

Of course, you wouldn't want to call this code in the release version. For this reason I suggest using the following code in every Init event of all your base classes:

```
IF Version(2) > 0   && 0 = runtime
   oInstanceCounter.LogInstance(THIS.Class,THIS.Name,;
      IIF(VarType(THIS.Parent)='O',THIS.Parent.Name,""))
ENDIF
```

This code checks for the Visual FoxPro version using the Version() function. If Version(2) returns 0, you know that this is the runtime version, and you don't count instances. However, there is a certain amount of overhead attached to this code. For this reason it would be better to use pre-compiler statements like so:

```
#DEFINE DEBUGMODE .T.
#IF DEBUGMODE    oInstanceCounter.LogInstance(THIS.Class,THIS.Name,;
      IIF(VarType(THIS.Parent)='O',THIS.Parent.Name,""))
#ENDIF
```

Usually you would define the DEBUGMODE constant in a header file to make it available throughout the application. This constant is useful in many other scenarios as well, so most likely you'll already have it defined.

# Metrics based on code complexity

Evaluating code complexity is the most basic way to measure progress. There are various ways to measure code complexity, the oldest of which was to simply count all lines of code. Later on, the impact of each line was considered as well, which resulted in information of higher quality. Without considering the complexity of each line of code (LOC), certain coding practices give a different result that others, even though the code might accomplish the same thing. Cascaded IF statements versus IF statements with complex expressions is an example of such a misleading scenario.

## Number of lines of code

As mentioned above, counting the LOC is the simplest of all metrics. It gave a great deal of information in the old days. But with the introduction of object-oriented development, counting lines of code was considered bad practice. There are some good reasons for that. Having many lines of code does not indicate progress, but improper use of object technology. For this reason, various other metrics were invented and developed.

However, I still believe LOC is a valuable metric and provides necessary base information for all kinds of other metrics. Only the goals and use of this measurement have changed. LOCs should not be used for scheduling or measuring progress. But if it's bad practice to have numerous lines of code, then we have a great and easy way to detect bad code. However, large projects will always have a huge number of LOC. Does that make them bad by default? No. So it doesn't seem quite as easy as we thought.

Lines of code are not a useful measurement by themselves. They only provide useful information in combination with other metrics. Knowing that a project has 100,000 lines of code doesn't tell us anything. But if we know that 100,000 lines are spread over 50 classes and 500 methods, then we also know that we have an average method size of 200 lines. That's quite a lot, and gives us a good indication that object-oriented technology might be applied improperly. At the same time, there might be only a couple of really huge methods while others have a small number of LOC. In this case, our 200-line average doesn't draw an accurate picture. Fortunately, the information is still valuable, because we can now easily spot those methods and fix them.

Calculating the number of lines of code is easy. In a Visual FoxPro application, you analyze all PRGs, the method and property fields of VCX libraries, and other metadata tables FoxPro uses, like menus and reports. There is some controversy about how to rate specific application components, such as menus. Do you rate the MNX file, the generated MPR, or both? In this case, I encourage you to use only the MNX file. The reason for that is the fact that the generation tool might change. Newer versions of the generator can create more lines of code, more comments, a different number of classes, and so on. In this case, any kind of measurement would reflect either progress or a step back, even though no changes were made to the project. The same applies for other types of metadata that might be converted in some kind of source code, be it something VFP uses internally, or some extension or tool written by yourself or a third party.

Even when you're simply counting every line of code, you shouldn't treat every line equally. Every program I've seen so far has a quite large number of blank lines. It's obvious that these lines should be left out of your statistics. You should also count the number of comment lines separately. It gets a little more complex when it comes to class, method, property, and function definitions. I never count lines that define classes, such as DEFINE CLASS and ENDDEFINE. Counting these lines would give you a different result when using source code classes and visual class libraries, because there are no lines for the class definition in VCX files. The same applies for ADD OBJECT because this command is not used in VCX files. This is also true for method definitions—they aren't needed in the VCX file. However, method definitions can contain parameter information. They are a crucial part of any application, so leaving them out would again produce a wrong number, especially because they may contain PARAMETERS or LPARAMETERS statements. For this reason I recommend counting method definitions if they have a parameter statement such as this:

```
FUNCTION Execute( lcId )
```

It is rather simple to figure out whether a method definition has a parameter statement. If it does, the line must include a parenthesis, in addition to some regular text after the open parenthesis.

I apply the same logic for regular functions that are not members of an object.

I never count the line that defines the end of a function or method definition, because it is optional; therefore, different coding styles would affect my measurements, and again, those lines don't exist in visual class libraries.

Property definitions are often overlooked in visual classes. They are regular lines of code in source code classes, but they're stored in the property field in visual class libraries. Make sure you count these lines as well. You can simply go through the property field and count all its lines, because the properties are stored line-by-line in plain English (see Chapter 5.)

Visual FoxPro's line structures are rather simple. There is no way to put several program lines in one line of text like there is in other languages. However, one program line can stretch across multiple text lines, using a semicolon at the end of each line. If you find a semicolon at the end of a line, you should not count the next line so that you can get an accurate result.

## Line complexity

Counting the lines of code as described above gives you a baseline number that you can use for various other metrics. However, there are a lot of additional issues to consider if you want to come up with a number that has some real statistical value. If you only want to see how your project evolves, and you don't change your staff of programmers, then the methods described above should be sophisticated enough. However, if you want results you can compare to other projects, or if you want to compare the statistics for various programmers, then you need to eliminate factors such as personal coding style and the like.

A good (but non-trivial) way to do this is to determine the complexity of each line and to rate it. This will eliminate, for instance, the difference between cascaded IF statements and IF statements with multiple expressions. To rate a line of code, you have to count the number of complexity indicators individually for each line. Indicators include the number of method and function calls, operators such as =, $, #, AND, and OR, as well as the main purpose of each line. When dealing with LOCATE statements, lines that contain two function calls are not necessarily twice as complex as LOCATEs with a single function call or only expressions. These lines might contain a simple LOCATE statement with compound search criteria. So no matter how complex a LOCATE might be, I'd always count it as one line of code. However, when using IF statements, lines with two function calls or expressions usually are twice as complex as lines that have only one expression. They are at least equal to cascaded IF statements, which have at least twice as many lines of code. They have ENDIF statements, and very often they have redundant code because ELSE branches might be needed more than once. For this reason I add a factor of 1.5 for every additional expression or function call I find in an IF line. So an IF statement with one function call would be counted as one line. IF lines with two function calls are counted as 2.5 lines; if I find three function calls, I count the line as four lines, and so forth. The REPLACE command offers yet another variety, because it can be used to replace multiple values.

Many different commands in Visual FoxPro need special treatment. Addressing all of them would be impossible, so I recommend finding a couple of command groups. Lines that are always counted as one line should be in one group. Another group might contain all commands that have the complexity of multiple lines, such as the REPLACE lines. Yet another group would contain lines with more complex statements, such as IF, CASE, and DO WHILE.

Considering all these factors gives you a more accurate picture that can eliminate the differences in coding styles. Unfortunately, you won't be able to come up with a perfect algorithm to eliminate all differences. But every little step toward more accurate and objective results is a good and valuable one.

Code complexity is measured in many ways. People often count lines of code and come up with a complexity factor. I prefer the method described above. It doesn't really tell you about the complexity, but it does give you a greater number of lines of code. This might seem incorrect at first (and in many ways it might be), but I think it is a lot easier to handle, and it also allows you to compare source code from different programmers without having a result that's influenced by personal coding style.

Knowing about the code complexity can also give you some interesting hints about personal preferences of each programmer. You can see who likes to impress himself by creating complex lines, and who wants to give others a chance to read and understand his code, by keeping it simple unless there is a good reason for complexity.

## Percentage of comment lines

Adding comments to source code is especially important in object-oriented applications. While you are counting lines of code, you also check whether everybody is documenting his code properly. Every time I see code with less than 10% comment lines, I get suspicious.

But again, differences in coding style make counting comment lines a little difficult. One programmer might like to use separate lines for comments, while another might add comments to regular lines using the && delimiter. The programmer who uses separate comment lines might like to use short lines and wrap comments over multiple lines. Yet another programmer might be known to create comment lines several hundred characters long. I try to compensate for all those differences by counting lines with attached comments (using &&) as two lines. When I encounter monster comment lines, I start to count everything longer than 80 characters as multiple lines.

If you use naming conventions, you can go even further and filter out certain types of comments. Some might be temporarily disabled code. Those lines should either be ignored all together, or they should be counted separately. Other comments could be function headers, documented changes, or just regular comments.

## Percentage of procedural code

Visual FoxPro is a hybrid language that allows combining object-oriented features with traditional procedural code. This is a great feature, but because the programmer is not forced to use object-oriented technology (as he is in languages like Smalltalk), it allows him to apply non-object-oriented techniques in scenarios where proper object design is desired.

Finding procedural code is simple. Simply count every line that is not within the boundaries of a class definition.

Having a large percentage of procedural code usually is a sign of insufficient knowledge or poor acceptance of object-oriented technology. Unfortunately, making that judgement is not quite that easy. Keep in mind that Visual FoxPro applications will always require some procedural code—the main program and menus, for instance. For this reason, you need to examine where the procedural code is located and what it is used for. But as a rule of thumb, there should be less than 1% procedural code in good object-oriented applications.

# Metrics based on class hierarchies

Metrics based on class hierarchies are of enormous value for object-oriented projects. They allow you to analyze the quality of source code, as well as estimate the amount of work remaining. Some of the metrics based on class hierarchies are among the most important software metrics I know.

## Number of classes

Counting the number of classes is relatively trivial and efficient at the same time. But counting is not enough. Classes need to be categorized and they need to be given a certain weight to determine their importance and complexity. In the following paragraphs I'll introduce various metrics that deal with different kinds of classes, measure class complexity, and so forth.

### Number of key classes

Key classes are the heart of the application being developed. They are usually discovered early during analysis. Because they are central to the application's main functionality, they are great indicators for the total amount of work that lies ahead. The quality of key classes is crucial for class reuse in later projects. Due to the importance of key classes, they are more likely to be reused than support classes.

Key classes resolve the majority of your application's business problems. Only on rare occasions are major technical classes (like handler or manager classes) considered key classes. However, there is no definitive judgement to be made whether or not a class is a key class. When you are uncertain, ask yourself the following questions:

- Would I still be able to develop applications for this domain without this class?
- Would I remove this class if I switched to another interface/back end?
- Would this object be of importance to the customer?
- Will I, or do I, reuse this class frequently? If so, is it designed to be reused?
- Does this class contain a lot of functionality, or is it only a lightweight subclass of the real key class?

Those questions should be of great help when rating your classes. Also, they can give you some hints about the quality of your design—key classes that aren't designed for reuse, for instance, generally aren't such a great idea. **Table 1** illustrates some problem domains and associated key classes.

*Table 1*. Problem domains and their associated key classes.

| Invoicing | Word processing | Banking |
|-----------|-----------------|---------|
| Invoice | Spell checker | Transaction |
| Line item | Text-rendering engine | Account |
| Tax calculation | Imaging subsystem | Currency |

As you can see, key classes can be more or less technical depending on the problem domain, but they are always related to the problem domain. The text-rendering engine of a word processor is relatively technical. However, it directly helps to solve the business problem, which is to display and print text in a certain way. The class that saves the created document to disk is solving a problem brought up by computers in the first place. It is extremely important for the success of the overall system, but because it is not connected to the problem domain, it is considered a support class.

In a typical business application, 20% to 40% of all classes are key classes. However, this number is influenced by a number of factors, one of which is the choice of implementation tool. In the case of Visual FoxPro, the number of key classes should lean toward the higher number. Visual FoxPro provides a lot of built-in functionality that allows you to focus on the business problem rather than on technical issues. In the case of C++, this number will be significantly lower. Another factor is the user interface. Interface classes aren't usually considered key classes, unless the interface also represents the main purpose—as it does in a word processor. If your application has a rich Windows interface, you will automatically have more support classes. If you use a simple, straightforward interface like HTML, the number of key classes might even be higher than 40%.

In Visual FoxPro, another factor influences the percentage of key classes: pseudo subclassing and instance programming. Using these techniques reduces the number of support classes significantly, because there is simply no need to subclass all the time. Therefore, depending on whether or not you use pseudo subclassing and instance programming (if you are unsure, then you do), the percentage of key classes can rise quite a bit.

A low number of key classes (less than 20%) is an indicator of poor design. Most likely, you started implementing too early and didn't discover much functionality or didn't explore gray areas of the system. In this case I recommend going back to the drawing board, continuing to work on your object model, and (yes, this is one of these rare occasions...) holding meetings to address this issue. One might argue that when an existing framework is used, the percentage of support classes is very high, because the framework provides all kinds of them. However, this is only partly true. The framework might have a large number of support classes, but you most likely won't use them all. In this case, you shouldn't count those classes. If, on the other hand, you use all provided classes, you are also very likely to create a huge project and therefore write a large number of key classes.

### Number of support classes

Support classes are typically not discovered until late in the analysis phase or maybe even during implementation. Discovering support classes during implementation does not always indicate poor design (unless you discover huge classes, such as an error handler)—they could simply be implementation issues that deal with technical challenges occurring only in a certain implementation tool.

Support classes usually accomplish small, problem-oriented tasks or resolve technical issues. Many of the support classes are interface classes. Others are database managers, file handlers, and so forth. They can also be non-problem-oriented behavioral classes. If a support class is problem-oriented, it usually accomplishes only a small task or one little step within a complex task. Many of those classes taken together might be considered a key class. However, counting each one of them as a key class would not give you an accurate picture of your application. A couple of programming practices create such scenarios—one of them is the use of the Strategy pattern. This pattern suggests breaking into a number of behavioral classes, complex operations that might follow many different branches. These classes should not be considered key classes.

The number of support classes is influenced by many factors, just as the number of key classes is influenced. In fact, these two kinds of metrics are closely related (as I describe in the next sections). For detailed information about influencing factors, see the section about key classes in this chapter.

## Average number of support classes per key class

The ratio between support classes and key classes is a valuable bit of information. It can tell you a lot about the quality of your design and also about the knowledge of the involved programmers. I've found that the ratio between key classes and support classes is somewhere between 1:1 and 1:3 for Visual FoxPro projects. As mentioned above, this factor is influenced by a number of other factors, in addition to personal coding style. For this reason, you might find slightly different results than the ones I just quoted. You might want to analyze a couple of your older projects to find a more accurate ratio that works better for you. However, keep in mind that different numbers typically indicate poor design or a lack of knowledge. So if you find your results to be significantly different from what I describe here, you should try to apply other techniques described throughout this book to get better results.

### Estimating project workload

Not only does the number of average support classes per key class indicate the quality of your design, it also helps you to schedule your project timeline. Typically, not knowing the number of support classes is the part that makes it hard to estimate a schedule. Key classes are discovered relatively early during the design. Knowing that a typical ratio between key classes and support classes is between 1:1 and 1:3, you can easily calculate how many classes you can expect to discover. **Figure 1** shows a graph that helps you to estimate the ratio for your project. The first two columns show the ratio in a user-interface-intensive application. The second pair of columns shows a regular Visual FoxPro application with a simple interface, possibly even an HTML interface. The third pair of columns shows a Visual FoxPro application that makes intensive use of instance programming and pseudo subclassing. Finally, I added an example for a C++ program.

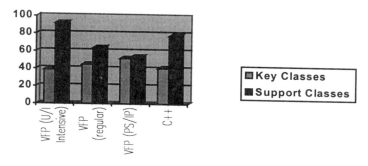

*Figure 1*. Sample ratios for various scenarios.

The results displayed in Figure 1 are based on my personal experience, and the number of analyzed projects is too small to achieve statistical accuracy. However, they seem to be in accordance with the results other people achieve, and I'm fairly confident that they have some significance. But as mentioned above, you might want to analyze your existing projects to get more accurate schedule estimations.

One might argue that support classes are less time-consuming to create and therefore the estimation would be wrong. For most support classes I have to agree. However, other tasks that are not captured by key and support classes have to be accomplished before finishing the implementation cycle of an application. Estimating all of them in great detail is non-trivial, and I found that I was better off basing my estimation on key and support classes (and by counting them equally) than by going into a great level of detail. Once I proceed further with my design, I will have a chance to estimate more accurately, but in an early design stage the key class/support class ratio estimation has served me well.

## Ensuring project quality

Let's talk a little more about project quality. Once you have all your key and support classes in place, you can use the ratio to check whether your design was done properly. A low number of key classes with a very high ratio indicates that you are creating "Swiss army knife objects." You are simply doing too much work in too few classes, making the classes hard to maintain and hard to reuse. Typically, these classes also have an enormous number of lines of code in a small number of methods. I'm not really sure why this is, but it seems that the mindset of a "Swiss army knife object programmer" is closely related to the mindset of the "monster method programmer."

When you find one of those "Swiss army knife objects," ask yourself what you can do to avoid it. Often you will find that the object combines behaviors that don't belong together. In this case, cut the object into pieces! If you find that the object serves only one purpose, you can create many behavioral objects, some that are additional key classes, and some that are not.

Ask yourself these questions when you encounter the Swiss weaponry:

- When I describe what the object does, do I talk about many different problem areas?
- Are there any other objects that could implement some of the functionality?
- If I split this object, what other objects would each resulting object work with?

Usually these questions will lead you to the solution of your problem. The last one especially tends to point out groups of objects that make the whole scenario clearer. If each of the resulting objects doesn't invoke a certain group of objects, you should split them up in another way.

The opposite scenario would involve more key classes than support classes. That should tell you that class hierarchies weren't properly abstracted and responsibilities got mixed up. In other words: Classes that are supposed to resolve a business problem deal with technical issues. That introduces problems when trying to change business logic, or even when you try to transport your code to another platform, interface or back end. Projects that show these symptoms usually are constantly out of date, simply because the design is too inflexible to keep up with the rapidly changing world of software.

In yet another scenario, you might have a ratio that looks perfectly fine, but if you analyze it further you realize that the ratio is incorrect for your kind of project. Let's say you create a middle-tier COM component that has no interface whatsoever. Let's also assume it uses another component that talks to data. The key classes/support classes ratio is 1:2.3. This would be perfectly normal in other scenarios. In this scenario, however, it isn't. Middle-tier objects are almost exclusively concerned with business logic. The ratio should be closer to 1:1. Most likely you are dealing with yet another variety of the Swiss army knife.

## Number of abstract classes

Using abstract classes is a great technique to create proper class hierarchies and code that's relatively easy to reuse. Studies show that projects that make proper use of abstract classes are more successful than projects that don't. A project with a high number of abstract classes is proof of proper use of inheritance as well as proof that somebody actually sat down and took the time to design and model his application. Therefore, a relatively high number of abstract classes is simply good.

When I say "a relatively high number of abstract classes" I'm talking about 8% to 12% of abstract classes. The framework you use influences this number. If you base all your classes on some class of an existing framework, you might end up with no abstract classes at all. That's fine, because you need to count all abstract classes in the framework as well. Together with the framework's abstract classes, you should end up with the same magical number again. If the number is too low, you could either have a huge application, or you could have chosen a bad framework.

This, of course, also suggests that if you are creating a framework yourself, you should have a significantly higher percentage of abstract classes.

A certain percentage of those abstract classes can be interface classes, which don't have any code at all, but only method and property definitions. I don't know how to judge a project based on the number of interface classes. Nevertheless, it's interesting to know. **Figure 2** shows a diagram that compares the percentages of abstract, interface and concrete classes in a particular project.

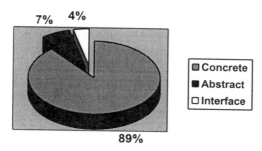

*Figure 2*. *Concrete, abstract and interface classes in a particular project.*

## Counting abstract classes

Counting abstract classes is not trivial at all. The easiest way to do this is to use the instance counter that I introduced at the beginning of this chapter. Once you have a log file that shows all classes that get instantiated, you can compare this to your total list of classes. Every class that wasn't instantiated is an abstract class, unless none of its subclasses was instantiated either. In this case it is a useless class. The percentage of those should be close to 0.

## Number of custom properties

The number of properties per class is a good indication of the complexity of each class. This is especially true when you also consider the number of methods per class (and the complexity of those methods). Counting the number of properties is relatively simple. If you use VCX classes, you can simply count the lines in the Reserved3 field of the VCX (see Chapter 5 for more information about the VCX file). If you use source code classes, it gets a little harder because the class header not only contains the new properties, but also the overwritten ones, so you need to go up the class structure to see what was there and what was newly defined.

There is no rule whether a high number of properties is good or bad. Certain types of objects typically have more methods than others. Interface objects typically have many properties that determine the object's visual appearance or its behavior when communicating with the user. If you use data objects, they will have a lot of properties as well, since one property usually represents one field in a table or other data source. At the same time, these objects hardly have any methods. Middle-tier objects (behavioral objects) usually have a low number of properties, or at least a low property-to-method ratio.

I usually count the number of properties for two different groups of objects: interface objects and behavioral objects. Data objects (if you use them) usually are created or retrieved at runtime and therefore are hard to analyze. At the same time, the number of data object properties doesn't tell you a whole lot.

Counting properties for behavioral objects can indicate your most complex classes. When I find objects that have a lot of properties (and a lot of methods at the same time), I reevaluate whether I should split the object into several smaller ones, which often is the case. However, behavioral objects deal with many different scenarios, some of which can be complex. So there could be a good reason for behavioral objects to have many properties and a lot of complexity.

When counting properties for interface classes, you get a first indication whether your class design is proper. When an interface class has many properties (especially newly defined ones), this can be an indication of improper separation of the interface from the behavior. In other words, you might have discovered a class that is an interface and a behavior object at the same time. This kind of scenario is a threat for three-tiered applications.

### Number of exposed properties

The number of exposed properties indicates the cleanliness of the interface design. If the number is almost as high as the number of all properties, the rules of encapsulation have been violated. However, many Rapid Application Development (RAD) techniques in Visual FoxPro encourage you not to use encapsulation properly. Instance programming and pseudo subclassing are typical examples.

Having a large number of exposed properties doesn't necessarily mean that many properties can be accessed from outside. The programmer might have been lazy and didn't protect those properties, even though nobody ever references them. This can produce problems later on, for instance if a new programmer joins the team, or if somebody simply doesn't remember whether or not he is supposed to access a property. For this reason, all properties that are not part of the interface should be protected or hidden. This will raise the overall quality of your code.

Up to Visual FoxPro 5.0, it was considered bad practice to have an interface with many exposed properties, because changing and accessing properties directly left few possibilities for changing things later on. With the introduction of access and assign methods, this is no longer a problem. Quite the opposite is true. I encourage you to create a property interface rather than Set() and Get() methods as often as possible (for performance reasons). However, you should not confuse a property-rich interface with internal properties that are exposed for no reason.

As you can see, this metric can help you to identify two different kinds of problems: improper design or bad implementation.

### Number of properties with access and assign methods

This is an interesting metric. Access and assign methods can be used for various things, including virtual properties and late binding. These techniques help to improve performance and resource management. But access and assign methods can also be used to compensate for bad design or incompatible classes. It is great that Visual FoxPro 6.0 allows this, because it greatly improves class and component reuse. Unfortunately, if access and assign methods are applied too frequently, it isn't all that great for performance. Counting the number of properties with access and assign methods gives you a good indication when it is time to start redesigning your object model.

## Number of methods

Counting the number of methods can give you a similar indication about class complexity. This, too, allows you to judge the complexity of each class to determine whether it has been abstracted properly for its purpose. If you find an interface class with a huge number of methods, the class usually does more than provide an interface. However, making this judgement is a bit harder than just counting the number of methods. Applying the template method pattern, for instance, would raise the number of methods tremendously, but it wouldn't necessarily mean that the interface class wasn't properly abstracted. For this reason you also have to measure the complexity of each method, and consider whether it is used to accomplish an entirely new task or only support another method.

### Number of exposed methods

The number of exposed (public) methods is usually a good indicator of whether a method is used for an entirely different task, or if it is only called internally. The number of public methods can also give you an idea whether the ideas of object-oriented programming (especially encapsulation) were applied properly. If almost all the methods are exposed, the programmer most likely isn't familiar (or comfortable) with private or hidden methods, and he should be educated. But keep in mind that using protected or hidden methods might not be possible if you use instance programming or pseudo subclassing.

When counting exposed methods, some people argue that all methods inherited from the FoxPro base classes are exposed, and therefore they have to be counted as exposed methods. I don't like this approach because many of these methods won't show up in my design or be used at all, but I can't make them disappear. Therefore, the results are quite a bit off. For this reason, I count methods inherited from a FoxPro base class only if they also have some new defined code.

If you are using VCX classes, counting methods is relatively easy because they are all listed in the VCX file. When using source code classes, it gets a little more complex because you have to search for all FUNCTION or PROCEDURE keywords that are located within the class definition. Unfortunately, it gets really tricky when trying to differentiate between methods that are inherited (maybe even from the FoxPro base classes) and newly defined ones. I usually don't bother with these issues when using source code classes.

### Number of supporting methods

Supporting methods are relatively interesting. To find them, you typically search for small methods that are called from another place within the same class. I like to analyze whether supporting methods are reused within an object (especially if it is complex) and whether they can be overwritten or reused in subclasses (otherwise they should be hidden). I like to see a lot of small supporting methods, especially when they are used within a template method pattern. This adds a lot of design flexibility. For this reason I like to see a 3:1 or even a 4:1 (or higher) ratio between exposed/main methods and supporting methods.

### Average method complexity

Traditionally, code complexity was a main point of interest when talking about software metrics—especially techniques like Function Point Analysis. Code complexity could be measured in many different ways. One popular way was to count the number of decision points (like IF or CASE statements). However, this metric lost most of its importance with the introduction of object-oriented technology. One of the main ideas behind object-oriented development is to reduce complexity. Methods are smaller than functions used to be. In fact, statistics show that the average method length in object-oriented projects is only six lines! One famous man once said that he only believed the statistics he faked himself, but the point I'm trying to make is that methods shouldn't be complex if they are split up! Maybe you can even create another behavioral object that gets invoked, rather than creating a monster method. Many great patterns, such as the Strategy pattern, can help to reduce complexity and introduce flexibility at the same time. In fact, object-oriented technology adds so much flexibility that some purely object-oriented languages (such as Smalltalk) don't even use CASE structures.

The only reason I would measure code complexity is to identify bad methods that need work. But measuring code complexity is not trivial, and I think it's not worth the effort. Therefore, I usually only search for methods with many lines of code, many of which are also overly complex.

### Average lines of code per method

Many people think counting code lines is stupid. I believe it's rather smart. But it all depends on what you do with the results you retrieve. The number of lines of code by itself doesn't tell you anything, other than the fact that maybe you are creating methods that are too complex (those with more than 60 or 70 lines are the ones I look into). Other than that, I only use the number of lines of code in combination with other metrics. Knowing that a class has a total of

5000 lines of code is useless information. However, if I know that I have a class with 100 methods and an average of 50 lines of code per method, it gives me quite a good idea about the size of that class. If I know further, that the largest methods have 200 or 300 lines, I know that I might have found an overly complex class that needs some work.

I like to keep my average number of lines of code per class at about 30 or 35 lines (not counting comments, blank lines, and the like).

### Number of new defined methods

This metric doesn't tell you much about code quality. Nevertheless, it is interesting to see how many new defined methods are in a class. Classes that have many new defined methods typically hold a lot of functionality; they might even be key classes to the entire system.

This metric is not meant to be used for average numbers, simply because the average number of new defined methods would be the number of all methods divided by the number of classes in your system. In other words: This doesn't tell you a whole lot.

Overall, it's nice to know how many new defined methods are in a class, but it's not incredibly important.

### Ratio of overwritten methods

In Visual FoxPro, programmers hardly ever intentionally overwrite (and wipe out) inherited behavior. Typically, if you define a class, its subclasses should inherit its entire behavior unless you are absolutely sure that they shouldn't. So in 99.99% of all cases, you should use DoDefault() or the scope resolution operator (::) when you add code to a method, to make sure you inherit the original behavior instead of replacing it. Unfortunately, it seems to be a widely accepted custom to "knowingly forget" to call the original behavior. There are various reasons for that: One is laziness, and another is the concern about performance. Of course, you experience a slight overhead when executing a DoDefault(). In Chapter 3 I discussed the fact that object-oriented programming introduces some performance penalties, which are a tradeoff for its great flexibility and maintainability. Well, this is one of those penalties. Since you've already accepted the fact that object-oriented technology is somewhat slower than procedural coding, you should use DoDefault() in all scenarios and not try to cheat your way through.

Another reason for not using DoDefault() is the fact that there is no code to inherit in the parent class. Well, this might change later on! If you add some code to a parent class and one of the child classes doesn't behave as expected, you have a bug that's extremely hard to find.

If you use inheritance improperly, you introduce a serious threat to your code quality and you also reduce code reusability and maintainability. These are some of the main ideas and advantages of object-oriented programming. Don't ruin them just because you forgot about the inherited code! Counting the number of overwritten methods is a great indication of improper use of inheritance. Every project will have a certain amount of overwritten methods, but if this amount ends up being more than 1% of all methods, I would be very concerned and take another look at these methods.

## Number of "Is-A" relations

Is-A relations (also known as inheritance) is a key concept of object-oriented programming. It's important to use it properly to ensure the success of any object-oriented project. There are many different opinions about what inheritance structures should look like. Some like shallow but wide structures; others like extremely deep and narrow structures. In my opinion, objects are supposed to reflect the real world, and I don't believe the real world is single-dimensional (no, the Earth is not flat!). I believe in deep and wide structures. I like all of my objects to be derived from a handful of my own base classes (not the ones FoxPro provides) so I can make global changes. At the same time, I have a common base that defines some standards. I like to compare this to electrical parts. They are all unique, but still they follow some standards, like using a certain voltage, and so on. Of course, I need great class variety throughout the system, so the structure becomes very wide at the second or third inheritance level. But then, I like to get more and more specific (step by step) until I finally have highly specialized classes at the bottom of the inheritance chain. **Figure 3** shows different kinds of strategies for inheritance structures.

This kind of structure is not as simple to create as a shallow or narrow one. There is quite some planning involved, especially to keep this structure flexible. In addition, certain patterns help to reuse classes that were not designed to work in this kind of environment (which is one of the major concerns when creating deep structures). Wrappers and proxies come to mind.

When counting the number of inheritance relations, you get a good overview of the nature of your application. Typically, you will also see great differences between different programmers. If some of your programmers create shallow structures while others prefer narrow ones, it is time to sit down and talk about some design goals. Mixing the two worlds is problematic and will only give you the disadvantages of both! The same is true for different areas of your system. Don't create one subsystem with one strategy and the next one with another.

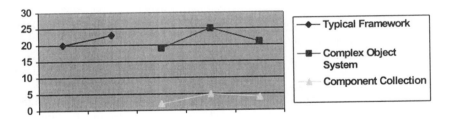

*Figure 3. Different strategies for inheritance structures.*

## Metrics based on objects

Metrics based on classes and source code can provide most of the information you'll ever need to help you estimate workloads and find problem areas in your design or implementation. Unfortunately, they do not necessarily tell you about the size and performance of your running application. Metrics based on objects can do this. They also can help you determine whether or not classes and objects are reused. You could retrieve the same information straight from the source code, but it would be quite a bit harder.

## Number of instances

Counting the number of instances tells you about performance and resource characteristics of your application. At the beginning of this chapter I introduced a simple mechanism that counts instances automatically. Once you have these numbers, you can identify resource-intensive parts of your application as well as performance bottlenecks.

There is no general rule about how many object instances you should have. Obviously, bigger applications have more instantiated objects than smaller ones. However, it is still interesting to see how many objects are instantiated and also how many objects are instantiated at any given point in time.

## Number of times a class is reused

Class reuse is key to successful object-oriented projects—not only across projects, but also within a single application (see Chapter 8). For this reason, it's important to know whether classes are reused properly. You can analyze source code to see whether they are instantiated or subclassed in many different places, but it's hard to tell whether that code is ever executed. When counting instances as described at the beginning of this chapter, it is easy to determine which classes have been instantiated how often, what their parent classes are, and so forth.

## Number of dependencies

When one object depends on another object, the first object gets harder to reuse. For this reason it is important to keep the number of dependencies as low as possible. If you have to have dependencies (and every system will need many), you need to know what they are. A good object model is a good and easy way to document object dependencies. If you have a good model, you don't need to measure dependencies at the implementation level, but if your model lacks some detail, metrics is another way to find and document dependencies. Unfortunately, this is a non-trivial task. Typically, you would scan the source code to find object checks (Vartype(x)="O") or object instantiation within a method.

However, due to the complexity of this task, I recommend working on a good model instead.

# Conclusion

Object and software metrics are a great way to track the progress of your project as well as its quality and other factors. Measuring facts makes me more comfortable than taking wild guesses. What fascinates me the most is the fact that you can actually measure the quality of source code by applying some of the most basic metrics—a task that could hardly be accomplished otherwise.

There is a wide variety of metrics you can use. I usually use only those described in this chapter. If you are interested in more information about metrics, I recommend reading *Object Oriented Software Metrics* by Mark Lorenz and Jeff Kidd (Prentice Hall, 1994, ISBN: 0-13-179292-X).

# Section 3
# Object Modeling

# Chapter 12
# The Unified Modeling Language

**Modern, highly complex applications are impossible to build without first analyzing the problem and modeling the solution. Many different notations and methods have been introduced to make this process easier. The latest, Unified Modeling, combines the best ideas from older methods and provides a unified and standardized way of object modeling.**

## Introducing the Unified Modeling Language

It's necessary to analyze and model applications before starting the actual implementation for an obvious reason: Modern applications are simply too complex to start implementing them out of the blue. You have to collect requirements, analyze the problem, come up with an attack plan, and finally implement the solution.

Most programmers are concerned with only the last step: implementation. Many different tools and languages, including Visual FoxPro, are available to implement solutions. Choosing an analysis tool is rather simple. It can be a word processor or even a simple sheet of paper. Choices become more complex when it comes to modeling tools, which help to create the "attack plan." Many different modeling methods and tools have been created, each of which has been treated almost religiously. However, differences in notation, methodology and processes among these modeling languages have made it difficult for programmers to arrive at a common standard for designing solutions.

## Some modeling history

In the beginning, the three most popular modeling methods were OMT (Rumbaugh), Booch (yes, the method and the man are the same) and OOSE (Jacobson). Each method had different strengths and weaknesses. OMT was powerful for design but weak for analysis. Jacobson's notation was strong in the analysis phase but didn't work as well for design. Over time, the creator of each notation looked over the fence and added strengths of other methods to his own. The methodologies started to converge. However, differences in some notation details made it difficult to switch from one notation to the other. One notation used a small circle to indicate aggregation, while another used the same symbol for multiplicity. This was extremely confusing.

This was the time when so-called *notation war* began. Looking back, the issues were rather trivial. Was it better to represent a class using a cloud or a rectangle? What was the right symbol for inheritance? I personally couldn't care less. These questions can never be answered because they are based on personal opinions and preferences. However, the need for a uniform way of drawing these items was rather pressing.

The creation of the Unified Modeling Language (UML) brought an end to the notation war. The first draft (version 0.8) was introduced in October 1995 and was created mostly by Grady Booch and James Rumbaugh. For the next version, the public's input was added to the notation as well as the experiences of Ivar Jacobson, who became the "third father" of UML.

This version was released in July 1996 (version 0.9) and the next in October 1996 (version 0.91). Version 1.0 was presented to the Object Management Group (OMG) for standardization in July 1997.

To serve everyone's needs, version 1.1 was introduced in September 1997. This version included input from many other well-known object people such as "the Gang of Four" (patterns), Odell (classifications), Shlaer-Mellor (object life cycles), Embly (singleton classes), Fusion (operation descriptions and message numbering), Wirfs-Brock (responsibilities), Harel (state charts), Mayer (pre- and post-conditions), and others.

## The ideas behind UML

UML aimed to take the best parts of each existing notation and combine them into one widely accepted and more powerful standard. In addition, the biggest problem, the difference in notations, was resolved elegantly. Everyone had a chance to give their own input and address their own concerns.

UML is a modeling language, not a method. Most methods consist of both a modeling language and a process. The language is the (mostly graphical) notation that the method uses to draw diagrams or describe a model in other ways. The process is the guideline for doing a design and getting to the diagrams (or other parts of the language).

We can compare the situation to Visual FoxPro, which should clarify the topic, since this is a more familiar world to most of us. The language would be the Visual FoxPro syntax. The process would be certain wizards (like the Application Wizard), builders, or just general steps that help to achieve the goals.

Usually, the description of the modeling process is rather sloppy. Also, I found that most people (including myself) who say they use a method really only use the language and rarely ever follow the process. In fact, I purposely don't follow the process. I think most processes are great, but I usually do things a little differently when I discover that the process doesn't entirely match my needs. I'll compare this to Visual FoxPro one more time: The Application Wizard is a great tool to create applications quickly. However, I still use my own framework, which matches my needs a lot better than the code created by the Application Wizard.

When talking about object design, it's not important to understand the process used to create the design. It is important, though, to understand the notation. Every process can only be a suggestion. Most of those suggestions are good, and you should familiarize yourself with them to get more out of object modeling. But do not treat these processes religiously.

UML does not have a standardized process. However, the "Three Amigos" (Booch, Jacobson and Rumbaugh) are also working on a unified process called *Objectory*. UML and Objectory don't depend on each other but they do work well together. I suggest taking a look at Objectory as soon as the Three Amigos publish their book, *The Objectory Software Development Process*.

## UML tools

Many tools are available to help create UML models. Compare this to the fact that there are several different tools (compilers) available to implement certain programming languages, like C++. I personally prefer to use Rational Software's Rational Rose.

The Three Amigos work for Rational Software, so they have a very good idea what UML is about. It seems that Rational plays the same role in the object-modeling world that Microsoft plays in the software business. Both companies work together quite closely. Rational even licensed a special version of Rose, called the Visual Modeler, to Microsoft. This is a "light" version of Rose that is optimized for Visual Basic programmers. Unfortunately, Visual Modeler can't handle the entire UML specification.

Both tools are integrated tightly into Visual FoxPro through the Visual FoxPro Modeling Wizards, which I'll discuss in Chapters 16 and 17.

All diagrams used in this book were created using Rational Rose.

# UML notation

UML notation is so rich that its creators had to write three books, rather than one, to describe all its details. And even that wasn't enough, so they edited a whole series of books that are additions to their own books.

It's obvious that this book cannot describe all the details of UML. It's not meant to do that, nor is it meant to compete with the other UML books. I wrote this book to describe object-oriented programming in Visual FoxPro. UML is part of that, so I will describe the aspects of UML that are important for Visual FoxPro programmers.

## Packages and package diagrams

Packages are a simple way to break a model down into smaller systems. Remember that we use modeling to design large and complex systems. It would be impossible to model a complex system in one single diagram. Such a huge diagram would only increase confusion and do more damage than good.

Packages categorize diagrams based on logical structures. Packages can contain sub-packages, as well as classes and any other UML elements. They should not be compared with Visual FoxPro class libraries. Classes located in one package can be stored in different Visual FoxPro libraries, and one FoxPro class library can host classes located in different packages. **Figure 1** shows a UML package.

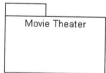

*Figure 1. A UML package.*

Packages can be displayed in regular class diagrams (in combination with other UML elements, that is). Typically, diagrams that contain packages show packages only to avoid confusion and keep everything simple. I like to call these diagrams *package diagrams,* although this is not a UML term. Package diagrams show packages contained in one view and how they relate to each other. **Figure 2** shows a package diagram that has sub-packages of the one displayed in Figure 1.

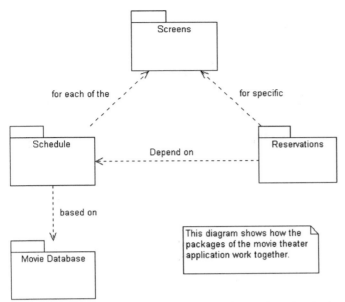

*Figure 2. A package diagram shows dependencies between packages.*

This diagram shows the four main packages (categories) into which our movie theater example is broken down. I added a comment that describes the current diagram.

The diagram also shows how the packages relate to each other. The dotted lines are called *dependencies*. Typically, some descriptive text is added to describe the relation. Usually, they are meant to be read together with the package name. Figure 2 shows that there is a "Schedule for each of the Screens" and the "Reservations depend on the Schedule."

Dependencies between two packages exist if there are relations between any two classes in the involved packages. For example, if any class in the Schedule package depends on another class in the Movie Database package, there is a dependency.

Dependencies have navigability, which means that the arrow must be drawn in a certain direction. In Figure 2, the Schedule depends on the Movie Database but the Movie Database can exist on its own.

There are some packages that almost every other package depends on. We'd create a mess if we drew a dependency from every package to one of these. For this reason, UML allows us to define packages as global, which is displayed with a remark in the actual package item (see **Figure 3**).

Using Rational Rose or Visual Modeler, you can define a package as global in the package specification. You can get to this specification by selecting Specification from the shortcut menu. The actual setting can be found on the Detail page, shown in **Figure 4**.

**Figure 3**. *A global package.*

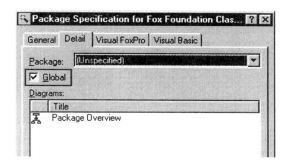

**Figure 4**. *Defining global packages in Rational Rose.*

What happens to sub-packages? Some say that a dependency on a package does not automatically mean that there is a dependency on sub-packages. In this case, you'd have to draw the dependency to the sub-package in a separate diagram or add the sub-package to the current one. UML diagrams can contain elements that are located in other packages (see **Figure 5**).

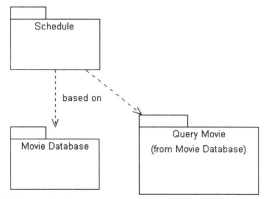

**Figure 5**. *Items can show up in more than one diagram, even if the diagram belongs to a different package.*

The package now has a comment indicating that it doesn't belong to the current package. However, this seems to complicate the diagram without adding any real value. For this reason,

I suggest treating this a little differently. Many argue that package dependencies are "transparent," which means that all sub-packages are automatically related to all packages on which the parent package depends.

UML does not define whether or not package dependencies are transparent. You have two choices. First, you can assume that it is either one way or the other and not worry about it anymore. This is perfectly fine, as long as the model isn't discussed with somebody who assumes differently. Secondly, you can use UML stereotypes, which allow you to define things that UML doesn't deal with. I'll discuss stereotypes a little later.

In the Rational Rose browser, packages are displayed as folders, as shown in **Figure 6**.

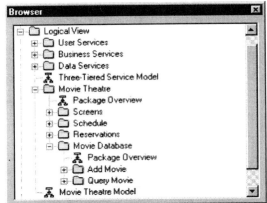

*Figure 6. Packages displayed in the Rational Rose browser.*

There is nothing like packages or dependencies in Visual FoxPro. Nevertheless, they are important for FoxPro programmers to understand, because they are the basic tools that help to get an overview of the whole application.

## Use Case diagrams

*Use Cases* are created during analysis. In fact, they are a big part of analysis so I will discuss them in great detail in Chapter 14. However, I still want to briefly summarize use case notations.

Ivar Jacobson first introduced use cases. Typically they contain a lot of text and therefore are not loaded with a lot of special notation. The typical tool to create use cases is a text processor like Microsoft Word. In addition, you can use Rational Rose to coordinate use cases and the parties involved (actors). Visual Modeler does not support use cases.

### Actors

*Actors* are not part of the system. They represent anyone or anything that interacts with the system. An actor might be a user who pushes the mouse, or another system or object that uses the described one. The UML symbol for actors is rather simple (see **Figure 7**).

Markus

*Figure 7. The UML symbol for actors.*

Well, as I said before: Simplicity is important…

I personally don't care for this notation. It seems to suggest that actors are always human users, but quite the opposite is true—actors are more often objects than people. But this statement is based on my own experience; you might find it totally wrong. Just keep in mind that actors are not necessarily human beings.

## Use cases

The UML element used to represent use cases should not be confused with the descriptive use case created in a word processor. The descriptive kind of use case can be attached to a use case element in a UML diagram (see below). **Figure 8** shows what a use case looks like in UML.

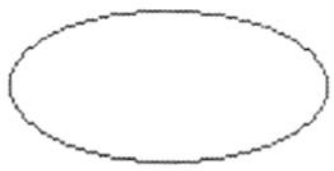

Add a Movie to the Database

*Figure 8. The UML notation for use cases.*

This notation is typically used to give an overview of all use cases that describe the system and the actors that use it. When using Rational Rose, you can attach files (such as Word documents) to these use cases.

## Use case diagrams

Use case diagrams describe how different use cases relate to each other, depend on each other or extend each other. **Figure 9** shows a part of the movie theater example.

One of the actors in Figure 9 is the Movie Master—a human user who updates and maintains the movie database on which the theater relies. Based on this diagram, we know that there is a use case that describes how a movie is added. Obviously it doesn't describe all the details, but it uses the use cases "Add Record" and "Check if Movie exists" to describe these general tasks. At the same time, the "Add a Reservation" use case also uses "Check if Movie exists." The actor involved in this use case is not human. It's some mechanism that deals with Web hits—maybe an ISAPI application or something similar.

The details about each use case (which are usually several pages each) are not located in this diagram. They are in documents that can be attached to each element of the diagram, if you use Rational Rose.

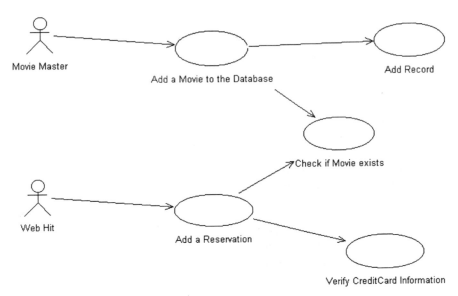

*Figure 9. A use case diagram.*

## Class diagrams

Class diagrams play a vital role in all modeling methodologies. They show classes, dependencies and inheritance relations. Typically, the largest part of an object model is its class diagrams. To deal with all this information, there are many different UML items and special notations. For this reason, I split the description of class diagrams into two: the basics and more advanced elements.

### Class diagram basics

Typically you'll be fine using only the basics. Once you are more familiar with these ideas, you'll be able to discover the value of specialized notation as described in the "Advanced class diagrams" section.

### Classes

The basic element of a class diagram is the class itself. In its simplest form, it's a rectangle with a name (see **Figure 10**).

*Figure 10. A simple class in UML notation.*

This simple notation is useful in large scenarios that show many different classes. It doesn't provide detailed information about the class, but UML allows you to display more information, as shown in **Figure 11**.

**Figure 11**. *A more complex class.*

This class has two properties and seven methods. The key icon indicates that the properties are protected. The Visual Studio method icon indicates that the methods are all visible to the public. The visibility of methods and properties can also be *private* (hidden) and *implementation*.

These classes, properties and methods can be translated directly into Visual FoxPro properties and methods. Visual FoxPro does not support the visibility "implementation," which is the only limitation to be aware of.

Visual Modeler and Rational Rose make it very easy to add classes to a model. You simply drop the class icon from the toolbar into a diagram, and the class is added to the current package. To add properties and methods, right-click on the class and select New Property or New Method from the shortcut menu. To change the visibility of a member, simply click the icon to the left of its name. This brings up a menu that offers the four different options I described above. For those who want more detailed information about the class, you can refer to the Class Specification dialog. To open it, either double-click the class or select Open Specification from the shortcut menu (see **Figure 12**).

The General page shows general class information such as the name and the stereotype (see below), as well as the verbal class documentation. It also shows the parent of the current class. In Figure 12, the class doesn't have a parent class, so the dialog displays the package this class belongs to (Data Access).

The Methods and Properties pages show more details about the properties and methods belonging to that class, in addition to all inherited ones (optional). **Figure 13** shows the Methods page.

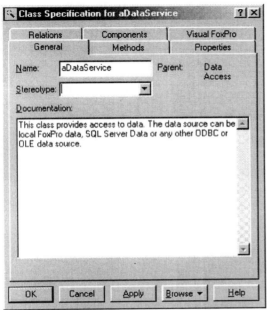

**Figure 12**. *Rational Rose's Class Specification dialog.*

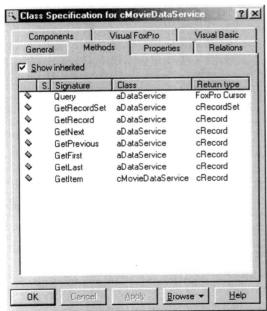

**Figure 13**. *Inherited and newly defined methods of a class in Rational Rose.*

This page has a complete list of all methods belonging to the class. It explains the method's visibility, its stereotype (see below), its name, the class it belongs to (which is important if inherited methods are displayed) and its return type. The Properties page is much like the Methods page (see **Figure 14**).

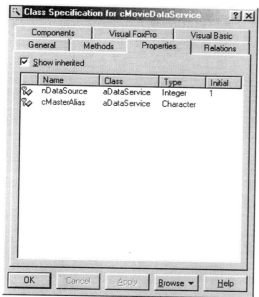

*Figure 14. Class properties in Rational Rose.*

Properties do not have a stereotype. Of course, they do have a type and they can also have an initial value.

Each property and method also has a specification dialog of its own, where you can define types, parameters and stereotypes. The Method Specification dialog's General page doesn't hold many surprises. It allows you to define the name, type, stereotype, visibility and the method's documentation. The Argument page is a little more exciting. It specifies the parameters and types that can be passed to the method (see **Figure 15**).

There is no parameter-specification dialog. You can simply enter all parameters directly into the grid. Unfortunately, there is no way to specify whether a parameter is optional.

The Property Specification dialog is rather simple. It looks a lot like the Method Specification dialog without the Argument page. The only difference is that it also allows you to specify an initial value.

Many of these dialog settings can also be displayed in the UML class diagram, as shown in **Figure 16**.

I don't like the UML class diagram much. I think diagrams become cluttered if they show too much information that detracts from the main information. For this reason I activate the display of that information only in very small scenarios.

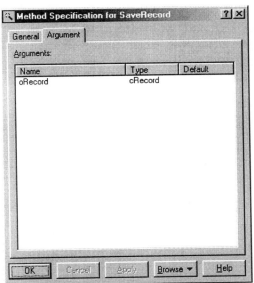

*Figure 15. Defining parameters for a method.*

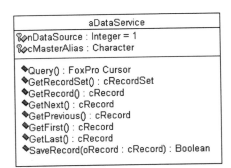

*Figure 16. A UML class showing properties and methods as well as parameters and initial values.*

### Classes and their dependencies

Now that you know how classes are displayed, you can examine their dependencies and relationships. **Figure 17** shows a simple class diagram that illustrates how the objects that form our movie database application work together.

We have two forms (*cMovieList* and *cMovieEditForm*) that are subclassed from the class *cDocumentForm*. This is just like an *Is-A* relationship in Visual FoxPro (inheritance/subclassing). This class belongs to another package and is displayed in this diagram only for documentation issues.

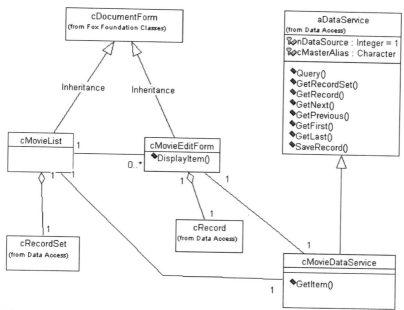

***Figure 17**. A class diagram.*

The line between the two form classes is called an *association*. It tells us that these two classes know about each other. Perhaps they depend on each other or they exchange messages—we can't tell by this diagram. A *sequence diagram* (see below) would clarify the situation. The diagram specifies that one *cMovieList* class can communicate with "zero or more" *cMovieEditForm* classes. However, each edit form class can deal with only one specific list. The numbers at both ends of the association are called "the relation's *multiplicity*." There is no such thing as an association in Visual FoxPro. Nevertheless, it makes a lot of sense to use associations in the design because they clarify which classes know about each other.

Both form classes communicate with the *cMovieDataService* class to retrieve data. This class is a subclass of *aDataService*, which also belongs to another package. The data service retrieves data in an objectified fashion. It retrieves either a single record object or a whole record set. In Visual FoxPro, these objects could be created using the *SCATTER...NAME* command. In the movie theater model, these objects are attached to each form class. The diagram also specifies the object ownership. The record object as well as the record set is owned by each form. If the form is released, the record and record-set objects will be released as well. This is indicated by the diamond sign at the owner-end of the line. This kind of relationship is called *aggregation*.

This diagram hides a lot of information. It does not show that both the *cRecord* and the *cRecordSet* classes have associations to the data service. Neither does it explain that the *cRecordSet* class owns many instances of *cRecord*. A different, more generic diagram provides this information. Adding too much information (especially information that's provided elsewhere and therefore redundant) doesn't add value to the model—it just makes the diagrams harder to read. In fact, the diagram above holds information we don't really need. The fact that the specialized data service is a subclass of the abstract one, or that the form classes are subclasses of a general form, can be explained elsewhere. Even if we want to show these classes in the current diagram, we probably don't have to show all the inherited properties and methods unless they are crucial to the documented scenario.

**Figure 18** shows the same scenario as the more complex Figure 17. However, it assumes that details are explained in another diagram. Therefore, it doesn't replace the first diagram, but it's a valuable addition that provides a simple overview.

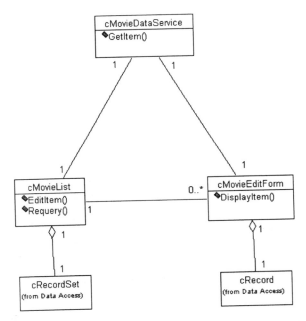

*Figure 18. The simplified version of the class diagram in Figure 17.*

Simplicity must be one of the main targets when creating object models. During the project life cycle, you won't get another chance to display scenarios as simply and easy to understand as in class diagrams (and other diagrams of the model).

### Generalization
Object modelers use the term *generalization* instead of *inheritance*. This is based on the fact that a parent class is a more general version of the subclass. The notation for inheritance (generalization) is an arrow that points from the subclass to the parent class.

Because UML is not specific to any implementation language, it has to support all mechanisms that are supported by any of these languages. That also means that UML can handle multiple inheritance (see **Figure 19**).

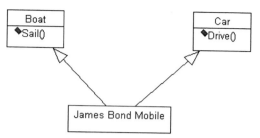

***Figure 19****. Multiple inheritance, the big no-no in Visual FoxPro.*

As I've already mentioned, Visual FoxPro doesn't support multiple inheritance. For this reason you should never create something that looks like Figure 19 if you want to use it for Visual FoxPro. Repeat after me: "I will not design multiple inheritance! I will not design multiple inheritance!" Good!

### Association
An association is a relationship between two classes. There is nothing in Visual FoxPro that represents the same kind of animal as an association. Object references could be seen as such; late composition is similar, too.

Nevertheless, associations are valuable tools when creating an object model. At an early stage in the modeling cycle, associations are very general. Later on, they are more specific. Associations can change into aggregation relationships. Typically, associations get navigability, which means they might not necessarily work both ways. One object might know about another that doesn't have a clue it's been watched or used. In fact, this seems to be the rule rather than the exception. Take Visual FoxPro forms, for example. They are well aware of all their members, but the members should be very generic. Therefore, they do not know about the forms they live in.

Sometimes associations also become generalizations (inheritance relations). This usually happens very early in the cycle; otherwise it requires some redesign. The reasons for changing an association into a generalization can be different. You might discover that two associated objects don't have much unique behavior but cover similar topics. In this case you might combine them into one class. To keep changes minimal, you'd create subclasses of this class in order to provide the previously defined interface. Everything defined later in the cycle can use that new class, and eventually, when everything is cleaned up, the subclasses can be removed and all classes in the system will use the new class that combines the two original classes. In other scenarios, you might discover that a class needs the entire functionality of another class rather than just the ability to send a couple messages to it. In this case, you'd make the class that needs the whole functionality a subclass of the more general one that shouldn't be changed or polluted with the methods and properties of the specialized one.

### Aggregation
Aggregation seems simple—a car has an engine, a form has buttons, and so forth. Unfortunately, it's more complicated than that. The example with the *cRecord* class demonstrates this quite well. Does the record really belong to the form? Maybe not. It could

just as well be handed over to another object that will take care of that record. In this case, we'd be talking about an association rather than aggregation.

Well, I'm not ashamed to admit that I get confused every now and then myself. Even gurus like The Three Amigos can't agree on the same issues in certain instances. If worse comes to worst, I go back and redesign my model. Not exactly a fun thing to do, but hey … everybody has to bite the sour apple from time to time.

There is also a specialized kind of aggregation called *composition*. It is usually drawn much like a regular aggregation but with a filled diamond (see **Figure 20**).

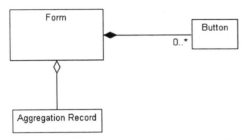

*Figure 20. Aggregation and composition.*

It's easy to tell that the button is contained in the form, and therefore owned by the form. In UML, this is called *aggregation by value*. The record object, on the other hand, does not belong to that form. It can use it as long as needed, but other objects can also access it. Furthermore, when the form is released, the record can remain in memory if required. It's pretty much an independent object that just happens to serve the form class. This is called *aggregation by reference*.

Aggregation can be translated into Visual FoxPro easily. Every kind of containership is aggregation by value. Objects that are tied together using object references demonstrate examples of aggregation by reference. Quite simple, isn't it?

Often people ask me why aggregation can't be imported to Visual FoxPro by the connection wizards. The answer is rather simple: Aggregation in modeling is at a higher abstraction level than composition in FoxPro. They are actually "incompatible." Consider **Figure 21**.

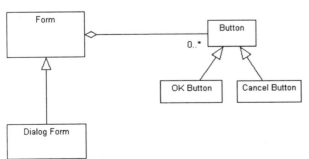

*Figure 21. Two form classes that may or may not contain buttons of various types.*

This simple diagram would be impossible to translate into FoxPro code. We basically know that the *Form* class can contain "zero or more" buttons. This by itself is vague from an implementation point of view, while it's perfectly fine for the model. It gets even worse than that! Figure 21 also tells us that all subclasses of the *Form* class could contain an undefined number of instances of the *Button* class or one of its subclasses.

Now imagine how this would work when you "round-trip" your model. The diagram has to be converted into FoxPro code, the programmer works on it for a while and updates the model with the changes he's made. In this case, the wizard had to analyze the *Dialog Form* class (for instance) and count the buttons. At that point, it had to figure out whether or not one of the parent classes of the button already was specified as a member of the class or of any parent classes. If so, it had to be smart enough to understand whether or not this relation already described the fact that the button is in the *Dialog Form*. There are a couple of problems here. First of all, scenarios get "slightly" more complex than the one above. Also, understanding a model is not trivial. The wizard would need to have full knowledge of the entire UML specification, including stereotypes and other equally complex ideas. Furthermore, it would have to understand the process applied by the modeler. And even if it knew all of that, the modeler might have altered a couple of things just a little bit, which would result in a scenario the wizards couldn't handle. The risks of misanalyzing a model and breaking it while updating changes are far too great.

### *Dependencies and instantiation*

Objects often depend on each other. In class diagrams, this is indicated by a dotted line, just as in package diagrams (see **Figure 22**).

This example shows not only which objects depend on each other, but also which classes create (instantiate) others. This is very important to know. In this example, the *cMovieList* class depends on the *cMovieDataService*, but it doesn't create it. The application object takes care of that. I simply use the description to indicate whether or not a dependency also means instantiation.

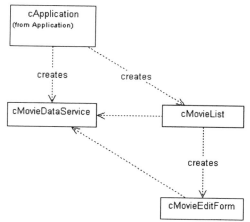

**Figure 22**. *Objects and their dependencies.*

## Multiplicity

I have used the term *multiplicity* in several examples. It can be attached to many kinds of relations, and it deals with the fact that one class can be instantiated several times.

When using aggregation, one class can contain many instances of another class or one single, specific instance. A car, for example, has one and only one engine. A plane, on the other hand, might have zero or more engines depending on its type. While a glider doesn't have an engine at all, a large passenger plane might have three, four, or more engines. This information is important for the design of the plane.

It's just as important to know how many instances of an object are involved in a certain relationship. UML allows you to indicate this using numbers at each end of a relation. **Figure 23** shows an example.

This demo shows a form class (*EditForm*) that may or may not contain some buttons (zero or more). We do know that it contains one, and only one, Save button. The form depends on some data service. We can tell by this diagram that many forms depend on the same service object. Each of these service objects can deal with an undefined number (zero or more) of record objects.

Now imagine this diagram without the multiplicity information. It wouldn't tell you a whole lot, would it?

## Relations at a glance

When using Rational Rose, there is a simple way to see all relations of a class. The Relations tab of the Class Specification dialog contains this information (see **Figure 24**).

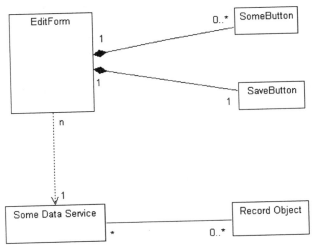

***Figure 23.*** *The EditForm class contains one Save button and optionally an unspecified number of other buttons.*

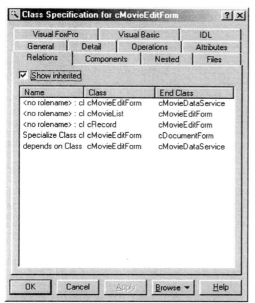

***Figure 24***. *Rational Rose shows relations to other classes.*

This page can get cluttered because it shows all kinds of relations in one list. Nevertheless, it holds valuable information. It is easy to spot classes that might be hard to reuse because they are involved in many relations. It is also easy to see what classes might be influenced by changes in the current class. And if a class is to be reused, this page holds all the information about classes that have to go with it. To get more information about a certain relation, just double-click an item in the list.

I found this information to be some of the most valuable in the whole product. It's the information I use most when going back to a model that has already been implemented but needs to be changed or maintained. Often I have to make changes to projects that are not my own, and it's difficult to know what parts of the system might be influenced by those changes. The relationship information clarifies this. I sometimes also have problems with my own projects. Who can ever remember what classes have to be brought over to another system when reusing code? This dialog helps a great deal with all these issues.

## Advanced class diagrams

By now you are familiar with the most important class diagram concepts. However, you may have encountered scenarios you couldn't model to your total satisfaction. This might be due to the fact that you don't know all the details yet, or you simply try to do something the UML can't handle. For all those cases, I can offer you solutions.

### *Interfaces and abstract classes*

Interfaces and abstract classes have the same meaning in object modeling as in Visual FoxPro. An abstract class will never be instantiated directly, but its subclasses will. An interface class is a special case of an abstract class. Its only purpose is to define the interface of its subclasses. An interface class does not have any behavior (code) attached; the behavior will be added in the subclasses. **Figure 25** shows how we could model the abstract screen class used as an example in previous chapters.

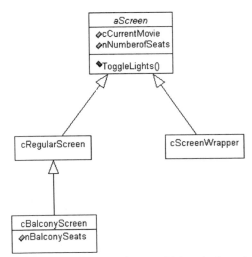

**Figure 25**. aScreen *is an abstract class in this diagram.*

The abstract class is indicated by the italic font style of its name. When drawing this on a whiteboard, it might be hard to illustrate italic fonts. In this case you can add "{abstract}" after the name of the class.

Interface classes are just a special case of abstract classes. Often you won't really know whether a class is abstract or an interface. For FoxPro programmers, it doesn't really matter. However, if you want to define a class as an interface class, you can use the interface stereotype (see **Figure 26**). See below for more information about stereotypes.

### Actors

Actors can be used in class diagrams as well. However, most scenarios documented in class diagrams don't need actors. Actors typically deal with objects rather than classes, but in some rare instances they might come in handy. See the section "Use Case diagrams" for more information about actors.

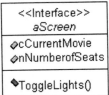

**Figure 26**. *A class using a stereotype.*

## Derived attributes

Derived attributes are those that can be calculated from other attributes. If you know the birthdate of a person, you can calculate the person's age. Therefore, the age would be a derived attribute. If we want to reuse our movie theater example, it might be handy to use derived attributes for the reservation class (see **Figure 27**).

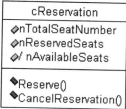

**Figure 27.** nAvailableSeats *is a derived property.*

The attribute *nAvailableSeats* is derived, which is indicated by the slash in front of its name. Unfortunately, this is not obvious and it's hard to see, especially in combination with the Visual Studio property icon. On the other hand, whether or not a property is derived is close to being an implementation issue. Therefore, it should not clutter the design too much.

In Visual FoxPro, derived properties can be implemented using access and assign methods. Instead of returning the property value, you calculate the requested value and bypass the accessed property. Here's some sample code:

```
FUNCTION nAvailableSeats_access
    RETURN THIS.nTotalSeatNumber - THIS.nReservedSeats
ENDFUNC

FUNCTION nAvailableSeats_assign
    LPARAMETERS lvNewValue
    ERROR 1743  && We fake a regular FoxPro error
ENDFUNC
```

## Association classes

Association classes allow you to add objects, methods and operations to associations. In **Figure 28**, a customer is associated to a screen. The association involves a reservation record that has more information about that association.

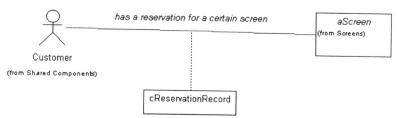

**Figure 28.** *Use of an association class.*

Diagrams like this are highly abstract. Figure 28 is a simplified version of **Figure 29**.

***Figure 29**. The same scenario as in Figure 28 without an association class.*

Simplicity is one of the greatest powers you can give to an object model. The version that uses the association class is a lot easier to read (at least for those who are familiar with the concept).

Each association can have only one association class. If you need more than one association class, you have to turn them into regular classes. In this case you lose the advantage of the simpler notation.

Due to the high level of abstraction, association classes are specific to the modeling tool. In Visual FoxPro, you'd probably write a lot of code to create the described scenario. Especially for this reason, this notation is very valuable.

### When to use class diagrams

Class diagrams are the core of every object modeling methodology, which is also true for UML. You'll find yourself using class diagrams more often than every other UML diagram.

The great danger is to overuse the notation and to clutter your diagrams. Keep in mind that the greatest advantage of class diagrams is their simplicity. Try to keep only the most crucial information in each scenario, and don't use all the available notations at once. If in doubt, create two different diagrams documenting different areas of the scenario, rather than drawing one huge diagram that's difficult to understand.

Class diagrams that are kept simple are fairly easy to understand, which makes them good candidates for meetings and demonstrations.

## Interaction diagrams

Interaction diagrams describe how objects work together. They typically show a small scenario, usually based on a single use case. The diagrams show a couple example objects and how they communicate with each other. The diagram may or may not specify the classes that make up these objects.

There are two kinds of interaction diagrams: *sequence* and *collaboration*.

### Sequence diagrams

These diagrams are one of my personal favorites. They show objects and the messages they sent, and describe the timeline they follow.

Objects are rectangles aligned from left to right at the top of the diagram. Attached to each one is a dotted line that represents time. This line is also called the object's *lifeline*. Messages are represented by arrows between the lifelines. They usually have some descriptive text attached, normally the name of the method that is called. Sometimes parameters or other issues are described there as well. Arrows can point from an object back to itself, which would represent a message an object sends to itself.

**Figure 30** shows a simple sequence diagram, which shows how the user can edit an existing movie that's stored in the movie database. It shows the human user like another object in the diagram. When the user wants to edit an item (by double-clicking in a grid, for instance), the EditItem() method of the MovieList object is called. This method then makes a call to a special EditForm object. It is not specified whether this object is created by the list object or already exists. The EditItem() method sends a DisplayItem() message to the edit form, which causes this object to retrieve an item from a data service object and to refresh itself in order to display the correct item. Afterwards, this sequence of messages is over, which is indicated by the rectangles attached to the lifeline of the objects. They inform us about the runtime of each message or method. At the end of each rectangle, the method is finished.

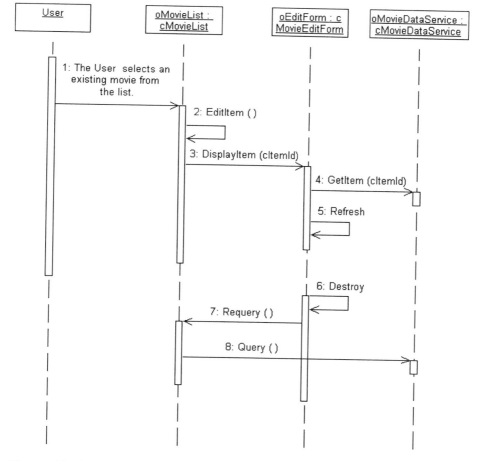

*Figure 30. A sequence diagram.*

There is more information in this diagram. It also tells us that the Edit Form sends a Requery() message to the list form to make sure all the contents are displayed properly. The list form uses the data services Query() method to retrieve an updated set of records.

This diagram is already rather specific to Visual FoxPro because it takes care of the fact that you need to issue a refresh to make sure all data is displayed properly. That's what we call an *implementation issue* that shouldn't really show up in the design. Implementation issues are concerned with special behavior in the implementation environment. The fact that Visual FoxPro doesn't necessary update all its fields when retrieving new data wouldn't be of concern if we'd implement the scenario in a different language. Also, workarounds or performance issues should not show up in the design.

However, the fact that the edit form sends a Requery() message to the list form is not FoxPro specific. That's how we designed our system. Imagine what would happen if the application ran against a SQL Server back end. No matter what language we used, we'd have to requery the data displayed in the list.

There are two bits of control information you can add to a method arrow. The first one is a condition, which has to be checked before the method is executed. **Figure 31** shows an example—the list form is updated only if changes were made in the edit form. If no information changed, updating the list form would be a waste of time.

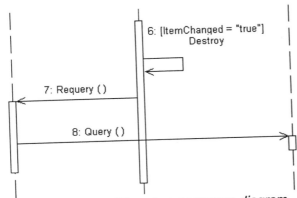

*Figure 31. Preconditions in a sequence diagram.*

The second bit of control information is the *iteration indicator* (*). **Figure 32** deals with the fact that the list could allow multi-select, and therefore an edit form would have to be opened for each selected item.

Sequence diagrams can also be used to document where values are returned from a method. Some people think that a Return should be drawn at the end of every method, as in **Figure 33**.

I don't often use return arrows. They look a lot like regular messages, which confuses me. After all, it's easy to see where a method ends, since the bar ends right there. I add an arrow for Return only when something special is returned—such as a particular item in Figure 33.

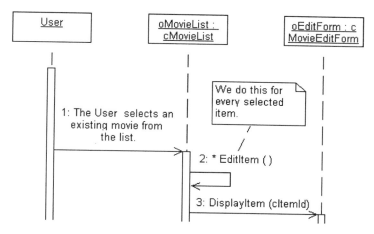

**Figure 32**. *The asterisk (*) indicates iteration.*

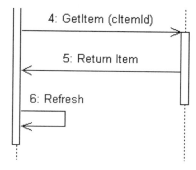

**Figure 33**. *Return values documented in a sequence diagram.*

One issue I consider very important is to indicate where objects get created. Unfortunately, there is no special notation that allows you to document that important event. I use a regular arrow labeled with the keyword "new" to signal that an object is created in this step (see **Figure 34**).

Sequence diagrams are easy to read and understand. They show object interaction in an orderly fashion, which is a great strength. One of the hardest things to understand in object-oriented projects is the overall flow of control. Sequence diagrams help to illustrate that.

When using Rational Rose (Visual Modeler doesn't support sequence diagrams), *message trace diagrams* (the old term for sequence diagrams) are also of great help when it comes to discovering gray areas of the system and adding new methods. When you specify a class for the used objects, you can right-click on a message arrow and select one of the existing methods. This makes it obvious when methods are missing. Rose allows you to add these methods to the classes right in the sequence diagram. This is a great feature, and I use it to discover most of my methods. This feature alone makes it worth the upgrade from Visual Modeler to Rational Rose.

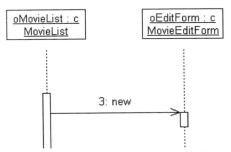

*Figure 34. Object instantiation indicated in a sequence diagram.*

### When to use sequence diagrams

For me, sequence diagrams are the second most important diagrams (after class diagrams). They have several different uses, one of which might be to demonstrate object interaction within a specific use case. Another would be to document the behavior of a few objects after triggering an action such as sending a message. In this case, sequence diagrams show very well what messages are sent when to what object.

I often use sequence diagrams to discover methods. I simply drop objects of a specific class onto the diagram and start to model the actions that take place. This way I can discover missing methods very quickly.

Sequence diagrams always document interactions based on a timeline. If you want a more general overview that shows a larger scenario—possibly across different use cases—use activity diagrams instead. If you want to track one specific object in a generic fashion and in large scale, consider state diagrams.

Sequence diagrams are easy to read. The basics can be explained within a couple of minutes. For this reason I like to use them in meetings and demonstrations.

### Collaboration diagrams

*Collaboration diagrams* are also concerned with object interaction. They use numbering to indicate the message sequence, rather than lifelines. This makes the timing much harder to read than in sequence diagrams, but collaboration diagrams display other things much easier. **Figure 35** shows an example of the same scenario I used in the sequence diagram.

As you can see, the collaboration diagram makes it easier to see which objects communicate with each other and how they are statically connected. At the same time it's a lot easier to see the message-firing sequence. The runtime of each method cannot be determined easily by this diagram because there is no optical clue where a method ends unless it has a return value. Of course, the method runtime could be determined in most cases by carefully analyzing the diagram, but it's much easier to use sequence diagrams instead.

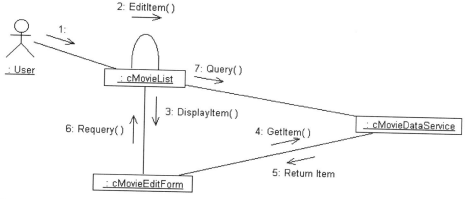

***Figure 35****. A collaboration diagram.*

Whether you use collaboration or sequence diagrams will depend on the scenario you model and what you are trying to show. In addition, personal opinion will influence your decision. I prefer sequence diagrams in most cases because I like to see what happens in what order, but as you can see in Figure 35, collaboration diagrams tend to be smaller and therefore appear simpler. Simplicity is good. Typically I will create both diagrams. The collaboration diagram provides a quick overview, and if I need details I can always go to the sequence diagram. For this reason, I don't put a lot of detail in collaboration diagrams. If you examine Figure 35 more closely, you'll see that I didn't bother to add object creation or conditional messaging, even though these features are supported by collaboration diagrams.

### When to use collaboration diagrams

Use collaboration diagrams when you want to get a quick overview of the general flow of events and object relations. Do not use them when you want to get a good idea of timing or message sequencing. You might also find these diagrams useful for larger scenarios, because sequence diagrams tend to be huge.

## Component diagrams

Component diagrams define how classes should be grouped together in the implementation. Typically, but not necessarily, all classes of one package go into one component. **Figure 36** shows a simple component diagram for the theater example.

In languages like C++, all classes in one component would go in one header and one CPP file. In Visual FoxPro, the classes of one component would be stored in one class library, which could be either a VCX or a PRG file. Sometimes it's also handy to assume a component is just like an Automation Server. You can specify that using a stereotype.

Rational Rose makes it easy to assign classes to a component. You simply drag and drop from the browser to the component in a diagram. All assigned classes are then displayed selected in the Realizes tab of the Component Specification dialog (see **Figure 37**).

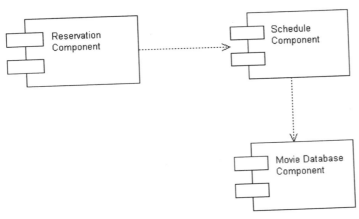

*Figure 36. A component diagram.*

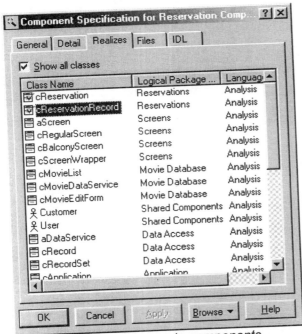

*Figure 37. Adding classes to components.*

The Component Specification dialog shows all classes that have been created in the model. The ones assigned to the current component show a red checkmark, like the first two items in Figure 37. Classes can be assigned to components by selecting Assign from the shortcut menu. A class can be part of more than one component. The Class Specification dialog has a Components page as well (see **Figure 38**).

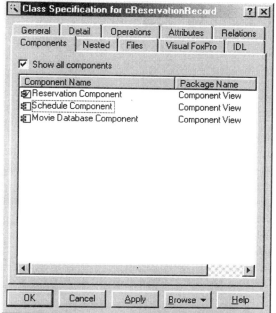

*Figure 38. Component specifications for classes.*

You can also assign classes to components from this dialog.

### When to use component diagrams

Use component diagrams to specify how an application can be broken down. Often components are later associated with certain devices in deployment diagrams.

Component diagrams are also used to specify where classes should be stored when using source code generation tools. However, the Visual FoxPro Modeling Wizards support other ways of doing that, as I will describe in later chapters.

## Deployment diagrams

Deployment diagrams describe how the application will be deployed, possibly across several computers using different connections and protocols. **Figure 39** shows how we plan to deploy our movie theater application.

Typically there are only one or two deployment diagrams per model, if they are used at all. I have to admit that I don't ever use them myself, and I've hardly ever seen them used by others. But I expect that they become more and more important when more large-scale Internet applications are created, or when people start to use technologies like Microsoft Transaction Server or DCOM on a more frequent basis.

### When to use deployment diagrams

Use deployment diagrams when you create an application that is not just one single EXE that runs on a single computer. I've found that deployment diagrams are only of value when I'm doing something new that I have to demonstrate to other team members or to upper management. I wouldn't bother making a deployment diagram when creating a simple network application with a data server and a couple of workstations.

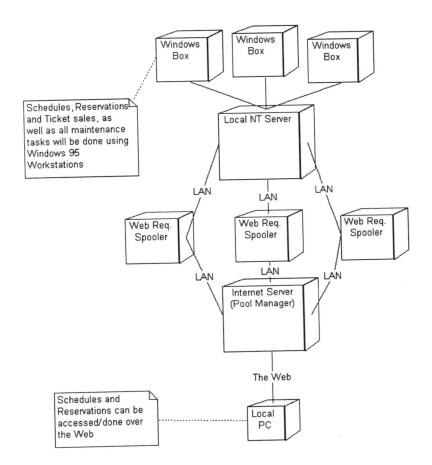

***Figure 39.** A deployment diagram.*

## Stereotypes

Rebecca Wirfs-Brock first introduced stereotypes, which have been added enthusiastically to UML. UML stereotypes are somewhat different than those originally introduced, but the basic idea is the same.

The original idea was to provide a high-level classification of an object that gave an indication of the kind of object it was. The Three Amigos reused that idea and turned it into a general mechanism to extend and customize UML. In fact, this became a very important UML mechanism because it guaranteed that UML could satisfy all needs, even if the creators didn't think about certain issues.

UML stereotypes allow controlled extension of the internal UML elements. They build an additional layer at the root of the UML metamodel. In theory, the whole UML could have been built of *Things* and *Stereotypes*. Stereotyping the class *Thing* could derive all other elements used in the language. I like to compare stereotypes to regular classes. Instead of using a native UML element, you take care of your needs by subclassing existing elements. This would have been confusing, though. Imagine modeling classes using classes. For this reason, the special term "stereotype" is used.

Typically, stereotypes are indicated by the special <<...>> naming convention. **Figure 40** shows an example of a stereotyped class.

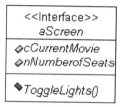

***Figure 40**. Use of a stereotype for a class.*

By the special naming convention you know right away that this is an interface class. You can even go a step further and define your own icons for the stereotypes you create. When using tools like Rational Rose, this is not trivial because the tool itself has to be extended. Rose comes with detailed documentation that explains how to do that, but it's still not simple. I have to admit that I've never done it myself. I found the naming convention to serve my needs well.

Stereotypes can be used for almost any UML element. You could create special dependencies, for instance, such as a "Relation" and a "Table" stereotype that could be used to model relational databases in UML. The possibilities seem to be never-ending...

## Conclusion

The Unified Modeling Language has been accepted as the standard notation for object modeling extremely rapidly. It is extremely powerful and extensible. Most of the UML may be used for Visual FoxPro modeling efforts. However, some of the used terms are different from the terms used in Visual FoxPro. This chapter gives you an overview of all the UML elements that have counterparts in Visual FoxPro, and it explains how to use them. There are only a few UML items that don't make sense in the FoxPro world. They are results of oddities or specialties found in other object oriented systems. We shouldn't use those things if we are modeling with Visual FoxPro in mind.

Throughout this book (especially in the following chapters), I use the UML extensively. Because of its simplicity and its acceptance as a standard, I hope this makes my diagrams easier to read.

# Chapter 13
# Collecting Requirements

**Collecting the requirements is the first step to creating a good application. It's a small step, but as a wise old Chinese man once said: "Even the longest journey starts with a single step."**

## What we try to achieve

Requirements seem to be a simple thing. They are often overlooked, even from people that buy into analysis and object modeling. Nevertheless, requirements are the very base of every application. How can you analyze a problem if you don't even know about it? How can you know about the customer's business unless you talk to him? You can save yourself a lot of trouble by simply spending a little more time collecting requirements to make sure everybody fully understands the situation.

Requirements have a very unpleasant characteristic: they are constantly changing. This will influence your project throughout its lifecycle. The later in the cycle that changes have to be made, the harder those changes will be to make and the worse they are for the morale of the troops. Unfortunately, changes are usually more frequent later in the cycle, simply because it has been quite a while since the original requirements were put together and the world has been changing since then.

What you need is a simple way to collect requirements, manage changes, and trace them to use cases, models and the implementation. This will help to predict the impacts of changes before implementing them. It will also help to find all the places that are affected by a change. In this chapter, I introduce techniques that help to resolve these issues.

## Collecting the requirements

The first step when collecting requirements is interviewing customers. How this is done depends a lot on the individual project. When creating custom database applications, you typically put on a nice suit, drive over to the customer's office, write down what he needs and that's it. The situation is very similar when creating in-house applications. The difference is that, instead of customers, you interview coworkers and usually you don't need a suit. When creating shrink-wrapped applications, this process is a little different because you usually don't get a lot of direct input.

### Research for shrink-wrapped applications

When creating standard software that sells off the shelf, you usually don't have customers that provide a lot of input. In this case you can do surveys, listen to complaints and requests about previous versions of the product (if there was a previous version, of course), make educated guesses or simply look at the feature lists of competitors. Very often, the marketing department replaces the customer and provides the input you need. Usually, this will be based on management decisions rather than on users' needs. But this is a different topic that should be discussed in a different place.

Normally, a company that creates standard software is somewhat knowledgeable about the domain they develop for. So from a starting point, their situation looks a lot better than for the company that creates custom software. The next steps are a little harder, though. Research has to be done, and there are many different ways to do that. Domain experts and external consultants can be brought in, which isn't cheap. Another way is to do surveys, which is resource intensive. No matter how you do it, you have to talk to many different people because you are trying to create an application that fits many different needs. One difficulty attached to this process is filtering out requests that wouldn't be in many people's interest or that are simply stupid. You don't want to add feature number 4079 to your invoicing application just because one person would appreciate it. However, when creating custom applications, the users (theoretically) know exactly what they need, and that's what you have to give them. When creating shrink-wrapped applications, you'll have to compromise and try to satisfy everybody.

On the other hand, once you have your list of requirements, which is based on extensive research, the list of requirements for shrink-wrapped applications is less likely to change. This takes out one of the major difficulties for managing requirements.

## Interviewing customers

Most FoxPro programmers are not in the shrink-wrap business. For this reason I will focus on custom applications. Whenever the need for a custom application arises (be it in-house or for a customer), the future users have a pretty good overview of their business problem. Typically, they are not able to express their needs clearly. Issues that are obvious to them are by no means obvious to you. Also, they are not aware of the possibilities, limitations and traps that the software world features. If they were, they wouldn't hire you to take care of possible issues, would they?

Your job is to make sure to get all the input you need to fully understand the situation. Your job is also to educate the customer about his options. If you are hired as a consultant, you should not blindly follow all the requirements the user writes down. Don't be afraid to fight battles over issues you consider critical. I've never had a customer who got mad at me because I argued about some issues. After all, he hired me to make sure everything went well. I have to admit that these arguments get emotional every now and then, and the customer might get upset. But that is far preferable to having an easy time during development, and delivering a product in the end that doesn't meet the expectations of the customer. Programmers are not paid big bucks to have an easy development time; they are paid for the final product they deliver. Keep that in mind when you interview your next customer...

Every customer I've met so far has at least two reasons why he needs this new product: One reason that looks good, and the real reason. The list of such cases is long. The most common scenario seems to be the "upgrade scenario." Somebody calls you up and tells you he really needs to convert his database application into Windows, because his business grew a lot lately and he wants to take advantage of all the cool "new" features like WYSIWYG word processing, OLE and others. The old version works fine, but he'd like to use the new system to send out this mass mailing at the end of next month...

Sooner or later you find out that the business didn't grow quite as much as he told you. The old application that "works fine" really loses a dozen records every day, the original programmer took off to enjoy the sunset in the Bahamas and now nobody can write an export routine to Word or recover the damaged database. The mailing turns out to be extremely critical, because unless the company makes a lot of sales in the next three months it will file bankruptcy, in which case you won't get paid. Had they told you sooner, you could have tackled the main problem right away, the mailing would have been ready even earlier than needed and everybody would be happy. Of course, this is a little exaggerated, but I'm sure you've seen similar scenarios.

A clear sign for such cases are extremely short deadlines for no apparent reason. If you can't figure out that reason, don't start the project (unless you are getting paid up front). You'll save yourself a lot of trouble. Every day, a couple of hundred thousand people across America need a software problem resolved. Don't pick the one who isn't even willing to tell you what he wants to achieve!

Another scenario is the "old-fashioned guy." He tells you how much he likes graphical user interfaces and all the other modern technologies. But as the project evolves, you discover that many of the features he wants don't really make sense in their environment. Sooner or later, you figure that the guy doesn't even like graphical interfaces all that much. Really and truly, he secretly never wanted to give up the command-line interface that he had used since his early pioneer days, when his company was the first one in the area to use computers.

In such projects you might discover requirements like a command-line interface that allows entering Visual FoxPro commands such as browse and edit (just in case, you know...). Maybe the customer even wants some non-objectified code in the core pieces of the system so he can maintain it himself. Another obvious symptom is the DOS-prompt shortcut he drops on your active desktop every time he uses your computer for five minutes because he couldn't imagine living without it. (Not that I don't use it myself every now and then, but don't mess with my settings, for heaven's sake!)

This mindset can also become obvious during the first presentations of prototypes or early implementations. You might demonstrate a feature that exports the current customer database to an HTML file, publishes it automatically on the Web and sends an e-mail to all your contacts informing them about the news. However, the customer might not be impressed by that feature (most likely because it was slightly over his head), but he might really like the hotkey you used to start the customer form.

I'm not saying that any of these scenarios is completely bad. The point I want to make is that you have to make sure you follow the correct targets. If the customer wants a DOS-like interface, I'd try to educate him about the advantages of the Windows interface. If he doesn't like it, fine. I can then decide whether or not I want to work on this project. If you discover after six months or one year that you've been hunting a phantom instead of achieving a simple goal, you'll end up very frustrated and accompanied by an angry customer.

## What you can prepare beforehand

Before I visit a customer for the first technical meeting, I make sure I have a very basic overview of the general problem. Usually, I ask the customer to send me some written information or other material that might be helpful in understanding the situation. Having some initial knowledge usually impresses the customer and makes him more confident. The atmosphere is more relaxed and the customer talks more naturally about his situation, which helps us get to the point more quickly. It also gives me a basic idea of whether I have any code or design I might be able to reuse. Usually I do, so I take notes and documentation and maybe even some demos with me, which allows me to evaluate those things at the customer's site if necessary.

### What you can expect

Your customers usually have a good idea about their needs and excellent knowledge about their business. This means that you have all the resources you need for your research. The main difficulty is getting the customer to provide this information—not because he isn't willing to share it, but because issues might be obvious to him but strange to you. Also, it will be very hard for him to share all his knowledge with you in the limited time you have to work together. For this reason, he has to pick what seems to be the most valuable knowledge and provide that to you. However, what seems to be valuable to him might be less valuable for you, and vice versa.

Customers know what they need—at least in general—but often they aren't sure about the details. It's your job to make them think about those details in order to find logical pitfalls.

In addition to these issues, there is the fact that the requirements change. I will discuss this issue in more detail a little later.

## Lay a good foundation

Keep in mind that the list of requirements you put together is the foundation of your project. If the list is weak, your application won't be any better. Don't leave room for interpretations. After creating the list of requirements, you need to go back to your customer and make sure it meets his expectations. (You might need to go back several times.) Insist that the customer takes the time to read over all those items and re-evaluate them in detail. Make sure he understands every single item that's on your list. Also, make sure you understand every item on that list. If something isn't entirely clear, don't make educated guesses. Just ask him! You might end up asking a stupid question every now and then, but that's nothing compared to the embarrassment of implementing a requirement entirely wrong.

A well-maintained list of requirements allows you to manage changes and trace them through several layers to the actual implementation. If you don't have a good way to maintain requirements, you lose those links right at the beginning of the development cycle.

## Hitting a moving target

Often I see programmers and designers getting upset because the customer changes requirements. I have to agree that this is a frustrating part of our work, but nevertheless, it's natural and maybe even important.

There are several reasons for requirements to change. One I see very often is that requirements are simply collected poorly. But there are more serious reasons than that. Customers usually aren't familiar with the possibilities in modern software development. How could they be? Even we ourselves don't have a good idea about the possibilities if we are lazy with our reading for a couple of months! Customers typically put their requirements together by looking at other systems or by looking at the weaknesses of the current one. Of course, there is also the real business problem that is to be solved, but usually it takes a while for the customer to explain all those details to you. As the project proceeds, customers see what you do, they learn about new possibilities and they always want to go a step further. On top of that, facts are simply changing over time. The longer a project takes, the more likely requirements are to change. At the same time, changes naturally have a more severe impact in larger projects.

All these factors are serious quality problems. They can lead to highly defective applications or to total failure. Normally, people try to avoid those changes as much as possible, which is the natural and simple solution. Talk to your customer and make sure every change is there for a good reason. Explain the related problems and the possible consequences. Very often, changes become less important when the customer understands all the impacts. However, you will never be able to eliminate changes completely, and I seriously doubt it would be good to do so. If changes didn't occur, every large undertaking would be hopelessly outdated when it's finished, and therefore would be useless. For this reason, you need to be able to manage changes and implement them without taking a quality hit.

When following the suggestions in this chapter, you should be able to eliminate the risk of poorly created requirement lists. Such lists leave you with customers that are unaware of possibilities and the changing business world. You won't be able to stop the world from evolving, but you can educate the customers somewhat. Don't spend weeks training them in the latest version of Windows, but give them an overview of the current options that might help to solve their problem. I typically give a two- to three-hour talk explaining the latest technologies from a user's point of view, which I've found to be well worth the effort.

There is no easy way to handle the evolving business world and its changing requirements. But I recommend evaluating—in a very critical manner—the reasons why a requirement changed. Often it turns out that changes can be avoided. You might even be able to postpone or ignore them entirely. If they have to be taken care of, you need procedures and tools that guarantee you can implement them without losing control over product quality. Avoiding delays seems impossible. Even small changes will cause serious delays. The later you are in the development lifecycle, the longer the delay will be. There is no such thing as a change that can be implemented "real quick" shortly before releasing your product.

## Managing requirements

For the issues discussed so far, you need a good way of managing requirements. Different techniques are used to do so, ranging from simple sheets of paper to specialized tools like Rational RequisitePro. Typically, some kind of text processor like Microsoft Word is involved in the process. Another popular way to manage requirements is to keep them in a database. This makes it easy to keep track of changes in requirements, sub-requirements, and related requirements. When using a database, you can track additional attributes of each requirement, such as groupings or level of importance.

Collecting requirements is an iterative process, just like every other part of the development lifecycle. The first step is to find external interfaces for the system. Typically, the customer has a couple of documents that describe the system in a very basic and often incomplete fashion. This document is usually good enough to be used as a starting point. If there is no such document, you need to ask the customer to write one. Systems often have more than one such document. The future users might write one, a domain expert might write another, and so forth. Needless to say, these documents often are inconsistent, but that's fine. It's your job to make sure the final list doesn't have inconsistencies. The fact that multiple documents are usually inconsistent actually works in your favor. Since two documents are different, one must obviously be wrong. If you had only one of them, an incorrect requirement might have made it to your list unquestioned. If you have multiple inconsistent documents, the discussion arises right away and you have the chance to get rid of potential problems early in the cycle.

You can use these documents to find "shall" sentences, which can be collected in a list. One standard you could use for your list is a Requirement Trace Matrix. I'll discuss different kinds of requirement lists in a little bit. For now we'll just agree on a very informal requirement list of unspecified format.

Collecting "shall" sentences is a simple and straightforward way to identify a basic list of requirements. For a more detailed list, you need to analyze the document more carefully. There is no set of rules to follow to identify further requirements that are supposed to be unique items. You should make an educated guess, plan ahead and imagine the future implementation, consult domain experts, and so forth. Wrong decisions (believe me, you'll make those at this point) can be corrected during later iterations. If you are in doubt, add a requirement to your list. It's easier to remove requirements or merge them together than to find requirements that were overlooked early on.

The result is a simple list that captures the most basic requirements and provides a rough overview of the whole system. Once this basic list is established, you can start to categorize and prioritize it. You can add headings in a Word document, or better, use attributes in a database. You might even combine the two using a tool like RequisitePro.

Once you organize your requirement list, take it back to the customer for a first review. He will either agree or disagree with the requirements you recorded. There should be no "maybes." If the customer hedges on a requirement, you should split it into multiple requirements to cover all the possibilities. You can keep the level of detail relatively low. Take notes about certain issues but leave the real description of each scenario for the use cases. (I describe those in the next chapter.) Focus on the current task! Remember that you're still collecting the requirements. You'll work out details of each requirement during later analysis.

After talking to the customer, you should revisit and correct the requirement list. Then go back to the customer with the new version to discuss it again. You should continue this loop until both parties are satisfied. When certain requirements are agreed on, you can start to analyze and work on the use cases, even if some requirements are still outstanding. If you wait until all the issues are resolved, you won't get to the next step. Keep in mind that requirements change, so only in rare cases will you have a requirement list with no unresolved issues.

There are two major differences between requirement lists and use cases. The first one is the level of detail. Use cases are far more detailed than requirement lists. The second difference is the way they are organized. Requirement lists are a very poorly organized list of typically independent items. Use cases combine requirements into scenarios. Also, use cases deal with the flow of events while requirements just capture the customer's needs from a business point of view.

## Requirement lists

There are many varieties of requirement lists. They can be informal or follow strict standards. I personally prefer to use advanced tools (as described next) to keep track of my requirements. However, every now and then I run across a consulting customer who wants to keep things simple by using regular Word documents, or something similar. In this case I create a Requirement Trace Matrix (RTM). An RTM is a regular Word table, just like this one:

| Entry # | Requirement |
|---------|-------------|
| 1 | A schedule shall be maintained that monitors the movies displayed on each screen. |
| 2 | A reservation database shall be maintained. |
| 3 | Tickets shall be sold at the ticket counters as well as on the Internet. |
| 4 | The software shall allow automating events like turning lights on and off in each theater. |
| 5 | Only supervisors shall be allowed to update automated tasks. |
| 6 | A movie database shall be maintained. |
| 7 | The movie database shall allow retrieving additional information about movies from the Internet. |
| 8 | The schedule shall be based on the movie database. |
| 9 | Credit cards shall be accepted and verified online. |

These are some requirements I would specify for my movie theater example. Of course, there are more possibilities, but in this example I'll keep the list short for simplicity. This is the initial list. It's very basic and loosely organized. In the next iteration I will organize it a little better and classify each requirement:

| Entry # | Requirement | Type |
|---------|-------------|------|
| 1 | A schedule shall be maintained that monitors the movies displayed on each screen. | SW |
| 1.1 | The schedule shall be based on the movie database. | SW |
| 2 | A reservation database shall be maintained. | SW |
| 3 | Ticket sales shall be monitored and organized. | SW |
| 3.1 | Tickets shall be sold at ticket counters and over the Internet. | SW,HW |
| 3.2 | Credit cards shall be accepted and verified online. | SW |
| 3.3.1 | The application shall continue to run while the credit card is processed, which usually takes a while. | SW,P |
| 4 | The software shall allow automating events like turning lights on and off in each theater. | SW,HW |
| 4.1 | Only supervisors shall be allowed to update automated tasks. | SW,SEC |
| 6 | A movie database shall be maintained. | SW |
| 6.1 | The movie database shall allow retrieving additional information about movies from the Internet. | SW,NTH |

This list shows more organization than the previous one because I defined sub-requirements. The requirement that the schedule should be based on the movie database is a sub-requirement of the one that defines my need for a schedule.

I also added requirement types, which will vary in every project. Make sure you document the requirement types you use. The codes in the above table are my basic set of types.

Here's what they stand for:

- SW = Software Requirement
- HW = Hardware Requirement
- P = Performance Requirement
- SEC = Security Requirement
- NTH = Nice To Have

In the next iteration I'll add even more detail and work on the requirements themselves (after talking to the customer). Since I don't have a customer around right now, I'll just assume the list above was fine, so I'll just add some more detail:

| Entry # | Requirement | Type | Importance |
|---|---|---|---|
| 1 | A schedule shall be maintained that monitors the movies displayed on each screen. | SW | High |
| 1.1 | The schedule shall be based on the movie database. | SW | Medium |
| 2 | A reservation database shall be maintained. | SW | High |
| 3 | Ticket sales shall be monitored and organized. | SW | High |
| 3.1 | Tickets shall be sold at ticket counters. | SW,HW | High |
| 3.2 | Tickets shall be sold over the Internet. | SW | Medium |
| 3.3 | Credit cards shall be accepted and verified online. | SW | Medium |
| 3.3.1 | The application shall continue to run while the credit card is processed, which usually takes a while. | SW,P | High |
| 4 | The software shall allow automating events like turning lights on and off in each theater. | SW,HW | Low |
| 4.1 | Only supervisors shall be allowed to update automated tasks. | SW,SEC | High |
| 6 | A movie database shall be maintained. | SW | High |
| 6.1 | The movie database shall allow retrieving additional information about movies from the Internet. | SW,NTH | Medium |

You can add as many columns as you want. I also like to add dependency information, which allows me to identify requirements that are based on other requirements but that aren't a sub-requirement of the current one. Here's how this would look:

| Entry # | Requirement | Type | Dependency |
|---|---|---|---|
| 1 | A schedule shall be maintained that monitors the movies displayed on each screen. | SW | 6 |
| 1.1 | The schedule shall be based on the movie database. | SW | 6 |
| 2 | A reservation database shall be maintained. | SW | |
| 3 | Ticket sales shall be monitored and organized. | SW | |
| 3.1 | Tickets shall be sold at ticket counters. | SW,HW | |
| 3.2 | Tickets shall be sold over the Internet. | SW | 3.3 |
| 3.3 | Credit cards shall be accepted and verified online. | SW | |
| 3.3.1 | The application shall continue to run while the credit card is processed, which usually takes a while. | SW,P | |
| 4 | The software shall allow automating events like turning lights on and off in each theater. | SW,HW | |
| 4.1 | Only supervisors shall be allowed to update automated tasks. | SW,SEC | |
| 6 | A movie database shall be maintained. | SW | |
| 6.1 | The movie database shall allow retrieving additional information about movies from the Internet. | SW,NTH | |

In this scenario, requirement 1 depends on requirement 6. Without a movie database, the schedule couldn't be maintained. Requirement 1.1 specifies this in more detail. Of course it depends on the movie database as well. Requirement 3.2 heavily depends on requirement 3.3. Without validating credit cards online, it will be hard to sell tickets over the Web. In fact, requirement 3.3 could also be a sub-requirement of 3.2, but we don't know that at this point. Requirement 3.3 could also be needed in more places and therefore be a totally independent requirement after all.

Another idea I find very interesting is to apply a simple function-point or action-point (AP) analysis. This technique will allow you to estimate the amount of work the application will need. Doing a function-point analysis might not be possible at this time, since it's a complicated way to rate requirements and we're missing too many details. Whil Hentzen's action-point analysis (first introduced in his *The 1997 Developer's Guide*) seems to work a lot better. It is based on the same ideas as the function-point analysis but it is a lot simpler. The results are not as accurate but at this early stage we won't be able to get accurate results anyway. The later you are in the development cycle, the more accurate this analysis will be. All we want at this time is a rough overview. Here's the table that makes use of this technique:

| Entry # | Requirement | Type | Importance | AP |
|---|---|---|---|---|
| 1 | A schedule shall be maintained that monitors the movies displayed on each screen. | SW | High | 3 |
| 1.1 | The schedule shall be based on the movie database. | SW | Medium | 1 |
| 2 | A reservation database shall be maintained. | SW | High | 2 |
| 3 | Ticket sales shall be monitored and organized. | SW | High | 1 |
| 3.1 | Tickets shall be sold at ticket counters. | SW,HW | High | 2 |
| 3.2 | Tickets shall be sold over the Internet. | SW | Medium | 5 |
| 3.3 | Credit cards shall be accepted and verified online. | SW | Medium | 4 |
| 3.2.1 | The application shall continue to run while the credit card is processed, which usually takes a while. | SW,P | High | 5 |
| 4 | The software shall allow automating events like turning lights on and off in each theater. | SW,HW | Low | 4 |
| 4.1 | Only supervisors shall be allowed to update automated tasks. | SW,SEC | High | 2 |
| 6 | A movie database shall be maintained. | SW | High | 2 |
| 6.1 | The movie database shall allow retrieving additional information about movies from the Internet. | SW,NTH | Medium | 1 |
| | | | | 32 |

Action points monitor the complexity of each requirement. Based on statistics and experience, you can now rate the application. I assigned 32 action points in the table above. Let's say it takes me about one or two days to implement an equivalent of one action point. In this case it would take me about two months to finish the application described above. Based on these numbers, I could rate the application and make a serious offer to the customer. If you want to find out more about action-point analysis, read Whil Hentzen's *Developer's Guide*.

Once you are done with the requirements and move on to the use cases, you can add this information to the requirement list as well:

| Entry # | Requirement | Use Case |
|---|---|---|
| 1 | A schedule shall be maintained that monitors the movies displayed on each screen. | Display Schedule<br>Maintain Schedule |
| 1.1 | The schedule shall be based on the movie database. | Display Schedule<br>Maintain Schedule |
| 2 | A reservation database shall be maintained. | New Reservation<br>Web Ticket Sale |
| 3 | Ticket sales shall be monitored and organized. | Regular Ticket Sale<br>Web Ticket Sale |
| 3.1 | Tickets shall be sold at ticket counters. | Regular Ticket Sale |
| 3.2 | Tickets shall be sold over the Internet. | Web Ticket Sale |
| 3.3 | Credit cards shall be accepted and verified online. | Web Ticket Sale |
| 3.2.1 | The application shall continue to run while the credit card is processed, which usually takes a while. | Web Ticket Sale |
| 4 | The software shall allow automating events like turning lights on and off in each theater. | Schedule Tasks<br>Turn Lights On/Off |
| 4.1 | Only supervisors shall be allowed to update automated tasks. | Schedule Tasks |
| 6 | A movie database shall be maintained. | Edit Movie<br>Add Movie<br>Delete Movie<br>Display Movie List<br>Display Movie Information |
| 6.1 | The movie database shall allow retrieving additional information about movies from the Internet. | Display Movie List<br>Display Movie Information |

This allows the developer to trace the requirements into the use cases. Whenever a requirement changes, it's relatively easy to trace those changes to the use cases. The use cases then have links to the object model, which has a link to the actual implementation. This is valuable information whenever requirements change, and as we've discussed, they change all the time.

# Rational RequisitePro

Rational RequisitePro is a requirement management tool that is tied tightly to Microsoft Word. The basic idea is to combine the two ways of managing requirements: the old-fashioned way of word processing and the promising new way of using databases.

Microsoft Word is used for the word processing part. I believe this to be one of the greatest strengths of RequisitePro. This way, the popular word processor can be used to create documents as usual. You can then use RequisitePro to add those requirements to a database and maintain it there. The other way around works as well. Requirements can be collected in the database and added to the document as needed.

**Figure 1** shows a requirement document in Microsoft Word.

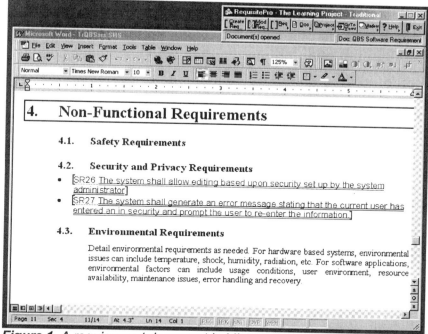

*Figure 1*. A requirement document in Microsoft Word.

The lines with the special format (which can be chosen) are requirements stored in the database. The additional window at the top is the actual RequisitePro toolbar. It always stays on top to allow easy access to all the features.

To see more detail about one of the requirements, move the cursor to a requirement in the text and select Req./Modify from the RequisitePro toolbar. This brings up the window shown in **Figure 2**.

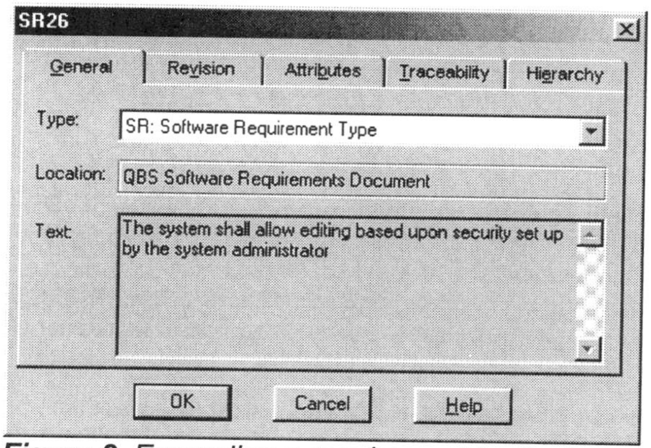

*Figure 2*. Expanding a requirement to display additional information.

This window provides detailed information about the current requirement. The General tab shows the classification (type) of the requirement as well as the text that shows up in the Word document.

The Revision tab shows the history of this requirement, which makes it easy to track changes. It remembers the changes as well as the person who made them, and annotations and remarks each person had about specific changes and their reasons.

The Attributes tab shows all the custom attributes we defined, as shown in **Figure 3**.

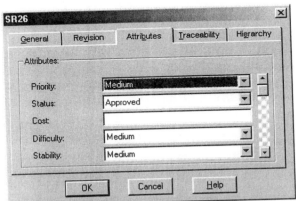

*Figure 3. The Attributes tab displays a variety of information about the requirement.*

RequisitePro comes with a predefined set of attributes, but you can create new ones. This is basically the same as adding more columns to an RTM as shown above. The Traceability tab in this dialog traces links to related requirements, which is very similar to the dependencies I demonstrated in the RTM. Finally, the Hierarchy tab allows you to define sub-requirements—also demonstrated in the RTM.

In addition to the Word interface, RequisitePro provides a database-typical view interface. There are three different view modes: The Attribute Matrix, the Traceability Matrix and the Traceability Tree. Within those views, you have many choices to customize them. **Figure 4** shows a simple Attribute Matrix.

The Attribute Matrix shows all requirements and sub-requirements in a treeview-like mode. It also shows the attributes in a grid view at the right-hand side. You have the option of filtering this view to reduce the displayed lines to certain items. Once you define such a view you can save it for later use.

The second type of view is the Traceability Matrix. It shows relations and dependencies between requirements (RequisitePro calls them Traceability Links). See **Figure 5**.

The third type of view is the Traceability Tree. It shows dependencies in a tree structure. In addition to that, it displays detailed information about each requirement. See **Figure 6**.

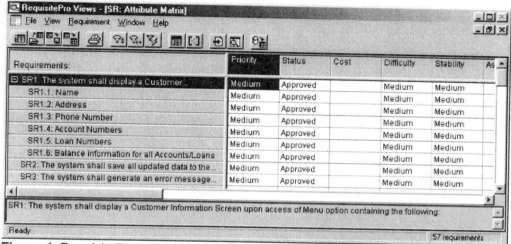

***Figure 4***. *RequisitePro can display the attributes for each requirement in a cross-tab-like view.*

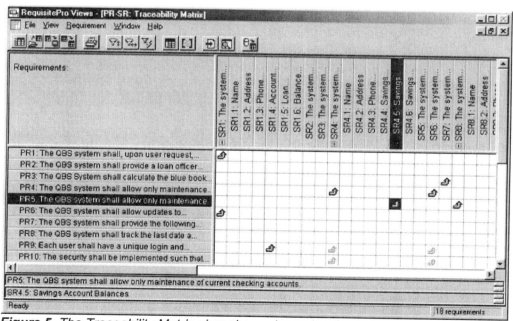

***Figure 5***. *The Traceability Matrix view shows dependencies between requirements.*

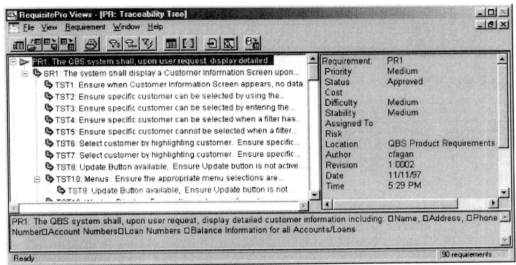

**Figure 6.** *The Traceability Tree shows dependencies between requirements and details about each requirement.*

RequisitePro fits very well in a series of development and modeling tools developed by Rational Software and Microsoft. It is actually the start of a chain that leads us to Rose, Visual Modeler and finally to the implementation tool—in our case, Visual FoxPro.

The next step after creating the requirement list is defining the use cases, which can be done using a word processor, a modeling tool like Rational Rose, or both. RequisitePro has a wizard that updates Rose models based on a requirement database and vice versa. This kind of tool is called a "roundtrip tool."

## Conclusion

The requirements you collect are the basis of the entire system you build. Mistakes made in this step are very hard to correct later on, and they will typically delay projects a great deal. The best time for the customer or user to give his input is while you are collecting the requirements. Make sure you interview customers and users regularly and try to get as many details as you can.

Using tools to collect requirements—rather than a simple sheet of paper or a word processor—is an essential step toward better software quality, easier maintenance and cheaper modifications. Tools help you to organize this process and give you valuable information about the impact of changed requirements, fixes and other modifications.

# Chapter 14
# Analyzing the Problem

**Once you have a requirements list, you know what the application is supposed to do in a somewhat unordered fashion. Now it's time to get your ducks in a row and describe the entire application in more precise terms and in a greater level of detail.**

## A Use Case-driven approach

Ivar Jacobson first introduced the Use Case as the main application-analysis tool. Use cases are excellent tools to describe applications, including all involved processes, actors and stimuli (see below for a detailed definition of these terms). Use cases describe all necessary user actions as well as required software reactions and modified data.

The most important part of use cases is documents. Typically they are accompanied by a couple of diagrams that provide an overview. Due to their great level of detail, use cases accurately describe an application's functionality, which gives you a good foundation for the next step—object modeling (see Chapter 15). Yet, because they are written in plain English, they are simple enough for users to understand and tell us whether the described scenario is accurate. In fact, use cases are so simple that both regular users and domain experts can help you write them.

## What exactly is a use case?

My description of use cases above sounds almost too good to be true, doesn't it? I'm sure you are anxious to find out exactly what they are (I know I was when I first heard about them). However, it's hard to find a good definition. I've read a number of books that discuss use cases exclusively, and I still had to read the entire book to find out what a use case was. When I started to write this book, I promised myself I wouldn't make this mistake. But here we are, at the beginning of Chapter 14, the magical place where I define the term "use case" as briefly and accurately as possible.

A use case is a text document that gives a step-by-step description of a scenario that an application must handle. A complete description of an application requires a number of use cases. Each scenario is described in detail, listing all involved actors, all stimuli and all data.

An "actor" is an entity that interacts with the system. It might be a human user or a piece of hardware, as well as some other software component that talks to your application. A "stimulus" is any kind of action an actor takes to interact with the application. The term "data" mainly refers to data stored in tables, but it could also be data in variables, files, or any other kind of data storage such as queued messages.

Use cases are well-formatted documents. They usually start with a section that gives a quick overview of the entire document. Then they list preconditions as well as all involved actors and their roles. The most important part of the use case is the actual scenario that lists all actions, followed by the software reaction. It is followed by special notes, post conditions, GUI sketches, a list of exceptions and references to use cases that describe these exceptions, a list of dependencies (mainly to other use cases), and possibly a couple of domain-specific sections such as timing constraints for time-critical applications or parts of those. Later in this chapter I'll show you a use-case template and an actual use case.

What got me confused when I started learning about use cases was the number of different names for them. At the purest definition, a use case is "a behaviorally related sequence of transactions." In other words, a use case describes a series of actions (reactions) taken by the system once an actor gives a stimulus. However, you will hear people say, "We are currently working on the use cases." In this case they are talking about the whole process of creating documents (containing all the sections I described above) and diagrams that contain the use cases as well as their dependencies. This is an inaccurate use of the term "use case." However, it might also be the most typical use of this term.

Use case diagrams are rather simple. They describe how use cases and actors are related to each other. The definition of each use case (the actual document) is still stored in a regular document (which can be linked to the diagram if a use case tool such as Rational Rose is used).

When I use the term "use case" in this book, I'm referring to the document that describes "behavioral-related sequences of transactions" (the scenario) as well as all the other sections I mentioned above. When I talk about diagrams, I'll refer to them as "use case diagrams."

Once you have a finished use case, you stick it in an envelope (figuratively speaking, of course) and put a label on it. You can now treat this use case almost as if it were an object. You can refer to instances of a use case in larger scenarios. Let's assume we want to describe the scenario of purchasing a ticket for a movie playing in our theater. There are actually a number of steps and actors involved in this process. We obviously have a customer and a salesperson—human actors. Note that I don't refer to them as "some person," but I give them a distinctive role. We also would have a use case that describes the process of checking whether a movie is playing and whether or not it's sold out, as well as printing the tickets. However, another use case might be involved if the user pays by credit card. Of course, we could describe the entire scenario in one large use case, but that wouldn't make a lot of sense because a credit-card use case is very generic. We could even reuse this use case in different projects. (Design reuse might even be more efficient than code reuse!) Along with this new use case, we also introduce a new actor: the credit card validation module. (Whether it is a piece of hardware or just a software component doesn't matter at this point.) **Figure 1** shows a use case diagram describing this scenario. See Chapter 12 for a description of the notation.

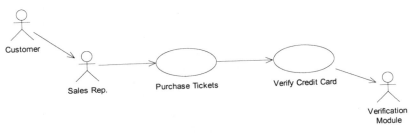

*Figure 1. A use case diagram gives a good overview of dependencies between use cases and actors.*

Treating use cases as objects or classes makes it easy for us to talk about the software to be produced. Instead of saying "If the customer pays by credit card, we use a verification module to verify the credit card and receive the payment," we can simply say "If the customer pays by credit card, we use the 'Verify Credit Card' use case." This not only makes it easier to talk about scenarios, but it also makes it more accurate, because the 'Verify Credit Card' use case defines the process in more detail than the first statement.

When treating use cases as classes, you might have the idea to subclass a use case, and indeed this is possible. For instance, you could create a use case that uses 'Verify Credit Card,' but it describes (very briefly) a slightly different scenario that uses a special kind of verification device (a software component instead of some hardware, for example) that requires some extra steps. It wouldn't be smart to rewrite an entire use case just because the software component required a password that the older hardware didn't require. However, keep in mind that we are still talking about regular text documents. "Subclassing" those documents isn't as straightforward as subclassing Visual FoxPro classes. You can simply put a remark in the "subclassed" document that mentions that another use case is to be used, with the exception of the facts in the current use case. For this reason, I recommend subclassing use cases only for small changes, or changes that can be described in a couple of continuous paragraphs. Don't subclass use cases and change nearly every other paragraph or sentence. This is very confusing and does more harm than good.

## Transition of a requirement to a use case

Making the transition from requirements to use cases isn't hard, as long as you follow a couple of guidelines. Basically, you bring your list of requirements in a well-organized form and enhance the level of detail. By doing so, you identify the actors and the stimuli as well as the software reactions. You are also likely to discover holes in the requirement matrix, but that's fine. You now have the opportunity to discover those gray areas of the system and put some light on them before they turn into real problems.

Let's have a look at the entire process step by step.

### Identify software use cases

The first step is to identify software requirements. All requirements not marked as software requirements do not qualify to get added to our list of use cases; however, they will influence use cases later on. The number of requirements that qualify for use cases can be enormous. However, you typically don't want a separate use case for every single requirement. This brings us to the next question right away: How many use cases do we need for our system? This question is one that people can never agree on. Some think a dozen use cases are sufficient for a two-year, 20-person project, while others aren't satisfied with 1200. It depends on your personal preference.

However, experience shows that too many use cases is more beneficial than too few, simply because large use cases are harder to maintain, handle, and understand. Also, the more use cases you have, the easier they are to group and reuse. For typical Visual FoxPro projects (18 months, up to five programmers), I try to keep the number of use cases in the two-digit range. Obviously I have more than 100 software requirements in most projects, so I typically start out using only the main requirements (for instance, I'd use requirement 1, but not 1.1) and add the other requirements to the Notes section of my use case (see below). This keeps the number of use cases low at the beginning.

However, some additional requirements that are only a note at this point end up as additional use cases later on, when I start to describe the scenarios. There is no real rule to identify additional use cases. This depends on your personal preference. There are various reasons why I would create a new use case. Large scenarios would be one; reusable scenarios would be another. The "Verify Credit Card" requirement might be a sub-requirement in a number of use cases. For this reason I export it into a separate document. Taking this approach, the quantity of use cases seems to emerge quite naturally.

Once I establish a first list of use cases (and a document for each one of those, of course), I start to describe the scenarios in the most detailed way possible. This includes all actors' input and all system reactions, including information displayed on the screen (and every other output media) as well as the required data manipulations.

While doing that, a lot of additional information surfaces, such as a list of actors, stimuli, preconditions, required GUI, dependencies and more. I add this information to the appropriate sections of my use case (see below) as soon as it emerges.

### When to start creating use cases

Frequently, people ask me whether they have to find all requirements before starting the use cases. The answer is no. You can start writing use cases as soon as you have a fair number of requirements. However, defining a "fair number" is not quite as straightforward. Requirements often depend on each other, which also means that they change use cases dealing with other requirements. I recommend establishing requirement groups before starting with use cases. Once this is done, you can start writing use cases for the requirement groups that are completed or close to completion. This way, changes in other requirement groups are less likely to influence your work.

The process of converting requirements into use cases is an iterative one. As you create use cases, you will find shortcomings in the requirements that will force you to go back and add missing information. Typically you'll have to talk to the customer or a domain expert to do so. At this point of development, it is important to keep customers and domain experts involved—not only to help with requirements, but also to approve use cases and possibly help develop them. As mentioned above, one of the great strengths of use cases is that they are very detailed and technically informative, yet easy for non-programmers to understand.

### Establish standards

Before you start creating use cases, you should establish some standards and guidelines to follow in all use cases. Remember that all use cases together build the entire description of your system. It wouldn't be very helpful if every use case had its own naming convention, level of detail, sections in the document, and so forth.

One of the first things you should agree on is the naming convention for use case files. The convention I adopted is "UC### Use Case Name." The triple pound sign (###) stands for the use case number with zero filling. So the two use cases in the example above would be called "UC001 Purchase Tickets" and "UC002 Verify Credit Card." The file extension would typically be DOC, TXT or HTM, depending on your text processor and output format.

I recommend using one template for all use cases (see below). This makes it easy to find your way around in all use cases so you can focus on understanding information rather than finding it. It also makes all required information available in each use case.

Finally, you should establish some standards about the things you want to mention in your use cases. You should agree on what kind of stimuli you want to describe in your use cases. Some people think only human actors and hardware can cause stimuli. I believe that all kinds of actors can cause stimuli, including other software components or events within current applications. You also need to determine a base set of preconditions that must be fulfilled. You don't want to describe every single precondition in every use case, because the list would simply grow too long. However, many preconditions are true for most parts of the system. For instance, I wouldn't mention in every use case that the hardware has to be turned on. While this might be a stupid example, there are many other examples that aren't quite as obvious, but still just as stupid. Nevertheless, they are needlessly mentioned in the set of preconditions, making the use case unnecessarily complex.

## Identify involved actors and stimuli

As mentioned above, actors and stimuli usually emerge while describing scenarios. To identify and properly document them, we have to look at the characteristics of actors and stimuli.

Let's start with the actors. As you already know, an actor can be anybody or anything that interacts with the system—a human user as well as any kind of hardware and software component. When you identify actors, make sure you describe the role they play. Typically this isn't a problem when the actor is a hardware or software component, but it seems to be a bit more difficult when the actor is a human user. Often I see human actors labeled "User," which is inappropriate.

You need to identify the role the user plays. In the example above, "User" could be either a customer or a sales rep. The difference is quite significant. It makes a big difference whether a customer or a sales rep tries to change the price of a ticket. Had we simply labeled both of them "user," we wouldn't have found a possible security leak or other shortcomings. You might now think that the customer wouldn't have a chance to initiate something such as changing the ticket price because he stands at the other side of the glass. However, this is true only in scenarios where the customer actually walks up to the box office. If he orders his tickets over the Web, he would have simply been "yet another user." This could have given us a lot of trouble had we mislabeled him initially. Giving the customer a specific role prevents such mistakes.

Assigning roles to actors also makes it easier to deal with scenarios where the same human user might play different roles. In the evening a person might be a sales representative, while he wipes the floor or maintains system machinery during the day. By creating multiple actors with distinct roles, we don't care whether we're dealing with one or more people. This helps to avoid a lot of confusion.

Make sure you list all the actors and a description of their roles in the appropriate section of your use case—including a brief description of the role they play as well as all their rights and responsibilities.

Now let's move on to the stimuli. A stimulus is any kind of interaction with the system, be it a mouse movement or click that requires some reaction, some text entry, a system event or a message sent by a hardware or software component. It's essential to describe all stimuli, no matter what. Don't just assume certain things (unless you previously agreed on them and documented them). It might be obvious to you that a dialog has some kind of OK button the user must press to proceed, but this might not be so obvious to another programmer.

Eventually, the other programmer might end up implementing a system that proceeds once the user selects an option in an option group, without waiting for the user to click OK or Cancel. It may seem difficult to imagine all possible stimuli, but in reality it isn't all that hard. Every time you describe something the system does without being triggered by a stimulus, you are missing some information. Depending on the format of your scenario description (see below), this is more or less difficult. If you find yourself tempted to skip stimuli, use the tabular format instead of plain text. This format makes such shortcomings very obvious.

## Develop scenarios

Scenarios are the most important part of use cases. They describe, step-by-step, all the actions taken by the actors (stimuli) and all the reactions coming from the software. This is done in plain English, so the scenario is easy to understand, even for non-programmers such as the customer or domain expert. In fact, customers and domain experts can help to develop scenarios. (They can also help to describe actors and their roles. Beyond that, use cases are the responsibility of the analyst.)

When starting to develop scenarios, create a rough draft first and fill in the details in later iterations. The UML standard allows multiple scenarios per use case. However, it seems easier to describe only one scenario per use case. This makes use cases easier to understand and maintain, and it is also easier to find common functionality throughout the system. Later on, it is easier to trace requirements through use cases if there is only one scenario.

Remember that the process of developing use cases is iterative. With each iteration, more details will evolve. Make sure to validate the additions of each iteration with domain experts. This gives you a great opportunity to find and resolve problems early in your development cycle.

Let's look at an actual example. The requirements in **Table 1** came from the list we developed in Chapter 13.

*Table 1. Some entries of the requirements matrix developed in Chapter 13.*

| Entry # | Requirement | Type | Importance |
|---------|-------------|------|------------|
| 3 | Ticket sales shall be monitored and organized. | SW | High |
| 3.1 | Tickets shall be sold at ticket counters. | SW, HW | High |
| 3.2 | Tickets shall be sold over the Internet. | SW | Medium |
| 3.3 | Credit cards shall be accepted and verified online. | SW | Medium |
| 3.3.1 | The application shall continue to run while the credit card is processed, which usually takes a while. | SW, P | High |

Each requirement in Table 1 is at least partially a software requirement, so we need to consider all of them directly in our scenario. As mentioned above, requirement 3.3 (which is very generic) will be described in a separate use case, though we wouldn't know that when we first started developing our use cases. In the following example, I refer to another use case, which means that the example doesn't represent the first iteration. Here it is:

*The customer requests a certain quantity of tickets for a movie of his choice at the box office. The sales representative checks for the availability of those tickets. If they are available, the customer is told and payment is requested. The customer may pay by credit card (in this case, use case XXX is used to validate the payment) or cash. The amount is entered in the system by the sales rep and validated by the system. If the amount is valid, the tickets and a receipt are printed and handed over to the customer by the sales rep.*

There is still some detail missing from this scenario, but more details will be determined during a later iteration. The scenario uses two actors (customer and sales rep), which must be defined in the "actors" section of our use case, like so:

**Sales rep**: *A human user that interacts directly with the system. He is responsible for interacting with the customer. He may access the list of scheduled movies and he may access a list of available tickets (that he may sell). He may not change ticket prices.*
**Customer**: *A person who intends to buy tickets. He will not directly interact with the system, but only with the sales rep.*

Typically, use cases describe the normal flow of events, such as "The customer walks up to the box office and asks for a ticket for one of the movies playing. The sales rep checks for available tickets, reserves the desired quantity, takes the money and hands the ticket to the customer." Obviously, there are a number of things that could go wrong. For instance, the desired movie could be sold out. Unless this problem is a minor one (which it probably isn't in this case, since it destroys the rest of the transaction), the exceptional scenario would not be described in the current use case, but in a separate one. This makes it easier to follow the scenario without getting distracted by unlikely events or complex scenarios that might not be directly related to the one described by the current use case.

As you may have noticed, we haven't yet handled some of the requirements we intend to cover in the current use cases. We haven't dealt with the Internet scenario, for instance, nor have we handled requirement 3.3.1 (The application shall continue to run while the credit card is processed...). Requirement 3.3.1 can be handled as a simple remark in the "Scenario Notes" section of our use cases, like so:

*Execution of use case XXX (Credit Card Validation) may take a while. For this reason, all steps described in this use case shall be executed as a separate thread so it doesn't block the system, and so other sales representatives may continue to sell tickets.*

There is a good reason why this requirement doesn't end up in the scenario: Requirement 3.3.1 describes an "implementation issue." We only have this requirement because of hardware-specific issues (verifying credit cards may take a while)—not because the business requires a wait state at this point. (They'd be happy to verify credit cards more quickly.) However, use cases should not be cluttered with implementation issues. We'll take care of those in later steps, such as the object modeling step or (more likely) the implementation step.

The fact that the requirements mention the Internet as a possible medium is a different story. Earlier I mentioned that use cases could be treated as classes and could be subclassed, and the Internet requirement would be a good example for using this technique. We can simply create another use case that refers to the first one. This should be done in the "Preconditions" section of the use case. Here's how:

*This use case subclasses use case XXX (Selling Tickets). All statements made in use case XXX are valid for this use case, with the exception of additional statements and definitions found in this document.*

There are only a few more things that we have to explain in this new use case. First of all, the role of the sales rep changes. This actor is no longer a human user, but an Internet component (application) that communicates with the main system in a similar manner as a human sales rep. A number of technical issues arise with this change—most likely, the entire architecture will change. A three-tiered model would be nice. We could have a middle-tier component that handles all logic, and we could have two different interfaces. The human sales rep could use one graphical user interface, and the Internet component could talk to a programming interface. However, at this point we shouldn't be concerned with technical aspects of the system we are going to build. We'll worry about these issues in the modeling step (see Chapter 15).

In addition to redefining the actors, we need to add a minor change to the actual scenario. It's obvious that an Internet component can't just hand tickets over to the customer. For this reason, we have to add some information about how the user will actually get his ticket. We have three options: 1) the user gets an electronic ticket with a confirmation number, 2) the customer can pick up the ticket at the box office, and 3) the customer can receive his tickets by mail. Each one of these options is complicated enough to require its own use case. We will simply refer to these use cases in the scenario. (I will not define these use cases here due to the amount of space it would take.)

So far, we used a simple "descriptive format" to describe our scenarios. In other words, we used regular English sentences in no particular format. However, that's only one of the possible options. The other option is to use a "tabular format." Let's have a look at both options in more detail.

### Tabular format

The tabular format organizes scenarios in a table. It lists scenarios in two columns: actions taken by the actors (stimuli) and reactions from the system. **Table 2** shows a template.

*Table 2. A template for a scenario table.*

| Action (Stimulus) | Software Reaction |
|---|---|
| 1. <Stimulus given by an actor> | 1. <Description of the software reaction> |
| 2. <Stimulus given by an actor> | 2. <Description of the software reaction> |

Typically, a scenario table is organized as a two-column table. However, in scenarios that have a lot of descriptive text, you might be more comfortable with the format shown in **Table 3**. This format consists of a narrow first column listing the number of the interaction, and a wide second column containing the description of the scenario. For every interaction, we reserve two rows: one for the stimulus and the other for the reaction.

**Table 3**. *A scenario table that's more readable if you have lots of descriptive text.*

| Interaction | Description |
|---|---|
| 1 | <Stimulus given by an actor> |
| | <Description of the software reaction> |
| 2 | <Stimulus given by an actor> |
| | <Description of the software reaction> |

However, it seems that the format used in Table 2 is easier to understand. For this reason I recommend using this format unless you have an extremely large quantity of text. I use the two-column format in most of my use cases. (Make sure you use the same format in all use cases belonging to one project; otherwise they can be difficult to read and compare.)

Table 4 shows the same scenario discussed above, but in tabular format. As you can see, it's a lot easier to identify stimuli, the overall flow of events, and missing information.

**Table 4**. *Our sample scenario in tabular format.*

| Action (Stimulus) | Software Reaction |
|---|---|
| 1. The customer walks up to the box office to purchase tickets. The sales rep starts a new ticket purchasing process. | 1. The system displays an entry form with a selection box for all scheduled movies. |
| 2. The customer chooses a movie, and the sales rep selects it in the displayed form. | 2. The system retrieves information about the quantity of available tickets for the selected tickets. |
| 3. The customer tells the sales rep the number of tickets he wants to purchase. The sales rep enters this information in the system. | 3. The system checks whether the number of requested tickets is still available. This repeated verification is necessary, because other sales reps may have soled a number of tickets since step 2 was executed. The system calculates the price for the tickets and displays them on the screen. |
| 4. The sales rep tells the customer the price and collects the money. If the customer pays cash, the user presses a "Cash" button (see GUI sketch) and enters the amount received. | 4. The system calculates the change and displays the amount. It also prints the tickets and the receipt, which are handed to the customer by the sales rep. |
| 5. If the customer chooses to pay by credit card, the sales rep presses a "Credit Card" button. | 5. The system invokes use case XXX (Verify Credit Card). Once the card is verified, the tickets are printed. |

As you can see, tabular formats tend to be better organized and provide more information. They make it very easy to identify steps that must be taken by the actors and reactions that you will have to program once you start to implement the application. I recommend using the tabular format especially if you are just starting to work with use cases. Table 4 shows a direct translation of the example I used earlier, but it contains much more detailed information. If I didn't include these details, the table would have appeared empty and it would have been obvious  information was missing.

There are some disadvantages that come with this format. Most importantly, it is harder to subclass tabular scenarios than descriptive ones. But overall, the advantages seem to outweigh the disadvantages. I use the tabular format in all my use cases.

### *Descriptive format*

The descriptive format (as I used in some examples above) seems a lot easier to write. Writing text in simple paragraphs rather than tables seems to be more natural. However, this format efficiently hides shortcomings and information holes. As I mentioned earlier, I prefer the tabular format over the descriptive format in any case. I can only recommend the descriptive format for extremely experienced analysts. For everybody else, failure seems to be preprogrammed.

### Preconditions

Most use cases have preconditions that must be fulfilled before the described scenarios can occur. Typical preconditions include other parts of the system that have to be executed first, hardware that has to be in a certain state, or business rules that have to be fulfilled. In our "Purchase Tickets" use case, preconditions would be that the movie schedule has to be up to date, and the credit-card-verification hardware has to be connected (possibly online as well) in case we decide to accept credit cards. Beyond those technology-related preconditions, there might be some business-related aspects—maybe we are not allowed to sell certain tickets before a certain date and time, and so on. Purists might now argue that I'm mixing different kinds of preconditions. In fact, the precondition that the credit-card module has to be online is entirely different from the precondition that tickets can't be sold more than three hours before the movie starts. This precondition is complex enough to require its own use case. However, in favor of the simplicity of this example, Ill leave it at that.

All preconditions must be listed in a special "Preconditions" section of our use case document. Do not make the mistake of explaining preconditions in the actual scenario. Preconditions just don't match the "action-reaction" format in which scenarios are written. It simply clutters the clarity of the scenarios. Also, you might end up reading and analyzing the use case and spending a lot of time with it, until you realize that the preconditions haven't been fulfilled. Having a separate section allows you to find use cases that match certain preconditions much more quickly and painlessly.

Never assume that programmers are aware of preconditions. It might be obvious that a movie schedule has to be set up before we can actually start selling tickets. However, during design and implementation, this might not be as obvious. Programmers might think they can sell the same kind of ticket every evening (which may or may not be true), or facts that seemed obvious during analysis might simply be forgotten during later phases when they're focusing on other challenges (such as technical issues or actual lines of code). The only preconditions you can assume to be known are those that are set and documented for the entire project.

### Post-conditions

Post-conditions describe the status of a system after the scenario has been executed, including tasks that have been accomplished in the scenario that aren't yet clear. In our example, this includes the fact that the number of purchased tickets is subtracted from the number of available tickets. Basically, post-conditions provide a summary of things that changed while the scenario was executed.

## Dependencies and relations

Use cases often refer to other use cases, as I mentioned above with the "Validate Credit Card" use case in our scenario. We can reference other use cases in more places than just the scenarios. Preconditions regularly refer to use cases. The precondition that states that a schedule has to be set up should refer to the use case that describes the scheduling process. We might have a note about this fact in the "Preconditions" section, but we should also list this use case in the "Dependencies and Relations" section. This allows us to quickly get an overview of all other use cases that describe a similar kind of scenario—or those that are at least somehow related to the current one.

Other sections that might include references to other use cases include (but aren't limited to) the description of actors and stimuli, as well as the general use case overview, post-conditions, notes, and other sections.

## GUI specifications and draft GUI sketches

Part of a use case is the actual description of the interface to be used, which is initially done using only words. Later in the process, you can (and should) create some draft sketches of the user interface. This will give the customer a rough overview of what he can expect to receive, and it will give the programmer a rough guideline for the actual implementation.

There are different ways to sketch interfaces. You can use scanned hand-drawings or graphical tools such as Corel Draw, or any other drawing program. I don't recommend using pixel-oriented tools such as MS Paint, because they don't allow you to change your sketches easily later on. I often use Visual FoxPro to design interface prototypes because it allows me to create them so quickly. When creating a Web-based application, I recommend Microsoft FrontPage or Visual InterDev (or any other HTML editor) to create a very rough version of the final interface. I've found that creating sketches that look like real interfaces, rather than just hand drawings or abstract versions of the final product, help to avoid confusion on the customer's end. However, I never tell the customer that the interface sketches are actual FoxPro forms or HTML pages. Customers usually confuse these early prototypes with the final product and expect too much too soon, so I leave them thinking that they are looking at nothing more than simple images.

## Use case diagrams

Use case diagrams provide a quick overview of dependencies between use cases and actors. Figures 1 and 2 in this chapter show examples of such diagrams. Both diagrams were created using Rational Rose (see below). Use case diagrams are nice to have, but they are not an essential part of a typical set of use cases. In other words, you could easily do without use case diagrams, but your entire set of documents would be worthless without the scenarios. Nevertheless, use case diagrams provide a nice and easy-to-read summary of all facts listed in the "Dependencies" and "Actors" sections of the documents. For more information about UML use case diagrams, see Chapter 12.

## A sample use case

Now that you have a lot of theoretical knowledge about use cases, you should examine an actual example. But first I'll provide a use case template as I promised earlier.

### A use case template

The following template has always worked well for my use cases, although you might feel more comfortable with a slightly altered version. You can download an actual use case template in Microsoft Word format from the Developer's Download Files at www.hentzenwerke.com.

---

**Use Case XXX: Use Case Name**

**Overview:**
<Provide a brief overview of the scenario described by the use case.>

**Notes:**
<This section is used for author notes. Typically, this section is deleted when the use case is finished.>

**Actors:**
<Describe all actors with their rights and responsibilities.>

**Preconditions:**
<List all preconditions that must be fulfilled in order to execute the scenario.>

**Scenario:**

| Action (Stimulus) | Software Reaction |
|---|---|
| 1. <Stimulus given by an actor> | 1. <Description of the software reaction> |
| 2. <Stimulus given by an actor> | 2. <Description of the software reaction> |

**Scenario Notes:**
<Special issues regarding the scenario.>

**Post-Conditions:**
<Describe the system status after the scenario is executed.>

**Exceptions:**
<List all possible exceptions and their consequences.>

**Required GUI and GUI Sketches:**
<Briefly describe the required interfaces (possibly illustrated by interface sketches).>

**Dependencies and Relations:**
<List all use cases that are utilized (or referred to) in sections of this document.>

**Additional sections to be added as needed...**
<Add more sections here if required...>

---

### UC001: Purchase Tickets

Now that you know how a well-formatted use case document should look, take a look at an actual use case. Below is the entire "Purchase Ticket" use case that we've used in several examples in this chapter.

---

**Use Case 001: Purchase Tickets**

**Overview:**
This use case describes the process of purchasing tickets at the box office.

**Actors:**
*Sales rep*: A human user that interacts directly with the system. He is responsible for interacting with the customer. He may access the list of scheduled movies and he may access a list of available tickets (that he may sell). He may not change ticket prices.
*Customer*: A person that intends to buy tickets. He will not directly interact with the system, but only with the sales rep.

**Preconditions:**
- A movie schedule has to be set up (as described by use case 021).
- The sales rep has to be logged into the system (see use case 018).
- The scenario described in this use case cannot be executed more than three hours before the movie starts.

**Scenario:**

| Action (Stimulus) | Software Reaction |
|---|---|
| 1. The customer walks up to the box office to purchase tickets. The sales rep starts a new ticket purchasing process. | 1. The system displays an entry form with a selection box for all scheduled movies. According to one of the preconditions, only movies that start within the next three hours will be available. |
| 2. The customer chooses a movie and the sales rep selects it in the displayed form. | 2. The system retrieves information about the quantity of available tickets for the selected tickets. |
| 3. The customer tells the sales rep the number of tickets he wants to purchase. The sales rep enters this information in the system. | 3. The system checks whether the number of requested tickets is still available. This repeated verification is necessary, because other sales reps may have sold a number of tickets since step 2 was executed. The system calculates the price for the tickets and displays it on the screen. |
| 4. The sales rep tells the customer the price and collects the money. If the customer pays cash, the sales rep presses a "Cash" button (see GUI sketch) and enters the amount received. | 4. The system calculates the change and displays the amount. It also prints the tickets and the receipt, which are handed to the customer by the sales rep. |
| 5. If the customer chooses to pay by credit card, the sales rep presses a "Credit Card" button. | 5. The system invokes use case XXX (Verify Credit Card). Once the card is verified, the tickets are printed. |

*Use Case 001, continued*

**Scenario Notes:**
- Reaction #5 shall not block the server component while processing the credit card, to enable other sales reps to continue selling tickets.

**Post-Conditions:**
- The number of purchased tickets has been subtracted from the ticket pool.

**Exceptions:**
- Action 2 and/or 3 could be impossible if there aren't enough tickets left. In this case, the customer is told so and the use case starts over.
- Step 5 might fail if the credit card isn't valid. This scenario is handled by use case 003 (Invalid Credit Card).

**Required GUI and GUI Sketches:**
The interface required for this scenario is rather simple. One of the main targets is to make it very easy to use. Sales reps at the box office might be students hired for short-term periods, so they won't receive extensive training. The interface could be implemented as a regular Windows interface or as an HTML page. The following two figures show examples of both versions.

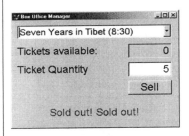

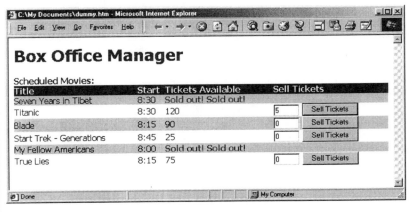

*Use Case 001, continued*

Both interface components show the first step of selling a ticket. Once we've decided what kind of interface to use, in a later iteration we will describe other interface components required by this scenario.

**Dependencies and Relations:**
UC002: Verify Credit Card
UC003: Invalid Credit Card
UC018: User Login
UC021: Maintain movie schedule

# Use case tools

Use cases don't require a lot of tools. In theory, you could write your use cases on a regular sheet of paper. In the real world, of course, this is impractical. You need some kind of text processor to create and maintain use cases; I use Microsoft Word, but any text processor will do. In addition to Word, I like to use Rational Rose. Let's have a look at both tools and how I use them to create my use cases.

## Microsoft Word

Using Word (or any other kind of text processor) is the minimum requirement for writing use cases. Word is considered a standard now, and I feel confident that almost everybody can read use cases stored in Word format.

 I like to use Word's template feature to reuse existing use case templates (and even stored macros). You can download my use case template from the Developer's Download Files at www.hentzenwerke.com. Future updates will be available at www.eps-software.com. Even though I feel confident about other people being able to open Word documents, I also use Word's export-to-HTML feature to create HTML documents from my use cases and publish them on the intranet or on secure Web sites.

## Rational Rose

Unlike its little brother (Microsoft Visual Modeler), Rational Rose can create use case diagrams. (You can read more about use case diagrams in Chapter 12.) Figures 1 and 2 in this chapter show examples of use case diagrams. I use Rational Rose as my modeling tool; it's rather pricey, so I wouldn't recommend buying it only for use case diagrams. But once you get used to these diagrams you won't want to be without them.

Rose allows you to create separate entities for use cases and actors. Each of those entities can have any number of documents assigned to it. (I usually use only one document to keep things simple.) This way, Rose provides a nice way to turn your loose collection of documents into an organized system specification.

Rational Rose introduces a number of nice features to use cases, such as stereotypes, abstraction and inheritance, or *generalization* as the modeler likes to call it. Chapter 12 provides a detailed definition of these terms. **Figure 2** shows a subclassed actor and a subclassed use case.

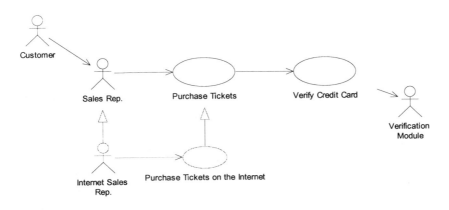

*Figure 2. A more advanced use case diagram that demonstrates subclassing of use cases.*

Rose also allows you to split huge use case diagrams into smaller scenarios to provide a simpler view. Luckily, none of the details gets lost because you can simply double-click an item to get a detailed description—including all dependencies, relations and linked files.

Overall, Rational Rose is a tool I wouldn't want to be without when creating use cases, but as I mentioned above, it's expensive; besides that, you might already have a tool of choice for the modeling process.

# Chapter 15
# Object Modeling

**By now we've specified all the requirements for our application and analyzed the problem in a great level of detail. In other words, we have a pretty good idea of what we want our application to do. Now we only have to figure out *how* it will do that.**

## Object modeling—an overview

*Object modeling* is the step in which we architect our application. Similar steps can be found in most undertakings, such as building houses, bridges and concert halls, flying into space, or simply setting up a plan for the day ahead. However, there is one major difference between the planning step in software development and the planning step in all other aspects of life: Software planning steps are often skipped. To me, this is unbelievable! Can you imagine building a skyscraper without consulting an architect first? I wouldn't set foot on the second floor of that building. In fact, I wouldn't get anywhere near its construction! Or can you imagine flying into space without planning the mission first? Going through a day without having a proper plan (schedule) can be disastrous enough (even though programmers are known to be quite accustomed to this scenario).

For software projects, the lack of a plan is equally disastrous. However, most people don't seem to care. "It takes too long," they usually say. "I have to earn a living and cannot spend weeks doing object modeling!" they continue. And they have a point! Modeling takes awhile, just as it takes awhile to plan a house. Nevertheless, nobody would seriously skip this step in the construction business. If we explore the scenarios further, we soon recognize that building a mid-size application is far more complex than building a house. This makes it even more surprising that object modeling is such a hard sell in most projects. In the end, this lack of respect for the planning phase makes up a major part of the incredibly high percentage of canceled or failed software projects.

Beating the odds of finishing a project (maybe even on time and under budget?) is a major step in making a career in software. I model every application I build for myself, and I try to talk every customer into modeling as well. Of course I need to set aside time for this step. But is this time spent in addition to the "regular" development time? Absolutely not! Quite the opposite is true. Modeling my projects saves me a ton of time during implementation and testing. In fact, it saves me so much time that I'm able to write a book while working on other projects.

## A picture is worth more than a thousand words

What exactly is an object model? Typically, a model is a bunch of diagrams describing the architecture of an application in a great level of detail. The diagrams show classes and objects as well as their relations (including inheritance), dependencies, properties, methods and interactions.

Object models are abstract and technical. Unlike use cases, the customer or domain expert typically doesn't understand object models. (And those who think they do typically are the most dangerous.) This also means that every shortcoming in the use cases is unlikely to be detected from this point on. Testing usually is the next quality milestone that discovers such problems. That's rather late, of course, so do everything you can to make sure quality milestones are met before you start to model. Make sure people take time to validate use cases and to point out and resolve problems.

Similar to use cases, object models describe an application in scenarios. Modeling scenarios are technology oriented. A scenario could describe how data is queried, for example. This scenario might show an interface object that uses business logic to retrieve data from some kind of storage mechanism. With use cases, I recommend sticking to one scenario per use case document to keep things simple. In the modeling step, this is no longer true. We typically have many diagrams describing similar (or even the same) scenarios, looking at them from different angles. One scenario might describe the inheritance situation using a class diagram, while another scenario describes objects used and their dependencies. Yet another diagram might show the messaging that occurs while the scenario is executed, using some kind of interaction diagram. Of course, the entire application could be described in two or three large diagrams. In fact, most customers expect to see a global diagram at some point. However, this is not practical. There is simply too much going on in most applications to show everything at once. However, I do recommend creating some "guiding diagrams" that provide a map of all scenarios organized in categories (or "packages" as they are called in the UML).

An object model must be an accurate and technical description of an application. This seems to be one of the hardest points for most modelers. Drawing diagrams is easy, but it's not so easy to make sure that the diagram can be implemented as drawn. Always keep in mind that every "box" you draw will become a class or object in the final product, so you have to consider FoxPro base classes and other issues. Of course, at this point we reach a level where a model is not entirely language independent, but that's fine, as long as such considerations aren't introduced too early in the modeling phase (see below). There are a number of things that can be helpful when creating the object model, including reusable model files. You can have a file with the entire set of Visual FoxPro base classes that you can use to subclass all your classes. This doesn't prevent errors automatically, but it makes it easier to detect problems. For instance, an object that's supposed to be a form, but that's instead somewhere in a chain of custom classes should make you suspicious.

There are a number of modeling notations. I use the newest and most widely accepted one: UML, the Unified Modeling Language. This notation has become extremely important in the last couple of years. In fact, I think it is so important, I spent an entire chapter (Chapter 12) explaining most of its aspects.

## Object modeling tools

Object modeling requires specialized modeling tools, and there are many different ones available. The obvious choice for Visual Studio developers is Microsoft Visual Modeler. However, Visual Modeler isn't a very advanced modeling tool because it was developed and packaged for Visual Basic developers. Due to the lack of certain object features in Visual

Basic, Visual Modeler lacks a number of features as well. Among them are sequence diagrams, which are essential for proper object modeling.

Fortunately, Visual Modeler has a big brother called Rational Rose. In fact, Visual Modeler is only a small version of Rational Rose that has been licensed to Microsoft. The similarities go so far that even the COM objects have the same names. Unfortunately, the similarities stop at the product price. Rational Rose is rather pricey. Nevertheless, you'll need a sophisticated modeling tool if you want to do serious modeling.

# From use cases to objects

So far, our development cycle hasn't produced any real challenges. We created the requirements matrix, and we made the relatively straightforward transition to the use cases. All of these steps were done in plain English, following some simple rules. Now we have to make the transition from written text to objects and classes. This step isn't quite as straightforward. Experience is a major factor, and you can't get experience by reading a book. However, note that this isn't a real modeling issue. Whether you create an object model or start implementation right away, you always have to somehow make the transition from requirements in plain English to source code (which typically involves objects and classes). So chances are, you already have quite a bit of experience and only need to know how to convert all your imaginary objects into the proper format.

Speaking of the way you think of objects: Don't change the way you think about applications. In the following sections, I'll present a three-tiered approach that closely matches my personal preferences. However, the purpose of this chapter isn't to teach you three-tiered development (see Chapter 9 if you are interested in this topic) or my way of doing things, but I want to demonstrate how an application is planned.

The ultimate goal of making an object model is to determine what objects we have, what classes they are created from, what methods and properties they have, when objects are instantiated, how they interact, how they depend on each other, and more. This is a lot of information, and the only sources of information we have are use cases written in non-object terms. The only real way to tackle this problem is to split up the task and start with small steps. The easiest thing to do is to identify objects without worrying about classes or any other issues.

As mentioned above, I like to develop my applications using a three-tiered architecture. This kind of architecture splits an application into three different layers—the user interface, the business logic and the data storage. I started using this approach to get a more flexible and easier-to-maintain implementation. However, it turns out that this logical separation of object types works out great for modeling as well. In fact, it works out so well that I recommend splitting any application into these three groups (logical and organizational groups, that is), even if the final implementation won't be three-tiered. There is a simple reason for this recommendation: Identifying objects in some tiers is easier than identifying objects in others. Objects are extremely easy to identify in the interface layer, so this is the place to start.

## Identifying interface objects

Interface objects are well defined in our use cases in several places. The most obvious examples of interface objects are the GUI sketches. All the forms we identify there can be assumed to be objects. We then have the scenarios where we can easily see all stimuli given by the actors. In order to give those stimuli, actors need some kind of interface. So identifying those objects isn't difficult. Sometimes, interface components are also described in the software reactions or other parts of the use case. However, this information is typically duplicated and can be found in the list of stimuli as well.

Let's have a look at the sample use case we created in the previous chapter. Here are the relevant parts that define interface objects:

---

**Use Case 001: Purchase Tickets**

...

**Scenario:**

| Action (Stimulus) | Software Reaction |
|---|---|
| 1. The customer walks up to the box office to purchase tickets. *The sales rep starts a new ticket purchasing process*. | 1. The system *displays an entry form* with a *selection box for all the scheduled movies*. According to one of the preconditions, only movies that start within the next three hours will be available. |
| 2. The customer chooses a movie and the sales rep *selects it in the displayed form*. | 2. The system retrieves information about *the quantity of available tickets* for the selected movie. |
| 3. The customer tells the sales rep the number of tickets he wants to purchase. *The sales rep enters this information in the system*. | 3. The system checks whether the number of requested tickets are still available. This repeated verification is necessary, because other sales reps may have sold a number of tickets since step 2 was executed. The system calculates the price for the tickets and *displays it on the screen*. |
| 4. The sales rep tells the customer the price and collects the money. If the customer pays cash, the sales rep *presses a "Cash" button* (see GUI sketch) and enters the amount received. | 4. The system calculates the change and *displays the amount*. It also *prints the tickets and the receipt*, which is handed to the customer by the sales rep. |
| 5. If the customer chooses to pay by credit card, the sales rep *presses a "Credit Card" button*. | 5. The system invokes use case XXX (Verify Credit Card). Once the card is verified, the tickets are printed. |

...

**Required GUI and GUI Sketches:**

...

...

---

As you know by now, we would have more interface sketches and more descriptive text in a complete use case, but we don't need this for the current example. I highlighted all interface definitions in the use case using bold and italic type. The actual interface sketch is another interface definition, of course, but as you can see in this example, the information can already be found in the actual scenario.

By now, we have identified the following interface objects (I already removed the duplicates):

- Ticket purchasing form
- Movie selection combobox
- Ticket quantity display component
- Ticket quantity entry form
- Price display component
- Pay-by-cash button
- Pay-by-credit-card button
- Ticket printing component
- Receipt printing component

As you can see, this list is still somewhat disorganized. It includes entire forms as well as single controls, and screen-interface components as well as print components (after all, printing is also part of the interface). The list even includes some objects that might be one and the same object in real life, such as the "Ticket quantity display component" and the "Ticket quantity entry form." Our application most likely has one form that displays the number of available tickets and allows us to specify the number of tickets to be purchased.

However, none of these issues are of concern at this point. We have identified the most important objects, which was the main goal. At this point, we have some duplicate objects but we are also lacking detail. Having too many objects is never a problem. We can always merge objects later on. Lacking detail isn't a real problem, either. We do not yet know all the objects we will use in our form, but at this point we aren't concerned whether a form is closed with an OK button or a link on a Web page. That's what we call an "implementation detail" (see below). However, we do need to know that there is an interface component that allows us to see all scheduled movies and the number of available tickets. We also need to know that there is an easy way to differentiate between payment by credit card and payment by cash. (At this point we've identified these components as buttons, but we'll abstract that further in the next iteration.) This information is essential to our design. No matter how we finally implement it, we will always have those components.

**Figure 1** shows the first object diagram that documents these basic findings. I organized the objects we've identified by putting them in a three-column layout. Column 1 shows everything that's supposed to be a form, column 2 shows everything that's some kind of important object on a form, such as buttons and comboboxes, and column 3 shows all objects related to printing.

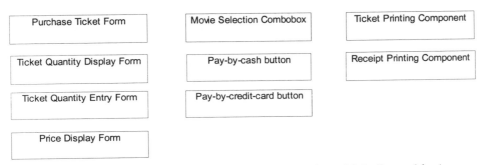

*Figure 1. The beginning of an object diagram showing all interface objects identified so far.*

Note: I manually created a package called "User Services" in my Rose model. However, Rose also supports three-tiered diagrams (the Visual Modeler uses them by default) that organize classes in various views automatically. This is nice for small projects and demos, but I don't like it for real-life modeling challenges because three-tiered diagrams do too many things automatically and it is hard to create proper packages. You can optionally switch Rose (and Visual Modeler) into three-tiered-diagram mode using the Diagram tab of the Options dialog.

**Figure 2** shows the Rose browser and the current packages and classes. With the exception of the Use Case View node, this view would be very similar when using Visual Modeler or three-tiered diagrams.

*Figure 2. The Rational Rose browser shows the current structure of our model.*

Note that all the objects identified so far have well-formatted class names, but this is not often the case. Initial class names typically are very relaxed and don't follow a lot of conventions or rules (like "Purchase Ticket Form"). This is fine at this point. In fact, for Rational Rose, "Purchase Ticket Form" is a valid class name. Keep in mind that Rose isn't a

Visual FoxPro-specific tool, and after all, there could be a tool that allows spaces in the class name. It's up to you whether you want to use descriptive names or more Visual FoxPro-like names. At the beginning of the modeling stages, it might be more intuitive to use descriptive names, but this is only my personal preference. In the following examples, I will start to use proper class names according to our definitions in Chapter 6, mainly because it makes writing this book much easier (I'm not writing everything sequentially, you know).

Now that we have all the objects, we can start to work with them. We can already identify classes that have things in common (I already did that by grouping them properly) and we can merge some classes because we already decided that the two ticket-quantity forms should really be only one object. **Figure 3** shows a more organized class diagram.

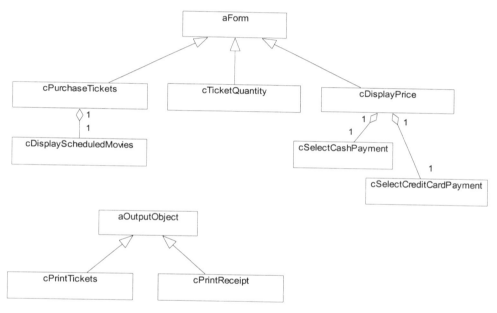

**Figure 3**. *Starting to organize our model, introducing generalization (subclassing) and aggregation (containership).*

If you compare Figure 3 to Figure 1 you'll see some drastic changes. In fact, I'm sitting here trying to decide whether the transition was too rapid. However, I really didn't do very much. Let's have an in-depth look at the changes.

First of all, I introduced two new classes: *aOutputObject* and *aForm*. When I looked at Figure 3 it was rather obvious that all the forms were, well, forms. As you know by now, all Visual FoxPro forms should be subclassed from another form class rather than starting from scratch every time. For this reason I introduced an abstract form class that I use as a parent class for the forms I've identified so far. Later on, we will add more subclasses, and the inheritance structure will possibly grow more complex. For now, this level of detail is enough.

I also introduced a parent class for both print objects, because in all my projects I subclass a standard print object to implement the exact details. Even if I didn't use this object, I would still recommend using it. But then again, I'm just documenting my way of doing things. If you don't use a common print object and if you wouldn't have identified one, it would be fine.

Figure 1 also contains a third group of objects: the interface controls. You might now wonder why I didn't create a common parent class for these objects. Well, there is a very simple reason: Just step back for a moment and think of the diagram as classes you will actually implement in Visual FoxPro, rather than just a diagram. What base class would those classes be made of? Buttons? Well, what about the list of scheduled movies? This would hardly be a button. Comboboxes? Not the payment-selection components! The truth is, we don't know what classes they are going to be made of, and at this point we don't even care. This is yet another implementation issue that we don't need to solve immediately. It's just important to have a reminder that these objects are essential. For this reason I modified these classes slightly. I stopped calling them buttons or comboboxes to make them a little more abstract.

There's only one last detail to explain: the relationship between the interface controls and the actual forms. I introduced aggregation relationships (in Visual FoxPro we would call this "containership"). The diamond end of the line points to the container (or the object that owns the other object). Using aggregation, I defined that the *cDisplayScheduledMovies* object lives inside the *cPurchaseTickets* form. I even specified the multiplicity and defined that one form has exactly one instance of this list. (In Rose you can do this by simply right-clicking the end of the line and choosing "Multiplicity.") I did the same thing with the payment-selection objects.

Figure 3 provides quite a bit of information, including a number of classes, inheritance structures and other relationships. And all we did was to examine the stimuli we defined in our use cases. It's been a fairly smooth transition so far.

## Identifying the data services

Now it gets a little harder: We need to identify the data that is involved in our actions. The use cases describe data in various places, which makes it a little harder to find. The software reaction column describes some data, but typically it provides too little detail and accuracy. Post-conditions often hold more information because they summarize what has been changed. Also, the precondition section will list data that must exist when we start our scenario. However, the sections that describe data aren't limited to the ones I just mentioned.

The next page shows our example use case with all references to data highlighted in bold and italic. As you can see, use cases typically describe data vaguely—and coincidentally, UML doesn't provide a default notation for data. You can simply describe a record as an object, describe the fields as properties, and create your own stereotypes for data, but that doesn't get you too far. To do serious data modeling, I recommend using one of the specialized tools for this field. However, we still need to document the data part in our object model. We do this at a very simple level, identifying all data objects and dependencies.

**Use Case 001: Purchase Tickets**

...

**Preconditions:**

- *A movie schedule has to be set up* (as described by use case 021).
- The sales rep has to be logged into the system (see use case 018).
- The scenario described in this use case cannot be executed more than three hours before the movie starts.

**Scenario:**

| Action (Stimulus) | Software Reaction |
|---|---|
| 1. The customer walks up to the box office to purchase tickets. The sales rep starts a new ticket purchasing process. | 1. The system displays an entry form with a selection box for *all the scheduled movies*. According to one of the preconditions, only movies that start within the next three hours will be available. |
| 2. The customer chooses *a movie* and the sales rep selects it in the displayed form. | 2. The system retrieves *information about the quantity of available tickets* for the selected movie. |
| 3. The customer tells the sales rep the *number of tickets he wants to purchase*. The sales rep enters this information in the system. | 3. The system checks *whether the number of requested tickets is still available*. This repeated verification is necessary because other sales reps may have sold a number of tickets since step 2 was executed. The system calculates *the price for the tickets* and displays them on the screen."" |
| 4. The sales rep tells the customer *the price* and collects the money. If the customer pays cash, the sales rep presses a "Cash" button (see GUI sketch) and enters the amount received. | 4. The system calculates *the change* and displays *the amount*. It also prints the tickets and the receipt, which are handed to the customer by the sales rep. |
| 5. If the customer chooses to pay by credit card, the sales rep presses a "Credit Card" button. | 5. The system invokes use case XXX (Verify Credit Card). Once the card is verified, the tickets are printed. |

...

**Post-Conditions:**

- *The number of purchased tickets* has been subtracted from the *ticket pool*.

...

Here's a list of all data entities I found in the above use case:
- Movie Schedule
- Movies
- Ticket Pool per Theater
- Tickets Purchased
- Total Price
- Ticket Prices

During data modeling, we would identify a number of tables and relations, and we would see that some of those items are simply fields in another table (such as the number of tickets purchased and the total price). Again: Those things would be determined in a data-modeling step that I won't cover in this book (how convenient). **Figure 4** shows an object diagram that documents the existence of data and some basic relations that have been discovered in the data-modeling step.

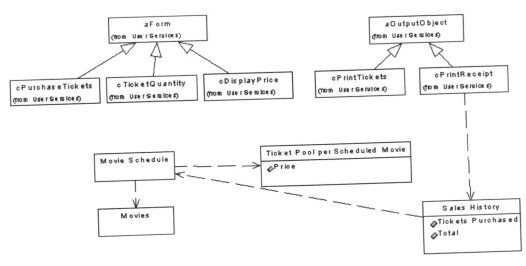

***Figure 4.*** *We create another scenario to document some of the data issues, but we leave further details to specialized data-modeling tools.*

Note that Figure 4 isn't a modified version of the first diagram, but a completely new diagram describing only this particular issue. In fact, I even created a new package called "Data Services" that I use to organize all data entities. If you look closely, you'll see that some of the items in Figure 4 have a remark because they are from a different package. Rose adds this remark automatically.

In this diagram, I left out some details such as the objects contained in the forms. I could have also left out the inheritance relationship to the abstract form and the abstract print object, but I thought it might help me to find my way around my own diagrams. (I'm not a good artist. Can you tell?)

When creating this new diagram, I reused the classes I already had. To do so, I simply dragged the classes from the Rose browser and dropped them on my diagram. Rose automatically knows about all relations previously set up, such as inheritance in this example. I then added new objects for the data items. Don't just add new objects to a diagram using the toolbar. In this case, Rose creates new classes that it manages internally. If you then update the previously created classes, those updates will not show up in your second diagram, which would defeat the purpose of modeling altogether. **Figure 5** shows the Rose browser displaying the entire model structure so far. If your model (given that you follow the examples on your computer at home) shows more classes, you've done something wrong and your model won't work (see below how Rose handles classes)!

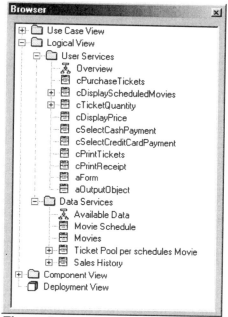

*Figure 5.* The Rose browser displaying our model.

## Identifying the middle tier

So far the ride has been pretty smooth, but it's about to get bumpier. I've always found it more difficult to identify the middle-tier objects (the logic) and to put them in an order that makes sense. The basic idea is to identify all places where the application is required to do something by itself as a reaction to a stimulus. So in theory, we can simply look at the second column of our use case scenario to find all the behavioral objects. In real life, however, it's more difficult. If we investigate our use case closely, we see that some of the required information is scattered over the entire use case. For instance, we know we'll need to invoke the "Verify Credit Card" use case if the customer pays by credit card. Of course, the system should be smart enough to do this automatically. However, we didn't describe this particular requirement in the reaction column (column 2), but rather in the stimuli column (column 1). To find these logical steps, look for phrases such as "if...then...", "...checks for...", "...calculates..." and the like.

The next page shows our use case one more time, with all descriptions of middle-tier objects highlighted in bold and italic.

**Use Case 001: Purchase Tickets**

. . .

**Preconditions:**
- A movie schedule has to be set up (as described by use case 021).
- The sales rep has to be logged into the system (see use case 018).
- The scenario described in this use case *cannot be executed more than three hours before the movie starts*.

**Scenario:**

| Action (Stimulus) | Software Reaction |
|---|---|
| 1. The customer walks up to the box office to purchase tickets. The sales rep starts a new ticket purchasing process. | 1. The system *displays an entry form* with a selection box for *all the scheduled movies*. According to one of the preconditions, only movies that *start within the next three hours will be available*. |
| 2. The customer chooses a movie and the sales rep selects it in the displayed form. | 2. The system *retrieves information about the quantity of available tickets* for the selected movie. |
| 3. The customer tells the sales rep the number of tickets he wants to purchase. The sales rep enters this information in the system. | 3. The system *checks whether the number of requested tickets is still available*. This repeated verification is necessary because other sales reps may have sold a number of tickets since step 2 was executed. The system *calculates the price for the tickets* and displays them on the screen. |
| 4. The sales rep tells the customer the price and collects the money. If the customer pays cash, the sales rep presses a "Cash" button (see GUI sketch) and enters the amount received. | 4. The system *calculates the change* and displays the amount. It also *prints the tickets and the receipt*, which are handed to the customer by the sales rep. |
| 5. *If the customer chooses to pay by credit card*, the sales rep presses a "Credit Card" button. | 5. The system invokes use case XXX (Verify Credit Card). Once the card is verified, the tickets are printed. |

. . .

**Post-Conditions:**
- The number of purchased tickets *has been subtracted from the ticket pool*.

. . .

Looking at this use case, we can identify the following objects:
- Check for Scheduled Movie Time object
- Retrieve Scheduled Movies object
- Retrieve Number of Available Tickets object
- Calculate Price object
- Calculate Change object
- Initiate Printing object
- Invoke Credit Card Processing object

As you might recognize immediately, many of these objects don't make sense. Why would we have two different objects to check for scheduled movie times and for scheduled movies? Most likely, this would be one object. Why would we have two objects to calculate the price and the change? On the other hand, would we really have only one object to initiate printing the tickets and the receipt? I'd say we need at least two different objects to take care of the job. But then again: Should those objects be defined in this scenario, or would they be defined by some other use case? The same is true for the credit card object.

This is where the ride gets bumpy and your experience needs to come in. A number of the questions I raised above can be answered right away by making some educated guesses. I can tell you right away that we only need one object to handle the movie schedule and another one to calculate prices and change. The answers about the print and credit card objects are harder to answer. I'm pretty sure those objects are defined elsewhere, but how could we know yet? For this reason, I would design them as separate objects at this point. Having too many objects is better than having too few. Consolidating objects later on is much easier than introducing new ones. So as a rule of thumb, always create separate objects if you are in doubt. In a later stage of design, you can identify objects with common behavior and consolidate them. Over time, you'll develop a pretty good feeling about such issues, and designing the middle tier will be much more straightforward.

Here's a list of all middle-tier objects I would identify using my experience:

- Movie Schedule object
- Ticket Pool object
- Price Calculation object
- Ticket Printing object
- Receipt Printing object
- Credit Card Processing object

This list is essentially different from the list above, but if you think about it, it makes more sense to have one object to maintain the movie schedule. This object can easily be capable of telling us what movies are scheduled, whether we are in the three-hour range and other things the current scenario doesn't require, such as setting up the schedule. This object might even be able to handle the ticket pool for those movies. However, we don't know that yet (and of course it depends on your personal preference). I designed a separate ticket pool object.

**Figure 6** shows our new object model, including all middle-tier objects and a first indication of their dependencies. Unfortunately, it doesn't give an indication of the flow of events and the relation to the other objects we've already identified.

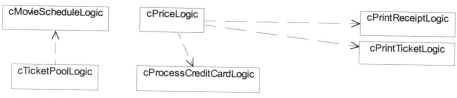

**Figure 6**. *Some business logic objects and a first indication of their dependencies.*

Now we need to figure out how these objects fit into our interface and data scenario. **Figure 7** tells us more about that.

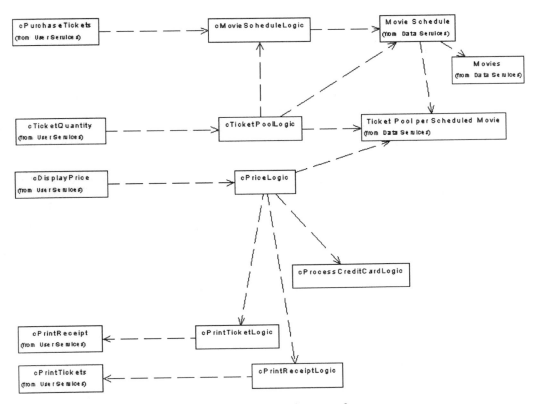

*Figure 7. An overview of the most important objects so far.*

This diagram might be somewhat confusing at first sight, but it really isn't. Here are some guidelines I used when drawing the diagram: First of all, I placed all the interface objects to the left. I didn't display all the details, such as the contained objects. These things were well documented in a previous diagram, so there is no need to repeat them here. In the middle, I placed all the middle-tier objects (as the name suggests), and to the right, all data objects. In this case, a three-tiered diagram would make this more obvious, but as I mentioned above, these diagrams have some serious restrictions, so I organize regular class diagrams as if they were three-tiered diagrams.

Figure 7 also gives us a rough overview of dependencies. Note that these dependencies are somewhat different than the ones shown in previous diagrams, because I changed them to invoke the new objects. Previously we had direct dependencies from the interface objects to the data objects. Now, all the dependencies go from the interface to the middle tier, from the middle tier to the data, or they stay within one tier. Every dependency that skips the middle tier would be a potential problem and defeat the purpose of three-tiered development (see Chapter 9).

Whenever I dropped existing objects on my diagram, the previously defined dependencies were automatically displayed. In Rational Rose, you can simply click on a dependency and press the Delete key, and it disappears. However, this doesn't mean that the dependency is deleted. It is only removed from the current diagram. If you really want to delete a dependency (as in this example), press Ctrl+D. This deletes the dependency from the model so you can create new and more appropriate dependencies. When you go back and look at the previously created diagrams, you'll notice that the dependencies have been removed from them as well. That's where the beauty of a modeling tool that adds meaning to the graphical diagrams comes in. The same is true for all items in Rational Rose.

## Identifying methods and properties

By now we have a pretty good idea of all the objects we need. However, we know little about the sequence of events or the methods and properties we need. Properties are relatively easy to define because they are mentioned in the use cases as part of the data. When you discover data you want to attach to an object, simply add it by selecting "New Attribute" from the right-click menu. Note that all attributes are created as hidden by default, because this is how things work in most object-oriented environments.

Discovering methods is somewhat more difficult, but you still might be able to guess a fair amount of methods by reading through the use case. In the example above, we could easily guess that the movie-schedule object has a method to retrieve all scheduled movies within the next three hours.

However, there is a better way to discover this information: Sequence diagrams.

### Sequence diagrams

Sequence diagrams define, in a very detailed manner, what objects are sending what messages to other objects (see Chapter 12). Because sending a message at the sender's end means calling a method at the receiver's end, we will automatically discover all the methods by simply thinking through the scenarios.

Creating sequence diagrams in Rose is trivial—simply drop the existing objects (classes) onto the diagram. Note that sequence diagrams deal with object instances, while all our diagrams so far have dealt with classes (even though I called them *objects* because we haven't yet thought about our class structures and hierarchies). This means that a sequence diagram can show multiple instances of the same class. (I'm not using this capability in this scenario, but it's still important to know the difference.)

**Figure 8** shows a simple sequence diagram. It doesn't describe the entire scenario as we've defined it in the use case, but only the first couple of steps.

Let's see what the diagram actually tells us. First of all, the user opens a form. We do not yet know how this happens. This information will be added in a later iteration. When the form gets created, it automatically updates an object that displays all movies scheduled for the next three hours. The object actually retrieves this information from yet another object by calling the GetMoviesForNext3Hours() method. Note the difference between the interaction initiated by the user and the methods that are called. The description "Opens" is simple text that I added. For the methods, I right-clicked on the arrow and chose "New Operation." This opens a dialog that allows defining a new operation (we'd call it a "method" in Visual FoxPro) and all details such as parameters. Once I've done that, I right-click the arrow again. Now, the shortcut menu shows the newly defined method and I can simply select it. The beauty of this is that I can now go back to my previously created class diagrams, and the new operation will show up there as well (given that I turned on the display of operations).

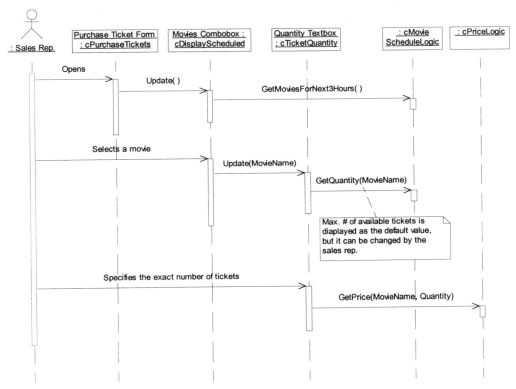

***Figure 8.*** *A sequence diagram describing all messages that are sent.*

Going through the entire scenario step-by-step guides me to all the important methods and parameters quite naturally. That's why I like sequence diagrams so much. Unfortunately, they are supported only by Rational Rose and not by the Visual Modeler.

## Identifying common scenarios

The steps described so far have to be repeated for every use case and every scenario. Eventually, you will end up with a detailed description of all objects and their methods. However, you can only program classes—not objects. In fact, all the "objects" we have identified so far really are classes, but we treated them as if every class were instantiated only once. As you know, this isn't how object-oriented applications work. Quite the opposite is true! We want to reuse as much as possible and create class hierarchies.

To discover those hierarchies, you need to analyze the diagrams you've created so far and look for objects with common properties and methods, and for common scenarios. The easiest way to do this is to create diagrams that provide generic scenarios that are not directly related to the scenarios described in the use cases. A typical example would be to create a general scenario about how print operations work. **Figure 9** documents such a scenario.

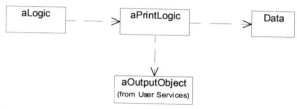

***Figure 9***. *A generic print process.*

In this scenario, some logic invokes special print logic that's responsible for gathering data, and finally an output object is invoked to print the result. Note that most of these classes haven't been introduced so far—or have they? Well, in a way they have. Some classes we've created so far are specialized versions of the ones described in Figure 9. The *cPrintTicketLogic* and *cPrintReceiptLogic* classes are specialized versions of the print logic, for instance. This means that we can make them subclasses of the *aPrintLogic* class. **Figure 10** shows this inheritance relation as well as some others we would discover if we followed the approach described above for other classes.

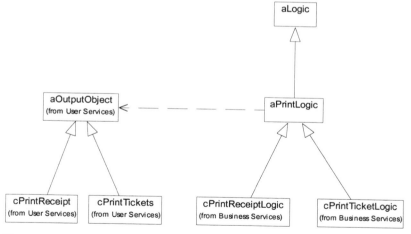

***Figure 10***. *Some inheritance trees we've just discovered.*

When discovering common parent classes, you need to go through all methods and properties and move the common ones to the parent class, rather than leaving them in the subclasses (after all, this is the idea of object-oriented programming, isn't it?). I recommend turning on the display of attributes and operations, so it is easy to see duplicates in the class diagrams.

## Putting things together

The example above was the first step toward putting things together in the technical sense. You need to model scenarios that are not described in the use cases. Creating a generic print scenario was one example. How did I actually know I needed to model this scenario? Well, the need for that pretty much arose automatically. When creating sequence diagrams, for instance (which seems to be the most obvious place to discover missing information), you'll often discover that you have a good idea of what's supposed to happen, but you don't have a clue how to do it. This is a good time to start thinking about the missing information and to add scenarios that give a clear description.

After taking this step and the one described above, you'll manage to make the transition from single scenarios to an entire application or complex object system.

## You don't want three-tiered models?

In the examples I've described so far, I've used a three-tiered approach because I like three-tiered applications. I recommend using this kind of architecture for all your business applications; however, if you don't like this approach, you can still do object modeling. This means that you may (or may not) take an entirely different approach to discovering your classes. You can still use the approach I described above to discover your objects in a three-tiered fashion, but you could then merge objects (typically the logic and the interface layer) to form an old-fashioned architecture.

## Implementation details

Often you'll discover issues that are important but that shouldn't be included in the object model. Those issues are called "implementation details." We've already discovered a number of them. The question whether certain interface components should be buttons isn't relevant for the object model, for instance. Other typical implementation details would be properties and methods that have to be implemented because of some oddities of the used implementation tool. You wouldn't mention that an update method that gathers data to display it in fields has to call the form's Refresh() method, for example. If you used a different implementation tool (not Visual FoxPro), this would no longer be valid.

Identifying implementation details gets easier with more experience. However, it's not too hard to discover them if you keep questioning whether the objects, methods and properties you design would be the same if you'd used an entirely different implementation tool.

Nevertheless, implementation details shouldn't be forgotten, even if you are not quite at the implementation phase. The best thing to do is to add a comment to the item documentation or to stick a note in the diagrams. (Rose has special note items. See Figure 8.)

## Keeping things language independent

In theory, the entire modeling step should be language independent. However, I've found this to be true only to a certain extent. The closer you get to completion of your model, the more language specific the model will become.

A number of different things influence the development environment or language in which a model can be implemented. Class naming is an obvious factor. Some languages are case sensitive, while others (such as Visual FoxPro) are not. Because Rational Rose has to work with all languages, it is case sensitive. This means that you can create two classes with identical names, but with different uppercase and lowercase settings. For Rose this is perfectly legal, but it would cause major problems in Visual FoxPro. And there is more to naming conventions—some languages might support special characters, while others will not. Again, Rose supports them all.

Inheritance is another factor that makes models language specific. Of course, there are a number of object-based languages (such as Visual Basic) that don't support inheritance at all. A model that uses inheritance would be useless in those environments. Even if you intend to use a language that supports inheritance (as in the Visual FoxPro case) you need to be careful with your inheritance design. Some languages such as C++ support multiple inheritance, but others (such as Visual FoxPro) do not.

The number of issues continues. What about visibility? Visual FoxPro 6.0 supports hidden properties and methods, but Visual FoxPro 3.0 does not. So the idea of language-independent modeling doesn't work all the time. In the first iterations, you probably won't have trouble staying independent, but as soon as you start to consolidate classes and create inheritance structures, you'll need to make a decision. Fortunately, most people know which implementation tool they want to use. The only scenarios in which I've discovered that things must be kept language independent is when prototypes are created with a different implementation tool than the actual application.

## How Rose handles items

At first sight, it appears that Rose is just a graphical tool that allows you to create diagrams. Once you start using Rose more regularly, you'll discover that there is more to it. Every item you put on a diagram is created internally as an actual class, inheritance relation, or whatever the item was. This item can then be reused in many different diagrams. Rose invokes items automatically when you add other items to a diagram. Let's assume you dropped two classes on a diagram, one of which was a subclass of the other. In this case, Rose automatically adds the inheritance relation to the diagram. You can then decide whether the diagram should display this relation or not. You can remove the relation (or every other item) from the diagram by selecting it and pressing the Delete key. Note that this removes the item from the diagram only! The inheritance relation is not deleted from the model. Other diagrams that show the same classes might still document the relationship. If you want to delete an item from the model, you have to press Ctrl+D. This will also remove the item from all other diagrams.

When you drop an item onto a diagram, Rose automatically creates this item internally. When creating multiple diagrams describing the same scenario (or at least showing an existing class), this holds the danger of creating the same class (or any other item) twice. To avoid this, you can double-click the item name to get a list of all previously defined items, and you can choose the one you want to keep. You can also drag and drop items from the Rose browser, rather than from the toolbar, which is my preferred method.

## Reusing design

Reusing code is great, but reusing design is better—simply because it is one step earlier in the development cycle and it therefore saves even more work and time. Typical reuses of design are patterns (see Chapter 10). When doing proper object modeling, the design is where all the brainpower is. Once you have a proper design, creating the code typically means filling in the blanks (coding the actual methods, that is).

Reusing design also is much simpler than reusing code, simply because it is more abstract and you don't get caught up in implementation issues and details. Often, the organization of class libraries, variable and reference naming, and other implementation details make it very hard to reuse code (see Chapter 8). Those problems don't apply when reusing design. Good designs are more abstract and therefore more applicable to "classes" of applications and/or application modules.

When you reuse design, reusing code typically is just around the corner (given that you implemented an existing design at least once). By reusing design, you keep systems compatible, which makes it much easier to reuse code.

# Chapter 16
# Implementation

**Our current project is coming along well. We have collected requirements, created use cases and planned the application using object-modeling techniques. Now it's time to take the last step and implement the actual application.**

## Creating Visual FoxPro code

Creating Visual FoxPro code for a model already created means mostly filling in the blanks. In the real world, this means coding the actual methods and writing additional code such as startup programs or non-object parts of the application such as menus.

Most parts of the application are simply created as specified in the plan (model). In most languages, this means sitting down and typing in all classes and objects already designed. It also means redoing a lot of work. Visual FoxPro provides a much easier way with its Visual FoxPro Modeling Wizards. If you are a registered Visual FoxPro user, you can download these wizards from the Microsoft VFP Web site free of charge. The wizards will automatically generate Visual FoxPro code and even update existing models from the code you created.

In the actual implementation, the application details—and even larger parts such as entire classes or modules—might differ from your object model. In a perfect world this wouldn't happen, but in real-life scenarios it does. Here's one example: The object model could have a number of classes and objects that deal with menus. This might be fine in many languages, but not in Visual FoxPro because it has no object-oriented menus. For this reason, the implementation can differ. That's fine. However, you should document these things once they are implemented. The easiest way is (again) to use the two Visual FoxPro Modeling Wizards because they can analyze entire projects and update existing models. In this chapter I'll introduce only the Code Generation Wizard. The next chapter deals with the Reverse Engineering Wizard.

## The Code Generation Wizard

Both Visual FoxPro Modeling Wizards are compiled into one application (VFPModel.app), which is one of many files you receive when downloading the wizards from the Microsoft Visual FoxPro Web site. The site states that the wizards are for use with Visual FoxPro 5.0. In fact, they were shipped long after Visual FoxPro 5.0 was done, but too early for Visual FoxPro 6.0. For this reason, they work well with Visual FoxPro 6.0.

When using Visual FoxPro 6.0, you should install the Modeling Wizards into the following directory (given that you installed Visual FoxPro 6.0 in the default directory):

```
C:\Program Files\Microsoft Visual Studio\VFP98\Tools\Modeling
```

The actual installation process is simple. The setup program copies files only into the specified directory. You can move them to other directories at any time without having to set additional parameters or properties.

Run the Visual FoxPro Modeling Wizards like so:

```
DO Home()+"Tools\Modeling\VFPModel.app"
```

This brings up a dialog that allows you to choose the wizard you want to run (see **Figure 1**). After you run the wizards once, they register themselves in Visual FoxPro as regular Visual FoxPro wizards, and they're available from the Wizard Selection dialog under the Tools/Wizards/All menu item. **Figure 2** shows the Code Generation Wizard in the regular wizards dialog.

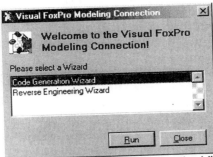

*Figure 1*. The launch pad for the Visual FoxPro Modeling Wizards.

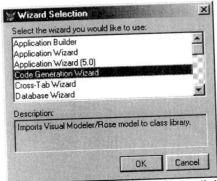

*Figure 2*. The Wizard Selection dialog shows the Code Generation Wizard.

You can also install the wizards in the Tools menu (my preference). To do so, simply call VFPModel.app with "0" as the first parameter. Here's an example:

```
DO Home()+"Tools\Modeling\VFPModel.app" WITH 0
```

I added this line of code to my startup program, so the wizards are automatically added to the menu when I start Visual FoxPro. **Figure 3** shows the new Tools menu with the installed Modeling Wizards.

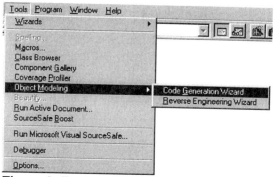

*Figure 3*. *The Modeling Wizards as a new item in the Tools menu.*

## Importing your first model

Before we explore the details of the Code Generation Wizard, let's import a model and generate some source code. To do so, start the Code Generation Wizard using one of the possible starting options I introduced above. **Figure 4** shows the first step of the wizard.

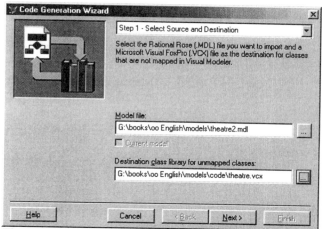

*Figure 4*. *In step 1 of the Code Generation Wizard, specify the model and a class destination file (library).*

First we specify the model file we want to import. We also specify a default class library where we want to store all the generated classes. (Note that the wizard creates only visual classes. If you wanted to see real source code, you'd have to use the Class Browser's source-generation feature to create low-level source code.) The specified destination file is only a default setting and might be overwritten in a number of places (see below). The library I specified in this example didn't exist, so the wizard automatically created it for me (after I approved it, that is).

Once we move on to step 2, the wizard actually starts to import and analyze the entire model. For this reason, moving from step 1 to step 2 can take some time. Still, it's lightning fast compared to writing all the code by hand. **Figure 5** shows step 2 with an imported model.

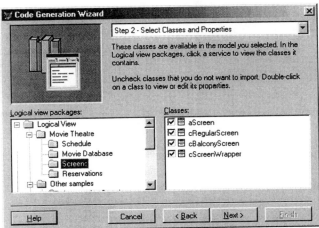

***Figure 5**. The entire model has already been imported internally. We can now choose the classes we want to generate and/or update.*

The tree shows all the packages we created in our model. Once we select a package, we see all the classes belonging to it. Initially, all classes are selected. However, we can deselect classes if we don't want to import them. As you'll see later on, a lot of additional functionality is hidden in this step (see below), but for now we'll move on to step 3a (see **Figure 6**).

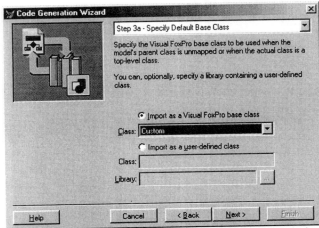

***Figure 6**. Selecting a base class for the imported classes.*

Step 3a allows us to select a base class for all imported classes. Typically this would be *Custom*, but you could also select any other existing Visual FoxPro base class. If that isn't enough for you, you can also select any user-defined class.

The selected class will be used as the default parent class for all imported classes. Not all classes will be of the same Visual FoxPro base class, but you can specify this in other places (see below). The class we specify in step 3 will be used only for classes that have no base classes specified and no other parent classes in the model that would define the base class.

Step 3b (see **Figure 7**) requires choosing some additional base class settings.

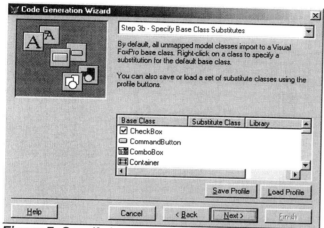

**Figure 7**. *Specify base class substitutes to use your own set of base classes.*

Step 3b allows you to substitute your own base classes for the default FoxPro base classes for each of the model elements. As we have discussed before, it is dangerous to inherit directly from base classes. In this dialog we can specify that the model use *cMyExtraordinary-FormClass* for all forms it encounters as it imports the model. To specify base class substitutes, simply right-click on the class you want to redefine and select a new class from the dialog.

Typically, different sets of base classes are used for different projects. Reassigning all those classes every time you run the wizard wouldn't be practical. For this reason, the Code Generation Wizard allows you to create reusable profiles. Once you define a set of base class substitutes, simply click the Save Profile button, assign a new profile name, and preserve the set for later use (see **Figure 8**). You can define as many profiles as you want.

In well-designed models we'd be done already. The next regular step is the Finish step of the wizard. However, if there are conflicts in the model, we need to resolve them before we move on. I'll discuss resolving conflicts later, so let's assume the model we are importing is flawless. **Figure 9** shows the final step of the Code Generation Wizard.

The options in the last step don't influence the way the source code is generated, but they do allow you to specify how the created code is displayed and what other files are generated and updated. The option group on top defines whether the classes are only imported, or whether they are displayed in the Class Browser right away. I recommend starting the Class Browser at once, since you will always want to see what has been created.

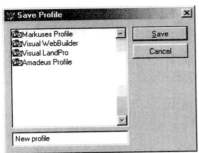

*Figure 8. The profile manager.*

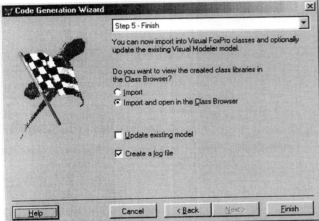

*Figure 9. Almost done! The last step of the Code Generation Wizard allows us to set some additional options.*

At this point you can also specify that the existing model should be updated, in case you changed anything. This would be important if you had conflicts, in which case those changes would be written back to the model right away. This can be dangerous in some situations, so be careful with this feature (after all, it changes your actual model). No conflicts occurred in our example, so this setting won't have any effect.

The wizard also suggests creating a log file. This is always a good choice. Remember that the wizard touches source code. It can't be bad to know the details of what it did.

As mentioned above, the wizard imports the entire model on the way from step 1 to step 2, so when you click Finish, the wizard only writes buffered data in the specified files. This happens rather quickly. Once this is done, the log file is displayed (if you chose to create one) and the results are displayed in the Class Browser (see **Figure 10**) if that's what you requested.

As you can see, all classes have been placed in one huge class library and they're all based on the Visual FoxPro base class *Custom*. This doesn't make a lot of sense for most projects. In the rest of this chapter I'll explain how to create more sophisticated models and how to specify details.

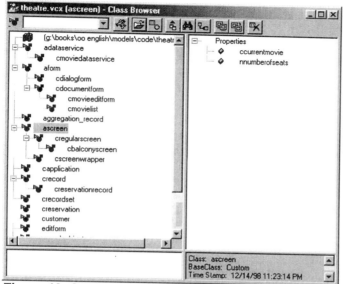

**Figure 10**. Our first generated class library displayed in the Class Browser.

## Selecting model files more efficiently

Visual FoxPro communicates with the modeling tool using OLE Automation. The wizards are smart enough to figure out what modeling tool you are using (Rational Rose or Visual Modeler) and they know how to deal with each tool. If you have both tools installed, the wizards invoke the one you used last. Every time Rose or Visual Modeler shuts down, it adds an entry to the Registry, indicating that it is the standard modeling tool from now on. So if you want to influence the tool to be used, start the tool of your choice and shut it down right away. Then start the Modeling Wizards.

If you are currently working on a model, and an instance of the tool is running, the wizards allow you to use the current model, rather than asking you to select a model file (see **Figure 11**). This is the option I use most frequently. It makes everything much easier, and it also speeds up the process.

## Step 2's secret options

Step 2 looks simple at first sight. It shows all the packages and, once you click on them, all the classes in each package. You can select and deselect classes by simply clicking on them. If you deselect a class, it won't be imported. This feature was implemented to give you the option of leaving out classes that you have already imported and that haven't changed (see below for more information about updating existing code). This is very important because it can take a long time to import a large model.

You might also encounter other reasons for deselecting a class. One would be to exclude classes that are not meant to be implemented in Visual FoxPro. Data or menu objects are typical examples. However, step 2 is not the place to do that. After all, you'd have to do that every time you wanted to update your libraries. It is much better to set these options in the model, where those settings are persistent. (See below for more information about this.)

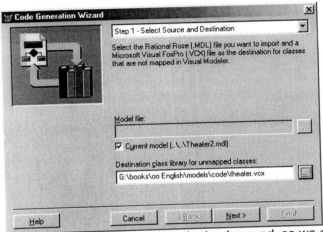

**Figure 11.** *Rose is running in the background, so we can choose to import the current model.*

Step 2 hides quite a bit of additional functionality. If you double-click a class, you get a Class Properties dialog (see **Figure 12**) that displays properties in the modeling sense. This shouldn't be confused with properties of Visual FoxPro classes. Basically, this is an options dialog for each class.

The General tab contains some basic information such as the class name, base classes, parent class, the class library in which to store this class when implemented in Visual FoxPro, and whether the class should be implemented at all. You can also set these options in the model file (see below).

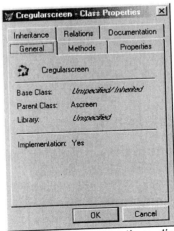

**Figure 12.** *Class options displayed in the Properties dialog.*

The Methods tab (see **Figure 13**) shows—you guessed it—all methods of the class and a brief description (if a description was defined in the model). The Properties tab does the same for properties. Thanks to the displayed icon, we also have an indicator of the visibility of the method or property.

*Figure 13. All methods of the selected class.*

The Inheritance tab gives more information about the inheritance structure. It lists all the parent classes of the class (see **Figure 14**).

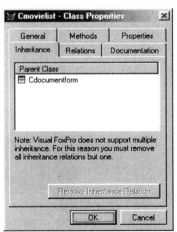

*Figure 14. The inheritance structure of our class.*

As you might have noticed, there is space for a list of parent classes, but Visual FoxPro supports only one parent class, so this seems to be a waste of space. Or is it? Well, not really. Multiple inheritance might not be allowed in Visual FoxPro, but it is allowed in the modeling tools. For this reason, the wizard needs to be ready to handle multiple-inheritance scenarios. If more than one parent class was defined, they would all appear in this list. See below for more information about multiple inheritance and inheritance conflicts.

If you want to see more information about a class, simply double-click on it to display the class properties. This way, you can work your way up the entire inheritance tree.

The remaining two tabs hold some information about relations to other classes and the written documentation as specified in the model. Most of this information is better viewed in the modeling tool.

## Resolving conflicts

Models are not necessarily compatible with Visual FoxPro's object model. Modeling tools have to be able to handle all kinds of object-oriented languages and environments. Some of them support features others don't. In Visual FoxPro, the two main areas of concern are class naming and inheritance structure.

### Naming conflicts

Naming conflicts can occur as a result of illegal characters (typically spaces in class names) or Visual FoxPro's case-insensitivity. Both issues are handled differently in other object-oriented languages.

Naming conflicts are automatically identified by the Code Generation Wizard and displayed in step 4a (see **Figure 15**).

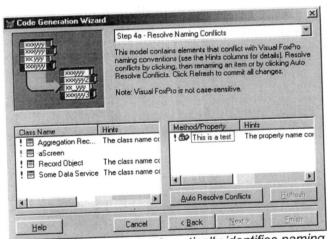

*Figure 15.* The wizard automatically identifies naming conflicts.

Step 4a shows two lists with items that raise issues. The left-hand list shows classes; the right one shows methods and properties belonging to each class. Red exclamation points indicate immediate problems, while gray ones point out that some properties or methods may have invalid names. Each item also has a brief description that explains the problem that occurred. As you can see in Figure 15, spaces are usually the main reason for conflicts, as well as duplicate class names caused by the fact that Visual FoxPro isn't case sensitive.

You can manually fix naming problems by clicking the item (hold the button for a little while) and typing a new name. When you are done, you have to click the Refresh button. The wizard will then revalidate the entire model. This can take awhile for large models. Checking for conflicts is a non-trivial task. Every change you make can cause additional conflicts, so the entire model has to be scanned and analyzed again. Doing this after every little change would take way too long. For this reason, you can resolve a number of conflicts at once before pressing the Refresh button, which initiates a batch update before the model is checked for conflicts again.

If you don't want to resolve naming conflicts by hand, click the Auto Resolve Conflicts button. The wizard will then do its best to rename the classes in a way that still makes sense to humans. However, you will get better results by changing class names yourself.

Once all conflicts are resolved, the wizard automatically moves on to the next step.

### Inheritance conflicts

The only problem that can cause inheritance conflicts is multiple inheritance, which is not supported at all by Visual FoxPro.

There are two different ways to deal with multiple inheritance. In step 2, you can look up class details and see whether you have multiple inheritance problems (see **Figures 16** and **17**).

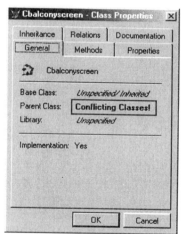

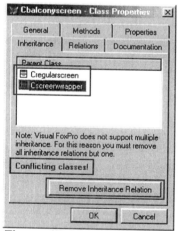

*Figure 16. The parent class can't be identified because of conflicts.*

*Figure 17. Multiple parent classes aren't good! Here you can remove them right away.*

In the Inheritance tab of the Class Properties dialog, you can remove additional parent classes. However, step 2 of the Code Generation Wizard lets you get away with inheritance conflicts. After all, it doesn't even know about the conflict unless you look up the details, and that's okay. Resolving conflicts isn't why step 2 was created in the first place. Step 4b was created to handle this (see **Figure 18**). You won't get past this step unless all inheritance conflicts are resolved.

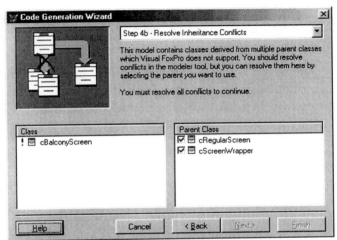

***Figure 18.** Resolving inheritance conflicts.*

In step 4b, all classes that have inheritance conflicts are pointed out to you. Once you select a class, the right-hand list shows all parent classes. You can now simply deselect the classes you don't want. Once all the conflicts are resolved, the wizard automatically moves on to the next step.

Unfortunately, resolving inheritance conflicts isn't as easy as removing one (or more) of the parent classes. You might be able to satisfy the Code Generation Wizard, but you most likely won't be able to create a working set of class libraries. Usually, multiple inheritance is designed for a good reason. By simply removing parent classes you also remove functionality that is likely to be substantial to the class. Therefore, you severely damage your model. I suggest stopping all attempts to generate code as soon as you encounter inheritance conflicts and going back to the drawing board to redesign your model!

## Setting Visual FoxPro options in the model
Setting options in the Code Generation Wizard is cumbersome. Microsoft realized that as well and gave us the ability to set Visual FoxPro options right in the modeling tool, whether it is Rational Rose or Visual Modeler. **Figure 19** shows the VFP page of the Class Specification dialog in Rational Rose.

This might surprise you, because after all, neither Rational Rose nor Visual Modeler are Visual FoxPro-specific tools. Fortunately, both tools are quite extensible, which allowed the Visual FoxPro team to modify the Class Specification dialog in a generic way. The additional options are stored in a property file (see below).

### Understanding property files
Property (.pty) files allow you to add new properties to Rational Rose or Visual Modeler items. These properties are not properties in the Visual FoxPro sense of the word, but they are additional options that can be stored with any item.

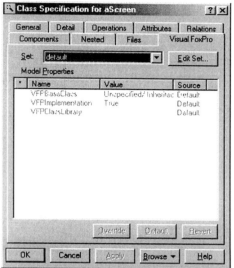

***Figure 19.*** *Visual FoxPro-specific settings in the Class Specification
dialog of Rational Rose.*

There are three property files that ship with the Visual FoxPro Modeling Wizards: Rose.pty, Msvm.pty and VFP.pty. All three files are essentially the same because they contain additional options specific to Visual FoxPro. However, Rose.pty and Msvm.pty also have options for Visual Basic, and in the future might include options for other Visual Studio members. Other than their names, the files are identical. They're named differently so that Visual Modeler users won't have to use a file called "Rose" and vice versa. The VFP.pty file contains only Visual FoxPro options. If you plan to implement your app in Visual FoxPro only, you can use this property file.

To set a property file, open the Tools menu, select Model Properties and then Replace or Add. Now select the property file you want to use. In Visual Modeler, the menu item is confusingly called "Visual Basic Options."

### Base class settings
One Visual FoxPro option you can set is the base class. The option is called "VFPBaseClass." When you click on this item, you'll see a combobox with all Visual FoxPro base classes. Simply select the base class on which you want the current class to be based.

You don't have to specify the VFP base class for every single class you use. Whenever a class is subclassed from another class in the model, it will automatically inherit the class's base class. Additional settings made in the options will be overwritten by inherited information. All base class settings you define in the model will overwrite defaults you specify in the Code Generation Wizard. This allows you to generate different kinds of classes.

You cannot specify your own classes in the model. If you need to do that, select a Visual FoxPro base class and base class substitutes in the Code Generation Wizard (see above).

## Implementation-specific settings

You can also specify a couple of implementation-specific settings right in the model. Purists might point out that this kind of information shouldn't be stored in the model, and they have a point. However, keep in mind that this information is only in addition to the regular information and does not influence the implementation in other languages, tools, or any other aspect of the model. Typically, this information is added when the model is done, so it doesn't influence or clutter the actual design.

First of all, we can specify whether a class should be implemented in Visual FoxPro at all. This is done through the *VFPImplementation* property, which is either True (default) or False. If you specify that a class is not supposed to be implemented in Visual FoxPro, the wizard will ignore it. However, the class will still show up in step 2 and you could force the wizard to implement it. This might sound stupid, but sometimes it's important. A typical example would be a class that was incorrectly defined as a non-VFP class. Nevertheless, that class might have a number of subclasses that are supposed to be implemented, but obviously those classes would not work without their parent class, so the wizard (correctly) refuses to import them. This scenario might sound somewhat constructed, but I encounter it all the time. I'm glad I can simply overwrite the mistake made in the model.

If a class is supposed to be implemented in Visual FoxPro, you can specify a class library using the *VFPClassLibrary* property. Again, this setting overwrites all defaults specified in the Code Generation Wizard.

## Updating existing libraries

Rome wasn't built in a day and neither are object models. However, customers seem to expect entire applications to be built in this timeframe, so in order to save time, people start to implement while they are modeling other areas of the system. That's fine.

Unfortunately, while continuing to model, you might also find that parts you've already implemented have changed. The Code Generation Wizard allows you to update existing source code, which might scare you. After all, an automated process is messing with your sources! Fortunately, there isn't a reason to be nervous. The wizard only adds new items to the system. It will not touch your actual code or remove parts that are not in the model. If it finds properties or methods that aren't in the model, it simply assumes they are implementation details and leaves them alone. Of course, this might leave things in the source code that were supposed to be deleted because the model changed. If so, you have to delete those items manually because the wizard will not do so. Another scenario it will not handle correctly is the relocation of classes. If you move classes to different libraries, the wizard will create new classes in new libraries, but it won't remove existing ones from their old locations. Again, this is a task you'll have to do manually. The danger of breaking existing code is simply too great.

# Filling in the blanks

Once you've used the wizards to create source code based on your model, you simply have to fill in the blanks and add the actual code to the empty methods. This might sound like a lot of work, but since you've already figured out all the required tasks and the flow of events, it's rather trivial and straightforward. It still surprises me how quickly I can move on and complete my project from this point forward. Try it yourself—you might be surprised!

# Chapter 17
# Documenting Existing Projects

**Looking back at our achievements in the last couple of chapters, we should be very satisfied. We've gone through a well-organized development cycle and can be confident that we've built a high-quality application. But are we done yet? Not really! We should make sure that we can maintain this level of quality from this point on, and we should also aim for ease of maintenance, ease of support, low total cost of ownership, and ease of implementing further changes.**

## Going back to the modeling tool

You're probably thinking, "Why does this book have another chapter? We've already implemented our application. What more can we do?" Well, there's a good reason why I sat down to write yet another chapter. Software development isn't over when you're done with the implementation. Most likely, you'll have to do another version or implement new features or changes. Even if that is not the case, you will definitely have to maintain your application. And on top of that, keep in mind that you might have to do ongoing modeling while working on the implementation.

All of these reasons will take you back to the modeling tool, either to add missing parts or to update the model with changes that occurred during implementation, so you have up-to-date documentation and a solid basis for the next version's development cycle.

Differences between the implementation and the model are the most likely reason for going back to the model and updating it. These changes and variations are caused by various factors, such as implementation details, greater levels of detail in the final implementation and (of course) because things sometimes don't work out as planned.

Microsoft provides a wizard to help you make these changes and update your Rational Rose or Visual Modeler object model. Called the "Reverse Engineering Wizard," it's one of the Modeling Wizards that you can download from the Microsoft Visual FoxPro Web site. Installation instructions are described in the previous chapter.

## The Reverse Engineering Wizard

Let's have a general look at the Reverse Engineering Wizard and all its steps. **Figure 1** shows the first step, which allows you to select the class libraries that you want to reverse-engineer.

There are two ways to select code to be reverse-engineered. The first is to select single class libraries, and the second is to open an entire project. In this case we'll analyze the entire project and select all its class libraries.

I'm frequently asked whether it is possible to reverse-engineer Visual FoxPro forms (not to be confused with form classes!). The answer is easy: "No, it isn't." The reason is simple. Forms are similar to classes, but they aren't real classes. With forms, the techniques of instance programming and (to a degree) pseudo-subclassing are used heavily. Those techniques are unique to Visual FoxPro and are not supported by any modeling tools.

Once the source code is selected, we can move on to step 2 (see **Figure 2**).

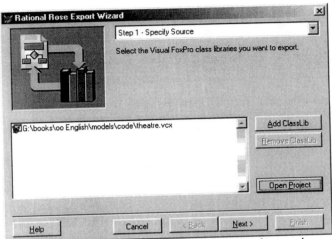

*Figure 1. Selecting code to be reverse-engineered.*

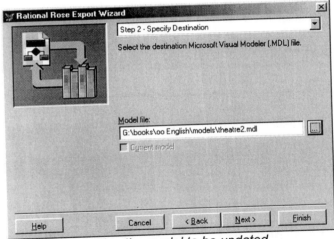

*Figure 2. Selecting the model to be updated.*

Again, you can either select a Rational Rose or Visual Modeler model file, or you can chose to export to the current model if the modeling tool is running in the background with a model file loaded. If you specify a model that doesn't exist, it will be created automatically as an empty model.

When moving from step 2 to step 3 (see **Figure 3**), the model file has already been analyzed, as has the source code to be exported. Step 3 shows the structure (packages) of the model file as well as all classes to be exported.

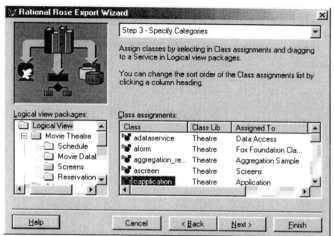

*Figure 3. The model structure and all classes to be exported.*

The purpose of step 3 is to organize your model. The tree shows the packages that already exist in the model. You can add new packages, and rename or delete the ones you've just created (see **Figure 4**). But you cannot rename or delete existing packages—you need the modeling tool to do that.

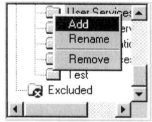

*Figure 4. Creating, renaming and deleting packages.*

The list at the right shows all classes that have been chosen to be reverse-engineered. You can see the name of the class, the library it's located in, the model package the class is assigned to and the Visual FoxPro base class. You can now drag and drop classes into packages in the tree to assign those classes to individual packages. You can click on the list headers to re-sort the list and you can select multiple classes at once. This makes it easy to select all classes of a certain base class or all classes that are stored in the same library, for instance.

Classes that you don't want to reverse-engineer (even though you might reverse-engineer other classes in the same library) can be dropped into the Excluded node. This just means that they will be ignored at this time but not removed from the model.

If classes were imported earlier from the model, they will already have packages assigned. Even if you assign those classes to different packages, they won't be relocated because they already exist in the model. You can relocate classes in the actual modeling tool.

When the wizard encounters a class that hasn't been imported from a modeling tool, it assigns default packages, such as "User Services" for all interface objects. It will do so even if a package of this name doesn't exist (keep in mind that the wizards were initially designed for Visual Modeler, which always has those packages). You need to reassign these classes to existing packages before you start to export.

Once you have decided the location of your classes in the model, move on to the final step (see **Figure 5**).

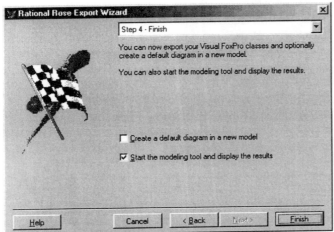

**Figure 5**. *Click Finish and you're done.*

Step 4 offers two additional settings, one of which is to create a default diagram. I do not recommend this, for reasons explained below. The other option allows you to start the modeling tool right away so you can see what has been accomplished. Obviously, this is a good choice.

## Creating diagrams

Just because you export classes to the modeling tool doesn't mean that you'll find diagrams showing those classes. As discussed in previous chapters, models are split into a number of small, scenario-oriented diagrams. There is no way for the Reverse Engineering Wizard to create useful scenario diagrams. Nevertheless, it offers the option of creating a default diagram that shows all exported classes. This is useful if you are creating a new model from scratch. Any time you update an existing model, you should not create a default diagram, because the wizard will add yet another diagram every time you run it.

Whether or not you create an existing diagram, you'll always have to do some editing afterward. You'll see all the exported classes in the Rational Rose/Visual Modeler Class Browser of the modeling tool. You can then simply drag and drop classes into a diagram. All the relations and dependencies will be drawn automatically, so this task will challenge your artistic skills above anything else.

## Updating existing models

Typically, the Reverse Engineering Wizard will update existing models with changes made in classes that you've previously imported to Visual FoxPro. The wizard is actually quite smart, because it reliably remembers the class mappings even if classes are renamed to resolve conflicts. The wizard analyzes the additions you made in source code (visual classes, that is) and adds those to the classes in the model as well. This is an extraordinary tool to keep object models up to date.

No matter what the wizard encounters, it will never remove anything. It simply assumes that the classes, properties, methods or relations have yet to be implemented. For this reason, you always have to remove items by hand in the source code as well as in the model (otherwise they will show up again eventually).

### Round-trip engineering

In a typical engineering cycle, you'd create an object model, implement the model in Visual FoxPro (or any other tool of your choice), make additional changes in the source code, update the model from those changes, possibly make more changes to the model and update the source code from those changes, and so forth. This cycle of going back and forth between the modeling tool and the implementation environment is called "round-trip engineering."

The Visual FoxPro Modeling Wizards fully support this kind of development cycle. The Code Generation Wizard creates new Visual FoxPro code or updates existing code. The Reverse Engineering Wizard updates existing models (or creates new ones as described below). This is an ongoing cycle that you can continue even over multiple versions of your application. In fact, the wizards allow you to work on both parts (model and implementation) simultaneously. In this case you have to run both wizards to update the source code and the model with the changes that occur in the other part. This scenario occurs frequently in real-life development cycles.

## Creating new models

The Reverse Engineering Wizard also allows you to create new models based on your existing source code. This is a great way to impress your friends, your customers and your boss. They'll never know that you didn't do any real modeling (of course, you'll start doing this from now on, right?).

Creating new models from existing code isn't much different than updating models. The major difference is that all classes are created from scratch. In order to get a well-organized model, you'll have to create a number of packages in step 3 of the Reverse Engineering Wizard (see Figures 3 and 4) and assign classes to them.

For small to mid-sized applications, you might consider having the wizard create a default diagram. This diagram will be huge even for a small application, but it usually gives you a good starting point.

Creating models, even if you haven't done proper modeling, has a number of advantages (even beyond impressing your friends). First of all, it gives you quick, hassle-free, accurate documentation of your application. Programmers usually skip creating this kind of documentation because it's time-consuming and difficult to keep up to date. This is not an issue with the Visual FoxPro Modeling Wizards, thanks to their round-trip-engineering capabilities. As if this weren't enough, there are even more advantages—especially for future iterations of your application, and also for maintaining and supporting the existing program.

# Beyond basic modeling

In the last couple of chapters, I gave you an overview of object modeling and the software development life cycle. My goal was to explain the necessary steps in a way that relates to Visual FoxPro and is easier to understand than the usually abstract definitions and explanations. It obviously isn't possible to cover—in a single book or even a series of books—everything that's involved. That's why so many books have been written about this topic. In fact, even the three main brains behind the UML (Grady Booch, Ivar Jacobson and James Rumbaugh) wrote three books to explain the details and then edited a number of others. And, as we know by now, the UML is only part of the entire development cycle.

With the knowledge I gave you in this book, you should be ready for your first successful modeling adventure. However, I still recommend reading some additional books and articles on this topic. You now know how things relate to Visual FoxPro and you're familiar with all the important terms. This should make it much easier to understand the high-level books. Check out my Web site (www.eps-software.com) for a continually updated list of further recommended reading.

## A glimpse of the modeling future...

The ideas behind object modeling aren't new. However, many of the tools and notations are. The UML is rather young; in fact, we just received the first version that covers everything the average modeler needs and that has been widely accepted. Rational Rose was around for a while, but it didn't support UML, nor did it tie into any of the Visual Studio components until recently. Visual Modeler first appeared with Visual Studio 97. The Visual FoxPro Modeling Wizards are available in their first incarnation today.

These facts make us hope for further acceptance and more advanced tools. One thing I'd really like to see in Visual FoxPro (and the rest of the modeling cycle) are traceability links. These links allow tracing requirements all the way from requirements lists through use cases and object models to the actual implementation. If we clicked an item in the requirements matrix, the modeling tools would automatically highlight all Visual FoxPro classes that are somehow related to this requirement. The advantages are obvious: Changes could be made with high confidence. We'd know exactly how long it would take to work on those changes. We'd also know exactly what to change, and we wouldn't run the risk of forgetting one of the involved components, which would cause a drop in overall product quality.

When the Visual FoxPro Modeling Wizards were created, the UML wasn't fully defined. I'm confident that the next version of the Modeling Wizards will support additional features, allowing us to automate more steps in the development process and to document existing code at a more detailed level.

# About the Author

## Markus Egger

Markus Egger is the owner of EPS Software, a software development firm founded in Salzburg, Austria, with offices in Salzburg and Houston, Texas. He specializes in object-oriented development, Internet development, training and consulting. EPS does most of its development using the Microsoft Visual Tools family, with an emphasis on Visual FoxPro.

EPS has worked on numerous software projects for Fortune 500 companies including Philip Morris, Qualcomm and Microsoft. Markus has also worked with well-known FoxPro developers and companies including SBC, F1 and Micromega. He is a contractor for the Microsoft Visual FoxPro team, focusing on object modeling and other object-related technologies.

Markus is an international speaker and has presented sessions at numerous Visual FoxPro conferences, including DevCon '97, DevCon '98, FoxTeach 1996, the European Visual FoxPro Conference, the Dutch Lowlands conference in Amsterdam, the Great Lakes Great Database Workshop in Milwaukee, and several FoxExpress conferences in Las Vegas.

Markus has written numerous articles for *Fuchs*, *FoxTalk* and *Microsoft Office & Database Journal*, and is the owner and editor of *Software Developer Magazine*, a European Visual FoxPro publication (www.eps-software.com/sdm). He is the author of several well-known tools such as GenRepoX, PowerBrowser and Visual WebBuilder.

Markus received the Visual FoxPro MVP Award ('96, '97, '98, '99) from Microsoft for his contributions to the FoxPro community. His application Visual LandPro 98 was a finalist in two categories for the Visual FoxPro Excellence Awards, 1998. You can reach Markus at megger@eps-software.com or www.eps-software.com.

## Malcolm Rubel, Technical Editor

Malcolm C. Rubel is president of Performance Dynamics Associates, a business applications consulting firm with offices in New York City and Bar Harbor, Maine. He is the author of several books on the Xbase language, including *FoxPro 2.0 Power Tools*. He is a contributing editor to *FoxPro Advisor* and has had a monthly column appearing in at least one publication for the past 11 years. He is the author of the FoxPro Power Developer's Library, a cross-platform suite of utilities for FoxPro 2.5/2.6 and Visual FoxPro; Raidar, the Development Debugger for FoxPro 2.5/2.6; and Visual Raidar for Visual FoxPro. Malcolm has spoken at many national and regional conferences and has been a Microsoft MVP for the past four years. You can reach Malcolm at 212-972-2330 or mrubel@compuserve.com.

# How to Download Source Code, Sample Files, And .CHM files

Several additional resources are available to you from Hentzenwerke Publishing's website. They include: source code referred to in the book, sample data sets, and the .CHM file of the entire book.

**To download the files:**

1. Go to our website:

   www.hentzenwerke.com

2. Click on **Books by Hentzenwerke Publishing** and follow the prompts.

As a protection to your investment (and ours!), there is a password scheme in place to prevent the downloading of these files without purchasing the book.

**You will need to have the book with you
in order to download the files!**

Note: the .CHM file is covered by the same copyright laws as the printed book. Reproduction and/or distribution of the .CHM file is prohibited.